HISTORIC CAMDEN

PART ONE

COLONIAL AND REVOLUTIONARY

BY
THOMAS J. KIRKLAND
AND
ROBERT M. KENNEDY
CAMDEN, S. C.

Southern Historical Press, Inc.
Greenville, South Carolina

This volume was reproduced
from a personal copy located in
the Publishers private library

Please direct all correspondence and book orders to:

www.southernhistoricalpress.com
or
SOUTHERN HISTORICAL PRESS, Inc.
1071 Park West Blvd.
Greenville, SC   29611

southernhistoricalpress@gmail.com

Originally printed: Columbia, SC   1905
:ISBN #978-1-63914--022-0
All rights reserved
Printed in the United States of America

TABLE OF CONTENTS.

	PAGE
Prefatory	5

Chapter I.
Municipal......... 9

Chapter II.
Indian Era......... 37

Chapter III.
Pine Tree Hill......... 67

Chapter IV.
Camden......... 90

Chapter V.
"Not Revolt—Revolution"......... 104

Chapter VI.
The Battle of Camden......... 146

Chapter VII.
Aftermath......... 171

Chapter VIII.
Interim......... 199

Chapter IX.
The Battle of Hobkirk Hill......... 221

Chapter X.
Gleanings from Hobkirk......... 243

Chapter XI.
The Cornwallis House......... 274

Chapter XII.
An Honored Tory......... 281

Chapter XIII.
Agnes of Glasgow......... 291

Chapter XIV.
Daniel McGirtt.................................297

Chapter XV.
Washington's Visit.............................306

Chapter XVI.
Citizen-Minister Genêt........................314

Chapter XVII.
Joseph Brevard................................321

Chapter XVIII.
Minton's Mill.................................327

Chapter XIX.
Early Representative Families.................340

Appendix A.
The Diary of Samuel Mathis....................399

Appendix B.
James Kershaw's Diary.........................404

PREFATORY.

The history of but a small community will be found no easy task, especially if the only available time for research be the remnants of otherwise busy days, as has been the case with us. Thus hampered, the work is infinitely extended.

To end delay and the skepticism of some expectant friends as to whether the proposed history of Camden would ever materialize, we have decided to wait no longer for completion, but to divide the subject, and to publish this, the first part, imperfect as it is, retaining for further revision enough matter for another volume. The second part will relate mainly to Camden of the nineteenth century, embracing chapters upon such periods and subjects as the War of 1812, Visit of Lafayette, Nullification Times, Mexican War, Secession, Civil War, Churches, Schools, Courthouse, Professions, Commercial Matters, Newspapers, Duels, Slaves, with sketches of the many men of those days, in the various walks of life, whose careers give distinction not only to Camden, but to the State.

In our laborious quest for data we have explored, as thoroughly as limited opportunities would permit, the ancient documents of the State archives in Charleston and Columbia, the oldest newspapers, State and local, and the records of our Court, back to earliest times. We must thank in general terms the many who have kindly aided us. From collections found in the families of Salmond, Williams, Boykin, Alexander, Meroney, and Man, we were enabled to bring together almost complete files of the Camden newspapers from 1816 to date, and secured one specimen of a paper so early as 1802, apparently the first local journal.

There seems to be a prevalent opinion, on the part of residents and visitants, that Camden's history is of such significance and interest as to make it peculiarly worthy of record in a permanent and accessible form, and we thus feel not unwarranted in adopting what some might regard as a pretentious title. Allowance must be made for a local pride, which all Camdenites believe to be well founded and justified.

This work should have been undertaken by some more competent hands prior to the Civil War, which wrought such havoc with documents and relics, and whilst the elders of preceding generations survived, who could have related much that has grown dim or is buried beyond recovery. We are fully aware that this attempt of ours will be unsatisfactory to those who feel an interest in the subject. But we trust our effort will be of some value, and shall be quite content

"If something from our hands have power
 To live, and act, and serve the future hour."

THOS. J. KIRKLAND.
ROBT. M. KENNEDY.

Camden, S. C., June 25, 1904.

PLAN OF CAMDEN
1904

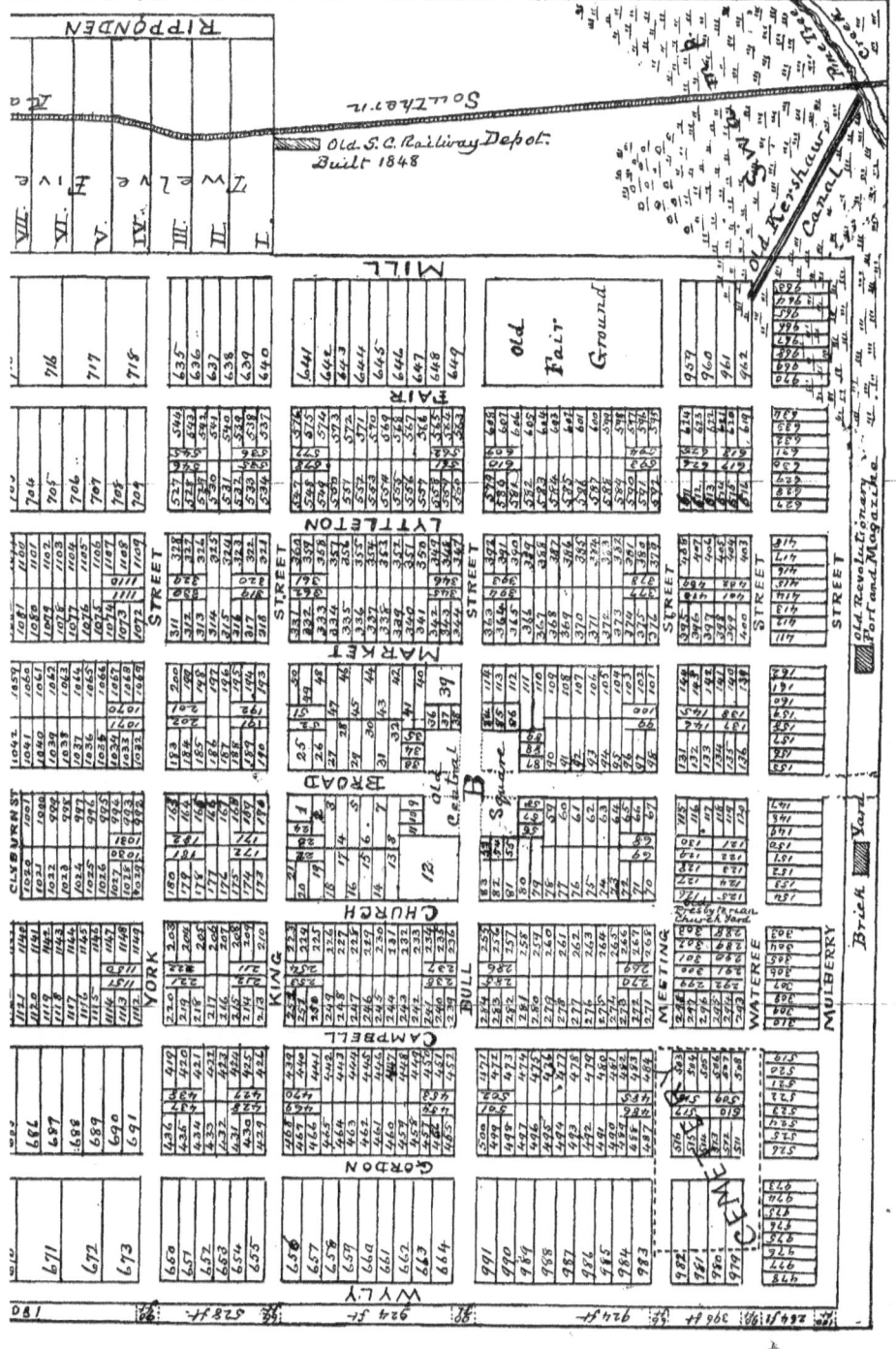

HISTORIC CAMDEN.

CHAPTER I.

MUNICIPAL.

In this chapter will be attempted a concise account of the evolution of Camden in its municipal features, from its inception to the present. Its earliest settlement, here mentioned only in outline, will be treated with more detail, further on, under the head of "Pine Tree Hill."

The germ of the city of Camden may be recognized in the resolution of the Royal Council on December 6, 1733,[*] wherein they employ James St. Julien, for the sum of £500, to survey a township on the Wateree River, at such point as he judged most convenient for settlement.

This act of the Council was in pursuance of the instructions of King George II, issued in 1730, to Gov. Robert Johnson, on his departure for the Province, "to mark out places in a proper situation for eleven townships," on the rivers of South Carolina, one of which, it was especially ordered, was to be located "on the River Watery." It was further directed that these townships should each be bounded by the river on one side, to be six miles square, and each contain 20,000 acres. It must have been little realized how formidable these river swamps were, for the King's precept continues:

"In each of these townships you shall mark out a proper place for the situation of a TOWN, contiguous to the river, to consist of so many lots, and of such quantity

---

[*] Council Journals, 1730-34, p. 673, State Records.

of land, as you judge convenient."* Surrounding these townships was to be marked out an area twelve miles square, the territory of which was to be reserved exclusively for those settling within the township.

The purpose was to attract immigrants, and land within the townships was granted only to colonists from abroad. Each comer was entitled to a donation of a town lot, and fifty acres for each member of his family.

According to contract, St. Julien, between December 6, 1733, and February 2, 1734, laid off, on the eastern side of the Wateree River, the township of FREDRICKSBURG. The name, which became obsolete after the Revolution, was given, no doubt, in honor of the then Prince of Wales.

Of the plats of these eleven townships established by the King in South Carolina, the one of Fredricksburg is the only *original* that survives. It is upon cloth, with the genuine tint of antiquity, and was found folded in a large book of copy-plats in the State archives. It is still legible in most parts. Diagram No. 1 is a reduced copy. It shows that even so early as 1733 "Sanders Creek" had its name, and "Pine Tree Creek" also. The latter, it is said, derived its name from the circumstance that the old "Catawba Path," which is indicated on the plat, and which is now Broad street of Camden, crossed the creek on a large pine log.†

The large exterior square represented on the diagram, the lower line of which is lacking,‡ marks the twelve-mile outer limits reserved for the town settlers. The small interior square, of which the northern line is wanting, lying south of Pine Tree Creek, was doubtless

---
*London Colonial Manuscripts, Secretary of State's office, Vol. 15, p. 202.
‡The absence of this lower line is due to the fact that the lower extremity of the plat was torn away along a fold.
†Judge James, Manuscript Memoirs.

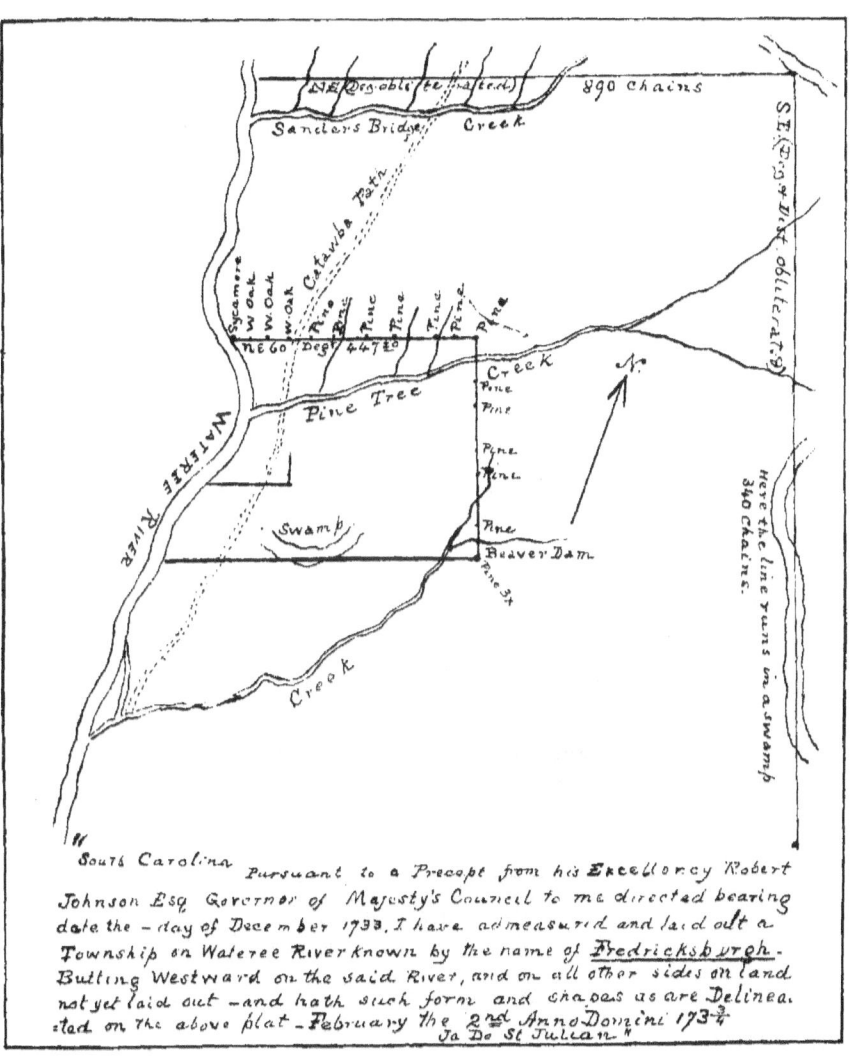

FREDRICKSBURGH TOWNSHIP.
Copied from old Plat in office of Secretary of State, Columbia, S.C.

DIAGRAM No. 1.

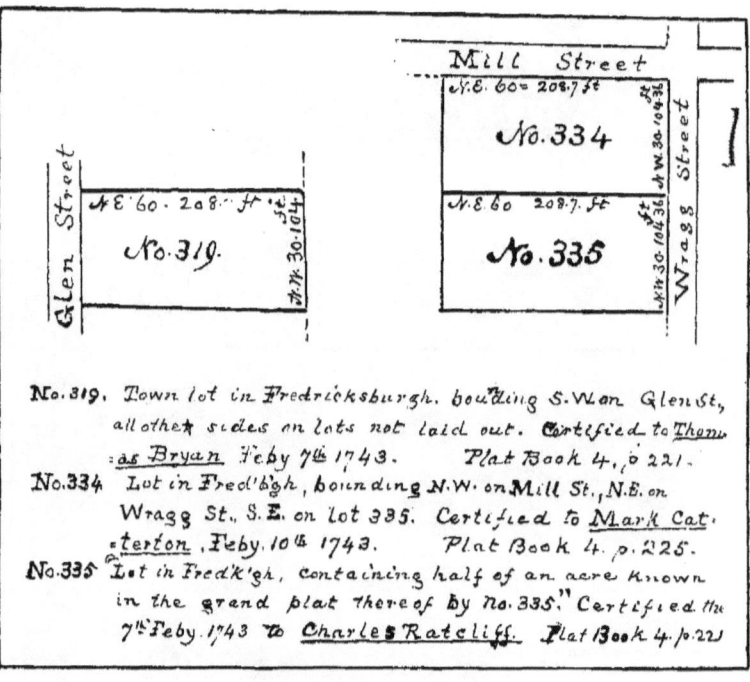

Lots in Fredricksburg.

DIAGRAM No. 2.

intended to indicate the TOWN of Fredricksburg, corresponding about with the location of Mulberry. Its southern boundary was not far north of Town Creek, which thus probably derived its name. The river, according to the King's precept, constituted its western boundary, so that the greater part of it lay in low swamps by no means adaptable to habitation.

The "grand plat" of Fredricksburg town, referred to in the grant of Lot No. 335 to Charles Ratcliff, February 7, 1743, has been nowhere discovered after zealous search. Plats of three several lots and adjacent streets have been found, of which a diagram (No. 2) is presented, by which we learn the names of three of its streets, Wragg, Glen, Mill. There seems to have been no demand for lots, for after grant of the three mentioned, the whole town was disposed of in tracts without reference to street or lot, and was taken up by John Williams, John Collins, George Senior, and others.

When in 1750 or 1751 the colony of Irish Quakers came to Fredricksburg, there was no semblance of a town population, only scattered plantations, and Indian camps. These Quakers, themselves, formed no town, but spread out along the river, both sides, for several miles above and below the present site of Camden. It was reserved for Joseph Kershaw and William Ancrum to plant the first rudiments of Camden in June, 1758. It was in that year that Kershaw came up from Charleston to Fredricksburg. On a tract of 150 acres, which was surveyed for William Ancrum on June 12, 1758, Kershaw established a store and called the spot PINE TREE HILL, now known to us as the Magazine Hill, in the southeast corner of Camden—the site, in former times, of the Cornwallis House. The land, while in the name of William Ancrum, who always remained a resident of Charlestown, was an asset of the firm of Ancrum, Loocock, Lance & Kershaw, the Pine Tree Hill branch of which was styled Kershaw & Company.

It is not until April 12, 1768, that any mention of CAMDEN is found, in an act of the Assembly of that date, establishing a Circuit Court at "Camden, lately called Pine Tree Hill." The naming is attributed to Joseph Kershaw, and was in honor of Lord Camden (Charles Pratt), then so cordially admired by the colonists for his pleas in Parliament in their behalf.

The very earliest plan of the town of Camden which the most diligent search reveals, is to be found in the State records, in an old book of town plats, a copy of which is shown in Diagram No. 3. The fact that it represents, in the "References" on its face, the Courthouse and Gaol as built, and a space "for the Fair," compels the conclusion that it does not date earlier than 1774, in which year the Fair was established. The Courthouse and Gaol were finished in 1771. Only those lots marked "2" had at that time been disposed of, seventy-two in all, all far south of the Courthouse, south even of Bull street, and near the creek swamps.

There is no trace of any municipal officers or organization in Pine Tree Hill or Camden prior to the Revolution. Like the other pine-stump villages of the interior, it seems to have been nothing more than a rural settlement, without corporate existence. The nearest approach to any charter rights, at this period, is a curious old commission, found as a waif among the ancient Probate records in Charleston.

It was issued October 28, 1774, in the name of "George the Third, by the Grace of God, of Great Britain, France, and Ireland, King, Defender of the Faith," and recites that:

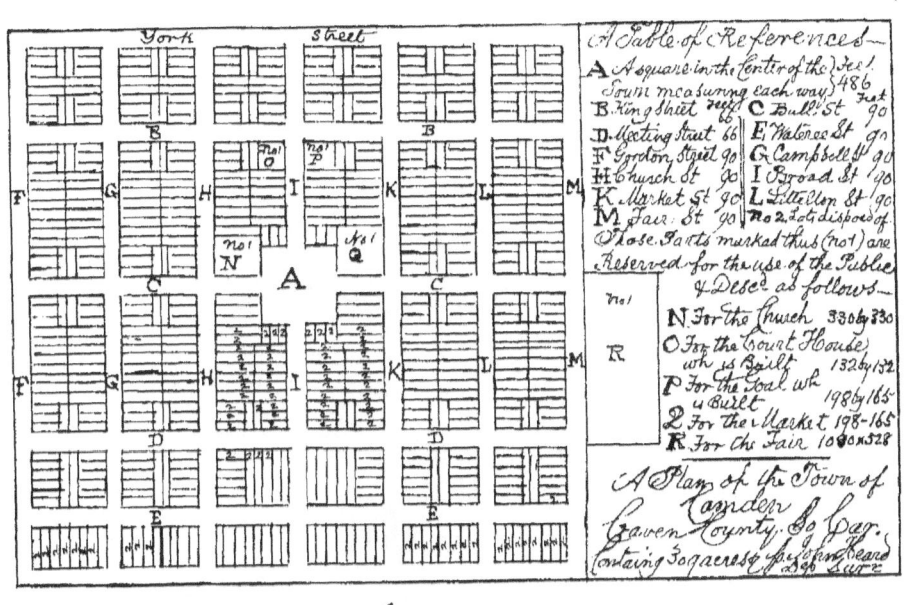

Earliest Plat of Camden 1774 —
From Coby-olat. State records Columbia S.C.

DIAGRAM No. 3.

"Whereas, it will greatly tend to the Benefit and Advantage of the Inhabitants of the interior parts of this Province, if Fairs were to be held at fit and proper places, whereto the said Inhabitants might Resort to sell or purchase Horses, Cattle, Hogs or other Commodities which they may either want or have to dispose of.

"And whereas, Joseph Kershaw, Ely Kershaw, John Chesnut, Wm. Ancrum, and Aaron Loocock, who are the joint proprietors of the greatest part of the said Town of Camden, have given and surrendered up unto us, our Heirs and Successors forever, a Piece or Parcell of Ground situated on the East side of Fair Street in the said Town of Camden, containing in front from the Northward to the Southward 1,080 feet, and in depth from the Westward to the Eastward 528 feet, as appears by Plan of the said Town hereunto annexed,* for the use and purpose of holding a Fair thereon.

"And being desirous of contributing to the Ease and Emolument of our loving subjects in our said Province of South Carolina, do grant unto the said Joseph Kershaw, Ely Kershaw, John Chesnut, Wm. Ancrum and Aaron Loocock, as tenants in common and as Joint Tenants, full power and absolute authority to proclaim and hold two Fairs, in each year forever hereafter."

These Fairs were to be holden in April and November of each year, on second Tuesdays, and to last three days, the first to be held April, 1775. Authority was also granted to the above-named parties "by sealed instrument to appoint a commissioner or manager" with the power "to have and hold a Court of Piepowder, with all liberty and free custom to the same appertaining."

The Court of Piepowder was an old English institution, having jurisdiction of disputes arising at fairs,

---

*This plat was probably the same as represented in Diagram 3, and to which we have assigned the date of 1774.

with summary process. The title is said by Blackstone to be derived from the old French word for "pedlar," he of the *dusty foot,* the badge of those resorting to such places. This unique tribunal probably was peculiar to Camden. This old fair ground is still municipal property.

It has been stated that so late as some years after the Civil War there hung on the walls of the Town Council Chamber a royal charter of incorporation, granted by King George III to Camden, said to have been issued in 1750, but which could not have antedated 1768. In the *Camden Journal* of 1883 the announcement was made that this unique old relic had disappeared from its place, in some way unknown, and Council offered a reward for its return. Extensive inquiry develops no clue as to its existence. Let us hope that this antiquarian prize may yet be recovered. So far as known, no other town of the State could lay claim to any similar parchment.

During the Revolution there is still no evidence of town government. During British occupation, which lasted from June 1, 1780, to May 10, 1781, martial law, of course, was supreme, which was rigid enough, judging by the diary of Samuel Mathis, from which it appears that the commonest transactions were subject to the scrutiny of military officers.

The first appearance of any municipal organization is found in the act of 1785, creating commissioners of streets and market in Camden. A quaint relic of this regime was discovered some years ago by Maj. E. B. Cantey, a "promise to pay" in blank, which bore on its face the following:

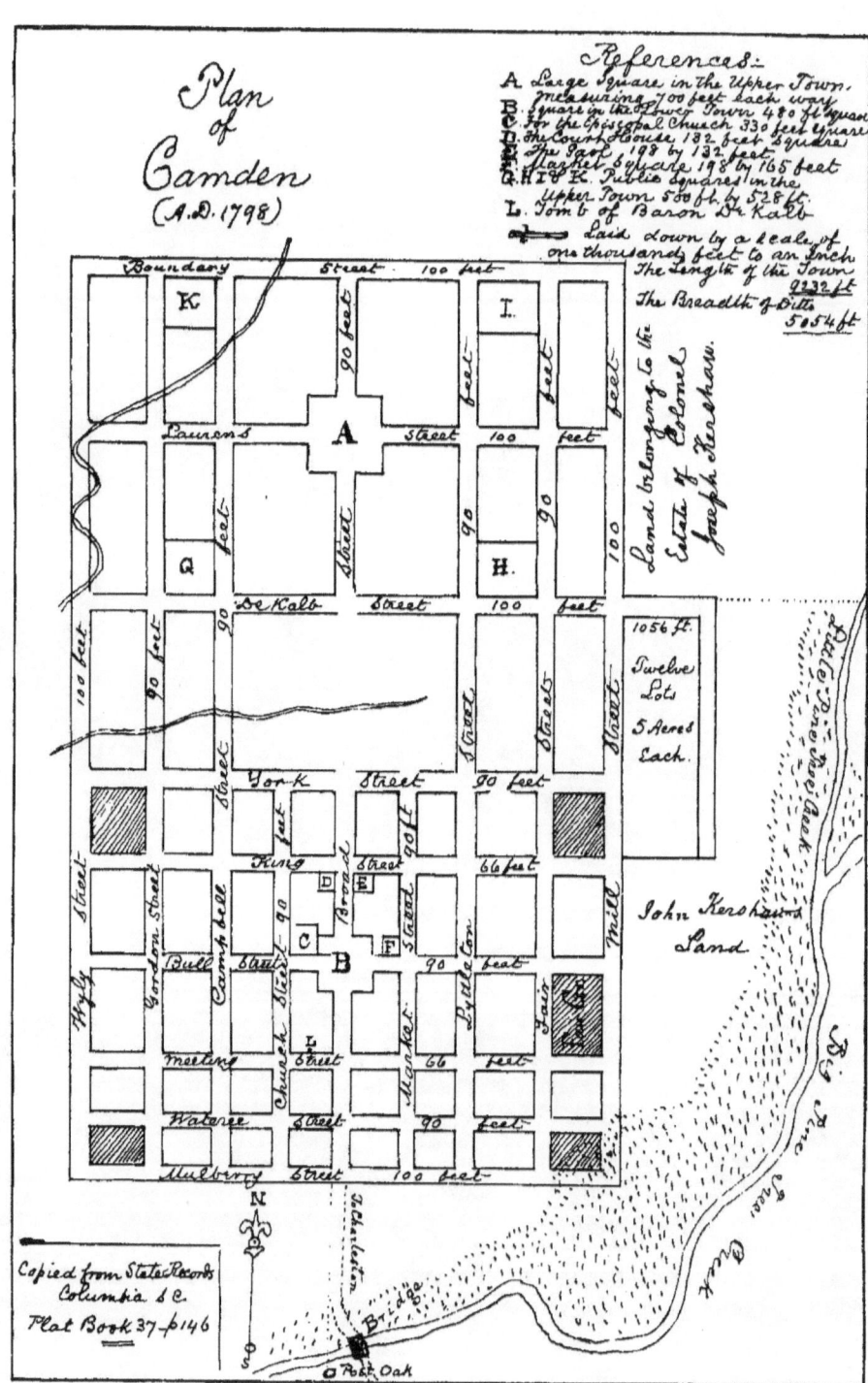

DIAGRAM No. 4.

Camden No......
The Commissioners of the Streets and Market of Camden Promife to pay the Bearer on Demand .... value received this .... 1788.

Here we have the first specimen of town currency, which so abounded in after years, resulting in each case from the stringency following upon war.

The era of formal corporate existence dates from February 19, 1791, when the legislative act of incorporation was passed. Camden was the first town after Charleston (which was incorporated in 1783) to receive that privilege. The government was vested in a town council, consisting of an intendant and four wardens elected annually on the first Monday of April. The municipal charter created by this act sufficed, with few amendments, for the government of Camden just one hundred years.

Boundaries.

The limits of the town as first defined in the plan of 1774 remained unaltered until 1798, when they were extended by legislative act, in conformity with the report of a commission, consisting of James Kershaw, John Kershaw, William Lang, James Chesnut, and Samuel Mathis, who were constituted "for the purpose of surveying and laying out, and ascertaining by metes and bounds, the boundaries of the town of Camden, according to the plan thereof laid out by the late Joseph Kershaw, commonly called the extended plan of Camden."

The plat accompanying the report of these commissioners is of record in the office of the Secretary of State at Columbia, in Plat Book 37, p. 146, of which Diagram No. 4 is a copy.

It is expressly declared by the act that the lands lying between Pine Tree Creek and the southern and eastern part of the town, from the bridge on the Charleston road to where DeKalb street continued intersects Little Pine Tree Creek, shall be within the jurisdiction of the town, so that the boundaries of the said town shall be as follows: "Beginning where DeKalb street intersects Little Pine Tree Creek, thence down the old bed of the creek, to a post oak on the bank of the creek below the bridge aforesaid."

It will thus be seen that the bed of the creek was the eastern and southern boundary of Camden, and *still is*, on the east, from the intersection of DeKalb street extended down to Mulberry street extended, though it seems a misapprehension has long prevailed that Ripponden street formed the extreme eastern limit of the town.

The "old bed of the creek," referred to in the act, is explainable in this way: Some of the early settlers, probably Robert Milhouse, for the purpose of a mill, had closed the original channel of Big Pine Tree Creek, just south of the bridge on the Charleston road. A small part of the water was carried from this point by a canal to a mill in the vicinity of the present Carrison Mill. The main waters of the creek, thus obstructed, sought another course nearer the Camden side. This new channel used to be called the Machine Creek, which, in former days, was no doubt applied to some sort of machinery.

The plan of 1798 shows a large vacant square area in the heart of the town, some ninety acres or more, with a stream issuing from it. This space was then a marsh, which at times became a pond. The Broad street of today then passed through it as a causewayed road. This is now the heart and business center of Camden.

DIAGRAM No. 5.

It was, however, the last part to be laid out in lots and streets. In 1801 it was purchased by Richard Lloyd Champion at a sale under judgment against the estate of Joseph Kershaw. Shortly after, Rutledge street was established through it, and the "Big Ditch" cut to drain it. Lots were sold off rapidly, and an old plat of Champion's, dated 1808, shows that many had then been taken. Kershaw and Champion may, therefore, be regarded as the designers of Camden.

Samuel Mathis, Intendant, on March 25, 1799, considerately placed of record in the Clerk's Office, Book A, p. 316, a plan of the town of Camden, as recently established, showing that portion which had been laid out into lots and streets. This was done, as stated in the record, "for the convenience of the inhabitants, and others who may own or wish to buy, or sell, or convey lots in the said town." It does not, however, represent the run of the creek, or that portion of the town's jurisdiction between the creek and the easternmost streets, and has therefore contributed to an erroneous impression as to the boundaries. So constantly has this recorded plan been thumbed for a century, that it is the worse for wear. The photographic copy herewith shows that Rutledge street, and the lots of the middle portion of Richard L. Champion, are by a different hand and evidently after-insertions, according with the fact that these were laid out after the record of the plat.

The boundaries, as defined in 1798, stood until the acts of March 9, 1871, and March 4, 1872, by which the town was extended north three-quarters of a mile, so as to include Kirkwood and Hobkirk Hill. But all the territory south of Mulberry street was thrown out, and that street, *extended east to the creek*, became the southern boundary, and so remains. The run of Big and Little Pine Tree Creeks, by said acts, constituted the eastern boundary, from Mulberry street up to the confluence of Horse Branch. Four granite posts, still in place, marked the northern limit of extension.

By the act of February 14, 1878, the extending acts were repealed, except as to the southern boundary, and otherwise the limits of Camden reverted necessarily to those previously existing, as established by the act of 1798. Consequently, between Mulberry and DeKalb streets, extended eastward to the creek, the run of the creek is the true eastern boundary.

A new legislative charter was granted to Camden, December 24, 1890, to meet modern demands, whereby it was elevated to the title of CITY, and under which it is now governed. The City Council consists of a Mayor and four Aldermen, elected biennially on the first Monday of April.

Log Town.

All that northern and more elevated portion of Camden between DeKalb and Boundary streets, and both sides of Broad, was granted to Joseph Kershaw in 1768, a tract of 250 acres. It was by him called Log Town, and is mentioned by that name in an old deed of 1777, the name attributable, doubtless, to the log houses of its first dwellers.* General Greene mentions, in a letter of 1781, taking position at "Log Town," a few days before his occupation of Hobkirk Hill, and Tarleton, in his memoirs, states that Lord Rawdon fell back from Lynches Creek, before the advance of General Gates, to "Log Town." It is frequently mentioned in the old municipal records as a distinct quarter of the town, which enjoyed its own warden, pump and fire engine.

---

*Mrs. Thornton, who came to Camden in 1804, relates in her memoir that the name originated from a small log house located somewhere between Monument Square and Lafayette Hall.

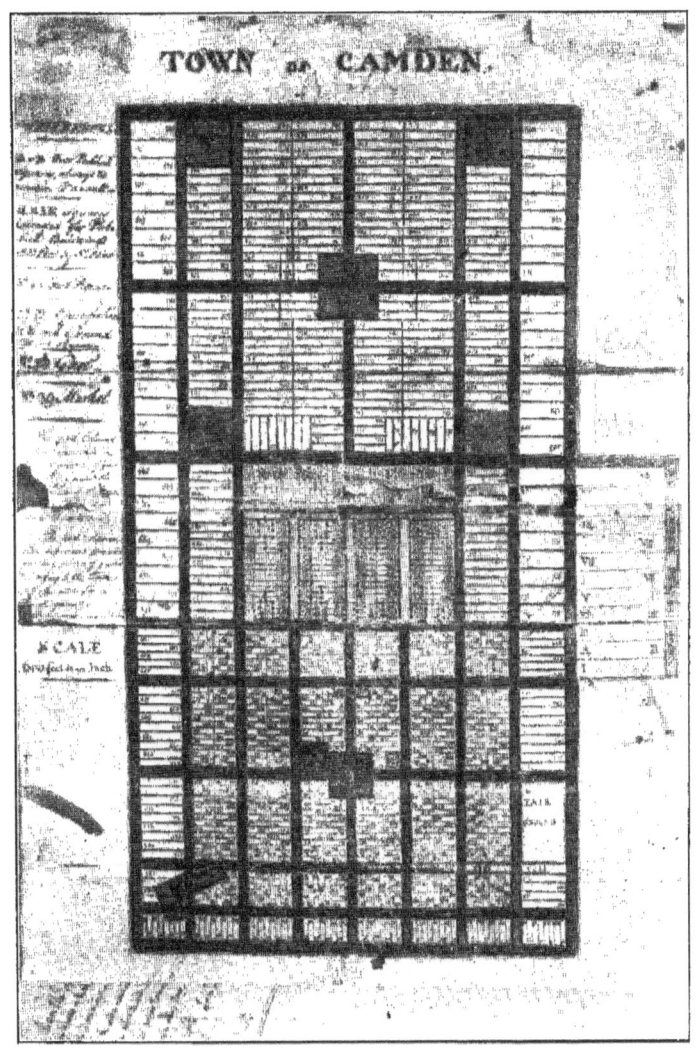

The Mathis Plan of Camden.

DIAGRAM No. 6.

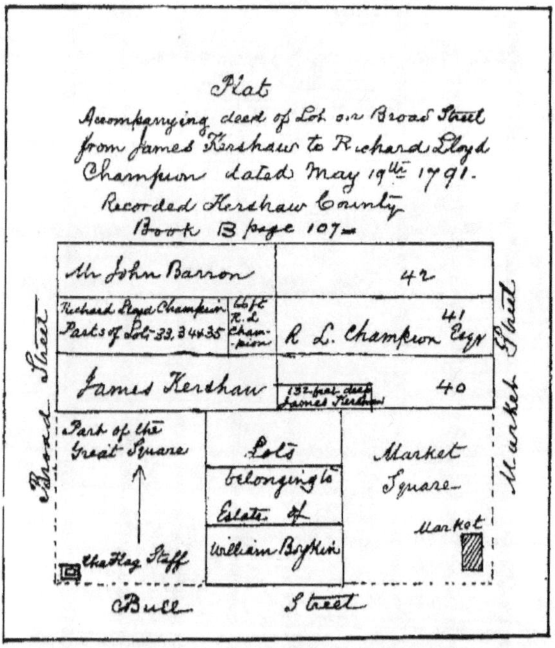

Plat
Accompanying deed of Lot on Broad Street
from James Kershaw to Richard Lloyd
Champion dated May 19th 1791.
Recorded Kershaw County
Book B page 107.

Mr John Barron		42
Richard Lloyd Champion Parts of Lots 33, 34 & 35	66 ft R. L. Champion	41 R. L. Champion Esqr
James Kershaw	132 feet deep James Kershaw	40
Part of the Great Square ↑ the Flag Staff	Lots belonging to Estate of William Brykin	Market Square Market

Broad Street — Bull Street — Market Street

DIAGRAM No. 7.

The Market and Hall.

The original market was located on the northwest corner of Bull and Market streets, Lot No. 39 in the Plan. It was there certainly in 1791, see Diagram No. 7, and probably earlier. This was destroyed in the fire of 1812, which swept away the two chief squares of the town. Shortly after, it was rebuilt on the site previously occupied by the Gaol, which perished also in the fire, just opposite and east of the Courthouse, Lot No. 25. It had been rebuilt by 1816, for in the *Camden Gazette* of April 4th, that year, it is stated that Camden possessed "a handsome brick market," and in the same paper Phineas Thornton advertises:

"Groceries and Cloths, Bow Strings, fine and coarse of an excellent quality, which will be sold low by the dozen, also Fresh Garden Seed from the North, *one door below the Market on Broad street.*"

There it stood until 1859, narrowly escaping the great fire of 1829. The upper floor served many purposes, as town hall, council chamber, Sunday School room, where all denominations met in common, also for the Library Society, founded in early days by Abram Blanding, and long a very creditable and flourishing institution. The appearance of this structure may be guessed from the reproduction of an old Camden Bank Bill of 1836. It was adorned, as the cut shows, by a steeple, one hundred and eighteen feet high.

The steeple was not finished until 1825, and scaffolding was still around it at the time of Lafayette's visit in March of that year. Funds for its completion were raised by a lottery under town auspices, as appears by the *Southern Chronicle and Camden Gazette* of September 4, 1822. Fifteen hundred tickets were sold for $7,500, the town reserving fifteen per cent. of the prizes.

Managers, Christopher Matheson, Capt. Peter Warren, Alexander Young, C. J. Shannon.

But Camden, in its steady progress northwards, left the market house in the rear, so that by 1859 its removal uptown became a necessity. Its new location was Lot 1178, west side of Broad street, a little north of its intersection with Rutledge. As in the old building, the second floor formed the town hall and theater. In front rose a graceful turret and spire, the base of which arched over the sidewalk, and through this archway the stream of passers flowed for thirty-three years. A print from an old ferrotype shows this steeple in course of construction, with the old Indian vane being elevated into position by a derrick.

The ambitions of the town again called for better municipal quarters, and the present Opera House, on Lot 1049, completed in 1886, resulted.

In making this change the market was divorced from the hall, but placed beside it, just south, on Lot 1048. The first idea was to place it *in Rutledge street,* at the intersection of Broad, facing east, and materials were actually being hauled to the spot, but the plan was abandoned upon the protest of some citizens. This market was abolished in 1901, the building removed, and stores erected in its place.

Indian and Clock.

The most distinctive object in Camden is the Indian figure which surmounts the Opera House turret. For nigh a century he has stood sentinel on the pinnacles of Camden, and as a work of art is nothing short of a masterpiece. It was designed as an ideal effigy of the noble Catawba chief, King Haiglar, who in the olden days, between 1750 and 1763, was a frequent visitor to Camden, then Pine Tree Hill. He is represented in fine

Old Market and Courthouse, 1836.

ILLUSTRATION A.

Tower of Present City Hall.

ILLUSTRATION B.

pose, with drawn bow and arrow, a quiver at his back, feathers in his hair, and a stag's horns at his feet.

In stature it is five feet one inch, cut from iron, with gilding, which from time to time is overcome by rust, needing renewal. When and by whom was it shaped? The author is known to have been one J. B. Mathieu, a Frenchman who flourished in Camden between the years 1815 and 1834. Capt. James I. Villepigue, who in his youth knew Mathieu well, has told us that he repeatedly heard him state that he had designed and executed the figure, and presented it to the town. Of this there is no doubt. That Mathieu was expert in the profile business appears from this advertisement in the *Camden Gazette* of April 4, 1816:

"PROFILES AT J. B. MATHIEU'S 50c.,
WARRANTED CORRECT LIKENESSES."

It is gratifying to know that this likeness of King Haiglar is warranted. (See figure, page 55.)

It is also a fact that its execution dates as early as 1826, in which year it was raised to the summit of the completed market steeple which stood opposite the Courthouse. There it presided till 1859, when it was removed, with the steeple, uptown, and stood on this second perch till January, 1886, when Alfred Humbert, a colored man, daringly climbed up and dislodged his majesty for removal to his present location, fortunately in time to save him from the fire of December, 1892, which swept away the old tower and market.

The prowess of this Indian warrior, our tutelary genius, against the elements, cannot be better expressed than in these graphic words of a well-known, now departed, citizen of Camden: "The old Indian, so dear to the hearts of the people, was never known to turn his back to the storm; yet I have seen him bend before the blast and quiver like an aspen leaf, while spectators, with bated breath, expected to see him hurled from his airy perch. But no, he would suddenly recover his equilibrium, boldly face the warring elements, and with pointed arrow bid defiance to the hurricane."

The TOWN CLOCK, with its four dials, is a contemporary of the Indian, has accompanied him in each migration from spire to spire, and as he presided above, has tolled off the hours of a century. The bell of this clock served in days of slavery for the curfew which rang at 9 P. M., as a market bell, and fire alarm. Alexander Young, the noted Camden silversmith, was elected first keeper of the clock. He was succeeded by his son, G. G. Young. Their service extended over seventy years. By an ingenious device of the former the bell signals were sounded automatically.*

Dots From the Minutes.

[Unfortunately the journals, minutes, and other town records prior to 1843 were destroyed in the Civil War. Fragmentary data of the earlier period have been collected from various sources, old newspapers principally.]

1792.—Joseph Brevard, Recorder and legal adviser, salary £10; Zach. Cantey, Treasurer. Town lottery instituted, profits to be used in bulding a church in Camden. Number of tickets 1,780 at $6.00 each. Prizes 894, aggregating $9,850. Town to receive fifteen per cent. of prizes, total profit $2,307.50.

1794.—No sales to be made in market till bell rung.

1795.—Further burials in Episcopalian churchyard, south of Courthouse, prohibited, "being in most popu-

---

*Upon the bell is the following inscription: "Cast by John Willbank, Philada., 1824." Upon the clock the following: "Lukens. Fecit. No. 11, Philada."

lous part of the town"; exceptions in favor of those having close relatives there interred.

1808.—Lot owners required to plant trees and construct "terraces or gangways, of gravel or sand, along margins of Broad street from the lowest lots or tenements, occupied by Zebulon Rudulph and Robert Mickle, ending at uppermost tenanted lot below the Big Ditch."

1809.—Assize of bread, regulating size, price, quality, and weight.

1816.—Paving of sidewalks of Broad street from Bull street to Big Ditch.

1819.—Paving of sidewalks of Broad street, from Big Ditch to DeKalb street.

1843.—Boy put in stocks till ringing of nine o'clock bell for throwing stick in street pump.

1846-47.—Stock taken by town in South Carolina Railway.

1849.—Council gives $20 for tablet to Samuel Mathis, "first white male born in Camden." Sidewalks of brick or gravel to be constructed by lot owners from DeKalb to Laurens streets, on Broad.

1850.—James Robert McKain, Intendant of the town, lost in burning of steamer Orline St. John, on Alabama River, March 5th; born November 3, 1811, in Camden. In this disaster also perished Mr. McKain's mother, Mrs. Vaughan and her daughter Virginia, Mrs. Sizer and her daughter, all of Camden.

1851.—Town pays A. L. Chattan (builder of many of the best houses in Camden) $252.00 for rebuilding bridge over Pine Tree Creek on Charleston road, which since 1798 had been in the corporate limits of Camden, and maintained by the town.

1853.—Railroad stock of the town sold for $13,942.50.

1855.—Memorial page to Warden Keith S. Moffatt, who died at Orange Springs, Florida, January 17th.

1856.—J. K. Witherspoon elected Recorder, served until 1877, longer connected than any other official in its history, with the municipal affairs of Camden.

1857.—Revenues of the town, $2,958.51. Town in debt, and proposition discussed of disbanding police force.

1859.—Old market house, opposite Courthouse, sold, except steeple and clocks.

1860.—R. A. Young, $16.00 for flag; Robert Man, $26.00 for repair of cannon. Permission given commissioners of public buildings to erect Courthouse on Public Square.*

1862.—Two six-pounders and a brass piece loaned to State (Revolutionary guns?). "Terebene" oil lamps for council chamber. Heavy export tax on provisions.

1863.—January 15th, $140.00 for entertainment of staff of General Villepigue, whose body was brought for burial.

1865.—SHERMAN'S VISIT. Anticipating arrival of invading forces, the town hall was converted into a hospital to save it from destruction. The town records were sent for safety into the country, where, along with vast quantities of other property, they were captured by the enemy and all books antedating 1843 lost; those of subsequent date recovered. On February 24, 1865, a detachment from main body entered the town. The town was fired in many places, but heavy rain and exertion of citizens checked the progress of destruction. The railway depot, the commissary,† and east side of Broad street from DeKalb to Rutledge, Masonic Lodge, jail, Cornwallis's house on old muster ground, grist mills near the town, and a number of other buildings, were burned.

---

*The Public Square here referred to is the one we now call Hampton Park. This permit was during the intendancy of J. B. Kershaw.

†This was situated on the southeast corner of DeKalb and Broad streets, and the fire consumed the square to the next corner south.

On the first of April the usual election for council was held, the following chosen: R. M. Kennedy, Intendant; J. A. Young, I. B. Alexander, W. E. Hughson, Robert Man, Wardens. Their first care was to clear the streets of rubbish, of brick and burnt cotton, everywhere prevailing. Alarms of fire were constant, caused by incendiaries left by the Yankee troops. In one of these fires the Theological Seminary and its valuable library perished.

On April 18th occurred another invasion by General Potter and his negro troops. They broke into the banks and safes, and during their brief stay made the time hideous. The next day they retired to meet a threatened attack of a small Confederate force. They did not return.

The Council at this time, for lack of funds, issued a currency dated May 15, 1865, receivable for taxes and all town dues. This circulation was suspended when the town was occupied by Federal garrison, June 14th, under command of Capt. C. W. Furguson, Twenty-fifth Ohio Volunteers. They encamped in the upper (Monument) square, and the commanding officer used the council chamber as headquarters. The Council were relieved of duty, and military rule prevailed.

The garrison guarded and protected the town strictly, restraining the license and depredation of the newly-liberated negroes. By proclamation of Provisional Governor Perry, the civil authorities of the town resumed their offices November 1, 1865. Intendant R. M. Kennedy and Warden Hughson resigned. At election on November 13th the following were elected: Intendant, Col. A. D. Goodwyn; Wardens, J. A. Young, I. B. Alexander, Robert Man, Leslie McCandless.

1866.—Federal garrison removed March 24th, and after occupation of nine months the provost-marshal,

Captain Reed, turned over the keys of arsenal and town hall to Capt. J. A. Schrock.

1867.—No election. Officers' resignations declined by General Canby. Use of public square on DeKalb, between Gordon and Campbell, granted to B. F. Whittemore for negro school, now Jackson School.

1868.—After a fierce contest against a mongrel ticket, the following officers were elected: Intendant, Dr. A. A. Moore; Wardens, W. D. McDowall, J. R. Goodale, H. C. Salmond, William Daash.

1874.—This year marks the advent of street lighting in Camden. Twenty gasoline lamps installed on streets.

1875.—Memorial page to James Dunlap, so often intendant of the town; born December 20, 1804, died February 25, 1875. Census taken by town shows 2,293 inhabitants (including Kirkwood extension).

1877.—E. E. Sill, Recorder, in place of J. K. Witherspoon, who retired after twenty years' service.

1896.—Telephone franchise, exclusive, granted for five years, extended to ten years.

1897.—Electric light and water contract with Frank K. Bull and E. E. Mandeville, later incorporated as Camden Water, Light and Ice Company; twenty years, exclusive. The burning of the power house of this company in May, 1902, which left the town in darkness and a prey to several disastrous fires during the ensuing summer while deprived of resource for water, has caused a modification of these contracts.

Fires.

Fires have been a potent factor in causing the steady progress northwards of Camden from its original location. Often and sorely has it been scathed, beginning with the torch applied by a certain renegade Westberry to the Courthouse and Gaol in 1779, soon followed by

Rawdon's more thorough work on May 9, 1781. A local bard thus sang of that event, in the *Camden Journal* of November 7, 1829:

> "Grim war from Camden moved today,
> Long felt was there his iron sway,
> The town was fired when Rawdon fled,
> Lo, on its site the embers red!"

Then came the fire of 1812, of which we have but a bare mention,* informing us that it destroyed the two principal squares of the town, that opposite the Courthouse and the one south of it. The Market and Gaol were consumed, and an appropriation was made by Legislature for relief of sufferers.

The conflagration of the night of November 23, 1829. was probably the greatest in our annals, and has been described for us by the graphic C. F. Daniels, then editor of the *Camden Journal*. The heart of the town, the two squares north of the Courthouse, between York and King, both sides of Broad, were laid in ashes. The fire started near the southwest corner of York and Broad, then occupied by Dr. William Blanding's drug store. A strong northwest breeze swept it down to the Courthouse and Market, which were several times on fire. Eighty-five considerable buildings, some handsome, were lost, including Goodman's Hotel and the Jackson Hotel. The later was a four-story brick building, the property of Col. William Nixon, costing $20,000. It stood on the northeast corner King and Broad. The paper tells:

"An incident connected with the burning of the Jackson Hotel was universally noted and talked about. The hotel sign was what purports to be a likeness of the

---

*From an entry in James Kershaw's diary it appears this fire occurred October 23, 1812.

General. It hung within a few feet of the walls of the house, between that and Goodman's. While both buildings were one sheet of flame, 'Old Hickory' stood his ground unscathed, as he has always done amid the fiery bolts of his foes."

An eyewitness of that fire, an old citizen, has told us that so embittered was Colonel Nixon against some citizens for taking sides against his son, Henry G. Nixon, who had recently fallen in the duel with Hopkins, that he declined their services in saving his house and cursed them off.

The work of the flames in February, 1865, has already been mentioned. In 1874 the northern half of the west side of Broad, between DeKalb and Rutledge, was burned, including the Mansion, or Kershaw House, on the corner. The lower half of the same square was destroyed in 1892, and again in 1902. In 1875 the "Meroney Block," on Rutledge and Broad, with other buildings and offices, was wiped out, and in 1877 the great "Ark" fire occurred. An immense old wooden building on the site of the present Opera House was known as the "Old Ark." It made a huge blaze, and half of the square on that side went up with it.

These many disasters were due to no fault of Camden's fire department, which has always been active and gallant. The earliest regulation found on the subject is an old ordinance of 1798 requiring each lot owner to have a well, a good bucket, and ladder. Four fire masters were appointed to preside at conflagrations, their insignia being a black staff with white tip. In 1816 the town had two fire engine houses.

Just before the great fire of 1829 the Independent Fire Engine Company had been chartered by the Legislature, and certainly did great service in saving the town hall and Courthouse. In 1830 a Hook and Ladder

Company was formed, and 1833 another fire company, the Hydraulion. In 1837 one Aaron Burr is mentioned as captain of the Independent Company, which operated an engine costing $800, with 24 feet of suction and 150 feet of delivery hose. This was a wonderful machine in that day, and excited great curiosity on its arrival, described by the town wag as a beast with a short tail behind and long one in front.

This Aaron Burr was for many years a merchant of Camden, a town warden, and prominent in fire circles. His advertisement of "cocoanut dippers" and other wares may be found in the old newspapers.

During the forties and fifties Camden had three fire engines, the Market engine for downtown, Hydraulion for the middle section, and Log Town engine for the uptown. During the seventies the town had besides the Vigilant, a white company, two colored companies, both very faithful and efficient.

In 1884 the hand engine gave place to a steamer, which, like the Hydraulion of 1837, was hailed as a savior. It was not, though a great "hummer," a special success, for it usually arrived on the scene of action an hour late. It gave way to modern progress with the advent of waterworks in 1897, since when a first-class hose and reel company has protected the town.

Squares.

The public squares of Camden have always been one of its attractive features. In the first plan of the town there was but one central square, south of the Courthouse, intersected into four quarters, by Broad and Bull streets. On the northeast quarter stood the flagstaff for patriotic occasions (see Diagram No. 7); on the southwestern the boys of old used to play cricket. All, except the northeast quarter of this square, has been abandoned to cultivation, being rented out by council.

In the upper or modern Camden are five squares. The large central one, known as Monument Square, is like that of old Camden, quartered by the intersection of Laurens and Broad streets. On the eastern side of the town, between Lyttleton and Fair streets, are Rectory Square, and Hampton Square. On the western side also, between Campbell and Gordon streets, are two squares, with pine groves, but without names. They should be designated in some way.

The land occupied by all of these squares was originally owned by Joseph Kershaw, or the partnership of which he was a member. No formal deed, by Kershaw or other person, conveying them to the town, has been found, other than the official plats of the town (see Diagrams No. 3 and No. 4), upon which they are marked as public squares, and they have been occupied as such by the town authorities over a century.*

Wards.

The first division of Camden into wards was in May, 1792, when they were termed quarters, and denominated the Northeast, Northwest, Southeast and Southwest Quarters.

The present division was made in March, 1892, as follows:

Ward One—All south of Rutledge street.
Ward Two—All between Rutledge and DeKalb.
Ward Three—All between DeKalb and Laurens.
Ward Four—All north of Laurens.

---

*It will be noticed that on the plan of the town (Diagram No. 6) authorized by Council and recorded in 1799, which we have referred to as the Mathis plan, the public squares, H, G, I, K, are marked as "Reserved for Public Buildings," and the central squares, A, B, "Always to Remain Vacant." These appropriations rest upon the authority of the Town Council. But in the legislative, and most authoritative plan, that of 1798 (Diagram No. 5), all of these squares are simply designated in general terms as "Public Squares."

The Streets.

WYLY.—This was not a street on the first plan of Camden, which we have attributed to the year 1774. It was added to the extended plan of 1798, and most appropriately named in honor of Samuel Wyly, one of the old Quaker settlers of Pine Tree Hill. His residence was probably at some point near the line of this street.

GORDON.—In honor, most likely, of Chief Justice Thomas Knox Gordon, who presided at the first Court in Camden, November 5, 1772. It may possibly have derived its name from some local resident, as we find Moses Gordon a subscriber to the grand jury presentment of the year 1773.

CHURCH.—So named because the earliest churches were all on this street. The Presbyterian churchyard blocked it at the intersection of Meeting, and two lots (287 and 288) were devised to the town by Joseph Kershaw, to give space for the street to go around to the west.

BROAD.—Though not so wide by ten feet as some other streets of the town, this was probably the main thoroughfare of the early settlement, as it remains today.

MARKET.—So termed from the fact that the original site of the market was on this street, at its northwest corner with Bull, Lot No. 39.

LYTTLETON.—In honor of Governor Lyttleton, of Indian hostility fame.

FAIR.—So called from the Fair Ground at its southern terminus.

MILL.—This street was originally named by Joseph Kershaw "Front street" (see deed 1786 of Joseph Kershaw to Benjamin Carter). Its later name was derived, no doubt, from the fact of its being the chief route to

Kershaw's Mill, at the site now occupied by the DeKalb Cotton Factory.

RIPPONDEN.—The derivation of this name is not known, but was probably suggested to Joseph Kershaw by that of the market town of Ripon,* in his native West Riding of Yorkshire, England. The name Edward Ripon appears in Charleston Council Journals, 1732. The name is spelt with two p's on the old Mathis plan, but we think should have but one.

BOUNDARY.—So denominated as the northern boundary of the extended Camden of 1798.

LAURENS.—In honor of one or both of the Revolutionary heroes, father and son, Henry and John Laurens.

DEKALB.—No explanation of the propriety of this name is needed. As appears by James Kershaw's Diary, this street was laid off by him, August 22, 1799.

RUTLEDGE.—In honor of John Rutledge, the Revolutionary patriot, and President of South Carolina.

YORK.—Named by Joseph Kershaw after his native Yorkshire. This was the northern boundary of ancient Camden, 1768-98.

KING.—Named in honor of King George, no doubt. The Courthouse, located on this street, corner of Broad, represented peculiarly the seat of authority and royal powers.

BULL.—After Governor William Bull, a man of sterling merit, highly esteemed in the province, and worthy the compliment.

MEETING.—Derived its name, doubtless, from the fact that it led direct to the Quaker meeting-house, which stood at its western terminus, on ground now occupied by the cemetery.

---

*This town was noted in ancient times for the quality of the spurs there manufactured. Hence the old expression: "As true steel as Ripon rowels." Ripon spurs are mentioned in "Rob Roy."

WATEREE.—The sole Indian name that survives in our midst.

MULBERRY.—This street, located along the very verge of the Creek Swamp, was doubtless marked by native mulberry trees, and its name thus suggested.

The above were all streets of old Camden, none later than 1799 except Rutledge, which, as stated, was laid out about 1802. The following are the more recently established streets:

HAILE.—Forty-two feet wide; granted to the town by M. H. Haile, October 7, 1887.

ARTHUR LANE.—Granted to town by W. L. Arthur and A. D. Kennedy in 1894.

CLYBURN.—Granted by Capt. William Clyburn and A. T. Clyburn, February 12, 1896.

LAFAYETTE AVENUE.—Granted by Egmont Von Tresckow, April 4, 1901.

The Town Shinplaster.

After the devastation and depletion following the military raids of February and April, 1865, the town authorities were driven almost from necessity to issue a local currency. A press was put in operation to create municipal money, a process begun May 15, 1865, and continued until 1877. During this period there was issued a total of $34,252.10. There was outstanding $5,292.30 on June 13, 1877. The Council in the latter year adopted a rigid policy of redemption. So complete was the work of extermination that we have not been able to procure a single specimen of this curious currency as a relic. It never went below par, and many were loath to surrender it for redemption. It became so dilapidated, however, that in 1880 the merchants refused to receive it, thus driving it into final retirement.

The Town Cow.

The municipal topic cannot be dismissed without mention of the Town Cow, as sacred to the city fathers as to the Hindoos. For thirty years a campaign was waged to banish her from the streets, but in vain. The grazing along the ditch banks and open lots was too valuable a feature of the Camden of the bygone generation to be dispensed with.

The agitation began in 1850, when the *Camden Journal* said: "We suggest to 'our City Fathers' the propriety of impounding straggling cows, as well as vagrant hogs, for one is as great a nuisance as the other." Nothing was done.

Many will remember how, in the years following the war, when dilapidation had overtaken old Camden, the cows, after ruminating all day upon the pastures of the "Magazine Hill," would take lodging every night in the basement hall of the Courthouse. A sportive allusion to this is found in the *Kershaw Gazette* of April 12, 1876:

"It is said the cows have more business in the Courthouse than anybody else."

"NOTICE TO COWS: You and each of you are hereby warned against using the hallway of the Courthouse as a place of nightly resort, under penalty of incurring the supreme displeasure of all *persons* having business in said building." Many will recall how the cows used to devour the cotton out of bales left on platforms in town over night.

Again in 1881 the same editor protests against the cow as an unmitigated nuisance, and tells of a gentleman returning home, the night being dark, made to assume a recumbent attitude on the sidewalk, by coming in contact with a retired cow. What was the response of Council to all this clamor? They passed an ordinance against cow bells. But the very next year higher powers intervened, for the law against roaming stock was passed by the Legislature of 1882, and thus the public career of the Town Cow came to an end.

Intendants and Mayors of Camden.

1791. Joseph Kershaw.	1840. J. M. DeSaussure.
1792. Isaac DuBose.	1841. J. M. DeSaussure.
1794. Isaac Alexander.	1843. Hayman Levy.
1795. Isaac DuBose.	1844. Hayman Levy.
1798. John Kershaw.	1845. J. C. West.
1799. Samuel Mathis.	1846. W. J. Gerald.
1801. John Kershaw.	1847. J. M. DeSaussure.
1802. Isaac DuBose.	1848. J. M. DeSaussure.
1805. James Chesnut.	1849. J. R. McKain.
1807. Isaac Alexander.	1850. James Dunlap.
1808. John Darington.	1851. James Dunlap.
1809. Peter Warren.	1852. E. A. Salmond.
1811. John Kershaw.	1853. John Rosser.
1816. Abram Blanding.	1854. E. A. Salmond.
1817. William Langley.	1855. W. J. McKain.
1818. Thomas Salmond.	1856. James A. Young.
1819. Thomas Salmond.	1857. John Rosser.
1820. Royal Bullard.	1858. W. D. McDowall.
1822. John Kershaw.	1859. Joseph B. Kershaw.
1823. Peter Warren.	1860. Joseph B. Kershaw.
1824. James Brown.	1861. Thomas J. Warren.
1825. Thomas Salmond.	1862. James Dunlap.
1827. Thomas Salmond.	1863. James Dunlap.
1828. Thomas Salmond.	1864. James Dunlap.
1830. H. R. Cook.	1865. R. M. Kennedy.
1831. H. R. Cook.	A. D. Goodwyn.
1832. John Boykin.	1866. James A. Young.
1833. John Boykin.	1867. James A. Young.
1837. H. R. Cook.	1868. Dr. A. A. Moore.
1838. H. R. Cook.	1869. Dr. A. A. Moore.

1870. W. Z. Leitner.
1871. James M. Davis.
1872. James M. Davis.
1873. W. C. S. Ellerbe.
1874. Joseph D. Dunlap.
1875. Joseph D. Dunlap.
1876. Joseph D. Dunlap.
1877. J. C. Rollings.
1878. D. C. Kirkley.
1879. D. C. Kirkley.
1880. J. R. Goodale.
1881. J. R. Goodale.
1882. G. G. Alexander.

1883. J. C. Rollings.
1884. James Jones.
1885. J. C. Rollings.
1886. C. J. Dunlap.
1888. J. R. Goodale.
1890. J. W. Corbett.
1892. H. G. Carrison.
1894. A. D. Kennedy.
1896. F. L. Zemp.
1898. F. L. Zemp.
1900. E. O. McCreight.
1902. E. O. McCreight.
1904. H. G. Carrison.

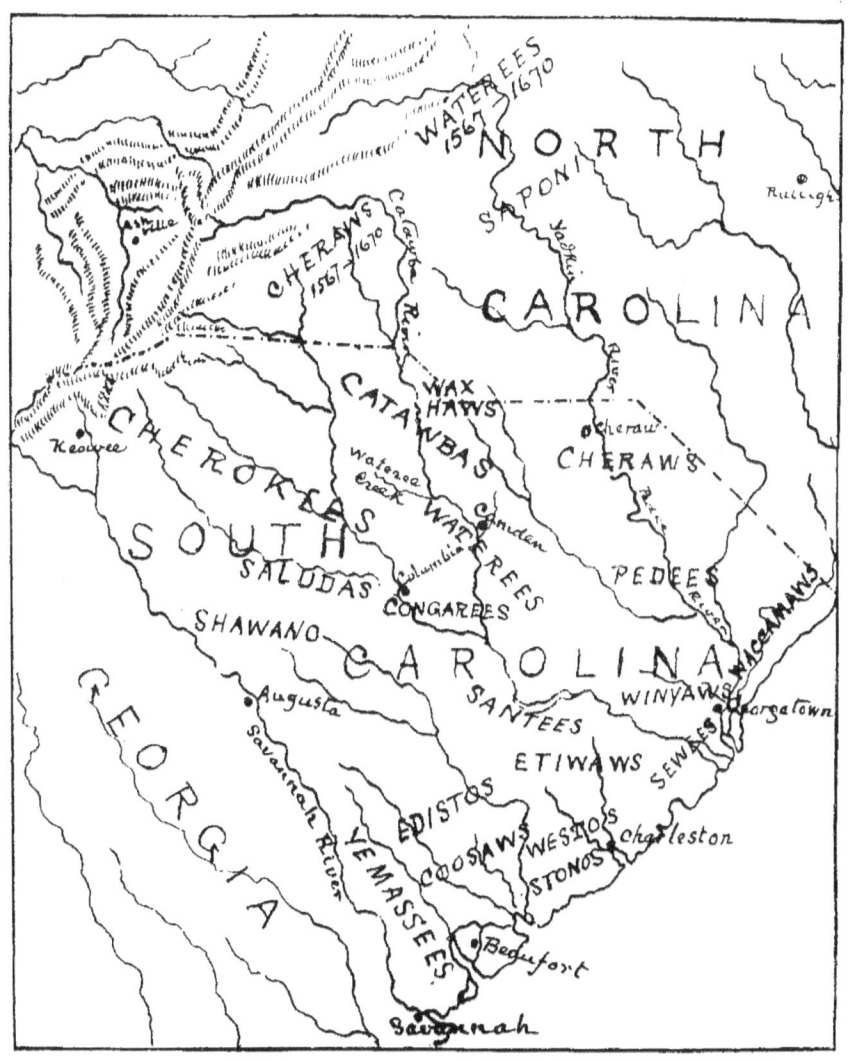

Chart of Indian Tribes.

DIAGRAM No. 8.

Chart of Indian Tribes.

DIAGRAM No. 8.

CHAPTER II.

INDIAN ERA.

The twenty or more Indian tribes inhabiting the triangular-shaped territory of South Carolina, at the time of its first settlement, according to the latest views of students of the subject, were subdivisions of the four principal races, Siouan, Iroquoian, Algonquian, and Muskhogean.* The locations of the South Carolina tribes are roughly indicated in Diagram No. 8.

The Cherokees, who occupied the hill and mountain corner, the northwest quarter of the State, and extending through the mountains of North Carolina and Tennessee, were a southern offshoot of the warlike and predatory *Iroquoian* race of the North, whose strongholds were in New York and Pennsylvania. The belligerent Tuscaroras of Eastern North Carolina were of the same stock. The Iroquoians were the constant enemies of the southern races. Indeed, their hands were against all others of the red men, and they lived a life of ceaseless warfare.

All those tribes lying between the sea coast and the Santee and Broad Rivers, of whom the Catawbas were the most powerful, have been proven by modern research to have been congeners of the *Siouan* race, which occupied the vast regions west of the Mississippi, to which belong the Sioux, Dacotahs, Osages, and the like. The theory is that the western tribes emigrated from the East, rather than the eastern tribes from the West, and more probably that the race had a common origin on the

---

*At the outset acknowledgement is hereby made to a publication of the Ethnological Bureau, by James Mooney, 1894, for the authority upon which statements are herein made as to the racial connections and locations of the Indian tribes of this State.

headwaters of the Ohio, and diverged in opposite directions. The South Carolina group of this stock comprised, besides the Catawbas, our own Waterees, the Cheraws, Waxhaws, Waccamaws, Pedees, Winyahs, Congarees, Santees, Sewees, probably also the Etiwaws (or Eutaws), whose tribal name is said to have been derived from the Catawba word for "pine tree"—*itiwa*.

As to the tribes in the southwest corner of the State, between Charleston and Savannah, such as the Yemassees, Coosaws, Edistos, they are rated as branches of the Muskhogean (or Creek) race, which inhabited the coast regions of Georgia and Gulf States. The Coosaws became incorporated with the Catawbas, but preserved a distinct dialect. The Yemassees and some of their neighbors were driven off by the colonists to Florida.

In early times there dwelt on the Savannah River, north of Augusta, a tribe of the Algonquian race, the Shawano (Shawnees), from whom the name Savannah is derived. It is said they left Carolina about the year 1700, and located in Pennsylvania. It was by a party of this tribe, as we shall see, that King Haiglar of the Catawbas was murdered.

So widely did the various tribes roam, and so often shift their habitations, that to follow and identify them, by the guidance of the confused geography and nomenclature of the early explorers, becomes an intricate task. For instance, a fragment of the Natchez of Mississippi, after their war with the French, about the year 1734, made their home in South Carolina, and are mentioned in our old records as "Notchees," or "Nouchees." In 1744 a party of them killed ten Catawbas, who were on their way to Charleston.*

*Letter of Governor Glen to Thomas Brown, Council Journals of 1744.

Within the period of historic certainty, the locality around Camden was occupied by the Waterees, extending along both sides of the river which bears their name, from Wateree Creek, twenty-five miles above Camden, to the vicinity of the Congaree River below. It seems doubtful whether this was their situation at the time of the Spanish expedition into the Carolinas under Juan de Pardo in 1567, who describes them, by the name "GUATARI," as residing near the mountain Cherokee tribe *Atali*, and which would indicate a position much nearer the mountains than Camden. He speaks of them as "ruled by two female chiefs who held dignified court with a retinue of young men and women as attendants."*

A century later, in 1670, John Lederer, a German explorer from Virginia, who has left a record of his journey, locates the Waterees up in North Carolina, on the headwaters of the Yadkin River (the Peedee in its lower course), apparently not far from the position assigned them by Pardo in 1567. Indeed it is thought by Gregg† that the name Wateree was originally applied to the Yadkin. Of the Waterees, Lederer relates this interesting incident: Their chief sent out three warriors with orders to kill some young women of a hostile tribe in order that their spirits might serve his son, who was dying, in the other world. In accordance with their instructions they soon returned with scalps and the skin from the faces of three young women. These trophies they presented to the chief, who received them with grateful acknowledgment.‡

Subsequent to Lederer's visit, the Waterees must have deserted their upper haunts, and come down to the Camden vicinity, some 150 miles south, where they were

---

*Narration of Juan de la Vendera, published 1569, cited in Siouan Tribes of the East, p 80.
†History of the Old Cheraws.
‡Siouan Tribes of the East, p. 81, citing Lederer, 12.

found by John Lawson in 1701, on his route through the Carolinas. From Lawson's statements it is difficult to determine whether his course lay up the eastern or western side of the Wateree River, and on which side he met with the Waterees. On a map of 1715 their town or village is put down on the western side, about Wateree Creek. In Moll's map of 1730, it is represented on the eastern side. They doubtless had several villages. On Cook and Monzon's map of 1771, an "Indian Town" is represented in the fork of Big and Little Pine Tree Creeks, adjacent to Camden on the east, just where the Camden Cotton Mill is situated. This spot also is indicated as "Indian Camp," upon the plat of a large tract of land conveyed in 1796 by John Kershaw to Duncan McRae and Zach. Cantey, and here we may reasonably conclude was once the headquarters of the Waterees.

Lawson designates them by the name of Wateree-Chickanee. No other writer mentions the latter half of the compound, which probably represented some co-tribe of whom nothing is known. He gives us this most quaint account of his Wateree hosts:

"The people of this nation are likely, tall Persons, and great Pilferers, stealing from us anything they could lay their Hands on, though very respectful in giving us what victuals we wanted. We lay in their Cabins all night, being dark, smoky Holes as ever I saw any Indians dwell in. Their nation is much more populous than the Congarees, and their neighbors, yet they understand not one another. They are very poor in English effects, several of them having no guns, making use of bows and arrows, being a lazy idle People, a quality incident to most Indians, but none to that degree as these as I ever met with.

"Their country is free from swamps and quagmires, being high, dry Land and consequently healthful, producing large cornstalks and fair grain.

"Next morning we took off our beards with a razor, the Indians looking on with a great deal of admiration. They told us they had never seen the like before and that our knives cut far better than those that came among the Indians. They would fain have borrowed our Razor, and they had our Knives, Scissors and Tobacco Tongs the day before, being as ingenious at picking of pockets as any, I believe, the world affords, for they will steal with their feet."

We may judge how wild was the country in the days of Lawson (1701) by this description of his camp near the river, some distance below the Waterees: "When we were all asleep, in the Beginning of the Night we were awakened with the dismall'st and most hideous Noise that ever pierced my Ears, endless Numbers of Panthers, Tygers, Wolves and other Beasts of Prey, which take this Swamp for their Abode in the Day." He also tells that there issued from this swamp at sunrise a "Gang" of several hundred wild turkeys, and that his Indian companion killed fifteen of them.

Yet, after such a picture, he states that on his way from the Waterees up to the Waxhaws, about fifty miles, he found not a spot of bad land and went through cleared ground all the way. This would not seem to tally with the indolent character given to the inhabitants, and leaves us puzzled at the transition. These clearings may have been the work of preceding occupants. Who were they and why did they leave?

When, in 1715, the Yemassees, incited by the Spanish, sent around the bloody stick, the signal for war, and fell upon the unsuspecting coast settlements, the Waterees, as did all the Carolina tribes, joined the coalition.* After the first surprise, in which a number were overtaken with torture and massacre, the colonists turned the tables on their Indian foes and inflicted on them condign punishment. In this contest the Waterees were doubtless much worsted and reduced.

We hear nothing more of them until we come upon an old entry in the State records, the Council Journal for February 28, 1743, containing the petition of a certain Indian trader, Thomas Brown, which is in substance as follows:

"That in the year A. D. 1735, and for several years before, having been a lycensed trader to the Cattawbaw Indians, he carried on considerable trade from the place of his residence near Congaree Old Fort,† and used frequently to pass and repass from said Congarees to the Cattawbaw Nation, by which means he became acquainted with the goodness of the lands upon the Santee and Wateree Rivers, particularly the Wateree lands, and the Indians living and residing upon the same.

"That there are very few inhabitants in that remote part of the country besides your petitioner's family, and to introduce whites, he proceeded to secure a body of land between Santee and Wateree Rivers, inhabited by Wateree Indians, not settled, inhabited or claimed by any white person. That by deed of Feofment, he purchased the lands of the Waterees, *as far up as Catawba Ford,* with livery of seizin, on March 13, 1735. That the Wateree Indians were the natural, rightful owners and possessors of said lands, had not forfeited same, and there was no law at the time prohibiting purchase of lands from Indians. But that a subsequent

---

*Carroll's Hist. Collections, Vol. 1, p. 198.
†About where Columbia is now located.

Act of Assembly declared all future and past purchases of lands from Indians void."

He proceeds to protest against this *ex post facto* law, and the subsequent loss of his Wateree domain, and presents as a bill against the government, the price he had paid for the lands, with interest and expenses, which he sets forth in the following grotesque account:

38 1-2 yds. strouds	@ £ 4	£154
16 yds. plains	@ £ 1 1-2	24
3 guns	@ £16	48
50 wt. gun-powder	@ £ 2	100
100 wt. bullets	@ £ 1-2	50
15 white blankets	@ £ 6	90
15 gals. rum	@ £ 4	60
1 bus. salt		3
40 doeskins, worth in ammunition for war		40
Beef and corn		12
		£581
Interest at 10 per cent.		451
Charges coming and going		100
Advice £25, conveyance £15		40
		£1,172

The Assembly without ceremony rejected Brown's petition, and the Waterees were so much to the good in the bargain. But they were to have little longer tenure of the land they had so foolishly sold.

As we have seen, the town of Fredricksburg, the antecedent of Camden, had just, the year before Brown's purchase, been laid off in the very heart of the Wateree country. We might expect them to become resentful at such signs of intrusion. Accordingly the records contain accounts of the hostile attitude of the Waterees, and we find this item, in the Council Journal of 1736, a letter of Lieut.-Gov. Thomas Broughton to the Assembly:

"Mr. Speaker and Gentlemen: I don't doubt but you have heard of the unfortunate Family that was cut off by some Indians near Pine Tree Creek. The neighbors thereabouts informed me that if something could not be done for their protection, they should be obliged to quit their Habitations. To prevent their removal I ordered a Lieutenant with eight men to range on the Back of those settlements." At the same time a petition comes to the Assembly from inhabitants of Fredricksburg alleging violent acts by the Waterees and asking horse paths to be cut to the other settlements.

The Assembly, in response to these appeals, resolved to send a guard among the Catawbas, "to demand satisfaction for the murder of the family on Pine Tree Creek, which the Council is informed was done by the Charraws. Late insults committed by the Waterees require satisfaction, those people being also sheltered by the Catawbas. That if they have any complaint they must come down here (Charlestown) and lay before Government, which will not suffer them to take their own satisfaction."

We thus see that at this date the Catawbas had already obtained the sovereignty or protectorate over the Waterees and Cheraws, as they finally did over the remnants of nearly all the Carolina tribes, and were held accountable for their behavior.

We catch few more glimpses of the Waterees as a distinct tribe. In 1740 Governor Bull sends to the Assembly a letter, stating that the Wateree Indians claim the lands of Fredricksburg township and demand satisfaction for same. He advises that compensation be made. But search through subsequent pages of the records does not show what payment, if any, was made to them. The only other entry found relating to them is as follows: "£3 to William Scott, planter, provisions supplied to Waterees on their visit to Charlestown; £3, 11s., 3d., to Mary Ann Jones for victuals and liquors to February 13, 1741, for Waterees."

From the above we may infer that they had gone down to see about payment for their lands. After this they became so merged with the Catawbas that their name disappears. They departed from their Camden haunts and moved up to the Catawba Nation, where they were found living, by Adair in 1743, still preserving their dialect.*

But no word of their dialect has been preserved to us. Even their tribal name, which attaches, as their sole memorial, to our river, is said to be derived from the Catawba word *wateran*, "to float in the water." Their name is also borne by Wateree Creek, which enters the Catawba, from the west, in Fairfield County, some twenty-five miles north of Camden, the name of the river also, at that point, changing to Wateree.

Two other names in our county may perhaps be of Indian origin. SAWNEY, the name of a creek in West Wateree, is very suggestive of *Shawnee, Suwannee;* and as some confirmation, we find in the *South Carolina Gazette* of January 12, 1760, mention of an Indian, of the Catawbas, by name of "Big Sawney," then in Charleston, enlisted for the Cherokee War. HYCO, the name of a locality near Pine Tree Creek, some seven miles northeast of Camden, is most probably Indian. In North Carolina, near the Virginia line, where dwelt

---

*Siouan Tribes of the East, p. 80, citing Gatschet.

the *Saponi*, is a river to this day known as Hyco or Hycootee, which, in their dialect, signified "Buzzard roost," Hyco being the Siouan for "buzzard," and *oti* for residence.* Some of the Saponi, according to Byrd, a Virginia author of 1728, came down and joined the Catawbas.† Is it unlikely that they dwelt in the section known to us as Hyco?

As the Waterees recede from view, our attention turns to the Catawbas. This unique tribe has a peculiar interest for us, since the ideal figure of their noted chief, King Haiglar, has so long been a conspicuous object and constant reminder in our midst. Besides, they were intimately connected with the early days of Camden, and within the memory of elderly persons they used to be familiar visitors here. Their small remnant have long been the sole survivors of the Red Man in this State, and they fairly illustrate the rule of the survival of the fittest.

The Catawba tradition, recounted by Schoolcraft, to the effect that they had been driven from Canada by the *Connewangos* and French, is pronounced by probably the best authority on the subject,‡ an absurd invention. They were found by Juan Pardo, in 1567, where they have ever since resided, that is the district corresponding with York and Lancaster Counties of this State. The name Catawba is not that by which they were known originally, or by which they called themselves. They were first mentioned by Vendera, in 1569, by the name of "Issa"; by Lederer in 1670 as "Usheree" (a perversion of the Catawba *Iswa-hĕrĕ*); and by Lawson in 1701 as "Esaw." These were all different forms of the Catawba *iswa* or *eswa*, meaning "river," their

---

*Siouan Tribes of the East, p. 46.
†*Ibid.*, p. 49.
‡Siouan Tribes of the East, p. 69, James Mooney.

name for the Catawba River being ESWA-TAROA, "the great river."*

Lawson mentions the *Kadapaus* (merely another form of Catawba) as a small tribe adjacent to the Esaws, of whom they were evidently a branch, and between them afterwards no distinction is traceable. Kadapau is said to have been the Indian name for Lynches Creek,† applied by Lawson, doubtless, to the tribe living thereon, just as Eswa, the name of the river, was transferred to the Esaws. Near to the Esaws, whom we will now call Catawbas,‡ dwelt the Waxhaws, the *Wisackys* of Lederer, who visited that section in 1672. He says they were then subject to the Catawbas, and virtually a part of them.

These Waxhaws were "flat-heads," and Lawson (1701), who tells a good deal about them, describes their process of compressing the infant heads. They claimed that by causing a prominence of the eyes the sight was sharpened. There is no reference to this practice among the Catawbas, who were, however, addicted to the ecstasy of the fire dance, thus described by Lederer (1672):

"These miserable wretches are strangely infatuated with the illness of the devil; it caused no small horror in me to see one of them wrythe his neck all on one side, foam at the mouth, stand barefoot upon burning coal for near one hour, and then, recovering his senses, leap out of the fire without hurt or singe."

Lawson says that in 1701 the Catawbas (by him called

---

*Mr. Hewitt, of the Ethnological Bureau, has kindly furnished us with this correct version of the name, which has heretofore been rendered as Eswa-*Tavora*.

†Gregg's Hist. Old Cheraws, p. 20.

‡In the State records, Indian Books, Vol. I, we find an entry of Orders from the Indian Commissioners to one John Wright to call a meeting of the headmen of the Wacsaw, Esau, and Cuttabau Indians, August, 1711.

Esaws, as stated,) were "a very large nation, containing many thousand people." Lederer, in 1672, says they were a "powerful nation" and their villages "very thick." Adair says that (about 1682) they numbered 1,500 warriors, and 6,000 souls. He also states that one of their old cleared fields extended for seven miles. Yet by 1743, after they had incorporated with themselves the remnants of twenty other tribes, their warriors numbered not more than 400. Such was their decline in half a century under constant warfare, smallpox, and the white man.

With the exception of a single early instance, when in 1715 they joined the Yemassee uprising, the Catawbas were ever devoted and constant friends of the colonists. Nothing could seduce them from this attachment. An old author speaks of them as "a noble race, fearless in war, in address surpassed by none." The good and wise Governor Glen writes of them to the Board of Trade in London, May 3, 1746: "The Catawbas are a very brave nation and entirely attached to the government. They are beset by enemies."

In 1754 Charles Pinckney writes to the London Board: "The Catawbas are a small but brave people, between South and North Carolina settlements. We often experienced the value of their friendship. They would to a man join us in any enterprise if their wives and children were secure. Perpetual enemies to the French Indians and by them frequently attacked, who, though sure to be worsted in every engagement, have reduced those brave people from upward of four hundred to about two hundred men."

Amid the mass of material which exists concerning these interesting Indians, enough to fill a large volume, it is difficult to select without wandering too far. From the *South Carolina Gazette* of June 2, 1746, we learn that the name of their King was Yenabe-Yetangway. He, with his headmen, attended a conference held by Governor Glen at a point near Columbia, for the purpose of dissuading the Pedees and Cheraws, whose chiefs were also present, from a breach with the Catawbas, which it seems was imminent. The paper relates that the Governor illustrated the parable of the bundle of sticks to show the strength of union, using pistol rammers for the purpose.

The name of their King in 1749 is mentioned as Essetaswa. To him succeeded Nobkehea, who, with five other Catawba headmen, one of whom was Haiglar, attended the great peace conference with the six Iroquoian nations at Albany, N. Y., in July, 1751. They made the passage by boat from Charleston, under escort of Gov. William Bull, whose graphic account of the ceremonials of the treaty is to be found in our State records. Among other things he states that the Oneidas and Cayugas were very loath to accede to the peace, because of an unavenged loss inflicted upon them by the Catawbas, who, in their last encounter, had killed seventy out of two hundred of their men, including their favorite warrior, Coronodawanah. By this we may judge the Catawbas to have been no easy antagonists.

At this conference it was agreed to end the inveterate hostilities that had ever waged between the Catawbas and the Iroquoians, and to bury the hatchet forever. The Catawbas were to return north the next fall and bring back all prisoners held by them, and to receive in exchange all captured from them. The following joint epistle was indited, November 23, 1751, by the headmen of the Mohawks, Amonidas, Tuscaroras, and other tribes, to the Catawbas, to which is appended a facsimile of some of their curious autographs:

"BROTHERS: We are very sorry to learn by your Paper that sickness has taken hold of your Nation, which you say has prevented your seeing us at Albany this Fall. We hope God will take the sickness from amongst you, that you may be able as you desire to meet us there next Spring, as soon as the leaves shall begin to adorn the Trees, and bring with you what people you shall have of ours. We thank you for the regard you express to preserve the Pledge of Peace we gave you at Albany."

Seth *his mark* Turtle   Rutt *his mark* Wolf

Paulus *his mark* Bear

Brant *mark* Wolf

The reign of Nobkehea, though marked by the Albany treaty, closed with a rather inglorious incident, related in a grotesque letter from the Catawbas, dated November, 1752, setting forth that a certain negro slave, who had been licensed to trade with them, had made their King drunk, and beat him so severely about the head "that he could not see out of his eyes for five or six days." It is not surprising to find another King in his place the next year.

Haiglar first appears officially in a letter written by him, as King of the Catawbas, to the Chickesaws, in the year 1753. Next is found this letter, dated March 14, 1756, to Governor Glen:

"The gentlemen of Virginia told us that if we would go and help, we with the other Force would cutt the French down like a great poplar and Top the branches. We are a small Nation, but our name is high, and if we go to war with the white People against the enemy, we shall drive them so far as that we shall raise many children, without any danger or molestation. I promised the gentlemen of Virginia who brought the Hatchet that I would go with them and the time is come, but I will stay and hold the Hatchet in my hand until I hear from you, which I hope won't be long."

Hagler a King of the Catawbaws

Haiglar kept his word well with the Virginians, for in an old *Gazette* of 1757, a "Gentleman on the Yadkin" writes that thirteen Catawbas had passed with four French scalps taken at Fort Duquesne, and again that seventeen "compleat Catawba warriors had passed on their way to war and that King Haiglar was to follow with 100 more."

It was just about the time of the accession of King Haiglar that the Quaker colony landed at the site of Camden, the Pine Tree Hill of those early days. Soon after arose the intimacy between Samuel Wyly, the leading Quaker, and Haiglar, headman of the Catawbas, who were frequent visitors at Pine Tree Hill. Their names come down to us closely associated. Wyly became the colonial agent in dealing with the Catawbas. We find an item in the old government accounts of £1,000 paid to him for surveying the 144,000 acres allotted to the tribe. He conducted their correspondence, and the signatures of Haiglar and the other chiefs were probably made with his pen.

James Adamson, another member of the Pine Tree

Hill colony, of whom more will be told, has left us a name memorable for his gallant service and tragic death among the Indians. It was with no little degree of satisfaction that copies of letters of this period by Wyly, Adamson, and Haiglar were found among the State papers. Some of them are here transcribed:

Haiglar to Governor Lyttleton:

Pine Tree Hill, 3 Jany., 1759.

DEAR BROTHER: Agreeable to our promise to you and Mr. Atkin, I and my warriors went out against the enemys of our Father the Great King George, whom we shall be always ready and willing to serve; upon our return we found the dry weather had entirely destroyed our crop and unless our good Brother the Governor will supply us with a little corn, our wives and children will perish. We are glad to hear that the Six Nations of Northward Indians has made peace with our Father the Great King George, which is all from your loving brother

King (his mark) Hagler

Samuel Wyly to Governor Lyttleton:

Mount Pleasant, 5th May, 1759.

May it please the Governor:

I received thy favour of the 27th April pr Capt. Johny* who seems well pleased. I did all I could to talk and feed them into a good humour. I informed

---

*A Cheraw chief. The Cheraws were then a component part of the Catawbas.

them of the woman that one of their party had abused, which I mentioned to thee in my last pr Joseph Kershaw, and they promised me that they would punish the offender according to the nature of his crime when they went home.

Two days before the Indians returned to my house there came down an Indian from the Nation and informed me there had been several murders committed on the upper settlement on our River, but as the Indian could not speak good English, I could not tell what to make of it untill this day there came two men from the upper parts and gave me the inclosed account and made oath that they knew the major part to be true and believed it all to be true (one of them went with the party in search of the murderers), says that it is the opinion of everybody that it is done by the Cherrockees; the Catawbas that were at home behaved very well upon the occasion, and the King, captain and warriors declared they would do all in their power to find out the murderers, and revenge it, they seemed to be greatly insenced against the Cherrockees and declared their firm attachment to his Majesty. I believe it will not be in my power to get anybody to build the chimney for Haiglar, and wait for their pay until the Assembly thinks proper to pay them. I have nothing more to offer thee but that I am thy real friend   SAML. WYLY.

Information on oath before Samuel Wyly:
Pine Tree Hill, 5th May, 1759.

On the South Branch of Catawba River one Dutch man named Conrad Mull, his wife and his son scalped by the Indians (supposed to be Cherrockees) on the No. side of said River in Wm. Morrison's settlement, eight children of a white man named Hannah, and two Familys on the Adkin River (name is unknown) Sunday

29th ulto. As soon as the Catawbas heard of the murder 22 of them went out to bury the dead and 15 of their warriors went voluntary under the command of Matthew Pool accompanyed by several white men in search of the Murderers. This intelligence was given under oath before me. SAML. WYLY.

Lieut. James Adamson to Governor Lyttleton:

Wateree, this 5th May, 1759.

SIR: To acquaint Your Excellency of the behaviour of the Cherrockees I went after three of our deserters where I heard they were in North Carolina within a few miles of the Adkin River and coming into their parts I found them all in arms by reason the Cherrockees had killed a Dutchman, Conrad Mull and his wife and son; on the north of said River, in William Morrison's settlement, they killed eight children, also killed two more familys on the Adkin whose names are not known, when the Catawbas heard of it they went out after them and I am certain they are very loyal. I would have staid and sent you a fuller account but having three deserters on my hands and no one to assist me that I came away and brought the men with me, where I await Your Excellency's orders, and am willing to go anywhere you please to send me, which is all from Your Excellency's Humble Servant to command

JAMES ADAMSON.

The outrages of the Cherokees, referred to in the preceding letters, were the prelude to the open warfare between that tribe and the colonists which very soon followed and lasted through several bitter campaigns. The Catawbas rejected the Cherokee overtures for alliance, and sided with the colonists. The Assembly

Effigy of King Haiglar—Vane on Tower of City Hall.

ILLUSTRATION C.

voted them £2,150, to be expended by Samuel Wyly for corn, blankets and equipment of fifty of their warriors. We also find a note in the *South Carolina Gazette,* of October, 1760, that provision had been made for "building a fort to protect their women and children to be erected within a few miles of Pine Tree Hill."*

They did valiant service in the Cherokee War, and although smallpox during 1759 had made terrible havoc among them, in December of that year a party of six presented themselves to Governor Lyttleton in camp at Keowee, with "Passes of Health from Samuel Wyly of the Waterees." In 1760 the *Gazette* states that "King Haiglar and some Catawbas were with the army." In October, 1760, ninety-nine Catawba warriors arrived in Charlestown, with eight Cherokee scalps taken near Keowee, for which they claimed a bounty. They went home extremely well satisfied, having, besides the ample provision made for them by the General Assembly, received their scalp money, and a reward equal to two scalps, for a prisoner taken by them.

Like many another distinguished career, that of King Haiglar was cut short by the assassin. On August 30, 1763, a lurking party of Shawnees poured a volley into him from ambush, and took his proud scalp. An explicit authority for this statement is found in the following letter (Council Journal, 1763, p. 89), from William Richardson to Richard Richardson:

"Waxsaws, Aug. 31st, 1763.

"SIR: You have heard of what devastation the Indians have done to the northward and they have extended them to these parts, have killed one woman on the south

---

*In the Council Journal, June 23, 1761, is found an entry of £700 paid by Assembly to Samuel Wyly, the amount advanced by him for building this fort for the Catawbas.

fork of Catawbaw, one man and two children and miserably cut a woman lower down the country. This has filled the inhabitants of Broad River with such fear that a great part hath fled hither. *Yesterday the enemy killed King Hagler almost in the midst of our settlement,* which caused such Terror that there was nothing but running and flying wherever safety could be had. Now, sir, you see to what we are reduced, and we think proper to apply to you to see if you could prevail with the Governor to allow us a small scout between Broad River and the Catawbaw, for as long a time as shall be judged expedient by his Excellency and as ammunition is very scarce, a little would be necessary, and indeed if some speedy assistance is not afforded, the Frontiers will, we are afraid, be immediately deserted and the prospect of Famine, as our crops are but poor, scarce able to maintain ourselves far less ourselves and the frontier inhabitants. Now Col. try to do us service at such a juncture and we shall be greatly obliged to you."

The choice of a successor to King Haiglar seems to have been subject to the supervision of Samuel Wyly, who, on January 29, 1765, writes to Governor Bull that he had "assembled the Catawbas, who had chose Capt Frow for their King," and sent to his Honor the following:

Talk from the Headmen of the Catawbas.
  To the Hon. Wm. Bull, Esqr., Lieut.-Governor in and over his Majesty's Province of South Carolina, this 29th day of January, 1765.
DEAR BROTHER: We met our Friend Samuel Wyly, who delivered your talk and we have unanimously chose Capt Frow to be our King. We are very glad and rejoice in our hearts that our Father the great King

INDIAN ERA. 57

George and our Brother the Governor and his beloved men are so good to us; as the boundary line leaves our nation on the North side we hope our Father the great King and Governor will keep us in the South government, our faces is always turned there and our hearts is also there, notwithstanding our land is run all round and marked there is several people of North Carolina settled within our line. Two families have lately built houses on our land. We remain your loving Brothers.

King Frow his Mark
Capt Thomson his ͻ Mark
John Chesnut his ₰ Mark
Wateree Jenny his G Mark

Our sense of poetic justice is gratified to find of record the retribution that befell the Shawnee slayers of King Haiglar. It is but proof of how assiduous the Indian was in pursuit of his revenge. In the Council Journal for May 31, 1768, is found the following entry:

"King Frow and twelve of the Catawba Indians being come to Town were called in, when they shook hands with his Honor and the gentlemen of the Board. His Honor asked Him what they had to say. King Frow then laid before his Honor six scalps of the Shawnese, according to custom come to harrass them and their nation and said that they had given them what they wanted.

"His Honor then told him we loved King Haglar because he was a friend to the English and are glad the man that killed him was killed by the Catawbas. He desired that they would carry their scalps home to make their boys brave men. * * I will give you (said the Governor) some Rum and Paint, powder and shot, and one saddle for the King, but I cannot give all his captains saddles."

In 1771 the Lieutenant-Governor informed the Board of a letter from Mr. Kershaw "at Cambden informing him that the Catawba Indians had lately been interrupted in their Hunting by some of the back settlers, which had given them great uneasiness, and that some persons, about six weeks ago had come to their camp,* destroyed their skins and beat them severe, which usage could not fail to inflame their minds."

But the fidelity of the Catawbas to their white neighbors did not falter. With the single exception of the Yemassee War in 1715, when all the southeastern Indians united in a vain effort to repel the invasion of the white man in its incipiency, the Catawbas remained loyal through all vicissitudes. In 1712 a party of their warriors, forty-one in number, served under Capt. John Cantey in the campaign against the Tuscaroras of North Carolina. Samuel Boykin, of Camden, commanded a company of one hundred of their braves at the Battle of Sullivans Island in 1776. Some of them served under Colonel Davie, and also in Col. Henry Lee's legion. In the Civil War they supplied twenty soldiers to the Confederacy.

It is within the memory of some of our citizens when parties of the Catawbas used to visit Camden. One recalls when Gen. Jim Kegg, their chief, dined at his

---

*Probably near Camden, where cotton mill is located across the creek.

father's house, and his men exhibited their skill in archery by hitting coins tossed in the air. Another, living on the old Waxhaw road running north of Camden, relates how they used to pass, returning from town, single file, all drunk except the leader, who kept sober to act as pilot.

The Catawbas, like all the other tribes, melted away under constant warfare, drink and smallpox. To the credit of King Haiglar, he strove to keep rum from his tribe. His protest to Chief Justice Henly of North Carolina, dated May, 1756, has been found in the archives of that State, in which he says: "I desire a stop may be put to the selling of strong liquors by the white people to my people. This will avoid a great deal of mischief." As to the smallpox, the *Gazette* of December, 1759, states that "the smallpox has lately raged with great violence among the Catawba Indians, and has carried off nearly one-half of that nation, by throwing themselves into the river as soon as they found themselves ill."

Their numbers have dwindled to seventy-five. Their domain is now but 800 acres. On July 31, 1900, the citizens of the nearby town of Fort Mill honored themselves by the erection, with ceremonies, of a monument in honor of the Catawba Indians. On the occasion Ben Harris (the tribe have adopted Christian names) spoke with rude pathos, in broken English, as follows:

"Love prompted White and Spratt to build monument. Much thank them good men. Indian love them. Glad Indian now getting education. Fifty years from now, if wanted, Catawba he make good speech as white man. Much thank to people for love shown. My forefathers show love by fighting and give life. I show love try to make a speech. All Indians grateful."

A few specimens of Catawba language, found in Mills's Statistics, are here inserted:

> My daughter..........*Non-yaw.*
> My son...............*Cow-re-dha-har-ree.*
> A fine boy...........*Cow-sin-nee-wi-ra.*
> A beautiful girl.......*Ya-wee-can-nee.*
> A baby..............*Cow-ri-dhagh.*
> I love you............*Ne-mough-sa-ragh.*
> My wife..............*You-e-go-jau.*
> My brother...........*Burrough-hend-ha.*
> The girl that I love....*Cun-re-har-ree-yaw-ee.*

Their latter-day trade names for the first ten numerals, as used in their former visits to Camden, reported by one who remembers, ran as follows:

	Modern.	Original.*
1	Coleman	*Ne-po-ya.*
2	Fillman	*Nau-pa-ree.*
3	Yallerbelly	*No-mon-da.*
4	Yang	*Purree-purree.*
5	Bang	*Puc-tree.*
6	See-see	*Ne-purree.*
7	Co-pa-lily	*Was-si-nee.*
8	Lem-me-go	*Ne-pis-saw.*
9	Debrico	*Pat-chaw.*
10	Pay-see	*Pitch-in-nee.*

The Cherokees also figure in Camden's early annals. Their territory once extended to this vicinity, and the neighboring counties of Fairfield and Richland were by them ceded to the State in 1775.† To them probably we owe the larger mounds along the river above Camden, one of the largest just a mile west of the town. This interesting object, which we shall designate the Adam-

---

*According to Mills's Statistics of South Carolina.
†Mills's Statistics.

son Mound, warrants a reference to the latest results of scientific investigation as to the authorship of mounds, long, and until recently, a subject of great controversy.

The conclusions reached by the Bureau of Ethnology, after long, careful and extensive explorations, are set forth in a Report by Cyrus Thomas, 1894, and may be briefly summarized as follows:

The links discovered connecting the Indians and the mound-builders are so numerous and well established that there should be no longer any hesitancy in accepting the theory that the two are one and the same people.

The statements of the early navigators and explorers as to the habits, customs and circumstances of the Indians are largely confirmed by discoveries in the mounds, this especially true of the Southern States.

Though the larger number of the mounds belong to prehistoric times, a number were built subsequent to the discovery of this country.

The large mounds in the vicinity of Camden, and the large, conical, flat-topped mounds of the South generally, were not originally used as places of burial, but were domiciliary, occupied by the council houses and residences of the chiefs. Mound testimony and history are in perfect accord on this point. However, later "intrusive" burials may have been made in these mounds.

The proof is apparently complete that the Cherokees were mound-builders.

Now, as Lawson reported the Waterees as so extremely indolent, and no authority as to their being mound-builders, we might be justified in attributing our larger mounds to the more energetic Cherokees. True, Lawson describes a burial of their king by the Santees, and states "that they build mounds of earth high or low according to the dignity of the person." These were probably humble hillocks, compared with our colossal domiciliary heaps, which, as stated, have no connection originally with burials.

Turning to our meager local discoveries of Indian archeology, we find by an item in the *Camden Journal* of 1850, that two large pots had been dug from the Adamson Mound, one being on exhibition at Mr. Alexander's shop. The same paper, June, 1886, describes the revelations made by the great May freshet of that year, at the Chesnut Mound, a short way south of Camden. The spot, it states, when examined, proved to be no mound, but a plateau, an old Indian burial ground covering some acres. Excavations about four feet deep, made by the waters, exposed quantities of pottery, pipes, and stone axes, mixed with dog and deer skulls, and jawbones and teeth of some unknown animal. Specimens of human jaw- and thigh-bones indicated the owners to have been of tremendous proportions.

Again, the record-breaking freshet of May, 1901, laid bare, in the vicinity of a moderate-sized mound on the river five miles above Camden, a lot of broken pottery, several human skeletons, and one very fine specimen of a pot, about five gallons capacity, intact except as to the bottom, which was broken out.

But other links than mounds and bones connect the Cherokees with Camden's history. Among the Irish Quakers of Pine Tree Hill, though not one of the sect, was James Adamson. A soldier by profession, he had served as captain* in the English contingent sent to aid Maria Theresa in her wars with Frederick the Great. This force was disbanded in 1748. Adamson married a

---

*Mrs. Ciples, who was an Adamson, a lady of olden Camden, had his commission in her possession.

lady of the Milhouse family, and probably came with them to Pine Tree Hill in 1750.

The military spirit of Adamson, as his letter to Governor Lyttleton in 1759, above cited, shows, led him into the adventures of Indian warfare. The atrocities of the Cherokees, to which he alludes, were their retort to the shocking slaughter of a party of their warriors by some of the Virginia colonists, whose stray horses they had presumed to capture and mount on their return through that province from war against the French. An implacable resentment was planted in the Cherokee heart by this brutality of their English allies. The feeling spread into South Carolina, where their young men went out in parties and used the tomahawk upon the settlers, causing general alarm throughout the colony.

The older Cherokee chiefs strove, it is said, to suppress the strife; and, apparently with honest purpose, sent a delegation under lead of Oconostota to interview Governor Lyttleton at Charlestown, the seat of government, under promise of a safe visit and return. Lyttleton, to his lasting disgrace, against the honorable protest of Lieut.-Gov. William Bull, treated them with despicable manners, and held them as prisoners. He summoned an army of 1,400, and at its head, with the chiefs captive, marched against the Cherokees as far as Keowee (Fort Prince George), in the mountain corner of the Province.

Here he waged, in December, 1759, a bloodless, but mortal campaign with the smallpox, which ravaged his ranks and proved very persuasive to a treaty with Atakullakulla, leader of the Cherokees, whereby Oconostota was released, but twenty-four chiefs retained as hostages, who were left in custody of a garrison at Keowee. The army then dispersed and Lyttleton returned to Charlestown with airs of a conqueror.

In a game of perfidy the Indians were not often bested. The troops no sooner disappeared than Oconostota, burning with his wrongs, planned revenge. He invited the commander of Keowee, Captain Cotymore, out to an interview, and slew him from ambush as he returned, also wounding two lieutenants. The incensed garrison put all the hostages to death. The war-whoop rose and massacre fell at once upon all the upper settlements. In one party alone, fleeing to Augusta for safety, fifty were slain, among them members of the Calhoun family.

Pine Tree Hill, in all probability, stood in danger of this bloody visitation, for the *Gazette* of September 12, 1760, contains a report of shocking deeds of the Cherokees within a day's journey of the village. It tells that on the 5th inst. the wife and daughter of McLaney were murdered on Fishing Creek, about thirty miles beyond Pine Tree Hill, by a party of eighteen Indians. McLaney was at "Pine Tree Store," on the way, with his wagons, to Charlestown, when he heard the dreadful tidings. Near the same place Thomas Hughes was found pierced by a ball and with several arrows sticking in his body.

Gov. William Bull succeeded Lyttleton, and had the legacy of Indian war on his hands. He sent against the Cherokees a force of regulars, who dealt out to them severe retribution. But the campaign was in rugged mountains, and relief could not be pushed through in time to save Fort Loudoun on the Tennessee. Here, an isolated garrison, composed of two South Carolina companies, Captains Demere and Stewart, and Lieutenant Adamson, having held out to extremity, surrendered to the Cherokees with promise of protection and safe return home. But the forfeit for the slain hostages of Keowee was now to be exacted. An eyewitness relates the incident in the *South Carolina Gazette* of October 27, 1760, in substance as follows:

On the morning of October 10th, just after beat of reveille, the garrison being ready to march, two guns were suddenly fired at Captain Demere, who fell. Lieut. James Adamson, standing beside him, instantly returned the fire and brought down an Indian. In a moment the war-whoop rose, and a shower of bullets and arrows from 700 warriors fell upon the garrison. All officers except Stewart were killed, also thirty privates and three women. Stephens (the writer of the account) was wounded in the side with an arrow. He states that the prisoners were horribly tortured. He, having a Cherokee wife and children, was spared and allowed to be ransomed. Captain Stewart, ancestor of the Beaufort family, was released through the personal friendship of their chief, Atakullakulla.

The remains of Lieutenant Adamson, according to a manuscript of Col. E. M. Boykin, his descendant, lie in our cemetery. Their recovery from such a remote point in those days would seem improbable, but Colonel Boykin states that he derived his authority from Mr. Lang, a grandson of Samuel Wyly. The Colonial Government granted Adamson's widow a pension of £200 per year. He left three daughters. One married her cousin, John Adamson, from whom a branch of the Boykin family are descended; the others married Robert and Joshua English, and to them several families of our community trace.

With a bit of legend the undue length of this chapter must close. It has been obtained from a former resident of Camden, and was delivered to us thus: On one occasion, whilst Samuel Wyly was on his rounds amongst the Indians, he came upon a party who were about to dispose of a captive with usual torture. The good

Quaker released the victim by a ransom. An author of colonial times has written: "The Indian will not soon forgive or forget injury, though very capable of gratitude, even to a romantic pitch."

Some years after, when the Cherokees were on the warpath, Wyly was one night awakened by rapping on his door, at Pine Tree Hill. There he found, on opening, the Indian whom he had rescued, and who warned him that the Cherokees were about to fall upon the unsuspecting village, which was thus saved from massacre.

The name of this Indian is not a part of the legend, or has faded out. Being free to speculate, we might ascribe to him any one of the Cherokee titles, such as Ousteneka, Hywassee, Tukassee-ke-wee. But such a gracious act comports better with the Catawba traits, and we prefer to attribute it to our patron saint, King Haiglar.

CHAPTER III.

PINE TREE HILL.

"Rest there, old fathers, in thy quiet graves."
—*J. Belton O'Neall.*

Mention has been made in the preceding chapters of the first settlements in the vicinity of Camden, but under this heading something more particular will be undertaken in regard to that obscure subject. There are few data to go upon, except such as may be extracted from original grants and ancient deeds, exhumed from musty trunks and the tomes of the State House. Few chronicles did those first comers leave behind, other than a cleared field or a deed of land.

That district for some miles above and below Camden, on both sides of the river, was early known as "The Waterees," a name which was sometimes used to designate Fredricksburg, the township on the eastern side. According to the petition of Thomas Brown, the Indian trader, his family was among the few inhabitants, in 1735, residing in "that remote part of the country."

So far as careful research reveals, the very first landowner in the vicinity of Camden was one James Ousley, who obtained a precept for 300 acres on the western side of the river, nearly opposite Camden, on January 17, 1733. Near the same site came Thomas Hanahan, August 16, 1735. The land of James Ousley passed to the Quaker, Nebo Gaunt, then to Joseph Kershaw, and now forms a part of the "Westerham" plantation of Henry Savage.

After close scrutiny of the township grants for evidence of the first settlers on the Camden side, none earlier can be found than February 8, 1737, on which date a group of families obtained precepts for land in Fredricksburg Township. Fifty acres being allotted for each member of a family, the number of individuals may be inferred from the number of acres granted to the head. The following may therefore be cited as the original prospectors of Camden:

Adam Strain	200 acres	4 in family
David Alexander	100 acres	2 in family
James McGowan	300 acres	6 in family
Hugh McCutchin	100 acres	2 in family
Michael Harris	50 acres	1 in family
William Seawright	250 acres	5 in family
Robert Seawright	50 acres	1 in family
		21

The unnamed family, mentioned in the Council Journal of 1736 as murdered by the Indians on Pine Tree Creek, belonged, no doubt to this little colony. We can but marvel at their hardihood in bringing wives and children into such surroundings.

Of these seven families, William Seawright and Robert Seawright settled in Belmont Neck, just south of Mulberry; Hugh McCutchin, Michael Harris, and James McGowen about seven miles southeast of Camden, on waters of Swift Creek; Adam Strain and David Alexander cannot be precisely located, but were probably within hailing distance of some of the others.

It is six years later before the records show any other arrivals in Fredricksburg, after which there is a small annual accession. A list of these comers, down to 1750, has been made up after much exploration of the old grant books, and is here presented as matter of curiosity:

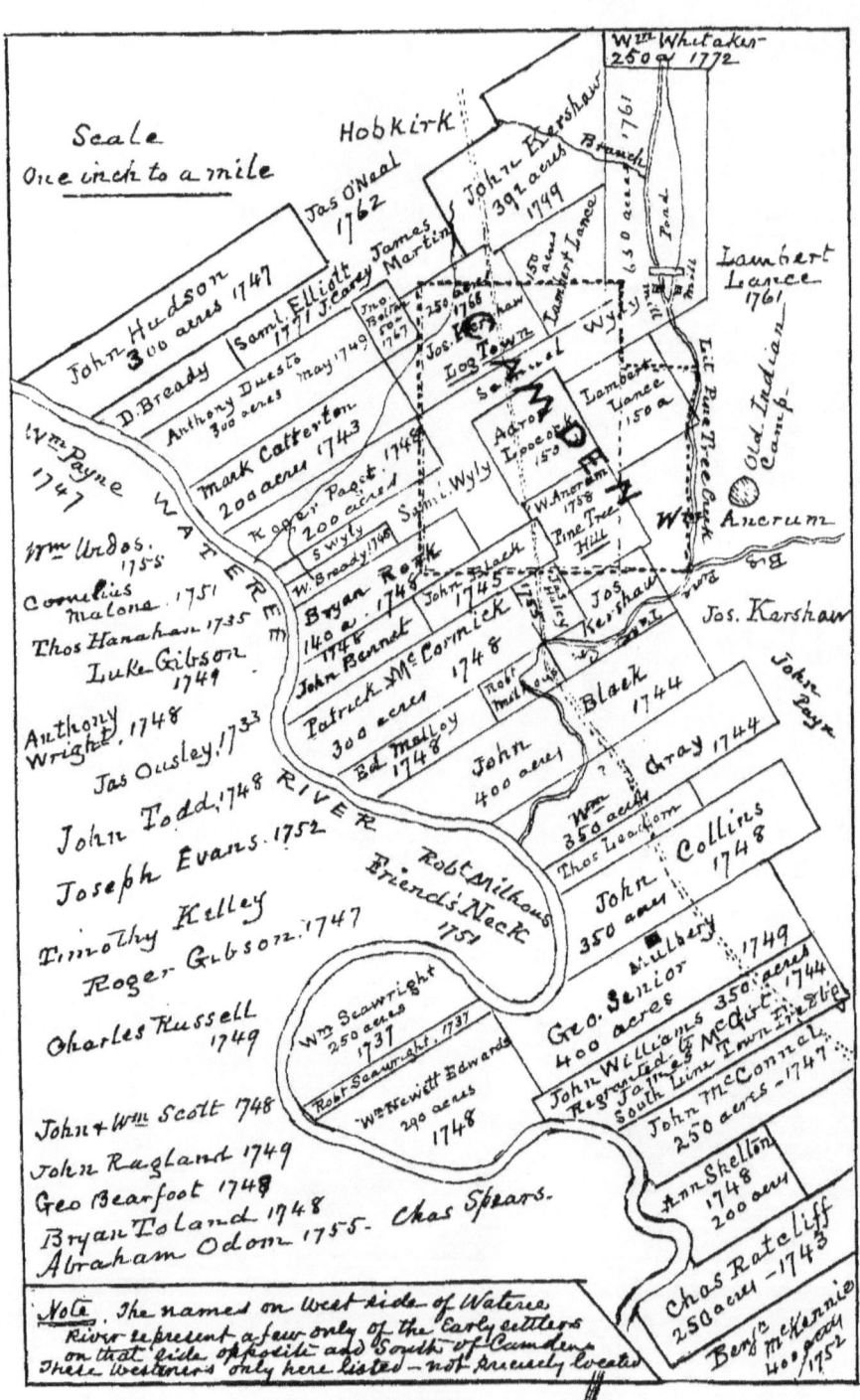

Grants to Earliest Settlers of Camden and Vicinity

DIAGRAM No. 9.

PINE TREE HILL.

Thomas Bryan,	100 acres, February 7, 1743.
Charles Ratcliff,	250 acres, February 7, 1743.
Mark Catterton,	200 acres, February 7, 1743.
John Williams,	350 acres, March, 1744.
John Black,	400 acres, October 6, 1744.
William Gray,	350 acres, October 6, 1744.
Michael Branham,	200 acres, October 6, 1744.
Ann Duyett (widow),	300 acres, November 2, 1746.
John Hope,	350 acres, November 2, 1746.
Benjamin McKinnie,	600 acres, November 2, 1746.
John Hudson,	500 acres, February 7, 1747.
John McConnel,	250 acres, May 15, 1747.
Edward Malloy,	150 acres, January, 1748.
Thomas McCormick,	*450 acres, January, 1748.
Patrick McCormick,	300 acres, January, 1748.
Paul Harlestone,	140 acres, January, 1748.
Thomas Leadom,	100 acres, January, 1748.
William Bready,	50 acres, January, 1748.
Daniel Bready,	100 acres, January, 1748.
Bryan Rork,	140 acres, January, 1748.
Roger Paget,	200 acres, February, 1748.
John Collins,	350 acres, February, 1748.
Ann Shelton,	200 acres, February, 1748.
Anthony Duesto,	500 acres, February, 1748.
Alexander Rattray,	500 acres, February, 1748.
William Newitt Edwards,	290 acres, February, 1748.
John Bennet,	100 acres, March, 1748.
Daniel McDaniel,	500 acres, June, 1748.
Samuel Neilson,	400 acres, November, 1748.
William Kelley,	550 acres, December, 1748.
George Senior,	400 acres, May, 1749.
Samuel Buxton,	50 acres, August, 1749.
Thomas Harper,	50 acres, October, 1749.
John Maddox,	300 acres, October, 1749.
William Guess,	200 acres, October, 1749.
Edward McGraw,	100 acres, October, 1749.

*Granted in 1768 to John Weatherspoon.

To illustrate this chapter, comparison has been made of the plats annexed to the original grants in Fredricksburg Township, found in the State archives. These have been fitted together, and the accompanying Diagram No. 9 constructed according to scale.

These settlers, with but few exceptions, located adjacent to the river, their lands joining one to another for some six miles above and the same distance below Camden. But three of the whole list, viz.: John Black, Bryan Rork, and Roger Paget, owned a foot within the present corporate limits, and that barely within the southwestern corner. They seemed to be attracted by the immense fertility of the river bottoms, and to ignore the uplands, except spots for their houses above freshets. Most of them resided so near the swamps that we can imagine they must have suffered seriously from malaria, disposing them to sell out to subsequent colonists, and accounts no doubt for the disappearance of most of their names from this locality.

Immediately west of Camden, between it and the river, located Anthony Duesto, Mark Catterton, Roger Paget, William Bready.

To the north of them, above the Indian mound, were Daniel Bready, John Hudson, Thomas McCormick, Samuel Buxton, Samuel Neilson, Michael Branham, Thomas Harper.

Just south of Camden came Bryan Rork, John Black, John Bennet, Patrick McCormick, Edward Malloy, whose name is still perpetuated by *"Malloys Pond";* William Gray, Thomas Leadom.

Around Mulberry: John Collins, George Senior, William Newitt Edwards, William Seawright, Robert Seawright, and John Williams, whose tract was acquired by James McGirtt in 1752.

On Town Creek were John McConnel, Ann Shelton,

Charles Ratcliff,* Thomas Bryan, Ann Duyett, Benjamin McKennie, ALEXANDER RATTRAY, William Guess.

John Hope had the courage to take his abode on the sandy and secluded wilds of Gum Swamp, northeast of Camden. A few other settlements of this date outside of Fredricksburg will be noted. In February and March, 1748, Edward Howard and James Gamble took grants at the mouth of "White Oak Creek"; Oliver Mahaffy and Michael Brannon, in 1749, on "Grannys Quarter Creek," and John Ragland, the same year, near the creek which bears his name. All of these streams had received their titles as far back as the dates of these grants.

On the western side of the river, opposite, were an almost equal number of settlers, among whom may be mentioned: Anthony Wright, whose name is preserved by "Wrights Branch," ROGER GIBSON, Luke Gibson, William Paine, William Harrison, Nathaniel Hill, Charles Russell, Richard Gregory, Thomas Paget, William Scott, Roger Roberts, John Arledge, John McKenzie, and some others.

In the above enumeration the names of Alexander Rattray and Roger Gibson have been "writ large," for the reason that from them alone of the number have we derived a contemporary narrative of the experiences of pioneer life. The following documents, extracted from the ancient State records, speak more graphically of the times than could be expressed in volumes of description:

Affidavit of Alexander Rattray† before Governor Glen, May 24, 1751: "That he has lived for Ten years

---

*On the plat attached to grant of fifty acres to Charles Ratcliff, dated April, 1745, is represented a stream marked "Sims Creek," which seems to correspond with Town Creek; also a mill dam, and house of one G. Davis. This was in all probability the very first attempt at a mill in these parts.

†Indian Book, Vol. 2, p. 65. State Records.

past near the Wateree River, and is at present captn. of the company there, in which there is one hundred men; that the country thereabouts was pretty well settled, and there would have been many more Inhabitants, had it not been for the Constant alarms from the Cherokees almost every year since he has been there. That at present the fear of the People in those outposts is so great that all the familys have left their habitations, and betaken themselves to Forts with their wives and children, and their most valuable effects. That numbers of them must lose their crops notwithstanding he takes all manner of care to Preserve them by sending parties of men from Plantation to Plantation, and so while one party works the other party guards them."

Roger Gibson to Governor Glen:*

Wateree, May ye 9th, 1751.

I am informed this day by some my Company just returned from the Congarees that the Inhabitants of 96, Seludy and upper inhabitants are fled to the Congaree Fort† for safety because of the Cherokees and Norw'd Indians who have killed several white People, and as my Company is the nighest to the enemy of all the Wateree Inhabitance‡ we are in most danger, and is at present altogether unprovided with ammunition, the people being mostly new settlers here, within these two years my Company having advanced from 35 to 83. We would therefore pray your Excellency to grant us such a supply of ammunition as may Enable us to defend ourselves and familys against these Heathens who Theateneth our Present Destruction. Without it (if attackt) we must fall a sacrifice to their Heathen Fury.

*Indian Book, Vol. 2, p. 51, State Records.
†The present site of Columbia.
‡As previously stated, Gibson was settled on west side of river, opposite Camden. Rattray was on Camden side.

One hundred wt. of Powder, one of Bulletts, and 100 lb. wt. of swan shot would supply our Present necessity.

ROGER GIBSON.

In another letter of July 22, 1751, this same Gibson complains to Governor Glen of the hardships of his men, and their poor pay: "My men also complain that the pay allowed them is too Little, that to Ride in the Heat, and often sleeping wett by Day and Night in the wilderness, 120 miles from their familys, having their Provisions to provide, and too farr to carry, their Horses Tyring and themselves often taken sick and no proper means to help them, as also Day and Night in danger of their Lives, requireth a better reward than £14 per month."

We now come to an important epoch in our story, the advent of the colony of Irish Quakers, in 1750-51, to whom, in all the sketches of Camden heretofore written, from 1816 downward, is attributed the foundation of Camden. But as demonstrated above, they were greeted by not a few white faces already on or near the spot, and while they were the most notable body among the early immigrants, they must share the credit for the origin of Camden with those who preceded and followed. As will be seen, it was not a Quaker who in fact located Camden, or even its antecedent, "Pine Tree Hill."

This band of Quakers most probably came by way of the river, as did most of the pioneers, and landed near the site of Camden, for we find them, soon after, distributed equi-distantly above and below this point. The precise date of their coming is not known by a twelvemonth. We should say, however, it was in the fall of 1751, for the earliest grants discovered to any of their number are those to Josiah Tomlinson, October 25, 1751, in West Wateree, and to Robert Milhouse, November

20, 1751, in "Friends Neck," also in West Wateree, a part probably of the Baum plantation.

How much we should like to know about them! But there are few authentic facts to relate, picked out of old records by slow and tedious process. Their very names are but partly known, and some of these have only been identified by the probate of some antique document wherein the witness, being a Quaker, *affirmed* instead of swearing, which was against their tenets. By similar roundabout means others have been ascertained, and thus we are enabled to make up the following imperfect roll:

Robert Milhouse, who has been accredited as the leader of the colony; Samuel Milhouse; Henry Milhouse; John Milhouse and Abigail, his wife; Daniel Mathis and Sophia, his wife; Joshua English; Robert English; Thomas English; Jonathan (or John) Belton; Abraham Belton, who, however, did not come out until probably as late as 1770; Joseph Evans; Robert Evans; John Wright; Samuel Kelly and Hannah Belton, his wife; Timothy Kelly; Walter Kelly; Samuel Russell; Josiah Tomlinson; William Tomlinson; John Furnass; Nebo Gaunt; Zebulon Gaunt; Zimri Gaunt; Samuel Wyly and Dinah Milhouse, his wife; James Adamson and John Adamson, who are classed as Quakers by Colonel Shannon, but by Doctor Boykin said not to have been of that persuasion, though connected by marriage with the Milhouses.

The following named, while they cannot be positively rated as Quakers, were probably such, judging from the date of their grants, their names, the adjacency of their locations to others of the sect, and various circumstances:

Anthony Wright; Samuel Thomas; Samuel Buxton;

James Haley; Thomas Moon; Cornelius Melone; William Widos; Timothy Plunkett; Timothy Morgridge; Archibald Watson; Bryan Toland; John Tod; John Cook; Jonathan Christmas; Moses Downing; Ann Dunsworth; Thomas Finin; Philip Fain; David Courson; John Cain, and others who might be added to this list, with names suggestive of Quakerism.

Strangely, it was some eight or ten years after the arrival of these Quakers before a single one of their number, or as to that, any other person, obtained a grant for any land now within the boundaries of Camden (aside from the small area already mentioned as falling within the tracts of Black, Paget and Rork). We are informed by Colonel Shannon, in his sketches of old Camden, that Daniel Mathis located with his family in that quarter of the town lying between the Courthouse and the Cemetery, although the records show no grant or conveyance to him of a foot of land anywhere. The statement, however, may be true, as his son Samuel was the first white male born on Camden soil. He may have occupied a spot of land, without grant, and omitted to obtain or record his papers.

Samuel Wyly, surveyor and merchant, of whom much has been said in the Indian chapter, acquired the tracts of Bryan Rork, Roger Paget, and William Bready, lying to the southwest of Camden, just beyond the Cemetery, now the Smyrl place. His dwelling must have been beyond the town limits, for although his son, Samuel, was born in 1756, yet Samuel Mathis, born four years later, is accredited as the first male native to Camden. He went first to Williamsburg, and came to Fredricksburg in 1752, a year later than his other "Friends," but from that time to his death, sixteen years after, he was the most prominent member of the colony, and his store its chief center and nucleus, until the coming of Joseph

Kershaw. The business of Wyly & Co., conducted by his sons, existed during the Revolution.

North of Wyly, between the river toll-bridge road and the Indian Mound, John Belton, surveyor, located, purchasing the tracts of Mark Catterton, now part of the Cureton place. The branch which rises at the southern foot of Hobkirk Hill, and flows through the northwest corner of Camden, and down through these lands to the river, originally called Harolds Branch, became known as Beltons Branch, a name which it should retain, though now almost obsolete.* Josiah Tomlinson purchased the adjoining tract of Anthony Duesto. These lands were conveyed in 1776 by John Belton to his younger brother, Abraham Belton, who, it is related, selected a situation for his home near the Indian Mound, upon the swamp edge, where he lost eight sons from malarious effects.

The Adamsons settled north of the Beltons, acquiring the lands of Daniel Bready, John Hudson, Michael Branham, and others, the property being still known as the Adamson place, subsequently owned by the Curetons and Dunlaps, now of Witte. The military tendency of the Adamsons would indicate that they were not of the persuasion of Friends, though they may have been of the "fighting" variety. The brave exploits of James Adamson in the Indian wars have been recounted. John Adamson was a valiant Royalist during the Revolution.

The Milhouses made choice of the lands around Mulberry, two miles south of Camden, purchasing from the

---

*This branch in olden days did not enter the river, as it does now, but made a great detour to the east and emptied into Pine Tree Creek just below the bridge on the Charleston road. Mr. W. W. Lang, when he became owner of the property, cut a channel and diverted it to the river as it now is. Its old course is marked by what is called "Baitman's Ditch."

first owners, John Collins, George Senior, and James McGirtt, who had acquired the John Williams tract. Robert Milhouse, for the purpose of a mill, obtained a grant of fifty acres on Pine Tree Creek, just below Camden, where now is Carrison's Mill, which is known to have been a mill site prior to 1780. The first mill, which was burnt by Lord Rawdon in 1780, was in all probability built by Robert Milhouse. Its site was on the creek, a few hundred yards north of the present one, and the trace of the old canal which led to it may still be seen. Robert Milhouse died in 1755. His son, or nephew, of the same name, died in 1771, at Camden, where he owned a tannery. The family gradually disappeared from these parts, and removed, it is said, to the Edisto, in Barnwell County, where descendants lived in recent years. We find the name in Camden so late as 1798. Their lands were purchased by the Kershaws and Canteys, and later by John Chesnut.

Thomas and Robert English settled west of the Milhouses, on Town Creek and Swift Creek. Joshua English selected Spears Creek, on the west side of the river, some thirteen miles south of Camden. He became a great landowner, and is said to have had grants for 70,000 acres. In the Revolution he was a Royalist, and letters of Lord Rawdon addressed to him were found in his old homestead, now destroyed. The letters, in recent years, were lost or mislaid.

Others of the Quakers settled in West Wateree, such as the Gaunts,* Kellys, and Evanses. Indeed quite half of their number seem to have taken post on that side. Their Meeting-House and Graveyard they established on the eastern side, on a spot within our present

---

*Nebo Gaunt became owner of the Camden Ferry, known in early times as Gaunt's Ferry. It was purchased by the Kershaws, and in the deed Nebo is designated as a "millwright."

Cemetery inclosure and within the limits of Camden. Samuel Wyly, in 1759, made conveyance to them of four acres, for this purpose, of which the following is a copy:

"*This Indenture,* made the sixth day of September, in the year of our Lord one thousand seven hundred and fifty-nine, and in the Thirty-third year of the Reign of our Sovereign Lord George the Second, of Great Britain, France and Ireland, King, Defender of the faith and so forth,

"Between Samuel Wyly of Fredricksburg Township in Craven County, in the Province of South Carolina, Esquire, of the one part and Timothy Kelly, Samuel Milhous and John Milhous of Craven County and Province aforesaid, of the other part, *witnesseth*

"That the said Samuel Wyly for and in consideration of the yearly Rents and Covenants hereinafter Reserved and contained on the part of the said Timothy Kelly, Samuel Milhous and John Milhous as Trustees for the People called Quakers in Craven County aforesaid, to be paid, observed and performed on the part of whatever Trustees shall be hereafter appointed and Nominated by the said People called Quakers,

"Hath Demised, granted and to farm Lett unto the said Timothy Kelly, Samuel Milhous and John Milhous for the use and in trust for the aforesaid People called Quakers in Craven County aforesaid,

"A Tract of Land containing Four Acres, situate, lying and being in Fredricksburg Township aforesaid and butting and bounding Southwestwardly and Northwestwardly by the said Samuel Wyly's Land, to the Southeast by Land granted to John Black, and to the Northeast by land not yet laid out (as by Platt hereto annexed may appear)

"Together with all and Singular the Houses, Buildings, woods, wells, waters, ways, paths, passages, easements, profits, Commodities, advantages, Hereditaments and appurtenances whatsoever, to the said Tract of land belonging or in anywise appertaining or accepted, Reputed, Deemed, taken, known and enjoyed, held, occupied, Leased or Demised as part, parcel or member of the same or of any part thereof,

"*To have and to hold*, the said Tract of four Acres of Land together with their and every of their Rights, members and appurtenances, unto the said Timothy Kelly, Samuel Milhous and John Milhous in Trust as aforesaid or unto whatever Trustees shall be appointed by the said people called Quakers as aforesaid from the day next before the day of the date of these presents, for and during and untill the full end and expiration of the term of Nine hundred and ninety-nine years thence next ensuing and fully to be completed and ended.

"Yielding and paying therefor yearly during the said term unto the said Samuel Wyly his heirs and assigns, the rent of one Pepper Corn, in and upon the first day of August every year if the same shall be lawfully Demanded.

"And the said Samuel Wyly for himself, his Heirs and Assigns, Doth covenant and agree to and with the said Timothy Kelly, Samuel Milhous and John Milhous, or with any other person or persons which shall be hereafter appointed as Trustees by the said people called Quakers That they the said Timothy Kelly, Samuel Milhous and John Milhous or other the Trustees appointed by the said people as aforesaid shall and may by and under the yearly rent and covenants herein reserved and contained peaceably and quietly have, hold, occupy, possess and enjoy the said Tract containing four acres of

Land, and all and singular the premises herein mentioned with the appurtenances in trust for the aforesaid people called Quakers, for and during the said term hereby granted, without Lett, Trouble, Hindrance, Molestation, Interruption and denial of him the said Samuel Wyly his Heirs and Assigns or of any other person or persons claiming or to claim by from or under him.

"And, moreover, the said People called Quakers shall have power to nominate and appoint other Trustee or Trustees in place and room of the said Timothy Kelly, Samuel Milhous and John Milhous at the time of their or either of their Deaths or at such other time as the said people called Quakers shall choose in order that the number of Trustees may be always kept up.

"In witness whereof the said parties to these presents their seals and hands have Interchangeably sett the day and year first above written.

Sealed and delivered
in presence of
John Gray
John Kennedy.

Samuel Wyly (Seal)
Timothy Kelly (Seal)
Samuel Milhous (Seal)
John Milhous (Seal)

"Endorsement

"At a meeting of the within named people called Quakers, held on the within mentioned premises the 23d day of the 10 month called October 1776, Have chosen and appointed William Tomlinson and Samuel Russell Trustees in the room of Timothy Kelly and Samuel Milhous Deceased, Two of the Trustees within mentioned. In witness whereof they have sett their hands and seals the day and year above mentioned.

Witness
Zn Gaunt,
Nebo Gaunt
Zimri Gaunt."

Samuel Russell (Seal)
William Tomlinson (Seal)

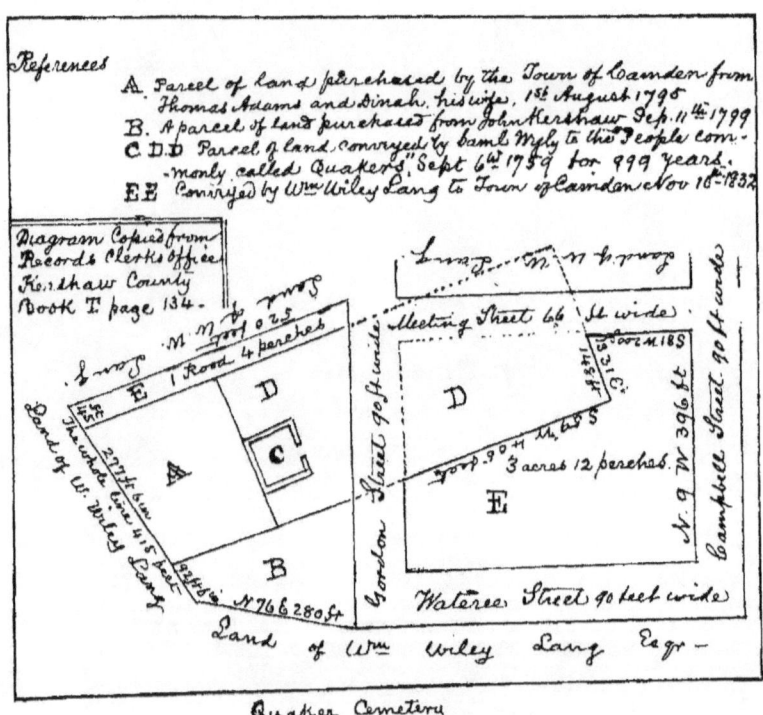

DIAGRAM No. 10.

Upon this four-acre tract, near its western end, was erected the Meeting-House, probably had been erected some time prior to the date and execution of the above deed, which mentions "Houses, Buildings." To its site Meeting street directly leads, probably so named from that circumstance. Around or beside the House, a small plot, surrounded by a ditch, was reserved for the burial of Quakers, indicated by the letter "C" in the annexed Diagram No. 10. The House and ditch have long since been obliterated, but their location might be very nearly fixed by survey.

The Quaker graves, too, have been encroached upon, but some of them, evidently ancient, may still be traced, marked by a mere arching of bricks. This plain people eschewed all forms and display, and did not indulge in monuments. With them the spirit was all in all. To their reserved half acre the lines of Wordsworth would have been truly applicable:

"Here's neither head nor foot stone, plate of brass,
  Cross-bones nor skull—type of our earthly state—
  Nor emblem of our hopes; the dead man's home
  Is but a fellow to that pasture field.
  The stone cutters, 'tis true, might beg their bread,
  If every English churchyard were like ours."

The Quaker lot was enlarged from time to time, until it has expanded into our present Cemetery, where all sects are interred. When we come into these precincts on memorial days, where the beauties of spring seem more ineffable than elsewhere, these few Quaker mounds deserve attention. Their tenants were the ancestors of our place, those who first "with the olive branch of peace and industry, made the lands of our district smile with examples of thrift and economy." We may well take pride in them, these disciples of George Fox, of whom Cromwell said: "They are a people whom I cannot win with gifts, honors, offices, or places." Odd though they were, no people were ever more staunch and incorruptible.

Judge O'Neall, himself a full-blood Quaker of Camden stock, has described some of their customs from his own observation, in his Annals of Newberry, and from him we quote:

"The meeting for worship was every Sunday at eleven o'clock. At that hour all entered the house and sat covered and in silence for an hour, unless the Spirit moved some Friend to speak. Any Friend may speak under the influence of the Spirit, but in general, only those speak in public whose gifts have been approved. If prayer be made, then the Friend who prays uncovers himself, and kneeling down utters the petitions which the Spirit prompts. The congregation rise and the men are uncovered during the prayer. As soon as it closes all take their seats covered."

In 1806 he witnessed the marriage of Robert Evans (who went to Newberry from Camden) and Keren Happuch Gaunt. As to the Quaker marriage he says: "A pair of young people about to marry are said to pass meeting by their purpose being announced at one monthly meeting, when a committee is appointed to inquire if there be any objections. At the next, if their report be favorable, Friends assent to the marriage, and on the succeeding fifth day (Thursday), it takes place, by the man and woman standing up and holding one another by the right hand and repeating the ceremony. The man says about as follows: 'I take this my friend to be my wedded wife, whom I will love, cherish and her only keep, until it shall please the Lord to separate us by death.' The woman says: 'I take this my friend to be my husband, whom I will love, honor and obey, until it shall please the Lord to separate us by death'."

The Quaker sect, after planting their settlements, received few accessions, and were steadily disintegrated or merged by marriage into other denominations. Another cause of their decline, as expressed by Colonel Shannon, was the "advancing civilization of slavery." Says O'Neall: "In the beginning Friends were slaveowners in South Carolina. They, however, soon set their faces against it, and in their peculiar language, they have borne their testimony against the institution of slavery as irreligious. Such of their members as refused to emancipate their slaves, when emancipation was practicable in this State, they disowned. Samuel Kelly, who was the owner of a slave or slaves in 1762, when he came from Camden, refused to emancipate his, on the ground that he had bought and paid for them; they were therefore his property; and that they were a great deal better off as his property. He was therefore disowned. His brother's children manumitted theirs."

A wise people in their day and generation! Their wisdom now shines like Portia's "good deed in a naughty world." Had all the colonists been as they were it is obvious their descendants would have escaped much of the calamities that befell them.

Again we draw from Judge O'Neall's storehouse of facts. Says he: "But it will be asked what became of the Friends? Between 1800 and 1804 a celebrated Quaker preacher, Zachary Dicks, passed through South Carolina. He was thought to have also the *gift of prophecy*. The massacres of San Domingo were then fresh. He warned Friends to come out from slavery. He told them that, if they did not, their fate would be that of the slaughtered islanders. This produced in a short time a panic, and removals to Ohio* commenced, and by 1807 the Quaker settlement had, in a great degree, changed its population. Newberry thus lost, from a foolish panic and a superstitious fear of an institution which never harmed them or any other body of people, a very valuable portion of its white population."

Whether this spirit of exodus infected the Camden Quakers we have no means of knowing, for alas, we cannot boast for our locality such an annalist as O'Neall. We learn more from him about the four Quakers whom he mentions as having gone from Camden to Newberry, than we know of all those who remained with us. We give here a short summary of what he tells of these four.

Samuel Kelly settled in West Wateree, north of Camden. He was from Kings County, Ireland, and his wife, Hannah Belton, of Queens County, a sister of John Belton. Samuel and Hannah removed to the large Quaker colony on Bush River, in Newberry County, about 1762. Their daughter, Anne Kelly, married Hugh O'Neall of Newberry, a Quaker, and their son, John Belton O'Neall, the distinguished jurist, was born April 10, 1793. John Furnass and Robert Evans went to Newberry from Camden (or what was soon after to be Camden) about the same time as did Samuel Kelly.

It seems quite warrantable to say that John Wright was originally one of the Camden colony, for he appears as witness on a deed of Mary and Robert English, dated May, 1760, and proven by him before Samuel Wyly, at Pine Tree Hill. He became, however, a resident of Bush River, Newberry. He lived to be aged, and, before his death, gathered around him his descendants, their husbands, wives and progeny to the number of one

---

*Ohio, the first State formed, in 1803, out of the Northwestern Territory, from which slavery had been excluded by the Ordinance of 1787.

hundred and forty. His two daughters, Charity Cook and Susannah Hollingsworth, were gifted with speech, Charity especially. She became a notable preacher, although mother of a large family, and in her mission work traveled through the States extensively and twice visited England. Her husband was not unlikely of the Camden family of Cooks; and to her with much probability may be attributed the following unique example of eloquence from the sermon of a Quakeress, extracted from the *Charleston Courier* of 1807:

"A Quaker Woman's Sermon.

"Dear Friends: There are three things I very much wonder. The first is, that children should be so foolish as to throw up stones, brickbats and clubs into fruit trees to knock down the fruit; if they would let it alone, it would fall of itself.

"The second is, that men should be so foolish and even wicked as to go to war and kill one another; if they would only let one another alone, they would die of themselves.

"And the third and last thing, which I wonder at most of all, is that young men should be so unwise as to go after the young women; if they would only stay at home, the young women would come after them."

Companion settlers with the Quakers, though not members of the sect, coming between 1750 and 1755, were several with names familiar to us, such as: John Cantey, 1752; Francis Lee, 1752; Richard Kirkland and Joseph Kirkland, 1752; Joseph Mickle, 1753; John Drakeford, 1754; William Boykin, 1755; and the catalogue could be greatly extended, did time and space permit.

It would perhaps be a matter of interest to many to

know the connections of our Camden families of today with the old Quakers. To trace these in all their ramifications would doubtless be too tedious for most readers, so that we will only attempt here to point out some of the leading lines of Quaker descent.

Daniel and Sophia Mathis left, so far as known, four children, Samuel, Israel, Mary, Sarah. A daughter of Samuel married Dr. Joshua Reynolds of Camden, their descendants being represented here (by Miss Sophia Zemp) and in other parts of the State. Sarah married Col. Joseph Kershaw. Israel practiced law at Camden in partnership with his brother, Samuel, until about 1810, when he moved to Sumter County. Mary married Capt. William Nettles. Of Samuel more will be told in the next chapter.

The Lang family, also the descendants of Dr. E. M. Boykin and Burwell Boykin, trace to Samuel Wylie and Dinah Milhouse through their daughter, Sarah Wylie, who married William Lang in 1775.

From John Belton, who married Mary, a sister of Joshua English, through their daughter, Martha, who married Maj. Joseph Mickle, are descended the families of John, Joseph and Robert Mickle, and of James Lyles. John Belton died in 1790. We are not quite sure Mary Belton was sister to Joshua English. She may have been a niece.

From Abraham Belton, who married Elizabeth Alexander before coming to America, through their daughters, Rebecca, who married Everard Cureton, and Ann, who married John Doby, are descended the families of Cureton and Doby. Abraham Belton died in 1826, aged seventy-eight.

From an old family Bible we gather something of the lineage of Joshua English, who married Elizabeth, daughter of Lieut. James Adamson. Of their children,

James married Nancy Darrington, whose daughter, Sarah, married James C. Doby. Sarah English married James Kershaw and, so far as known, left no descendants. Elizabeth English married Thomas Hopkins, whose daughter married Lemuel Boykin. Harriet English married a Singleton. Mary English married Austin F. Peay. From another son, Joseph English, who married Harriet Fitzpatrick, is descended Beverley M. English, of this county. Joshua English Sr. died in 1795.

Robert English (brother of Joshua) married another daughter of Lieut. James Adamson. Being a Royalist, he was banished from the colony at the end of the Revolution, and settled in the West Indies. His daughter married Isaac Lenoir, and to them trace the families of Lenoir and descendants of Benjamin Haile (the second).

John English (a younger brother of Joshua) in 1800 married Elizabeth Tucker, descendants unknown.

From Thomas English, who as early as 1761 settled on Town Creek, probably is descended the extensive Shannon family, through the marriage of Charles J. Shannon with Martha Allison English. It is possible that this Thomas English may have been the father of Joshua, Robert, Mary, John, and progenitor of the entire English family. We have been unable to obtain sufficient data to unravel this branch of English ancestry.*

The coming of Joseph Kershaw to Fredricksburg, in 1758, marks another stage in the evolution of Camden.

---

*Thomas English, son of the first Thomas, married Miss Allison, daughter probably of that Andrew Allison, one of his Majesty's Justices of the Peace for Craven County, and before whom, in 1763, Thomas DeLoach makes affidavit as witness to execution of a paper by Abraham Odam and Cibble, his wife. This old document found among papers of Dr. E. M. Boykin—Mouzon's Map, 1775—shows that Allison's lands were in West Wateree, on Cornals Creek, Richland County.

He found the country dotted with inhabitants along the riverside, and here and there on the creeks, but the area which is now Camden was unoccupied woods, except, perhaps, the spot in the southwest corner, where the Mathis family alone resided. He came up from Charlestown, with the purpose, it would appear, of establishing a country branch of the mercantile firm of that city, composed of William Ancrum, Lambert Lance, and Aaron Loocock. Soon after, he himself became a member of the firm, the local branch going under his name and management, as Kershaw & Co.

The other partners never became residents of Fredricksburg, and it is not known that they ever came up except to visit or prospect. But just after the time of Kershaw's arrival we find the territory now covered by Camden being granted in blocks to the individuals of this firm. On the plat attached to the original grant of 150 acres to William Ancrum, dated June 12, 1758 (see Diagram No. 9), is marked PINE TREE HILL. This settles beyond dispute that what we now call the Magazine Hill was the original Pine Tree Hill. The name must have been given at the time of the grant, which affords the first recorded mention of it so far discovered. By whom was it bestowed? It seems reasonable to attribute it to Joseph Kershaw, who was the local head of the business there established by him, and as appears by later documents, which will be cited, the land on which it stood was partnership property, though granted to one member, William Ancrum.

The name was probably suggested by that of the adjacent creek, and the hill was no doubt covered with a growth of sturdy primeval pines. The store here situated is mentioned in the old Charlestown papers as "Pine Tree Store." The firm continued to secure grants of many surrounding tracts of land, through Kershaw, who displayed great energy, and built up an extensive and prosperous trade.

Just where the store of Samuel Wyly was situated nothing has been found to determine. He became, however, quite a landowner, for in 1761 he obtained a grant of 650 acres, covering all the central part of Camden, including the present DeKalb Mill site and lake, and extending in a narrow strip to the river (see Diagram No. 9). But this body of land, too, the next year was purchased by Kershaw & Co. The diagram shows that so early as 1761 a mill was situated on this tract, just where it exists today, rebuilt, of course, on the pond which we call the "Factory Pond."

In 1766 Lambert Lance withdrew from the firm, conveying his interests to Ancrum and Loocock, who were then, it seems, the moneyed members. Just before this time the Chesnut family* came to Pine Tree Hill—John and James, with their mother and stepfather, Jasper Sutton. John entered the store of Kershaw & Co. as an apprentice, where he must have been very efficient, for after a brief service he became a partner.

In ante-bellum days there existed an official memorial of the origin of Camden, in the shape of the municipal seal, which, unfortunately, disappeared during the military occupancy of the Council Chamber by Federal officers in 1865. No document has been discovered showing an impression of this old device, which, it will be conceded, from the description, was appropriate, and evinced a commendable pride in our past. We are informed by the minutes of Council, wherein the loss is recounted, that it represented (undoubtedly an emblem of primitive Camden) "A Pine Tree on a Mound."

*For a full account of the Chesnut family see Chapter XIX.

CHAPTER IV.

CAMDEN.

For just ten years did the name Pine Tree Hill endure, from 1758 to 1768. So little disposed do the first settlers seem to have been to congregate, that during that decade there were not probably more than a dozen families within a radius of a mile around the present center of Camden. There is no evidence of the existence of the slightest division into streets or lots. However, tracts in the outlying district were being constantly occupied by newcomers.

As has been heretofore stated, the very first mention of the name of Camden is found in the Act of Assembly bearing date April 12, 1768, which provides for a court to be established at Camden, "lately called Pine Tree Hill." The bestowal of this name has always been assigned to Joseph Kershaw, and no doubt rightly. The same year he became the owner of a tract of 250 acres, which now constitutes the northern section of Camden, but which was not within the limits of the first town. This tract he named "Log Town." (See Diagram No. 9.)

The common statement that Camden was laid out into lots and streets by Kershaw in 1760 rests upon no proof, and seems improbable. The name certainly does not antedate 1765, and, as pointed out in the first chapter, the earliest recorded plan of the town cannot be given a date earlier than 1774. This plan, shown in a preceding diagram (No. 3), was the work of John Heard, deputy surveyor, and may be termed official. Kershaw

Lord Camden.

ILLUSTRATION D.

may have, before that, established a plan of his own, but there is no trace to be found of any such.

We are impressed by the rapid course of events as we review the past. Scarce had the feeble village of Camden begun to form, when the Revolution burst upon it. Indeed it was born of revolutionary spirit, and also of the spirit of law. The neglect of the Royal Board in London to heed the demand for courts in the interior of the province, and the consequent disorders, was a potent cause of dissatisfaction. The name of Camden makes its appearance with the establishment of a Courthouse. Just three years after it was built Justice Drayton and a grand jury there assembled, in November, 1774, announced the principles upon which the Revolution was fought.

The name has also another high association. It was given in honor of one of those four British champions of colonial rights, Camden, Chatham, Burke, and Fox. Here would seem an appropriate place to recall briefly the career of the statesman and jurist whose name and fame belong to us.

Charles Pratt was born in 1713, at Careswell Priory Devonshire, England. His father, Sir John Pratt, was an eminent lawyer. He left his family, however, in reduced circumstances. Charles attended Eton, and was a schoolmate of the great Pitt, of whom he was, throughout life, a personal and political ally. He was a finished classical scholar.

In 1735 he entered upon the legal profession. For many years he was without practice, the only knocks on his door being those of duns. In 1741 he wrote that he was "so poor that I have scarce money enough to bear me in a summer's ramble." But after nine years waiting an opportunity came in a case which befell him, the defense of a printer for breach of privilege of Parliament. In this he made a reputation and received popular demonstrations. He thereafter advanced with rapid strides.

In 1757, Pitt, having reached the premiership, appointed him attorney-general, and he won a seat in Parliament. His decision, as Chief Justice of the Common Pleas, against the odious "general search warrants," in the case of the celebrated John Wilkes, which, on account of the principles of personal liberty involved, had aroused the deepest feeling, was received by the population of London with a shout "heard with dismay at St. James."

In Parliament, July, 1765, he made that imperishable utterance against the declaration of the right to tax the colonies, a few sentences of which may not be out of place:

"I shall not criticize the strange language in which your proposed declaration is framed, for to what purpose, but loss of time, to consider the particulars of a bill, the very existence of which is illegal—absolutely illegal—contrary to the fundamental laws of nature, contrary to the fundamental laws of this constitution—a constitution grounded on the immutable laws of nature—a constitution whose center is liberty, which sends liberty to every individual who may happen to be within its ample circumference. Nor, my Lords, is the doctrine new; it is as old as the constitution; it grew up with it; indeed it is its support; taxation and representation are inseparably united. God hath joined them; no British Parliament can put them asunder. My position is this—I repeat it—I will maintain it to my last hour—taxation and representation are inseparable.

"There is not a blade of grass growing in the remotest corner of this kingdom which is not—which was not ever—represented since the constitution began; there is not a blade of grass which, when taxed, was not taxed by the consent of the proprietor.

"The forefathers of the Americans did not leave their native country, and subject themselves to every danger and distress, to be reduced to a state of slavery; they did not give up their rights; they expected protection, not chains, from the mother country."*

After this speech, the ministry, it is said, because of his great popularity, appointed him Baron Camden. The title was derived from the estate, Camden Place, whereon he resided, which had formerly belonged to the antiquarian, William Camden, and had been acquired by the Pratt family. The name Camden had no general notoriety whatever, until rendered famous by being attached as a title to Charles Pratt in 1765, and hence it is safe to conclude that it could not have been applied to our town until after that.

It may be excusable to explore somewhat further towards the source, and relate something about that William Camden, the old author with whom or whose family the name originates. In the South Carolina College Library, at Columbia, is a genuine and ancient "volume of forgotten lore," published A. D. 1610, being the second edition, the first having appeared in 1586. The title page reads as follows, and speaks for itself:

Britain
A Chronographicall
Description of the Most
Flourifhing Kingdomes, England
Scotland and Ireland, and the

---

*The degree of feeling in Carolina over the odious Stamp Acts may be inferred from these indicative circumstances: The *South Carolina Gazette* of October 30, 1765, appears in *mourning*, with the announcement of the arrival of STAMPS in Charlestown. In the issues immediately following are bold headings: "NO STAMPS TO BE HAD."

Ilands adioyning, out of the depth of
Antiqvitie
Beautified with Mappes of the
feverall shires of England
Written firft in Latine by William Camden
Clarenceaux K. of A.
Translated newly into English by Philemon Holland
Doctour in Physic
Finally revised, amended and enlarged with sundry
Additions by the Author

Londoni
Impensis Georgii Bishop
& Ioannis Norton
M D C X.

From the preface to this most quaint and curious production, wherein the author sets forth the difficulty of his task, we quote the following expressions, to which all who may have essayed even the humblest historical subject, will cordially subscribe:

"A painfull matter, I affure you, and more than difficult, wherein what toyle is to be taken, as no man thinketh, fo no man believeth but hee that hath made the triall."

In the year, we might almost say the day, of the birth of the town of Camden, on February 13, 1768, Samuel Wyly died, and was laid in the Quaker burial square. His death is announced in the *South Carolina Gazette* of March 17, 1768, as having occurred at "Pine Tree Hill," by which it appears the new name had not come into use, although, as we have seen, not a month later, on April 12th, the Act of Assembly mentions Camden as "lately called Pine Tree Hill." We should therefore be justified in fixing the christening of Camden between February 13, and April 12, 1768.

The materials for anything like a picture of the first six years of Camden are scant indeed. It seems to have been but a mere "neighborhood," without definite boundaries. The building here in 1771 of a Courthouse (located where it now stands), serving for a large district, known as "Camden District," now subdivided into nine counties, must, of course, have created an epoch, and together with the two stores of Kershaw & Co., Wyly & Co., and the Quaker Meeting-house, have been a powerful magnet for residents.

At this time, beside that of the Quakers, there was a Presbyterian church at Camden.* The system of parish government was in force, and elections of members of the House of Commons by the inhabitants were held under auspices of the Wardens of the Church of England. The Parish of St. Mark, in which Camden was situated, was very extensive, and there was then but one such church in its borders. We can but wonder at the isolation of the people at that day, which is strikingly depicted in the presentment of the grand jury at the first term of Court at Camden, November 5, 1772, wherein they set forth as a grievance:

"The Parish of St. Mark, in our District, being so extensive that the numerous inhabitants are deprived of the comfort of the Preaching of the Gospel and divine service, some of the Inhabitants being one hundred and Forty miles distant, and consequently subject to many

---

*Joseph Kershaw in his will (1788) devises as follows:
"To the Presbyterian Congregation the lots No. 287 and 288, with all my right title and property to that part of Church street laying south of the lot given to that Congregation prior to the town of Camden being laid out into lots as far down as Wateree street, not doubting but that ground will hereafter be vested in that Society by law and that Church street will not extend further south than the Meeting House ground."

evils too notorious to be overlooked in a Christian part of the world." They also mention "many villainies and Roberies committed."

The wild state of the country is thus picturesquely presented at the Camden April term, 1773:

"The want of Law to encourage the killing and destroying of Beasts of Prey, such as Wolves, Tygers, Bears &c., which, it is found, grow very numerous and of course detrimental to the inhabitants." Presentment is also made of "idle and disorderly vagrants constantly hunting in the woods and destroying Deer for their skins, especially when they do it in the night by fire light, whereby great numbers of cattle are destroyed, and the lives of the people endangered."

Among the subscribing jurors we find such names as: James Cook, Joshua English, John Witherspoon, Robert Carter, George Sanders, Glass Caston, John Chesnut, James McGirtt, Thomas Sumter, Robert Belton, James Cantey, Moses Gordon, John Gamble, Jasper Sutton, John Cantey, Joseph Kirkland.

In the *South Carolina Gazette* of December 10, 1772, Chief Justice Gordon and Justice Murray give an interview, just after return from the Camden Circuit, and express themselves as:

"Astonished with the views of a fine country, of whose value and importance they before had very inadequate Ideas, and highly satisfied with the reception they everywhere met with, as well as the general conduct of the Inhabitants, who, in those parts where they are termed in a great measure uncivilized, only want good Schools and School Masters, Churches and Ministers, and fit Magistrates to render them as valuable a people as any upon Earth."

The dissolution of the partnership of Ancrum, Loocock, Kershaw & Chesnut, in 1774, marks another important incident in the little community of Camden. In November of that year the property of the concern was offered for sale. It was only partially disposed of and another sale was made in April, 1777. This step was probably caused by the approach of the Revolution. A body of land containing 1,743 acres, which covered a great part of Camden, the DeKalb Mill tract, and the mills on the creek just south of the town, were purchased by Thomas Jones of Camden, for the aggregate amount of £26,605, equal to $133,025.00.* These transactions are of record in our Clerk's office. Jones, however, would seem to have been but a nominal bidder, for a few days later he transfers the property for the same figures, which appear quite huge for the times, to Joseph Kershaw. Thus in 1777 Kershaw became the owner of well-nigh the whole of Camden and adjacent lands. There is no record of any mortgage to secure the price, and that he should have been able to meet such a sum is an indication of prosperity in business.

As Aaron Loocock figures as one of the original owners, if not residents, of Camden, the following old letter written by him to Joshua English, discovered by chance, may be thought worthy of insertion:

Grandby Decr 8th 1774.

Joshua Inglish:

SIR: I have had not an opportunity of saying much to you, when I saw you last at Camden, about my planta'n at friends neck, which I hope it will not be Inconvenient for you to manage in the same manner and on the same footing as Coln. Thompson does for the People in Town who cannot be on the spot themselves—

---

*These figures are probably to be measured by a colonial standard, and not sterling.

so shall depend on your advice and assistance, now and then when it suits you to take a ride to Mr. Powers—whom I have a good opinion of on answer—he is to have two shares for himself and one negro—and as I have bought Mr. Hopes stock of Hogs—have also agreed to give him a quarter of the Increase of them supporting them 200 head—for his taking care of them—and as I have a great oppinion of the article of Madder, will soon become as much Planted and full as profitable as Indigo, I have offered him fifty pounds to plant out and take care of some plants I intend sending up, not to exceed Two acres. I must beg you to go to Mr. Powers and tell him to fitt Scipio out with his waggon and as many horses as he can bring down, to my Plantation at Goosecreek, he is to bring down Roger Rees and his wife and some Little furniture they have. He lives on Mr. Kershaw's place at the mouth of Pine Tree Creek. I have engaged him to plow at Goosecreek—he must also call at the store, and bring down Two plows and 4 large Iron forks or drags—for digging Madder with—w'ch are in the new store—shall send up by the waggon as many negroes as will make up 20 working hands w'ch is all I intend this year—here is a negro wench, Phillis, who will be sent over to Camden by the first waggon—she is to go to the Plantation and is wife to Ben the Baker—if anything be wanted for the Planta'n you may order it to be got at the store, or if you will be kind enough to write me, will send it from Town. I hope to be up in February or March—so for the present remain

      Sir your most humble servant
         AARON LOOCOCK.

To
Mr. Joshua Inglish
  at his Plantation
    Waterees.

While it is certain that Camden at the time of the Revolution was a very small community, it is now possible to name but a few of its few residents, among whom may be mentioned: The families of Joseph and Eli Kershaw; Samuel, Israel and Mary Mathis; John Cantey; the Wylys; William Lang; Joseph Clay; James Brown, Jasper Sutton, and the Chesnuts, John and James; Adam Fowler Brisbane; William Nettles; the Milhouses; the Adamsons; the Postells, and one P. Morong, in Log Town; Thomas Jones; Thomas Charlton; James Carey; John Cook; Richard Wadison; James Martin; Richard and William Tomlinson; probably John Belton; William Murrell, a schoolteacher; Bettie, a dealer; Murchison, a tailor; Thompson, a blacksmith; and one Castelo, a shoemaker. As to some of these we cannot be entirely certain, but all were in or near Camden, and of course there were others now unknown to us.

Having brought the meager narrative up to the Revolutionary period, before embarking into that broad field, we shall attempt here to record a brief memorial to the "first white person born in Camden," one well worthy a tribute on his merits, aside from the circumstance of his birth. The inscription upon his gravestone, in the old Quaker ground, reads as follows:

"The remains of SAMUEL MATHIS, son of Daniel and Sophia Mathis, Born 22nd March, 1760, Died 26th Sep. 1823, aged 63 years 6 mo., 4 days. The Departed was the first white person born in Camden. Naturally active and enterprising, and living in an age of extraordinary events and revolution, he passed through many chequered scenes which taught him this important truth: 'That all is vanity which is not honest, and that there is no solid wisdom but in early piety'."

The excellence of the character of Samuel Mathis is

also attested by another tablet to his memory, erected in 1849 on the wall of the Methodist Church, to which the Town Council contributed, in these words:

"Sacred to the Memory of SAMUEL MATHIS, the first male born in the town of Camden. He was an exemplary and useful citizen, and filled many offices of honor and trust, the duties of which were discharged with punctuality and fidelity. For many years he was an active and zealous member of the Methodist Episcopal Church of this place, and departed this life in the full assurance of a blessed immortality. Born 22nd March 1760, Died 26th Sepr. 1823."

It will be noticed that the epitaph and tablet differ slightly in stating, the former, that he was the "first white *person* born in Camden," the latter, "the first *male.*" It may be inquired by some how the statement can be true that he was born in Camden, and it be also true that there was no Camden until 1768? Both assertions may be reconciled upon this ground, that Samuel Mathis was the first white person born within that area included in the limits of Camden, defined and named a few years after his birth.

Although full-blooded Quakers, he and Samuel Wyly, who was four years his senior, joined the patriot ranks in the Revolution, and were captured at the fall of Charleston in May, 1780. The story of the cruel murder of Wyly by the British at Camden is told in a subsequent chapter. Young Mathis, being then but twenty, after his return home took care of the affairs and family of Joseph Kershaw, who had married his sister, Sarah, at the country place, Burndale, having been driven from the Camden home by the British. Here he struggled with the problems of the plantation, and kept a minute diary of his doings, fragments of which have luckily been discovered, and will be found in another part of this volume. In the midst of his plantings of corn, cabbage, peas, and potatoes, and worries with the slaves, he records the sound of musketry and cannon on Hobkirk Hill. When the British evacuated Camden, and his sister could spare his protection, he joined Marion's men.

Immediately after the war was over he opened a store in Camden. But in 1790 his name is found among the lawyers of the Camden bar, where for twenty years or more he was engaged in numerous and important cases.

He returned, however, to the mercantile profession, and in the *Camden Gazette* of June 20, 1816, we find the following advertisement:

Samuel Mathis & Co.

They have added to the stock which S. Mathis had, a considerable number of other useful and handsome
Goods
All which they are willing to exchange for Gold or Silver current Coin or good Bank Bills of any of the Banks of South Carolina, or the Bills of those Gentlemen in Camden, who issue Bills (while those Gentlemen support their credit as well as they have done). And they solicit the favor of their friends, acquaintances and all others to call and let them have a little of their loose cash, and not to pass by on the other side of the way (where nobody lives) as many do. They request the custom of the Planters, Farmers, and Mechanics, Lawyers, Doctors and Divines, &c., &c. And particularly invite the Ladies to call and see their GOODS. They will think it no trouble, but a pleasure to wait on them, even should they buy nothing, and hope it will be full as profitable and cost less than seeing the Panorama lately exhibited.

Camden June 20th 1816.

The "Co." above was one John Cessford Ker, of Charleston. In December, 1816, Mr. Mathis again advertises on his own hook a "small stock of goods *at the upper end of Camden.*" This location was probably near the southwest corner of DeKalb and Broad streets, where he then owned two lots. The following combination of articles advertised is rather heterogeneous (only a few here given):

"Copperas	Tin Cups	Bibles
Saltpetre	Tin Pans	Testaments
Pepper	Coffee Pots	Dictionaries
Alspice	Candlesticks	Almanacs
Ginger	Pepper Boxes	Hymn Books and
Brimstone	Dippers &c.	other Books."

The benevolence of this good man is bespoken by the two following clippings from the Camden papers of 1817 and 1820. They cannot now but excite a smile:

"CUTTINGS to Plant, of the Tree called the *Balm of Gilead,* to be had of Samuel Mathis, gratis.
"March 6, 1817."

"The
Sacred Songster
of Pilsbury
Sold for the benefit of the Widow, by
Samuel Mathis.
Camden, May 18, 1820."

The exemplary life of this honest and pious man is so well vouched for that nothing is lacking on that score. In 1790 he married Margaret C. Miller, a daughter of Andrew and Elizabeth Miller. The last named, by a second marriage, became Elizabeth McNair, and died at

Camden, 1831, aged eighty-four. A memorial stone to her, in our cemetery, was erected by her children, Elizabeth McLeod, Mary C. Taylor, Margaret C. Mathis, Thomas H. Miller, and John B. Miller. A daughter of Samuel Mathis, Sophia Elizabeth, married Dr. Joshua Reynolds, of Camden, and their daughter was the first wife of the late Dr. F. M. Zemp.

CHAPTER V.

"Not Revolt—Revolution."

Our narrow province permits but a hurried survey of the early years of the Revolution in South Carolina, prior to the fall of Charleston in 1780, only such important events being touched upon as bear, more or less directly, on our subject.

During the last year and a half of the war, the history of the State—we might say, of the United States—was making in that small district of which Camden was the capital. To this epoch, replete with local interest, we shall endeavor to give the full attention that it warrants. While it is true that northward of Camden, especially between Broad and Saluda Rivers, there was little or no sympathy with the agitation for independence, in this immediate vicinity the leading spirits, from the first, cast their lot with the colonists; such, for instance, as Joseph and Eli Kershaw, John Chesnut, Thomas Charlton, Duncan McRae, Isaac DuBose, Zach. and James Cantey, Willis and John Whitaker, and the three Boykins, Samuel, John and Francis. Many others might be named.

The Quaker element was divided. Some, from religious conviction, took no part in the contest. Others, such as John and Samuel Wyly and Samuel Mathis, are known to have sided with the patriots. Joshua and Robert English, John Adamson, Jonathan Belton, and a few others were active in the King's behalf.

Daniel McGirtt and Henry Rugeley were the most conspicuous Tories of these parts. The Carys were an English family living in Camden. They remained true to the crown. One of them, James, was a colonel in the Royal militia, and on his plantation, Cary's Place,* was fortified a redoubt which guarded Wateree Ferry, and which was named Cary's Fort. Here, doubtless, James Cary was in command, as we infer from the following old communication, recently discovered among the papers of the late Dr. E. M. Boykin:

November 15, 1780.

To Capt. Joshua English, Wateree.

SIR: I have sent my Negros Benjn. and Quash with some of my Mares and Colts to be left down in your swamp where you shall think best for the Purpose. They are to bring up for me the Horse which Herman Horn put somewhere down your way. I think it was in Mr. O'Quinn's Field. Pray let Mr. O'Quinn know that the Negros are sent for the Horse that they may get him. I had last night 6 of the Negros that were Thos. Taylor's either runaway or stolen, 2 fellows, 1 wench and 3 Children. they went off in the fore Part of the Night. I have sent Lieut. Thos. Hide and Strawder's Jack after them, tho' the Negros may be sculking in the Swamp.

If in your Power I beg that you would send up to me the two Bathenys or one of them at any rate, and any other Man or Men you can. I want them to scout for a Couple of Days. I think I can make some Discovery if I had a few good Men with me. I am convinced that there is Villainy carrying on. I should be extremely glad to see you before you set out for Town, if you can make it convenient to come up. I want a few Articles from Town, and I know I cant get them unless I see you before you go down. If it will not be hurtful to you,

---

*Mentioned in Mathis's Diary.

pray come & see me before you set off. I want to have a little Talk with you also and that very much. Hope all is well with you.

    I am, Sr., your Humble Servt,
          JAS. CARY,
         Colo. of Royal Militia.

Most of these loyalists, however, do not appear to have declared themselves until they deemed the rebellion crushed in the colony. Previous to that time, we shall find some of them joining with their neighbors in vigorous protest against Royal tyranny, and even in fortifying Camden against Tory or British attack. Their return to allegiance was due either to policy, because they believed further resistance futile, or, let us give them the benefit of the doubt, to the love that had never died out of their hearts for merry old England.

The Whig element, however, was always the more powerful here, apparently.

It will be recalled that a convention was held in Charleston, on July 6, 1774, to express the indignation of South Carolina at the closing of the port of Boston. Delegates were elected to the First Continental Congress, called to meet in Philadelphia the following September, and a committee of ninety-nine was appointed from the various sections of the colony to correspond with similar committees from the other colonies. No record, unfortunately, has been found of our representatives in this convention or on this committee.

On November 5th of the same year that lofty patriot, William Henry Drayton, presided at the sitting of the Circuit Court in Camden, and here delivered the first of those stirring charges to grand juries that were so effective in arousing the people of upper Carolina to a sense and assertion of their rights. Drayton was one of the King's Council, and was serving only temporarily on the bench until the arrival of the successor to Mr. Justice Murray, lately deceased.

In response, the Grand Jury of Camden District returned a veritable little Declaration of Independence,* antedating and not unfavorably comparing with those of Mecklenburg and Philadelphia.

The third clause of this remarkable document reads as follows:

"We present, as a grievance of the most dangerous and alarming nature, the Power exercised by the Parliament to tax, and to make Laws to bind the American Colonies in all cases whatsoever. We conceive such a Power destructive of our Birthrights as Freemen, descended from English Ancestors, seeing such freemen cannot be constitutionally taxed or bound by any law without their consent, expressed by themselves or implied by the representatives of their own election—a consent which the good people of this colony never have signified, to be taxed or bound by Laws of the British Parliament in which they never have had any constitutional representation.

"And whereas we rather choose to die Freemen than to live Slaves, bound by Laws in the formation of which we have no participation,

"So, now that the Body of this District are legally assembled, as one step towards the defense of our constitutional Rights, which are dearer to us than our Lives and Fortunes, we think it is our indispensable Duty, to the people of this District, to ourselves the Grand Jurors for the Body of the People, and to our Posterity,

---

*Similar presentments were later made at Cheraw and Georgetown, where Judge Drayton also presided.

thus clearly to express the sense of this large and populous District, touching our Constitutional Rights and the very imminent Danger to which they are exposed from the usurped power of the British Parliament, taxing and by Law binding the Americans in all cases whatsoever, being

"Resolved to maintain our Constitutional Rights at the Hazard of our Lives and Fortunes, we do most earnestly recommend that this Presentment, in particular, be laid before our Constitutional Representatives in General Assembly, who, we doubt not, will do all in their power to support us in our just Rights.

"We also recommend the publication of these our Presentments.

Mathew Singleton, Foreman,	David Neilson
Joshua English	Thomas Casity
Sylvester Dunn	John Perkins, Sen.
Jasper Sutton	Henry Cassels
John Payn	Samuel Bradley
Isham Moore	James Conyers
John Cantey	David Wilson
John Witherspoon	Aaron Frierson
John Gamble	Moses Gordon
Robert Carter	Samuel Cantey
Henry Hunter	Edward Dickey."

Here we have clearly set forth the cardinal principles of the American Revolution, the gist and substance of the Declaration drawn up by Jefferson nearly two years later. It does not announce that all men are born free and equal, but we need not look beyond this presentment for a statement of the causes of the war.

The sparks soon sprang into flame. On January 11, 1775, the Congress of the Province of South Carolina assembled in Charleston. This body the *South Carolina*

Gazette of that date pronounced "the most complete representation of all the good people throughout this colony that ever was and perhaps ever will be."

The delegates from that part of St. Mark's Parish, eastward of the Wateree, in which Camden was, were Col. Richard Richardson, Joseph Kershaw, Matthew Singleton, Thomas Sumpter, Aaron Loocock, William Richardson, Robert Patton, Robert Carter, William Wilson, and Eli Kershaw.

The Congress appointed a committee for effectually carrying into execution the Continental Association, determining upon law processes, etc. On it, from this section, were Col. R. Richardson, Messrs. Robert Carter, William Richardson, William Wilson, Matthew Singleton, Thomas Sumpter, Joseph Kershaw, Robert Patton, Richard Richardson Jr., John James Sr., Samuel Little, John Marshall, and Isaac Ross.

John Chesnut was a representative in this Congress, and on this committee, from the district between Broad and Saluda Rivers. This does not imply that his residence was there, the English custom of selecting delegates-at-large being then followed.

Charleston had thirty representatives in the Congress, and each of the other parishes six, except St. Mark's, which was divided into four districts, each being allowed ten delegates.

February 15th was set apart as a day of fasting, and prayer to the Almighty to defend the American people in their just title to freedom, and to avert the calamities of civil war. As an advisable precaution, however, the use and practice of firearms by the inhabitants was urged, in consequence of which advice the province was soon filled with the martial music of the fife and drum; even children, it is said, learned the manual of arms.

So far the agitation in this loyal colony was for

liberty, but not for independence. The expressed determination of the British government, however, to crush the rebellion by force, followed quickly by the affair at Lexington, Mass., hastened the crisis.

The Provincial Congress was again summoned to meet in Charleston, on June 1st. At this session, a "Declaration of Association" was drawn up and sent to be subscribed by every man in the province, the signers pledging themselves to be ready to sacrifice life and fortune to secure the freedom and safety of South Carolina, and holding all persons inimical to the liberties of the colonies who should refuse to subscribe to the Association.

The Congress further decided to raise two regiments of foot and a company of rangers, 500 men in each. Of the last-named corps, William Thompson, of Orangeburg, was elected lieutenant-colonel. Eli Kershaw was chosen one of the captains, Francis Boykin, a first lieutenant, and Thomas Charlton, a second lieutenant. Isaac DuBose, later a resident of Camden, was made second lieutenant in the regiment of foot.

John Chesnut and Joseph Kershaw were elected to the Committee of Continental Association from this part of St. Mark's, and Samuel Boykin from Saxe Gotha.

The famous Council of Safety was also created; it consisted of thirteen members, all residents of Charleston, with Henry Laurens president.

The Congress adjourned June 22d, leaving in the hands of this executive Council the entire reins of civic government, though the Royal Governor, Lord Campbell, was still in nominal authority.

Preparations were now openly made for war. Governor Campbell dissolved the Colonial Assembly, most of whose members had also served in the Provincial Congresses, and himself secretly took refuge on a British ship in the harbor. This was the end of Royal Assemblies in South Carolina.

We have stated that the people of the up-country had never been galled by the British yoke, and so saw no advantage to be gained by casting it off. Now, under such bold leaders as Pat and Robert Cunningham, Colonel Fletchall, and Moses Kirkland, they were raising armed forces to aid in suppressing the rebellion.

To win these people over, the Council of Safety had, in August, sent Rev. William Tennant and William Henry Drayton to go among them and try to convince them of the justice of the American demands. Joseph Kershaw and Rev. Oliver Hart joined this committee at the Congarees, and were doubtless able to render valuable assistance from their knowledge of the men and conditions of the district. The expedition, however, on the whole, proved a failure, few being induced to subscribe to the Association.

At this juncture of affairs, the Catawba Indians near Camden, mystified by the military preparations around them, sent two runners to Charleston to find out the meaning of it all. The Council of Safety explained to them "that our brothers on the other side of the water wanted to take our property from us without our consent, and that we would not let them, and that we expected their warriors would join ours." They were further asked to forward this talk to the Cherokees, who were then threatening trouble on the northwest frontier.

To avert an outbreak and appease the bad temper of the Cherokees, who were excited by British emissaries, the Council determined to send them a present of 1,000 pounds of powder and lead, for use in hunting. This ammunition was dispatched under the escort of a detachment of Rangers, commanded by Lieut. Thomas Charlton, a citizen of our town. This fact renders the incident of sufficient local importance to warrant its full narration, as given in the accompanying affidavit.*

South Carolina }
Ninety Six District }

Personally appeared before me, James Mayson, one of his Majesty's justices of the peace for the district aforesaid; Moses Cotter, of the Congarees, Waggoner, who, being duly sworn on the holy evangelist of Almighty God, makes oath and says, that, on Tuesday morning last, at about 9 o'clock, he left the Congarees, with his waggon, containing the ammunition that was delivered him in Charlestown, by the honorable the Council of Safety, to carry to Keowee under an escort of Col. Thompson's Rangers, consisting of Lieut.-Col. Charleton and Mr. Uriah Goodwin, a cadet, 2 sergeants and 18 privates, and continued on their journey there, without the least molestation or interruption, until about noon this day, when the deponent perceiving some men on horseback, ahead of the waggon, come towards him; a few minutes after, two of Patrick Cunningham's men, coming up to the deponent and asking him what he had in his waggon, the deponent answered, rum. Then up came a large body of armed men, in number, I suppose, at least 150, headed by Patrick Cunningham and Jacob Bowman. Cunningham ordered his men to halt, and then came up to the deponent and said, "I order you to stop your waggon in his Majesty's name, as I understand you have ammunition for the Indians to kill us, and I am come on purpose to take it in his majesty's name." He then ordered the deponent to take off his waggon cloth, which he refused; upon which Cunningham mounted the waggon himself, loosed the strings of

*Moultrie's Memoirs.

the cloth, and took up a keg of the powder. "There," said he, "is what we are in search of." I immediately took the keg from him and laid it in the waggon. Cunningham said, "It is in vain for you to attempt to hinder us from taking this ammunition, as you have no arms." Then he handed out every keg to his men who were alongside the waggon and prepared with bags to receive it. After they finished with the powder, he, with Messrs. Griffin and Owens, and several others, took out the lead, which they unfolded, cut into small pieces with their tomahawks and distributed it among the men. When the Rangers were at some little distance behind the waggon and were riding up pretty fast, Cunningham's party said, "There comes the liberty caps. Damn their liberty caps, we will soon blow them to hell," and such like scurrilous language.

Cunningham's men, as soon as Lieut. Charlton came up with his guard, retreated behind trees on the roadside, and called out to him to stop and not to advance one step further, otherwise they would blow out his brains; at the same time, a gun was fired by one of their men, but did no damage.

Lieut. Charleton, with his men, were soon surrounded by the opposite party, with their rifles presented, who said, "Don't move a step; deliver up your arms, otherwise we will immediately fire upon you." Lieut. Charleton continued moving on, when Cunningham's men marched up to him, with their rifles presented at him, and repeated, "Deliver up your arms without moving one step further, or you are a dead man." They then took his arms, together with his men's; afterwards they tied Lieut. Charleton, Mr. Goodwin and William Witherford, a private, by their arms.

Lieut. Charleton seemed very much displeased at their behavior, and said he would rather have been shot than used in such a manner, had he expected it; that he did not value his own life; thought he had acted prudent by not ordering his men to fire on them, as it would be throwing away their lives, without answering any good purpose; especially as their party was so numerous; that he was sorry to see them behave in such a base manner, and that he would very willingly turn out his party against twice the number of theirs and give them battle. Cunningham and Bowman, some little time after, asked Lieut. Charleton, whether, if they were to unloose him, he would be upon his honor not to go off; to which he replied, "I scorn to run, and all your force cannot make me." They then marched off with the ammunition and the "prisoners" as they called them, and left the deponent, desiring him to return to the Congarees; but, as soon as they were out of sight, he took a horse from out the waggon and came to Ninety Six, to inform me of what had happened, and where he arrived this night about eight o'clock. This unfortunate accident of taking the ammunition happened 18 miles below Ninety Six

MOSES COTTER.

Sworn, before me, this
3rd of Nov., 1775.
    JAMES MAYSON.

Thomas Charlton was a merchant in Camden prior to and after the Revolution.* His residence is designated on the chart of the Battle of Hobkirk Hill, made by Captain Vallancey (Diagram No. 15). It is marked "burnt," probably by the British.

We have seen that Charlton was elected a lieutenant in Thompson's Rangers, in 1775. He seems to have retired from active service in 1776—as the attached letter would indicate—whether permanently or not, we cannot say:

*See Diary of Samuel Mathis.

"Wm. Thompson to John Rutledge:

"Camp on Sullivan's Island, 11 July, 1776.

"SIR: Lieut. Charleton of Capt. Kershaw's Company, in consequence of a letter which he received this morning from Camden, did make application for leave to go there to secure his Family from a presumed insurrection of the Indians in that Quarter, which I did not comply with and he returned his commission into my hands. I hope your Excellency will not take it amiss in having received said commission. Several of the officers and privates have rec'd letters from their Friends in the Back Country on account of the Indians breaking out, which gives them a great deal of uneasiness in regard to their families. I for my part do not think that matters are half as bad as reported to be."

Charlton's name appears as a witness to a deed at Camden, in 1788. His death occurred here in 1795.*

Maj. Andrew Williamson, who was dispatched to recover the ammunition taken from Charlton, was himself besieged by the Tories for three days and nights in Ninety-Six.

The growing spirit of disaffection was so threatening that the Council sent Colonels Richardson and Thompson to crush it, which they successfully accomplished in the famous "Snow Campaign." Many of the Tory leaders were seized and their followers were scattered, some retiring to the mountains of Western North Carolina or to the loyal province of East Florida. Among the latter refugees was Daniel McGirtt, who soon reappeared as lieutenant-colonel of the Florida Rangers, a Tory organization that did much havoc in Georgia and Carolina.†

---

*Records of Camden Orphan Society.
†McCrady's South Carolina in the Revolution.

The passage of the Act of Parliament, December 31, 1775, confiscating the property of the Rebel Americans, denying them any further protection, and authorizing the capture and condemnation of all American vessels, removed the last link that bound South Carolina in spirit to the crown of England. She had shrunk from declaring her independence, in the vain hope that the difficulties might yet somehow be adjusted; but now the Provincial Congress appointed a committee to draft a new frame of government. This work was completed and approved, March 6, 1776, and South Carolina, first of the thirteen, became a free State. John Rutledge was chosen President and William Henry Drayton, Chief Justice. Joseph Kershaw was a member of the first Legislative Council, a body later styled the Senate.

One of the earliest acts of the new Legislature provided for the punishment of treason and rebellion against South Carolina. Courts of justice, which had been closed for twelve months, were reopened and other steps were taken to put the new constitution into active operation.

An effort was made to place Charleston in a state of defense for the expected attack from the sea, which came on June 28, 1776.

The glorious repulse of Sir Peter Parker's fleet by intrepid old Moultrie in his palmetto forts is too familiar to need rehearsal. One incident of this brilliant engagement was the landing made by Sir Henry Clinton, with 3,000 men, on Long Island, whence he attempted to cross the narrow channel, fordable at low tide, to Sullivans Island. The effort failed, owing to the gallant resistance offered by Col. William Thompson, who, with 750 men, had been stationed behind sand banks and shrubbery, to guard that point. Capt. Samuel Boykin, of Camden, with his company of Catawba

Indians, is said to have fought under Colonel Thompson in this action. The only seeming corroboration of this that we have found is in the statement of Maj. Samuel Wise,* who commanded troops on Sullivans Island in the engagement. Says he, in a letter, dated June 27, 1775, to Henry William Harrington of Peedee: "At eleven o'clock about twenty of the enemy, seemingly American renegade Tories, came down to the Oyster Bank with clubbed muskets, and took shelter behind it, at which time the Indians were on the return in a string from the point of Sullivan, and your humble servant was walking along the open beach to the point of Sullivan. At this instant, the enemy began to fire, and aimed their shot directly at the Indians, who caused us to laugh heartily by their running and tumbling, several of them whooping and firing their muskets over their shoulders backward. I confess, though the bullets poured round me, I laughed against my inclination. * * *

"I must to you do justice to Capt. F. Boyakin (nay I am in conscience bound to do it). He came down to us in the very hottest of the fire yesterday."

This was, of course, Lieut. Francis Boykin, of the Rangers, but Samuel Boykin, though not mentioned, was probably also there, in command of his Indians.

The origin of this noteworthy company of Red Men is explained in the accompanying letters:

"Col. Wm. Thompson to Council of Safety:
"July 22, 1775.

"Mr. Chesnut informs me that King Prow, with about 50 of the Catawbas, are now at Camden on a friendly visit. Mr. Kirshaw & I myself are both at a loss what

---

*Gregg's History of the Old Cheraws.
†Journals of the Council of Safety.

to do with regard to taking some of them into pay, for want of your instructions."

"John Rutledge to Joseph Kershaw.
"Charleston, July 25th, 1775.

"SIR: The Council of Safety have ordered me to acknowledge the receipt of your favor of the 8th instant, and to return their thanks for your assiduity in treating with the old men and head warriors of the Catawba Indians.

"Your assurances that those people are hearty in our interest, and your hopes that forty or fifty of them will cheerfully enter into the service of the colony, affords the Council additional satisfaction; and the design of uniting them to the Regiment of Rangers is a measure which they altogether approve of, but to be under the particular direction of a white man, agreeable to a resolution of the Congress in their late session.

"The Council request you to give them immediate notice when any body of the Catawbas are ready to march in order to join the Rangers, and that you recommend a white man well qualified to lead them in scouts and in action. Transmit your answer by the hands of such a one. The Council will give him a commission, and dispatch him with a letter to Col. Thompson, in whose camp he will meet the Indians."

Samuel Boykin was chosen, but, for reasons which he explains, was not at once able to take the field.

"Samuel Boykin to Council of Safety.
"Granby, Oct. 16, 1775.

"I am sorry it was nott in my Power to comply with your directions; it was occasioned by the Indians being taken very sick. One of them Died on his way home, and two more at their town, and several more very sick. A few days after I returned home, I was taken extremely ill with the feaver, or should have wrote you before this. I was at the Catawba Town a few days ago, and the Indians has gott much better, and are willing to come down at any time you may think proper, as the sickly season of the year is now over. I should be glad you would lett me know when they may be wanted again. By the desire of Mr. Thomas Ferguson, I have paid twenty five Indians under my command two hundred and fifty pounds, which is ten pounds each man, which sum should be glad you would pay Mr. Joseph Kershaw. I am, gentlemen,

"Your most humble servant,
"SAMUEL BOYKIN."

The following extracts are from the Minutes of the Council of Safety:

"Feb. 7, 1776.—Capt. Boykin attended and reported arrival of the Catawba Indians lately ordered within a few miles of Charleston."

"Feb. 20, 1776.—Ordered that Capt. Boykin with Catawba Indians do scout about the Parishes of St. George, Dorchester, and St. Paul's, as Capt. Boykin may receive advice or instructions from the Committee of either of those places, or to perform other public services in the line of their duty, from time to time, to the 10 of March following, time to get home on the last day, when said company is discharged. Capt. Boykin is desired to inform said Indians that, when their further services are required, the public will expect them to obey the call."

Another entry shows that Captain Boykin was allowed, in pay for himself and the Indians, £1,508 3s. 6d.

From the foregoing it is seen that the Catawbas were

discharged from service, subject to call, nearly three months before the Battle of Fort Moultrie; but they were evidently summoned out to the defense of Charleston, as Major Wise's letter would indicate, there being no other Indian company in the State, we believe, but Boykin's.

The obituary, in a local paper, of one Abram Kelley, of Kershaw District, who died in 1832, at the age of 85, states that he was a member of Capt. (Francis) Boykin's Rangers in the Revolution, that he served under Marion in various engagements, and that, at Sullivans Island, he gathered broken bombs fired by the enemy, thus keeping the artillery supplied when nearly exhausted.

The signal victory for the Americans in driving off Clinton and Sir Peter Parker secured comparative peace to South Carolina for nearly three years, from both British and Tories. It was a fitting prelude for the Declaration of Independence, proclaimed one week later, news of which was received with intense satisfaction by the more ardent patriots of South Carolina. The enthusiasm, however, was by no means universal.

At this time occurred the terrible uprising of the Cherokees, instigated by John Stuart and Alexander Cameron, British agents. Plantations in the up-country were abandoned, refugees retiring before the torch and tomahawk of the savage as far south as Orangeburg. The letter already given from Colonel Thompson in regard to Charlton would indicate that the people around Camden were also terror-stricken.

After doing much havoc, the Indians were finally defeated near Keowee River by Colonels Williamson and LeRoy Hammond, and a severe vengeance was wreaked upon them. Their lands were laid waste, their villages burned, many of their braves killed, and finally, when abjectly suing for peace, they were forced to cede to South Carolina all their territory eastward of the mountains, including the present counties of Oconee, Pickens, Anderson, and Greenville.

The alliance with France, consummated in 1778, increased greatly the hopes of the Whigs and kept latent the hostility of the Tories, so that South Carolina now enjoyed a degree of prosperity in marked contrast with the unhappy condition of her more northern sisters; but, at the close of the year 1778, the scene of action was transferred to the South, after Burgoyne's surrender at Saratoga, and from this time on to the end of the war no State was so harried and fought over as this. Savannah fell in December, 1778; Georgia was quickly overrun, and the frontiers of Carolina threatened.

Major-General Lincoln superseded General Howe in command at the South at this period.

A large number of the State militia were drafted by President Rawlins Lowndes, and put under three newly-made Brigadier-Generals, Richard Richardson, Stephen Bull, and Andrew Williamson.

On December 27th General Moultrie moved from Charleston to Purrysburg, a small village on the Carolina side of the Savannah River, not far from the city of Savannah. Here Lincoln assumed command and was joined by General Richardson with the militia, including the regiment from Camden District, commanded by Col. Joseph Kershaw. This militia was in a wretchedly undisciplined state, the men going off when they chose, and refusing to move without being told why and where they were going.

A striking illustration of their insubordinate spirit was afforded by an act of mutiny in Colonel Kershaw's ranks at Purrysburg. One of his men, a private, having been left upon guard, deserted his post for several hours.

For this he was rebuked by his captain. The soldier became abusive and was ordered under arrest. Upon this, he cocked his rifle and threatened to put a bullet through the captain's brain, being prevented from so doing by one of the guard, who threw up his gun in the nick of time.

For this grave offense, Colonel Kershaw asked that a court-martial try the offender; which was ordered by General Lincoln. General Richardson was appointed president of the court, the other members of which were also militiamen. Upon organizing for trial, however, several of the appointed judges refused to take the oath of office as prescribed by the Continental rules of war, claiming that the militia were not subject to the laws governing the Continental service.

The matter was referred to General Lincoln, who insisted that, as the men were in the pay of the Continental army, they were subject to its discipline; further, that, if they were not so, he certainly had no command over them, nor would he furnish them any more provisions, and, so far as he was concerned, they were at liberty to go home.

The trouble originated in the fact that by the militia laws there was only a small pecuniary fine for insubordination, while by the Continental rules the punishment was death.

This mutiny, which occurred in January, 1779, caused widespread discussion. Gen. Charles Pinckney regretted General Lincoln's determination in the matter, saying:

"I cannot help thinking that, with a little proper management, such as treating them as you would win a coy maid, by gentle methods, you may at last expect soldier-like performance of duty. Do not think of bringing free men to the halter for practices which they cannot be convinced are crimes. * * * They have never formally or voluntarily resigned the rights of citizens to the benefits of civil law, as is the case of the soldier in the regular service."

General Lincoln, in disgust and despair, turned over the command of the State militia to General Moultrie, as the only way out of the difficulty.

It was evident that something must be done by the General Assembly to remedy the evil. After wrangling a long while over the question, more stringent laws were made for regulating the militia, but it was expressly declared that they were not amenable to the Continental rules of war. So the incident closed.

The *South Carolina Gazette* of April 7, 1779, tells of a recent engagement on Beach Island, in the Savannah River near Augusta, between Lieut.-Col. Ely Kershaw, in conjunction with Colonel Twiggs of Georgia, commanding in all 200 men, and a body of the enemy under Major Spurgeon of the Carolina Royalists and Major Sharp of the Georgia Royalists. Both Spurgeon and Sharp were killed. The paper editorially comments: "If all our militia will only imitate these, how soon might we remove the enemy from our sister State and prevent a deluge of blood by the British King's Indian allies."

On April 20th, General Lincoln marched into Georgia, leaving at Purrysburg the North Carolina militia under General Rutherford and the regiment commanded by Col. Joseph Kershaw.

Thus the defense of Charleston was left to General Moultrie, with very insufficient forces. Seeing this, General Prevost,* who had long been awaiting such an opportunity, made a rapid march into lower Carolina

---

*Attached to Prevost was that savage Tory, Daniel McGirtt, whose life is elsewhere told in these pages.

and appeared before the capital on May 12th, summoning her to surrender.

The negotiations were protracted through an entire day and concluded with a virtual capitulation of the town, when, seemingly without reason, Prevost withdrew his forces. His withdrawal was the result of information, which fell into his hands, by intercepted letters, that General Lincoln was sending strong reinforcements to the aid of Moultrie.

The fright given by Prevost caused, however, a hurried mustering out of the militia, who were hastened from the interior to the coast.

General Moultrie writes, on May 21st, to General Lincoln:

"I am informed of 90 Catawba Indians on their march to join you. I cannot hear any more of Kershaw's 500 men."*

They were possibly at Camden, as we judge from this item in the accounts of the State with Kershaw & Wyly:

"May 12, 1779. To Sundrys supplyd the militia and Indians ordered to Dorchester, £425 1 9."

Capt. Sam Boykin had, it seems, once more called out his faithful company of Catawbas.

We next hear of the base desertion from their post at Stono Ferry of an entire company belonging to Kershaw's regiment—one captain, one subaltern, and twenty-seven privates. This occurred on June 8th, twelve days before the severe little battle at that point, in which, it is presumed, the rest of the regiment bore its part becomingly.

---

*As, by agreement, all numbers in official dispatches were doubled, it is inferred that Kershaw had only 250 men.

General Williamson's brigade, to which Kershaw's command belonged, had for days been dwindling away by such desertions, and, finally, as it was almost impossible to hold them together any longer, they were all discharged on July 8th.

At Stono Ferry, William R. Davie, afterwards so distinguished, and Major (or Cadet) George Ancrum, a near connection of the Ancrums who later settled in Camden, were both severely wounded. The latter subsequently died, as we learn from a letter written by William Ancrum,* of Charleston, to William Ogilvy, of date August 26, 1779:

"SIR: It is with much concern I inform you of the Death of your late friend, Mr. Geo. Ancrum Jr. The unhappy dispute subsisting between Great Britain and North America, that has occasioned the loss of many valuable lives, has put an early period to his, from a mortal wound he rec'd the 20 of June last. He died in two days afterwards, much lamented by every one of his acquaintances. Please to acquaint Mr. Wm. Marshall with my cousin George's death."

Count Pulaski, with his legion,† was present also in this fight. He had played a somewhat spectacular part at the time of Prevost's investment of Charleston, losing most of his infantry in a skirmish with the British advance guard outside the walls of the city.

Pulaski had passed through Camden on his way to the coast, as we gather from the account book of Kershaw & Wyly:

---

*Of the firm of Ancrum, Lance & Loocock. His letter book, a model of neatness, is in the possession of the Camden branch of the family.

†McCrady says that it was the remnant of a nondescript corps that had been cut to pieces at Little Egg Harbor, and that now consisted of but 120 men, lancers and infantry, called by courtesy a legion.

"Mch. to Aug. 1779. Forage furnished Troops Passing through Camden. A Field of Rye, Count Pulaski's Legion,

14 days pasturage, 160 Horse..............£ 23- 6-8
Bland's Dragoons, 14 days................£ 31- 6-8
635 Bushels Corn @ 3s. 6d...............£111- 2-6
900 Bundles or 75 Bushels Oats...........£ 8-15-0"

[A note to this entry states that Loan office certificates, in which payment was made, had depreciated forty to one.]

In February, 1780, Sir Henry Clinton landed troops within thirty miles of Charleston, and began those operations that culminated in its surrender.

In alarm, Governor Rutledge again hastily ordered out the militia. The fear of smallpox breaking out in the crowded city, says McCrady, deterred many from the up-country from going to its relief. It may have been this that impeded Colonel Kershaw's endeavors to get together his disintegrated regiment. Some troops were raised, as this pay certificate* will attest:

"State of South Carolina to Capt. Geo. Dunlap, Dr.

1780
April ye 21st to May 20, both days included } To 30 days under Col. Kershaw, in the foot service, at £3 5s. per day—£114-0-0 (I certify that the above duty was performed.   Jo. Kershaw.)"

The dire straits of the time, as well as Colonel Kershaw's inability to get his men again in the field, are set forth in the following letters:†

---

*From the "Rubbish Room" in the State House.
†Discovered among musty State records (1902). For prudence, no signatures were attached to official letters during the war.

A.

Joseph Kershaw to Governor Rutledge:

"Camden, Tuesday Morning,
"25th April, 1780.

"There is not a Grain of Corn to be Purchased here under 20 dollars p. bushel. On the Congaree I am told it is 16. it is unfortunate for the Publick that stores of Provisions were not laid in 4 or 5 months ago when it might have been done for much less than half the Price. The Publick Credit here is at a very low ebb. I shall be obliged to make all Purchases on my own Account. I am Pretty Largely in advance for the Publick for Supplys as Long ago as Christmas 1778. however I doubt not the Publick's doing me Justice as whatever I have done for them on this head has been without fee or Reward.

"Gen. Williamson sent four Waggons for Ammunition to this Magazine on Sunday last which was supplyd as far as we could. We had only about 1000 lb. of Lead of which sent him half tho' his Request was 2000 lb. there is nothing remaining in the Magazine but Powder Except about 30 Boxes Cartridges each containing abt 110 doz. and not a flint. this is a matter I thought necessary to mention to your Excellency lest you might depend upon a supply from this to supply the camp at Wright's Bluff.

"I inform you that a Colo. Beaufort is just arrived with about 300 Continental Troops. Our commissary is out of Money or Credit. No Rum or Sperits of any kind which they hanker after much."

B.

Joseph Kershaw to Gov. John Rutledge (Extract):

"I am sorry to say I have lost all influence & command amongst the People here, but shall do everytning in my power towards furnishing the Troops to be assembled at Wright's Bluff with corn flour, in which shall be assisted by my brother Ely Kershaw, but with respect to Beef it is not to be had in this quarter, the severity of the winter has carried off a great number of Cattell, and those which have survived are so miserable poor as scarcely to be able to get out of a Bog.

"Last Saturday Genl Caswell passed this place with about 500 men of his and Genl Rutherford's Brigade * * * and sent for ammunition which was supplyd him. We have at this place a quantity of Baggage waggons and six Brass field pieces belonging to Gen. Woodford's Brigade. We have thrown up some works about our Magazine to prevent any surprise from the disaffected.

"You may depend upon my utmost exertions for the carrying every desire of your excellency into Execution."

The authors have before them, unearthed from old State archives, the original "Pay bill of Artificers & Labourers employed in Erecting the Works for the defenses of the Magazine at Camden, 1780." It affords an interesting list of prominent residents of this neighborhood at the time, with some idea of their comparative wealth—or patriotism! Some of the contributors, as we have noted, were later avowed Tories—for instance, the Englishes, John Adamson, and the Carys. William Ancrum, a nonresident but large landholder about Camden, signed the address of congratulation to Clinton and Arbuthnot on the capitulation of Charleston.

"NOT REVOLT—REVOLUTION."

The pay bill is as follows:

James Brown, Engineer & Master Carpenter, from 27th March to 12th April, 1780,

		£	s.	d.
15 days @ 65s.		48	15	0
his negro carpenters 87 days @ 32s. 6d.		141	7	6
102 days		£190	2	6

Negroe Labourers, viz.:

Name	Days	Rate	£	s.
Joseph Kershaw's	74 days	@ 10s.	37	
John Wyly's	36	do.	18	
Joseph Habbersham's	114	do.	57	
Joseph Clay's	70	"	35	
Wm. Whitaker's, Senr	66	"	33	
John Pain's	9	"	4	10
James Bettie's	27	"	13	10
James Cary's	22	"	11	
Nathaniel Cary's	12	"	6	
Wm. Lang's	30	"	15	
Sam'l Elbert's	63	"	31	10
George McIntosh's	43	"	21	10
Joshua Dinkins'	24	"	12	
Burwell Boykin's	35	"	17	10
Samuel Boykin's	62	"	31	
Robert English's	12	"	6	
Joshua English's	25	"	12	10
William LeConte's	32	"	16	
Archibald Broun's	47	"	23	10
Abraham Belton's	9	"	4	10
Isabella Reed's	6	"	3	
John Hope's	6	"	3	
David Nelson's	3	"	1	10
James Seesom's	6	"	3	
John May's	3	"	1	10
John Platt's	2	"	1	
John Chesnut's	55	"	27	10

Wm. Whitaker's, Junr.	12	do	6	0 0
Richard Whitaker's	6	"	3	
Charles Ogilvie's	24	"	12	
James Whitaker's	18	"	9	
John Adamson's	24	"	12	
Ely Kershaw's	19	"	9	10
William Ancrum's	15	"	7	10
Malachi Murphy's	5	"	2	10
John Hutchins'	6	"	3	
	1,124	"	£701	2 6
To 1,124 Rations supplyd by Jo. Kershaw @ 4s.			224	16
To Timber Plank & Hauling of same			101	15
			£1,027	13 6

The remains of this old magazine, which gave its name to the hill at whose southwestern base it stood, are still plainly visible. Its location, as shown on the accompanying Diagram No. 11,* is about 150 yards east of the Charleston road, close to the spur-track of the Southern Railway running to the yard of the Camden Pressed Brick Company. It was built by Joseph Kershaw, in 1777, for the State, at a cost of about £9,000, as the accompanying estimate, also rescued from the "lumber room" of the State House, will attest:

Estiment of Magazine now building at Camden:
225,140 Bricks Maid & Deliverd at Foundation @ £7 14s.   £1688 11 2

---

*This diagram shows also the "Hermitage," with the canal cut by Joseph Kershaw to connect it with his town residence, and the pond and canals that supplied Colonel Kershaw's two mills. One of these, a flouring mill, was, as indicated, destroyed by Rawdon. The canal leading to this is still well defined, though long unused and almost concealed with thick undergrowth. The canal to the sawmill is now supplying Carrison's Grist Mill on the same site.

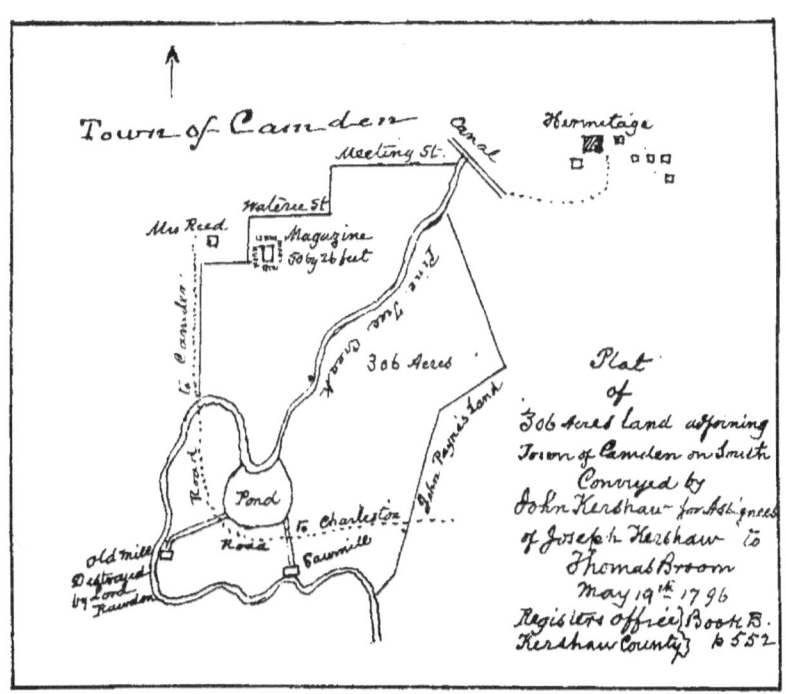

DIAGRAM No. 11.

45202½ Bushells of Lime Deliverd at Do.
   15s. per bu.   3,376 7 6
To Laying 225,140 Bricks with Teafolding,
   &c., &c., @ £7   1575 19 6
11000 Shingells Maid & Carted to Do. @ £12
   per M.   132
6000 ft. of Timber & Carting to Do. @ £5
   per C.   300
5600 ft. of 2-inch plank to Do. @ 80s.   224
600 ft of ½ Do. @ 50s. & 2300 ft of inch
   boards @ 40s.   61
         &c., &c., &c.,
   Total   £8,911 3 2

The above Estiment is exclusive of Nails, hinges, Boalts, Bars, Staples & Locks, which must be obtained to complet the Said Building.   Second Copy
                                        By Jas. Brown.

Jany 13, 1778.

N. B. The original made out & presented in April, 1777.

From the Treasury office, State House, we obtain this account:

Dr to Joseph Kershaw for Building Magazine at Camden, Viz—
1778, Novr. 17—To cash   £5,000 0 0
Octob. To Thomas Lenoar net pro-
   ceeds 40 pair cotton cards sold at
   Vendu   £524
To Publick Stow for 102 yards Sail
   Cloth @ 50s.   255
                                        ———   779 0 0
         To cash   2433 10 0
                                              ——————————
                                              8,212 10 0

1779—June 3—To Cash paid him on account of provisions purchased for the publick	25,000	0	0
Supro. Cr.	33,212	10	0
1778—Octob.—By Magazine of Gunpowder	3,212	10	0
	£30,000	0	0

Colonel Kershaw was the custodian of the Magazine until the town fell into the enemy's hands, and from its necessarily scant stores the troops operating in this section were supplied.

We have seen that, upon news of Charleston's prospective surrender, the Magazine was fortified with earthworks. At the same time, as an additional precaution, the ammunition and other supplies were removed to Charlotte, N. C., as proven by this item from the accounts of the State with Joseph Kershaw & Wyly:

"Feb., 1780—To 17 Wagons & Teams employed in removing Gun Powder & stores out of the Magazine at Camden and lodging them at Charlotte, No. Carolina, 10 days each is 170 days, with drivers & forrage @ £5 per day....£850"

When the British took Camden, they converted the Magazine into a redoubt, which, from its shape, was known as the "Star," and, from its location, as the "Southeastern," redoubt, guarding the road to the metropolis of the State.

On abandoning the town, in May, 1781, Rawdon partially destroyed the fortifications, including the Magazine, and the work of demolition was completed by Greene, for fear of their recapture by the enemy.

The original Magazine measured fifty feet by twenty-six feet. All that the visitor can now see is a heap of broken brick on a star-shaped mound, about 150 feet across from point to point, surrounded by a ditch that was deep and served probably as a moat.

* * * * * * * * *

The investment of Charleston by land and sea continued until May 12, 1780, when, cut off from all hope of help from without, the gallant little city yielded to the inevitable and capitulated.

Two days before, on May 10th, General Lincoln received several petitions from his exhausted garrison, urging surrender. We copy that from the men of our own section:

"To the Honourable Major General Lincoln. The Humble Petition of the Country Militia now in Charleston—

"Sheweth—

"That your petitioners being inform'd the difficulties that arose in the negotiations yesterday and the preceding day related wholly to the citizens to whom the British commanders offered their estates and to admit them to their parole as Prisoners of War & your Petitioners understanding it is an indispensable proposition that they can derive no advantage from a perseverance in resistance with everything that is dear to them at stake, they think it their indispensable duty in this perilous situation of affairs to request your Honour will send out a Flagg in the name of the People intimating their acquiescence in the terms propounded."

This was signed by a great many soldiers, among whom were the following from about Camden:

Zach. Cantey, Willis Whitaker, James Cantey, Samuel Wyly, Samuel Mathis, John Whitaker, John Chesnut, Isaac Dubose; and, on a similar petition of the same date, David Weatherspoon, John Witherspoon, Samuel Glasgow—familiar names in these parts.

All were dismissed as prisoners of war, and honorably observed their paroles until called upon, after the Battle of Camden, to take up arms against their own cause. This was more than could be endured, and few there were that did not join some one of the little patriot bands and strike once more for freedom, if with a halter about their necks.

After the fall of Charleston, Cornwallis was at once sent by Clinton with about 2,500 men to subdue the interior of the State, establish posts at Camden and other points and, perhaps, by a lucky stroke, to capture Governor Rutledge and his Council.

Cornwallis set out on May 18th. He encountered no opposition further than a delay at the Santee caused by the spiriting away of the boats. The route lay along the eastern bank of the river to Nelson's Ferry. At this point, on the 27th, Tarleton was detached with 40 of the Seventeenth Dragoons, 130 of his Legion, and 100 mounted infantry, and sent in pursuit of a party of Americans commanded by Colonel Buford, who had withdrawn before the advance of the British too rapidly to be overtaken by the main army. Each of Tarleton's troopers had an infantryman mounted behind him.

Col. Abraham Buford, with a regiment of infantry and an artillery company, mustering all told 300 men,* had marched from Pittsylvania, Va., to the relief of Charleston. They had set out early in the spring, reaching Camden on April 25th.† Here they rested, probably for two weeks; then, having been joined by

---

*See (ante) letter of Jo. Kershaw, A. Dr. Brownfield (James's Life of Marion) says that Buford had 350 men and Caswell about 700 North Carolina militia.

†See (ante) Kershaw's letter, A.

General Caswell, of North Carolina, with 500 of his own and General Rutherford's brigades,* they advanced as far as the Santee, before learning of the surrender of the capital.

Realizing the danger and futility of proceeding further, Buford returned to Camden, where he found Governor Rutledge† and two of his Council, Daniel Huger and John L. Gervais. The seat of government at that period was wherever these gentlemen found it safe to tarry long enough to hang up their hats.

They were now compelled to "move on," which they did under escort of Buford's regiment, of which General Huger assumed temporary command. Caswell left for the Pee Dee section.

In imagined safety, the Governor and his party proceeded to "Clermont," fourteen miles north of Camden, on the road to Charlotte, where they were hospitably entertained by its owner, Henry Rugeley. Here they came within one of being captured, being saved solely by an act of true chivalry on the part of their host, which must ever redound to his credit. Though himself a Tory, he aroused his sleeping guests in the dead hours of the night and warned them of Tarleton's near approach.‡ They barely escaped, hastening towards Charlotte.

General Huger accompanied them, turning over the command of the military escort to the ill-fated Colonel Buford, who proceeded more slowly, though with the utmost possible expedition, up the same road.

Meantime that brilliant, if bloody, young commander, Bannastre Tarleton, had made one of those remarkable

---

*See (*ante*) Kershaw's letter, B.

†Among Joseph Kershaw's papers is a receipt for one hundred dollars paid by him to Thomas Ruffington for bringing letters from Col. Thomas H. Brandon to Governor Rutledge at Camden, May 6, 1780.

‡James's Life of Marion.

forced marches for which he became later so famous, covering 154 miles in fifty-four hours. As his horses fell exhausted from the heat, others found along the road were impressed. On the 28th he reached Camden, where he learned the route taken by Buford. Resting a few hours, he left this place at two o'clock on the morning of the 29th, reaching Rugeley's at daylight. From that point, he sent a summons to Buford to surrender, greatly exaggerating the number of his own men and representing that Cornwallis was just behind him with nine British battalions.

Following close upon the heels of his messenger, he came up with Buford at about three o'clock in the afternoon, forty miles from Camden and twenty-six from Rugeley's.

Space forbids our entering into all the details of the horrible tragedy that ensued.

Underrating the strength of his adversary, Buford had discarded the suggestions of his officers either to surrender or to make a stand right there, and had pushed on. Captain Carter's company of artillery, a part of his force, was seven miles in advance, but, though necessarily aware of the desperate need of their comrades in the unequal conflict going on within earshot of them, they never stopped. Captain Carter's conduct was, we should think, more than "suspicious," particularly as Doctor Brownfield informs us that the whole command was paroled by Tarleton, after the battle, without injury. We are glad to be assured by the same writer that this was not Capt. Benjamin Carter, later of Camden.*

But, to return to the massacre; it may be as well, for its local color, to reproduce the account of it which ap-

---

*James's Life of Marion.

peared in the *Camden Journal* of June 18, 1845. This was prepared by a committee of citizens of Lancaster, of which James H. Witherspoon was chairman, and was intended to create interest in the movement to erect a monument* on the scene of the slaughter. The narrative, in general, follows that of Doctor Brownfield.†

"At the sound of Tarleton's bugle, the first intimation of the attack, Buford prepared for battle; but unfortunately it was in open woods, which highly favored the movements of the cavalry. Tarleton advanced with the infantry in the center and the cavalry on the wings.

"The rear-guard of Buford, commanded by Lieutenant Pearson, was cut to pieces; the Lieutenant himself was shot down—had his nose and lips cut off and his teeth knocked out; notwithstanding, he survived, by being fed with milk through a quill, for weeks.

"The main body received Tarleton with firmness, and was about beating his infantry back when they discovered his cavalry coming round in the rear.

"Then Buford ordered a flag to be hoisted, and to ground arms. Ensign Cruit, who bore the flag of truce, was cut down by Tarleton.

"History is silent as to what became of Buford, but tradition says he fled.

"Tarleton, totally regardless of the rules of civilized warfare, began an indiscriminate massacre and torture, which was continued as long as life was supposed to exist.

"Captain Stokes received twenty-three wounds; he was attacked by two dragoons, one of whom cut off his right hand, which was extended to ward off the blow aimed at his head—the other cut off the forefinger of the

---

*The memorial was unveiled in 1860.
†James's Life of Marion.

left hand; he was then cut down by a blow on his head and, after he fell, was transfixed four times with the bayonet; yet, strange to relate, he survived, and afterwards was promoted to a seat on the bench of North Carolina. Others of the wounded were pitched about with their bayonets and tortured to death. Even the dead were not spared.

"The loss of the Americans was 113 killed and 151 so badly wounded as to be left on the ground, being between two-thirds and three-fourths of the whole of their force. Tarleton himself reports it at two-thirds of the whole of the American force.

" * * * According to tradition in that neighborhood, Carter was at Silver Run, seven miles ahead. If he was sent on in advance by Buford, it was then Buford's error, and not Carter's fault. Except this company but few survived—in fact, the only survivors, whose names are known, were Captains Stokes, Lawson, and Hoard, Lieutenants Pearson and Jamison, Ensign Cruit, and Colonel Buford himself.

"It is a melancholy and much-to-be-regretted fact that the names of the unfortunate and fallen brave are to us unknown. Mr. Usher, whose father, in company with the Rev. Jacob Carnes and others, assisted in burying the dead, states that eighty-four, as well as he recollects, who were killed on the day of the battle, were buried in one large grave, and that twenty-five, who died of their wounds the next day, were buried in another grave about three hundred yards distant from the others. The wounded who survived were, in a few days, hauled in wagons to the Waxhaw Church as a hospital. There a number died, and are buried in the graveyard at that church, but now probably no person can point out their last resting-place.

"The loss of the British, according to Tarleton's account, was two officers and three privates killed, and one officer and thirteen privates wounded. So sanguinary and cruel was the battle and the conduct of Tarleton that he attempted to excuse himself by informing Cornwallis that, about the time of the surrender, his horse was shot and that his men became so infuriated, supposing he was wounded, that it was impossible for a while to restrain them; but the truth no doubt was that his thirst for blood induced him willingly to permit and encourage it. It was a fit occasion for an officer of his cold and obdurate heart to satiate his thirst for carnage upon a surrendered and armless foe—a thirst which characterizes him a cruel and sanguinary tyrant, and holds up his name and memory to eternal obloquy and scorn. 'Tarlton's Quarters,' which here had its origin, afterwards became proverbial throughout the country."

The massacre took place in what is now Lancaster County, where the old Salisbury road crosses that from Chesterfield to Lancaster.

Buford was tried by court-martial for his conduct in the fight, and acquitted.*

Fifty-three prisoners, all that could be moved, were brought down to the jail at Camden, to which point Tarleton fell back.

Here his reputation for monstrous cruelty was greatly increased by the assassination, at the hands of his myrmidons, of an innocent Quaker youth, Samuel Wyly, son of the pioneer of the same name.

Two versions of this murder are given by historians.

Ramsay says that, two days after the annihilation of Buford's regiment, one Tuck, a quartermaster of Tarleton's Legion, rode with a party of dragoons to the

---

*James's Life of Marion.

residence of Wyly, and, calling him out, charged him with having gone as a volunteer to the defense of Charleston. This was frankly admitted, whereupon Tuck and his men fell upon the inoffensive and unarmed boy and put him to death, despite the fact that the poor fellow exhibited a certified copy of his parole.

John Chesnut, who was a contemporary of Samuel Wyly, made a marginal note on this affair in his copy of Ramsay: "Tuck, the murderer, had a Mock Trial—by 3 Tory militiamen of Camden and 3 British officers. Part of these 3 Torys after made fortunes in Carolina. Dont name the men!!" Just enough to arouse one's curiosity!

James's* story is that Samuel was mistaken for his brother John,† the sheriff, whose crime was that he had superintended the execution of some men under the statutes of the time against treason.

Tarleton sent a favorite lieutenant, who always charged by his side, named Hutt,‡ to kill John Wyly. Two men were left concealed behind the two large gate-posts, while Hutt with the rest of his party broke into the house. Wyly was commanded to give up his shoe-buckles, and, while he stooped to obey, Hutt struck at his head with a sword. Receiving the blow on his hand, with the loss of several fingers, Wyly sprang up and dashed for the gate, where he was dispatched by Hutt's two accomplices.

Samuel Wyly's body is said to have been drawn and quartered and set up on pikes by the roadside, as a

---

*Life of Marion.

†John Wyly lived many years after the Revolution.

‡Note the different spelling of the name. This man was undoubtedly Capt. Christian Huck, who ended his cruel life in the night attack upon Williamson's House about a month later (see sketch of John Adamson).

Huck, says McCrady, was a Philadelphia lawyer, who joined the British in New York and came South with Tarleton.

warning to others. Family tradition further tells of the pitiful, but vain, appeals made to Lord Rawdon by Mrs. William Lang for the body of her brother. While awaiting an audience with Rawdon at Headquarters, this good lady's feelings were harrowed by the unconscious cruelty of some little Tory boys who were killing flies on the window panes, exclaiming, as each victim fell: "Ha, there goes another Rebel!"

The *Camden Journal* of July 28, 1824, gives the following anecdote from "the unpublished manuscripts" of Judge James. Major Cochrane, of Tarleton's regiment, made an effort to bribe young Zachariah Cantey, then seventeen years of age, to guide the British in pursuit of Colonel Buford. Cantey very honorably scorned the offer of money and promotion, saying that he had been paroled in Charleston and that under no circumstances would he betray his countrymen. He was turned out of his own house in the rain. Finally Cochrane gave him up as a "bad job." Afterwards Cantey was so persecuted by the British that, at the earnest instigation of his parents, who, like himself, had suffered many indignities, he broke his parole and joined General Greene, by whom he was made deputy quartermaster. This preferment was doubtless due to his having supplied Greene's army with fifteen wagonloads of flour and about 1,000 head of hogs, which he had driven from the Peedee section of South Carolina, skilfully evading both Cornwallis and the Tories.*

As the British army neared Camden, May 31st, two boys, Kit Gales and Sam Dinkins, were seized by Rawdon at the High Hills of Santee, for firing several shots at his troops. Gales was hanged on a tree, and Dinkins was brought in chains to Camden.†

*James's Life of Marion.
†Weems's Life of Marion.

Lord Cornwallis first entered Camden, with the main army, on June 1st. The citizens* met him outside the limits with a flag of truce and besought his protection; they were treated as prisoners on parole. To Stedman, who was with Cornwallis at the time, we are indebted for the following minute details† of the British occupation of the town:

"Upon the march to Camden, the British troops were supported from the country through which they passed. A number of negroes, mounted on horses, were employed under proper conductors in driving cattle for the support of the army, and, though they were in general very small, the army was plentifully supplied. The cattle were delivered alive to the regiments, who found their own butchers.

"On the first of June (1780), the royal army took possession of Camden, in a day or two after which Colonel Tarleton joined the army at Camden, distant nearly 100 miles from Charlestown.

"Upon the approach of the army to Camden, the author, who had the honor of being commissary to the troops under Lord Cornwallis, was by his Lordship ordered to move on in front, to post centinels and take charge of such stores as might be found in the town.

"In consequence of that order, a mill belonging to a Colonel Kershaw was taken possession of; in it was found a quantity of wheat and flour. In a store belonging to Joseph and Ely Kershaw was found a quantity of merchandise, 21 rice tierces, 3 hogsheads and a half of indigo, some tea, sugar, coffee and linen, which were sent to the general hospital; a quantity of salt, 20 barrels of flour, 18 ditto Indian corn meal,

---
*Ramsay.
†The History of the American War, by C. Stedman.

one hogshead of rum, a quantity of bacon and hams, butter, brimstone, axes and wedges, sent to the Engineer department. Rhubarb in root, damaged, sent to the general hospital. A number of hats and some green cloth, distributed to the troops.

"In a barn near the river 90 hogsheads of tobacco—part of which was destroyed by the troops; the rest was ordered by Lord Cornwallis to be sent to Charlestown. Near 100 head of cattle were found in and near the town, together with some sheep.

"Lord Cornwallis ordered the commissaries to give no receipt to Colonel Kershaw for the property taken from him, as he was deemed a very violent man, and who was said to have persecuted the loyalists."

Large quantities of silver plate, tobacco, indigo, and other stores, that had been sent from the low country to Camden for safe keeping, also fell into the hands of the enemy.*

The British proceeded to establish a well-fortified post at Camden, which was left in charge of Lord Rawdon, Cornwallis returning at once to Charleston, where he superseded Sir Henry Clinton in command on June 5th. We shall hear more of the works and garrison at Camden in a subsequent chapter.

Early in June,† Rawdon went up into the Waxhaws, carrying with him the Volunteers of Ireland and a detachment of his legion. He expected to find that section a prosperous Tory stronghold, but, disappointed in this, he hastened back to his post here.

Learning that Gates with a strong force was on the march towards Camden, in the early part of August, he called upon all the male inhabitants, in and around the

---
*McCrady.
†McCrady.

town, to take up arms in the British ranks. More than 160 nobly refused and, as a consequence, were cast into the small common jail, in the intense heat of the dog days. About twenty of them, gentlemen of the highest character and standing, were manacled. How unfortunate that the names of all these martyrs have not been preserved! Ramsay gives us an incomplete list, to wit: Mr. Strother,* Mr. James Bradley, Colonel Few, Mr. Kershaw,† Captain Boykin,‡ Colonel Alexander, Mr. Irvin, Colonel Winn, Colonel Hunter, Captain John Chesnut. Judge James adds the name of Mr. James Brown.

A lot of indigo, valued at $5,000, was taken from Colonel Chesnut, and, on the evidence of one of his own slaves that he had violated his parole by corresponding with the Americans, he was bound to the floor with chains. No wonder that this much injured man annotated the account of these indignities in his copy of Ramsay: "British cruelties in Camden, never to be forgot by their descendants!"

Mr. James Bradley, who had figured as a legislator and had considerable influence, was taken prisoner by treachery at his home near Salem,§ thirty miles from Kingstree. Tarleton, passing himself off as Col. William Washington, was unsuspectingly taken into his house by Mr. Bradley, and hospitably entertained. From his host, Tarleton drew the plans of the patriots to rid the country of the redcoats. He then asked Bradley to conduct him over two difficult fords of Black

---

*Mills ("Statistics") tells us that Mr. Strother, who was a decided and independent patriot, died in jail.

†This was certainly Joseph, as there is no evidence that Eli was taken in Camden, and the third brother, William, returned to his allegiance after the fall of Charleston.

‡Dr. E. M. Boykin thinks this was his grandfather, John Boykin.

§James's Life of Marion.

River; this Bradley cheerfully complied with, going as far as McGirtt's Swamp, when, as a graceful recognition of his courtesy, Tarleton had him put in irons and marched on to Camden. Here he was frequently carted out to the gallows to witness the execution of his fellow captives, and was warned that his time was coming. But he never flinched, either on these occasions or before courts-martial, warning his torturers that, in the event of his death, his friends with Marion would exact a heavy vengeance. This Spartan fortitude saved his life; but he was not liberated until the evacuation of Camden, the next year, and he bore to the grave the marks of his fetters. To Judge James, in after years, he showed these scars, saying modestly that he deserved no special credit for what he had done, as any man should sacrifice even life itself for the good of his native land.

CHAPTER VI.

THE BATTLE OF CAMDEN.

This, to the Americans, the most disastrous field of the Revolution, bears the name of Camden, though situated eight miles north of the town. It has also, to distinguish its location more exactly, been termed the battle of "Sanders Creek," or more properly still "Gum Swamp."* It occurred, actually, about a mile north of Gum Swamp, a tributary of Sanders Creek, and some three miles north of the latter stream. The term "Swamp" might give a false impression to one not acquainted with the ground itself, which, though almost completely inclosed by marshy streams, is well elevated above them, and afforded an ample arena of high, dry land for the troops engaged.

The American forces in Charleston under Lincoln, closely beset by the British from February to May, 1780, sent urgent appeals to Congress for succor. In response to these calls, a detachment of Continentals, two Maryland brigades, by license so termed, and a Delaware regiment, on May 16th started to their relief from Morristown, N. J., under command of Baron DeKalb, marched to Elk River, at head of Chesapeake Bay, and from there took passage by boat to Petersburg, Va. Thence they resumed the march overland for Charleston, via the Camden route.

The numbers of this detachment have been stated by most American authorities as 1,400, and by the British

---

*In some accounts this name appears incorrectly as "Green Swamp," and in others "Gun Swamp."

as 2,000, the latter being, as will be discussed hereafter, more likely correct.

It was July 6th when they reached Wilcox's Mill, on Deep River, near the center of North Carolina. Their progress had been painfully slow, owing to the lack of supplies, and Charleston had fallen weeks before, on May 12th. Further advance seemed deterred by the prospect of starvation in the lower districts of North Carolina, where the conflicts of Whig and Tory, nowhere else so bitter, had devastated the country. Old crops had been exhausted, the new still green and scanty enough, and the settlements sparse. At this point, therefore, about one hundred and twenty-five miles northeast of Camden, DeKalb halted and rested for three weeks, barely managing to subsist the troops.

Here on July 25th Gen. Horatio Gates arrived in camp, having been sent by Congress to supersede DeKalb and assume chief command in the South, now the main theater of the war.

The victor of Saratoga, still in high prestige, was hailed with welcome and salutes from the small park of artillery. Of handsome person, prepossessing address, and military experience, at the age of fifty-two it may well have been assumed that his was no mushroom reputation. With the halo of Stillwater, Behmus Heights and Saratoga about his name, he had come now to deliver the prostrate South. In him was none of the Fabius, and he proposed to meet the enemy at once and by the shortest route. Gen. Charles Lee, whom he had visited while on his way down through Virginia, doubtless detected in him symptoms of undue complacency, to be inferred from his parting monition: "Beware lest you exchange your Northern laurels for Southern willows." Prophetic words.

Indeed, the fault of his character, vainglory, was

about to yield bitter fruit. On his journey south he had also visited in Winchester, Va., General Morgan, who had been his best officer at Saratoga. Col. Henry Lee informs us that General Gates tried in vain to induce Morgan to accompany him into the Southern campaign about to open. Morgan was still offended at Gates's ungenerous omission of his name from the report of Saratoga, and resentful of his machinations against Washington. He promised, however, to come on later. As it was he did not arrive until after the army had been routed at Camden. Had he been there we may well believe the result would have been glorious. He did come in time to win the brilliant victory at Cowpens, to which the British historian Stedman attributes the loss of America.

The small force which greeted General Gates was in destitute condition. His advent, however, raised their spirits mightily. Dalliance may not be laid to his charge, but rather precipitancy, for he at once issued orders for the army to be ready to march on a moment's notice. He decided to proceed by the direct eastern route to Camden. It has been said that DeKalb protested in favor of the longer western circuit by way of Charlotte, where the country was more plentiful and friendly. The rejection of this advice is one of the long catalogue of errors laid to Gates by the critics. It may be remarked in extenuation, however, that General Greene, when similarly situated the following year after the Battle of Guilford, adopted the very same route to Camden.

Col. Otho Williams, who was Gates's adjutant, informs us, in his very interesting "Narrative," that he also presumed to expostulate with his general at the course he was about to adopt, and spoke in favor of that by way of Charlotte. Gates rebuffed him by saying he would

Line of Gates's March and Chart of Military Operations Around Camden.

DIAGRAM No. 12.

confer with the *general* officers when the army halted at noon. Williams adds: "Whether any conference took place or not, the writer does not know." Later in the journey, however, General Gates explained to Williams that he had felt compelled to take that line of march in order to form a junction with General Caswell, who, with the only other considerable body of troops, the North Carolina militia, was in the neighborhood of Cheraw, in danger of falling a prey to the corps of British regulars there posted. General Gates further said that Caswell "had evaded every order which had been sent him, as well by Baron DeKalb as by himself, to form a junction of the militia with the regular forces; that probably he contemplated some enterprise to distinguish himself and gratify his ambition, 'which,' said he, 'I should not be sorry to see checked by a rap over the knuckles, if it were not that the militia would disperse, and leave this handful of brave men without even nominal assistance.'" Williams adds, however, that Caswell's reputation stood high as a patriot and gentleman.

Again Gates has been much blamed for neglecting an offer of Colonels Washington and White, to recruit a corps of cavalry from his ranks. He seemed to set no store by cavalry. In the rugged hills of Saratoga he had won without cavalry, where they could not operate, but would have no doubt been of great service in the sandy plains about to be traversed. His only force of that sort consisted of a small body of sixty horsemen, composed, Colonel Lee tells us, of foreigners and deserters, commanded by Colonel Armand, a Frenchman (Marquis de la Rouerie), whom, however, Washington has commended as a very gallant and excellent officer.

The march from Wilcox's Mill began July 27th. On August 3d they crossed the Peedee in bateaux at Mask's Ferry. Here Colonel Porterfield, an officer of great merit, joined them with a detachment of 100 Virginians. On August 6th the borders of South Carolina were reached, and here General Gates indited a proclamation, in rather turgid style, of which the following is a paragraph:

"The exertions of the virtuous citizens of America, having enabled me under the protection of Divine Providence, to vindicate the rights of America in this State, and by the approach of a numerous, well appointed and formidable army, to compel our late triumphant and insulting foes to retreat from their most advantageous posts, with precipitation and dismay." He goes on to assure security to those who had been compelled by "all the arbitrary measures of military domination to make a forced declaration of allegiance and support to a tyranny which the indignant souls of citizens resolved on freedom, inwardly revolted at with horror and detestation." Those were excepted, however, from amnesty who had been "guilty of acts of barbarity and devastation, and such as hereafter give support to that enemy who but for the disaffection of many of the apostate sons of America, had long ere this been driven from the continent."

Moultrie says that this manifesto was placed in the hands of Francis Marion, who had come into Gates's camp with his "Ragged Regiment," to be disseminated through the State. This as yet unfamed hero, with his tattered troop, were so derided in the camp, that Gates concluded the best use of them was to send them back into their swamps, as distributors of his proclamation. We could wish he might have discerned the merits of this invincible little colonel. He might have saved the day on that fatal 16th.

Williams in his "Narrative" says: "Colonel Marion had been with the army a few days, attended by a very few followers, distinguished by their small leather caps and wretchedness of their attire. Their number did not exceed twenty men and boys, some white, some black, and all mounted, but most of them miserably equipped. Their appearance was in fact so burlesque that it was with difficulty the diversion of the regular soldiery was restrained by the officers, and the general himself was glad of an opportunity of detaching Colonel Marion, at his own instance, toward the interior of South Carolina."

On August 7th the army came up with General Caswell and his brigade of North Carolinians, fifteen miles east of Lynches Creek. In his camp they found a welcome supply of provisions and some wine. In the march to this point they had suffered sore distress. The two weeks' tramp had been a severe ordeal, through pine barrens, "sufficient," in the picturesque words of Weems, "to have starved a forlorn hope of caterpillars. What had we to expect," he continues, "in such a miserable country, where many a family went without dinner, unless the father could knock down a squirrel in the woods, or pick up a terrapin in the swamps?" He tells how the army, when they chanced to strike a patch of "roasting-ear" corn or an orchard, would rush in and devour it like a herd of hungry boars. Of flour there was none in camp, and some of the officers would use hair powder (those were days of wigs and perukes) to thicken their soup. On such diet it is a marvel they could survive, not to say march. Colonel Williams says the General and officers shared the hardships to the full extent with the privates.

With the united force Gates pushed right on to Lynches Creek, about twenty miles northeast of Camden, not far above Hough's Bridge. On the opposite side he found Lord Rawdon, strongly posted with three regiments. Rawdon had moved up to this point from Camden, and was here joined by the Seventy-first Regiment from Cheraw, under Major McArthur. Here skirmishes ensued, but the creek banks being steep, muddy and slippery, and the swamp wide, Gates determined not to attack in front, remarking that to do so would be "taking the bull by the horns." After waiting a day or two he moved up the creek and crossed above, whereupon Rawdon fell back near Camden, camping in Log Town. It would have perhaps been the true policy for Gates to have pursued right on after him and forced a fight. But he considered it more prudent, his troops being probably still exhausted, to await a junction with General Sumter, who was in the direction of Charlotte, and with a body of Virginians in the same quarter. With this object in view he moved across to Colonel Rugeley's, then called Clermont,* thirteen miles due north of Camden. Here he took post on the morning of August 13th.

Colonel Williams states that the army while at Lynches Creek was encumbered with a great multitude of *women and children,* with immense amount of baggage. To get rid of these an escort under Major Dean was formed, with wagons in which most of the women were sent off to Charlotte, but many remained behind to share the fate of the camp and witness the harrowing result of the battle.

On the 14th General Stevens arrived at Rugeley with 700 Virginians. Shortly after General Sumter came up, and to him General Gates detached 100 of the Maryland regulars and 400 North Carolina militia under Colonel Woolford. These raised Sumter's force to 800,

---

*This has been frequently confused in histories with Claremont, a locality some eighteen miles south of Camden, near Stateburg. Clermont was the name given to his residence by Colonel Rugeley.

The Battle of Camden.

with which he was ordered by Gates to proceed down the western bank of the Wateree, to capture the British fortified post opposite Camden, known as Cary's Fort,* commanded by Col. James Cary, and to cut off the enemy's supplies and reinforcements coming that way. This mission Sumter accomplished with great address and success. On the 15th he reports to General Gates that he had surprised the British post at Cary's Fort, killing seven and capturing thirty. He also intercepted a number of wagons coming in with supplies from Ninety-Six, and seventy recruits.

The American force under Gates, after the detachment to Sumter, amounted (Allen's History of the Revolution, Vol. II, p. 319,) to 3,663, including officers. The British authors estimate their strength at 6,000, but as to this Col. H. Lee remarks: "Cornwallis rated Gates's forces at 6,000, in which estimation his lordship was much mistaken, as from official returns on the evening preceding the battle it appears our forces did not exceed 4,000, including the corps detached under Colonel Woolford. Yet there was great disparity of numbers in our favor, but we fell short in quality, our Continentals, horse, foot and artillery, being under two thousand, whereas the British regulars amounted to nearly sixteen hundred."

Learning of Gates's approach, Cornwallis hurried up from Charleston, followed by a mounted detachment of the Sixty-third Regiment. He reached Camden the night of August 13th, the same evening Gates halted at Rugeley's. The British garrisons had been drawn in from Hanging Rock, Rugeley, Rocky Mount, and four companies from Ninety-Six. In the Camden hospital

---

*This fort was located at what is known as McCaa's Hill, not far from the old Camden Ferry, on land of the Whitakers.

were 800 sick, but his available force amounted in all to 2,331, including 237 officers and 40 drummers.

Cornwallis resolved to force a battle. No commander was ever readier to resort to the sword for relief from difficulties. Of portly and imposing presence, vigilant, combative, resolute, his skill had been fully proven on the desperate fields of New Jersey, with Washington for antagonist. His troops had implicit confidence in him.

Indeed Cornwallis was in a desperate predicament. Sumter had taken post in his rear, cutting off the main communications; swamps were all around him except on the north, and there was the American army. Says he: "Feeling little to lose by a defeat and much to gain by a victory, I resolved to take the first good opportunity to attack the rebel army."

Cornwallis took every precaution to procure information as to his enemy. He sent an emissary, according to Simms, one Hughson, into the American camp, who succeeded in gaining Gates's confidence and escaping with his observations. Colonel Williams confirms this, saying: "An inhabitant of Camden came, as if by accident, into the American encampment, and was conducted to headquarters. He affected ignorance of the approach of the Americans, pretended very great friendship for his countrymen, the Marylanders, and promised the General to be out again in a few days with all the information the General wished to obtain. The information he then gave was the truth, but not all the truth, which events afterwards revealed; yet so plausible was his manner that General Gates dismissed him, with many promises if he would faithfully observe his engagements. Suspicions arose in the hearts of some of the officers about headquarters that this man's errand was easily accomplished; the credulity of the General was not arraigned, but it was conceived that it would have been prudent to have detained the man for further acquaintance."

Tarleton relates that on the afternoon of the 15th he, with a scout of cavalry, ten miles above Camden, captured three American soldiers on the road to Rugeley's, making their way from Lynches Creek. These prisoners were placed behind dragoons and hurried full speed to Cornwallis, who learned from them that they were to have joined Gates that night on his march to Camden. Cornwallis, however, in his very full account of his plans and operations, does not intimate that he had any expectation of meeting Gates upon the road that night, but rather the contrary. He says: "I determined to march at ten o'clock on the night of the 15th and to attack at daybreak, pointing my principal force against their Continentals, who, from good intelligence, I knew to be badly posted, close to Colonel Rugeley's house." At the appointed hour (10 p. m.) the British army set out on the road to Rugeley.

The same day General Gates issued orders for march of his army on the same road towards Camden. The column was to be headed by Armand's legion, flanked on each side by Porterfield's and Armstrong's infantry, marching Indian file. Behind these were to follow the Maryland and Delaware regulars, the militia and baggage in the rear.

The possibility of meeting the enemy on the way seems to have been contemplated, as appears from the following portion of Gen. Gates's orders:

"The troops will observe the profoundest silence upon the march, and any soldier who offers to fire without the command of his officer must instantly be put to death.

"In case of an attack by the enemy's cavalry in front, the light infantry upon each flank will instantly move up and give and continue the most galling fire upon the enemy's horse. This will enable Colonel Armand not only to support the shock of the enemy's charge, but finally to rout him. The Colonel will therefore consider the order to stand the attack of the enemy's cavalry, be their number what it may, as positive."*

These orders were submitted to a council of the general officers called to meet in Colonel Rugeley's barn. Colonel Williams says that he busied himself, while the council was in session, making up a return of the number of available troops. This estimate he presented to General Gates as he emerged from the barn. The General cast his eye upon the paper, which showed just 3,052 rank and file present for duty. He expressed surprise at the small number, saying there had been no less than *thirteen* general officers in the council. "But," said he, "these are enough for our purpose." This purpose, Williams states, was not disclosed to him, the General only adding: "There was no dissenting voice in the council, where the orders have just been read."

Some authors have stated the object of General Gates in moving his army to have been to attack and surprise Cornwallis at Camden. But there seems no doubt that the real purpose was to occupy a new and stronger position, just six miles north of Camden, on Sanders Creek, selected by the engineer of the army, Colonel Senf, and Colonel Porterfield.† This is confirmed by the fact that the baggage was being moved with the army.‡

---

*Colonel Armand took great umbrage at these orders, as containing a distrust of his fortitude. The conduct of his men, whatever his own may have been, in the ensuing battle was pusillanimous to the extreme. After the defeat Colonel Williams tells us Armand blamed Gates in the severest terms. He certainly had an ample occasion to gratify any spleen against the author of the orders.

†Gates's Report of the Battle, and Garden's Anecdotes.

‡Colonel Williams says the American army was without spirits, as none had arrived in camp, "and as until lately it was unusual for troops to make

Battle of Camden.

ILLUSTRATION F.

The British and Americans thus set out on the same road at the same hour, moving towards each other. The advance guard of the British column of march consisted of forty cavalry, following them in order the Twenty-third and Thirty-third Regiments, Volunteers of Ireland, Hamilton's and Bryan's North Carolina Royalist corps, the Seventy-first Regiment and Tarleton's legion bringing up the rear. They proceeded in strict silence. In crossing Sanders Creek at twelve o'clock some disorder occurred, which was soon adjusted, and the march resumed. A little past two, about one mile north of Gum Swamp, a tributary of Sanders Creek, the vans of the two armies met.

Shots were exchanged at once, and flashing guns lit the night. Armand's horsemen reeled and fled, carrying confusion into the ranks behind. Porterfield's and Armstrong's light infantry, strung along the roadside, behaved well, and, according to the orders, volleyed into the British, wounded their officer, and drove them back. Musketry continued for a quarter of an hour. Colonel Porterfield was severely wounded, dying a few weeks later, probably in Camden. Prisoners were taken on either side, and from these it was ascertained the two armies were face to face.

The British had marched eight miles, while in the same time the Americans had traveled five. The difference was due no doubt to the fact that the British were hastening to reach Rugeley for the daybreak attack, unencumbered, while the Americans moved leisurely, with

a forced march or prepare to meet the enemy without some extraordinary allowance, it was unluckily conceived that molasses would for once be an acceptable substitute. One gill of molasses per man and a full ration of corn meal and meat were issued to the army previous to their march. But at this time a hasty meal of quick-baked bread and fresh meat, with a dessert of molasses mixed with mush or dumplings, operated so cathartically as to disorder very many of the men, who were breaking ranks all night, and were certainly much debilitated before the action commenced in the morning."

baggage, for a new encampment. Was the night moonless? No witness of the event has testified on this point. But astronomy has answered the question. There was a full moon on the 17th August, 1780.* So there was strong moonlight on the night of the 15th, but much shaded, we may suppose, by the pine forest then and there abounding.

Both armies had recoiled, and as by mutual consent ceased firing and proceeded to form line. Cornwallis in his report says that he was "well apprized by several intelligent inhabitants that the ground on which both armies stood, being narrowed by swamps on the right and left, was extremely favorable to my numbers. I did not chuse to hazard the great stake for which I was going to fight to the uncertainty and confusion of an action in the dark. But having taken measures that the enemy should not avoid an engagement on that ground, I resolved to defer the attack till day." The measure taken by Cornwallis to force an action consisted, probably, in advancing his line so near the Americans that they could not risk a retreat, but must needs stand to their ground.

Gates called a council of war. "What is now to be done, gentlemen?" said he to the assembled officers. There was silence for some moments, when General Stevens spoke: "Is it not too late now, gentlemen, to do anything but fight?" Silence again ensued, which implied assent. "Then," said Gates, "we must fight. Gentlemen, resume your posts."

An apocryphal incident, connected with this council, has been widely accepted, upon the authority, no doubt, of the romantic Weems, in his life of Marion. He rep-

---

*This has been computed by a thoroughly competent authority, to whom the question was referred for the purposes of this chapter.

resents that the Baron DeKalb protested against the proposal to give battle, and counseled retirement to Rugeley. Gates curtly suggested that the Baron was overprudent and overrated the danger. Stung by the innuendo DeKalb retorted: "Daylight will show us the brave," and with that indignantly returned to his command. This fable is disposed of by Colonel Williams, who tells that when he, "the deputy adjutant-general, went to call him (DeKalb) to council, he said: 'Has the general given you orders to retreat the army?'" He adds, however, "The Baron did not oppose the suggestion of General Stevens," which was to fight. As Gordon, the historian, has pertinently remarked, those officers who did not have the judgment or courage in council to oppose the proposition were not warranted, after the event, in condemning it.

The imaginative Weems has also fabricated for us two other dramatic and contrasting scenes on that fateful night, the one comic, the other pathetic. At headquarters, says he, an aide familiarly asked General Gates: "General, where shall we dine tomorrow?" quite a serious question with the army at that time. "Dine, sir," replied Gates, "why at Camden, sir, begad, and Lord Cornwallis at my table. I will make pilau of him in three hours, sir."

The other canvas of Artist Weems represents the veteran DeKalb in his camp conversing with his ardent young military disciples, Marion and Horry. The Baron recounts to them his life in France and his last visit to his aged parents before leaving for America; how he found his old father gathering fuel in the woods and his mother of eighty-three at the spinning wheel. He forebodes defeat. "Here are we, feeble and faint with fasting, they from high keeping strong and fierce as butchers' bulldogs. Our army is lost as surely as ever it comes into contact with the British."

Their discourse is broken by an order from Gates that Marion and Horry, with their swamp regiment of fifteen, set out at once, to go below Camden and smash all the boats on the river, thus cutting off British means of escape after their coming defeat. They part with the Baron in tears, who, "observing their eyes watery," took them by the hand, exclaiming, "No, no, gentlemen, no emotion for me. I will gladly meet the British tomorrow at any odds." The author adds that Horry, in his old age, declared to him: "With sorrowful hearts we left him, and with feelings which I shall never forget while memory maintains her place in this my aged brain." The veracity of which scene may be estimated by comparing the statements of Moultrie and Williams that Marion had left the army, at his own request, two weeks before, and was probably a hundred miles away.

But to return to the more certain grounds of history. The armies, formed in lines of battle through the woods, throbbing with expectancy, await the morning. Shots were being constantly exchanged as parties met in the night. The British lay upon the ground, but it is not recorded that any slept. Cornwallis describes the ground as "woody," and so it is today, except some small clearings. The situation is an elevated sandy plateau, about two miles long and one wide, sloping steadily from north to south, and rising to quite an eminence on the northwest. Streams, with boggy swamps, inclose it on the south, east, and west, and nearly so on the north. The road runs through the midst. Washington, passing over the locality on his visit South, in 1791, has recorded his opinion that neither army had any advantage of position, which should absolve Gates from having made any worse choice of ground than Cornwal-

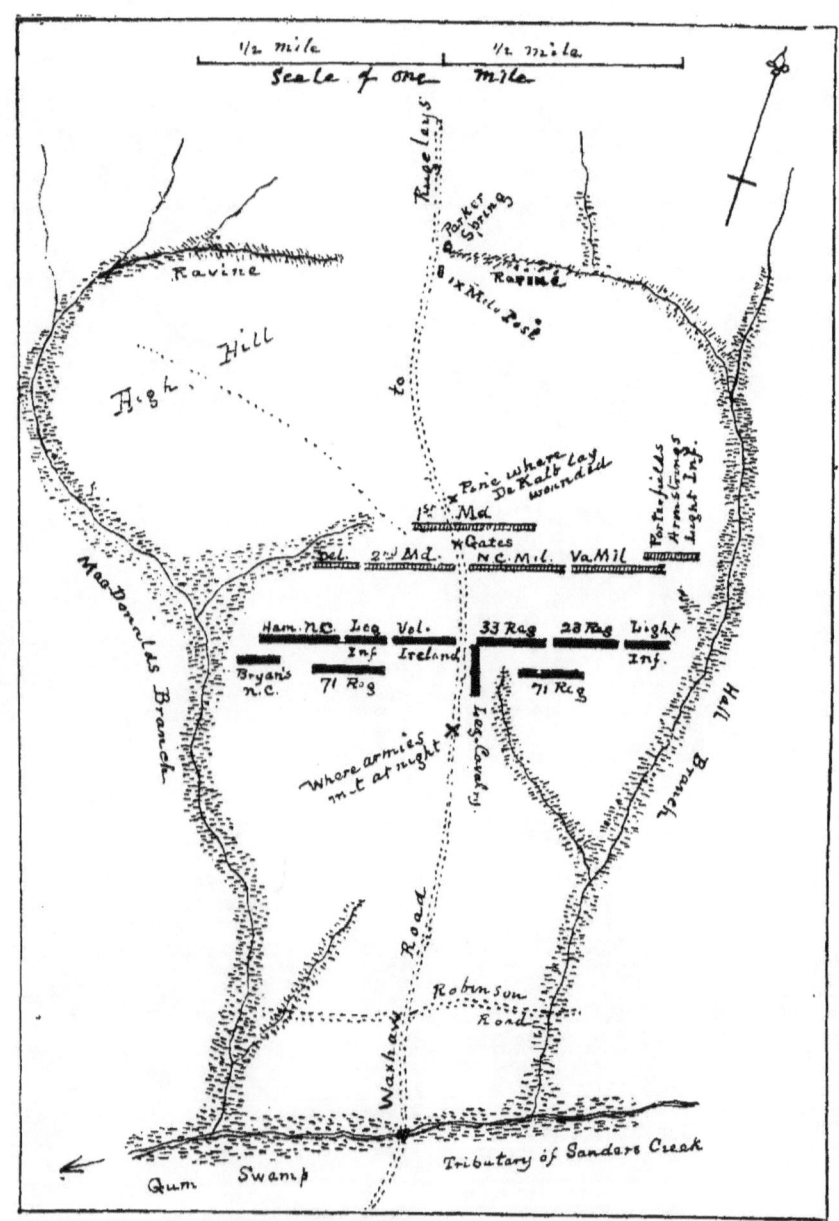

Battle of Camden, August 16, 1780.

DIAGRAM No. 13.

lis. For the forces engaged, there seems to have been room enough for deployment.

Colonel Williams has said: "Involved as Gates was in the necessity of fighting, the disposition which was made for the battle was, perhaps, unexceptionable, and as well adapted to the situation as if the ground had been reconnoitered and chosen by the ablest officer in the Army of the United States. It was afterwards approved by the judicious and gallant General Greene, to whom the writer had the solemn pleasure of showing the field of battle, and with whom he had the additional mortification of participating in the danger and disgrace of a repulse near the same place the very next campaign."*

The forces on each side were aligned east and west, across the Waxhaw road, the Americans in the following order: RIGHT WING, commanded by DeKalb, composed of the Delaware Regiment, Colonel Vaughan, and Second Maryland Brigade, General Gist; CENTER, North Carolina Militia, General Caswell commanding; LEFT WING, General Stevens commanding, composed of Virginia Militia, Armstrong's and Porterfield's light infantry. RESERVE, First Maryland Brigade, General Smallwood commanding.

The British were arranged thus: RIGHT, Webster commanding, the Twenty-third and Thirty-third Regiments and four companies of light infantry; LEFT, Lord Rawdon commanding, composed of Volunteers of Ireland, Tarleton's legion infantry, Hamilton's and Bryan's North Carolina Royalists; RESERVE, the Seventy-first Regiment and Tarleton's cavalry.

The accompanying Diagram No. 13 will more clearly

---

*Referring to Hobkirk Hill, where Greene was defeated, April 25, 1781. These comments from an officer of the distinction and ability of Otho Holland Williams, who was in the battle, should surely to some extent counteract the unmeasured censure which has been heaped upon Gates for the disposition of his troops.

indicate the relative positions.* It has been made from a careful inspection of the ground. The diagram contained in Tarleton's Memoirs, which seems to have been implicitly accepted and copied by many American historians, is very erroneous in its representation of the locality, made doubtless from memory and mere glimpses of the surroundings.

Dawn was the signal for battle. The air was still and thick with haze.† In the early light Colonel Williams sighted some British redcoats a short way down the road in front of the American artillery. He tells us that he ordered it to open upon them, and hurried back to General Gates, who was posted on the road between the front line and reserve, and suggested to him that the moment was favorable for an attack by the Virginians on the left. Gates approved, and Williams galloped over to convey the order.

General Stevens promptly responded by giving the command to his men to advance, himself going to the front to lead them. Williams called out a band of fifty volunteers and with these went ahead of all, to draw the enemy's fire and give the militia an object lesson in courage.

Cornwallis, ever vigilant, noticed the movement on the American left, and says, in his report of the battle, that he *supposed* it to be a change in formation taking place, affording him an opportune time to strike. So he ordered Webster to assail the American left, which was itself moving to attack. Webster with the best two British regiments went with a dash at the militia, shout-

---

*Just where the alignment of the Americans is placed in the diagram and a little south of the DeKalb pine, the writer has found grape shot and bullets in half-burnt and decayed trees.

†Tarleton, who was on the field, states in his Memoirs: "The morning being hazy hung over and involved both armies in such a cloud that it was difficult to see," etc. This afforded the worst possible conditions for the untried militia, and helps to account for their panic.

ing and firing, and with bayonets set, passed right on through Williams's advance skirmishers.

Stevens exhorted his men and called to them, "Come on, my brave fellows, you have bayonets as well as they." But their hearts failed. The steel of British veterans was fast upon them. At the critical moment an uncontrollable panic seized the whole Virginia brigade, and they broke in wild disorder. The North Carolinians next to them in line followed suit at once, and took to their heels, with the notable exception of a part of Dixon's regiment, who stood firm next to the Maryland regulars.* Colonel Williams has assured us that: "A great majority of the militia, at least two-thirds of the army, *fled without firing a shot.* The writer avers it of his own knowledge, having seen and observed every part of the army, from left to right, during the action."

What a deplorable spectacle to meet the eyes of the American commander! He states in his report that he was amazed at the sudden confusion. It was obvious that unless some of these militia could be induced to stand, his army must be beaten. With Caswell, Stevens and his staff, he strove desperately to stem the tide of fugitives. While thus engaged his aide, Maj. Thomas Pinckney, was dangerously wounded in the thigh and captured. Shortly behind and parallel with the American lines extended two marshy ravines, a narrow pass between, and just beyond some rising ground, favorable for a rally. Here he hoped to induce them to reform, and had probably reached this point with his aides. But Tarleton's terrible dragoons had fallen upon the panic-

---

*Of Dixon's North Carolina regiment, Col. Henry Lee, who was not in this action, writes: "In every vicissitude of the battle this regiment maintained its ground, and when the reserve under Smallwood, covering our left, relieved its naked flank, forced the enemy to fall back." Colonel Williams, however, only says in regard to their conduct: "A part of Dixon's regiment, next in line to the Second Maryland brigade, fired two or three rounds of cartridges."

stricken mass. Throwing away their guns unfired, they went like a torrent, bearing all before them, and scattered abroad in the woods. Tarleton's cavalry could thus close up the pass, and cut off Gates and staff, who must fly or be taken. Gates, well mounted, gets away, and with him Caswell. They cannot now return or get a word back to the troops within the ravines. A crown of thorns settles upon the brow of the victor of Saratoga.

Where were Armand's horse? At this moment they might have turned the scale. Simms has answered the question thus: "Swallowed by the woods." Colonel Williams says: "What added not a little to this calamitous scene was the conduct of Armand's legion. Whether it was owing to the disgust of the Colonel at general orders, or the cowardice of his men, is not with this writer to determine, but certain it is that the legion did not take any part in the action of the 16th. They retired early in disorder, and were seen plundering the baggage of the army on their retreat."

The Continentals were thus left to their fate, surrounded by swamps and British troops. No orders came to them, what must they do? Gates and Caswell had hastened back to Rugeley, the camp of the night before, thinking here enough of the flying militia might be stopped and led back to relieve the desperate pressure which must fall upon the Continentals.

Webster did not long follow the militia, who had melted before him, but leaving them to Tarleton's grace, wheeled to the left upon the exposed flanks of the Marylanders and Delawares. DeKalb, who was in command of this remnant, unaware of the utter rout of the militia,* was hotly engaged with Rawdon in his front. The

---

*Tarleton says: "Baron DeKalb, still ignorant of the flight of the left wing and center, owing to the thickness of the air, made a vigorous charge, and when wounded and taken would scarcely believe that General Gates was defeated."

staunch old hero was in the thick of the fray afoot, his horse having been killed under him. His men were driving the British before them and taking prisoners. But a heavy pressure comes upon them from the left.

The First Maryland Brigade, the reserve, greatly disordered by the rushing militia, had somewhat recovered, and was making a stubborn resistance to Webster.* The battle is not yet over, and the American artillery on the road is still dealing death in the British ranks. Cornwallis recalls Tarleton's cavalry from pursuit of the militia, and to deliver the final stroke, sends them in along with his reserve. These turn the scale and the weight of numbers prevail, but not without a desperate hand-to-hand struggle. Bayonets lock and blades meet. The woods ring with the clang of steel. The cry is raised: "Save the Baron DeKalb." The bayonets have reached him. DuBuysson, his aide, embraces him, to ward off the thrusts, some of which he receives in his own body. But no mercy is shown. DeKalb lies bleeding from eleven wounds. The battle is won and lost.

There is now but one way of escape, right through the boggy swamps in the rear. The Continentals, broken and routed, plunge in. Cavalry cannot follow here. Scattered through the dense thickets they dodge away, to live for future triumphs. Major Anderson, grandfather of that fine soldier of the Confederacy, Gen. Richard Anderson, "fighting Dick Anderson," was the only officer, says Williams, who rallied, as he retreated,

---

*Colonel Williams, in his narrative, has left quite a serious inference against the conduct of General Smallwood, who commanded the reserve. After the militia fled Williams made his way back to the reserve. Says he: "At this critical moment the regimental officers of the latter brigade (First Maryland), reluctant to leave the field without orders, inquired for their commanding officer (Brigadier-General Smallwood), who, however, was not to be found; notwithstanding, Colonel Gunby, Major Anderson, and a number of other brave officers, assisted by the deputy adjutant-general, and Major Jones, one of Smallwood's aides, rallied the brigade and renewed the contest."

a few men of different companies, and by his prudence and firmness afforded protection to those who joined on the rout.

Captain Kirkwood of the Delawares escaped, and thereafter commanded the remnant of that regiment. Colonel Vaughan and Major Patton of the Delawares were captured. Gist, Smallwood, Gunby, Williams, Hall, Ford, Howard and the principal officers of the Maryland brigades got away. The sun was barely risen when the fight was over. The rest was flight and pursuit.

Tarleton's dragoons returned to the pursuit. Passing rapidly up the road, they overtook the flying infantry, and with bloody swords chased them through the woods far and near. Many were killed and many captured. At Rugeley's bridge, over Grannys Quarter Creek, some officers had rallied a small force, but these were broken and routed by a charge of the dragoons. The tireless Tarleton carried his work of havoc on twenty-two miles further to Hanging Rock.

Says Tarleton, in his Memoirs: "Immediately after the action every possible assistance was given to the wounded of both parties. The loyal militia were ordered to explore the woods, and to collect the disabled. Wagons were afterwards assembled, in which they were placed with care, in order to follow the principal part of the British army, which fell back to its position at Camden. Lord Cornwallis, with the light and legion infantry, and the Twenty-third Regiment, moved forward to Rugeley's Mills, where he was joined in the afternoon by the legion cavalry on their return from Hanging Rock."

Says Colonel Lee: "The road was heaped with the dead and wounded. Arms, artillery, horses and baggage were strewn in every direction."

The British official reports give their own loss as 324 killed and wounded, including eleven missing, about fourteen per cent. of their whole force.

Cornwallis, Tarleton, Stedman, all British authorities, and on the scene, give the American loss in round numbers as 800 or 900 killed and 1,000 prisoners, many of whom were wounded, which would be sixty-five per cent. of those engaged. The booty captured is given as 150 baggage wagons, twenty ammunition wagons, 670 cannon shot, eight pieces of artillery, 2,000 muskets, 80,000 balls. Of the British estimate Colonel Lee says: "Although many militia were killed during the flight, this account must be exaggerated. While the Continentals kept the field, the loss in that quarter must have been about equal. The loss the Americans sustained could never be accurately ascertained, as no returns from the militia were received. Of the North Carolina militia between three and four hundred were made prisoners and between sixty and one hundred wounded. Of the Virginia militia only three were wounded, and as they were the first to fly, not many were taken. For the number engaged the loss sustained by the regulars was considerable. It amounted to between three and four hundred men, of whom a large part were officers. The British took such as were unable to retreat. This threw between two and three hundred Continental troops into their hands."

General Gates, writing from Hillsboro, August 30, 1780, says: "The militia broke so early in the day, and scattered in so many directions upon their retreat, that very few have fallen into the hands of the enemy. Seven hundred noncommissioned officers and soldiers of the Maryland division have rejoined the army."

All of these statements of the American loss are vague. But in regard to the Continentals something more authentic is furnished by Colonel Williams, deputy adjutant, in his Narrative. He gives a return made up at Hillsboro, some time after the battle. His statement is not free from ambiguity, but as we construe it, may be reduced to the following summary:

Maryland Division.

	Escaped.	Killed or Captured.
Colonels	3	
Lieutenant-colonels	4	3
Majors	5	2
Captains	38	15
Subalterns	50	13
Staff officers	24	2
Noncommissioned officers	85	52
Musicians	62	34
Rank and file	781	711
	1052	802

Delaware Division.

	Escaped.	Killed or Captured.
Officers	33	11
Musicians	11	
Privates	145	36
	189	47

He thinks that probably more were killed than captured. If his returns be not misunderstood, it appears thereby that the Maryland and Delaware troops, before the battle, amounted, officers and men, to the following total:

Marylanders—Escaped 1,052
              Killed and captured 802
Delawares—Escaped 189
              Killed and captured 47
                                                 2,090

This seems to confirm the British estimate of the strength of Continentals under DeKalb and Gates at the outset of the campaign. The number of them effective and present for battle may have been less. Certain it is that enough survived this terrible disaster to take an ample revenge at Guilford, Hobkirk, and Eutaw. It was this "noble six hundred" that drove the British from the Carolinas. All honor to the invincibles of Maryland and Delaware!

If one today, in leafy August, were to visit the scene of battle, he would exclaim: "Here indeed was a veritable 'war of the woods'." It has always been known locally as the "Parker Old Field," because of its ownership in former days by one Parker, although there are none of those badges in the vicinity always indicative of old fields. The present adjacent clearings are undoubtedly comparatively recent. At the date of the battle the ground was occupied by a close array of tall and stately pines, limbless to a height of forty or fifty feet. These, by the process of turpentining, have been reduced to a scanty few, so that not many of those remain that witnessed the battle. Their thinning has allowed to come up a growth of scrub oaks, which in summer obscure the view much more than did the pines. The British and Americans probably had a pretty fair view of each other at two hundred yards, while by the present growth they would have been concealed at fifty feet. Those living in that neighborhood have found amongst the leaves of the woods many an old buckle, button, bayonet, bullet, cannon ball, flintlock, and to this day diligent search will reveal some such *disjecta membra* of the encounter.

In the *Camden Journal and Southern Whig* of January 24, 1835, we find this curious item: *"Revolutionary Relic.* The musket belonging to Levi, a French negro, who was brought over by Lafayette and fought during the entire Revolution, was found bedded in the mud in Gum Swamp, where Levi had hidden it, being wounded at Gates's defeat. The barrel is badly eaten with rust, the bayonet eaten and broken. The powder flashed on being fired. Levi lived in Camden District for a long while after the war. The musket is now in the possession of Dr. William Blanding." A citizen of Camden says that Levi became a servant of the Whitaker family. His gun would be a prize today, could it be rediscovered. Dr. William Blanding died in Rehoboth, Mass., though many years a resident of Camden.

This historic field or woodland may now be conveniently reached by a railroad line which runs within a mile of it. The nearby station has been appropriately named DeKalb.

Gen. Horatio Gates.

ILLUSTRATION F.

CHAPTER VII.

AFTERMATH.

No victor's wreath was ever more completely blasted than that of Gates by this disaster. His military reputation was irreparably ruined.

Late in the night of the day of battle he reached Charlotte, with General Caswell, and the two, leaving directions to gather the fragments of the army, together kept right on to Hillsboro to meet the Assembly of North Carolina, then in session, and to concert with them some measures of relief. From Hillsboro, on the 20th, he writes to the President of Congress a report of the defeat, which begins with these dejected words: "In the deepest distress and anxiety of mind, I am obliged to acquaint your Excellency with the defeat of the troops under my command."

Seldom has such a load of chagrin, anguish, and derision fallen so suddenly upon the head of a popular favorite. His escape from the field, contrasted with the heroic conduct of DeKalb, had all the aspect of "caitiff flight." His rapid departure with the militia placed him in the same category with those renegades in popular estimation.

General Greene, writing September 17, 1780, to President Reed, says: "General Gates's late misfortune will sink his consequence and lessen his military character. He is bandied about and subjected to many remarks, the common fate of the unfortunate."

On September 6, 1780, Alexander Hamilton wrote these cutting comments to Duane: "But was there ever the instance of a general running away, as Gates has done, from his whole army? And was there ever so precipitous a flight? One hundred and eighty miles in three days and a half does admirable credit to the activity of a man at his time of life. But it disgraces the general and the soldier. I always believed him to be very far short of a Hector or a Ulysses. All the world, I think, will begin to agree with me."

In Wheeler's History of North Carolina we have an incident of General Gates's flight, related in the words of Maj. W. R. Davie, then a young officer in command of a small body of cavalry and coming down to join his force to the army. He met General Gates some distance above Rugeley's, hurrying up the road. "Gates desired Davie to fall back to Charlotte, or the dragoons would be upon him." Davie replied, "His men were accustomed to Tarleton and did not fear him." Gates had no time to parley, but passed on. Of General Huger, who then rode up, Major Davie asked how far the directions of Gates ought to be obeyed, who answered: "Just as far as you please, for you will never see him again." Davie again sent a gentleman to overtake General Gates and say that, if he wished, Davie would return and bury his dead. The answer of Gates was, "I say retreat; let the dead bury the dead."*

It has been stated that General Gates had no thought of General Sumter and failed to send him word of the defeat, so as to make a timely retreat. Colonel Williams, however, asserts that "he (Gates) therefore sent orders to Sumter to retire in the best manner he could, and proceeded himself, with General Caswell, towards Charlotte." Major Davie, seeing the rout. also took precaution to notify General Sumter, sending a Captain Martin on this mission.

---

*The only apology General Gates condescended to make to the army for the loss of the battle was: "A man *may* pit a cock, but he can't make him fight."—Williams's Narrative.

Dr. William Read, in his reminiscences, tells us that he met General Gates at Hillsboro and waited "on his fallen general in sympathy. General Gates was sadly low-spirited, and made every one unhappy that had to communicate with him. He (Read) saw him receive a dispatch from the North, and on reading a letter saw a good deal of feeling expressed. The General put the letter to his lips and uttered some words. The General received him graciously, and pointing to the letter said: 'Washington sympathizes with me in the loss of my son, and commands me to the right wing of the army'."

General Greene, who, on December 3, 1780, superseded General Gates, writes from Charlotte, January 9, 1781, to President Reed of Congress: "I overtook the army at Charlotte, to which place General Gates had advanced. General Gates had lost the confidence of the officers, and the troops all their discipline. The General and I met upon very good terms, and parted so. The old gentleman was in great distress, having just heard of the death of his son before my arrival.* The Battle of Camden is spoken of very differently here to what it is to the northwards, and as for regular retreat there was none. Every man got off the ground in the best manner he could. This is the account Colonel Williams gives, who was one of the last on the field. Indeed, the whole business was a short fight, and the greatest loss happened after the troops broke and attempted to make their escape.

"From all I can learn, if General Gates had stopped at Charlotte, little more disgrace would have fallen to

---

*This only son of General Gates, the pride of his life, Robert by name, died shortly after the Battle of Camden. This extract is taken from a letter from Gates to President Reed, written May 10, 1780: "Bob is reconciled to his disappointment" (the failure to receive an appointment) "and I would fain have him learn to be obscurely good; but youth and ambition will at his time prevail, and make him languish for the busy world."

his share than is common to the unfortunate. General Gates and Smallwood were not upon good terms, the former suspecting the latter of having an intention to supplant him. Smallwood has many enemies in the Maryland line, but upon the whole, I think him a sensible man and a good officer."*

It has been impossible to gather from such histories and narratives as we have had access to any satisfactory statement as to General Gates's personal conduct upon the field of battle, only such vague expressions as this: "The militia poured like a torrent and bore Gates with them."† Nothing more specific is contained in Colonel Williams's otherwise very detailed narrative.‡ William Gilmore Simms, in his "Partisan," which, though professedly a romance, in its historical features is authentic, may likely have derived from reliable source the following picture of Gates's efforts to save the day:

"He had only the native courage of his heart to fall back upon, he could only seek now to lead them back into the thickest waves of danger. Through the crowd, the torrent of confusion, with head uncovered and gray locks flying in the wind, he darted headlong, and his voice hoarsely rose over all the sounds of battle. He threw himself amidst the fugitives. He smote fiercely amongst them with bared sword, striking as if among foes only, and all in vain. Never were efforts more honestly, but idly, made, to compel the flying militia back to the standards which they had dishonored. In his fury, smiting down a refractory soldier, who offered much

---

*On December 7th, Greene had written to Washington: "General Gates sets out tomorrow for the northward. Many officers think very favorably of his conduct, and that whenever an inquiry takes place he will honorably acquit himself."

†Marshall's Life of Washington.

‡Williams does indulge a covert sneer, that "Gates and Caswell *soon* saw that all was lost," and got away.

more defiance to his general than he had done to the British bayonets, he vented his indignation in a torrent of oaths. 'Turn about, I say—turn, you d—d rascals, turn.' A tall sergeant, who was hurrying away with the rest, did not hesitate, with one stroke of his saber, to cut the bridle of Gates's horse, and set the animal free to a flight which he naturally followed with the fugitives. The fiery steed darted along up the route madly as the rest."

A mistaken criticism has been leveled against Gates, among a multitude of others, that he made the unpardonable blunder of changing the formation of his militia line at the very onset of battle. There seems no truth in this, or any evidence to support it, except in Cornwallis's report, wherein he says that just before the attack he observed on the American left what he supposed to be a change of formation. Tarleton repeats Cornwallis's error. Colonel Williams's minute narrative, so freely quoted above, gives no intimation that any such movement was made or contemplated, and Marshall* declares that Cornwallis was mistaken in his supposition.

Despite the detraction so freely vented against General Gates, some respectable apologies have been made for him. Col. Henry Lee,† in his Memoirs, says: "The general-in-chief, although deeply unfortunate, is entitled to respect and regard. He took decisive measures to restore the action by unceasing efforts to rally the fugitive militia, and had he succeeded, would have led them back to the vortex of battle and have turned the

---

*Life of Washington.
†Colonel Henry Lee, father of General Robert E. Lee, was not only a splendid soldier in the Revolution, but a man of high mental gifts and a finished scholar. He was the author of the immortal eulogy upon Washington: "First in war, first in peace, and first in the hearts of his fellow citizens."

fortune of the day, or died like the hero of Saratoga. This rapid withdrawal of Gates to Charlotte and Hillsboro has been generally supposed to diminish his reputation. Not so in truth. It does him honor, as it evinced a mind capable, amid confusion and distress, of discovering a point most promising to renew his strength, at the same time incapable of being withheld from doing his duty by regarding the calumny with which he was sure to be assailed."

It seems, so far as the imperfect accounts enable us to judge, and an inspection of the field, that General Gates, whilst mingling with the militia in a supreme effort to quell their panic, and rally them behind the ravines, was cut off from those troops who stood their ground, and became no doubt a conspicuous object for the pursuit of Tarleton's dragoons, who had fallen upon the broken militia, and his flight became the only alternative to capture. Pompey fled from Pharsalia, Hannibal from Zama. Gates had precedent. Well for his fame had he met the fate of DeKalb. In the words of Colonel Williams:

"If General Gates had fallen at the commencement of the action of Camden, the laurels of Saratoga would have been ever green on his brow, and history would have exulted in the merits of the hero. What difference in point of real merit would there have been (or could there be) between falling by an early, accidental shot, or submitting to the irresistible impulse of the militia, who went like a torrent from the field, forcing almost everything before them? And yet what a difference in the public opinion! Instead of praises, panegyric, and monumental honors, he was censured, calumniated and even condemned, unheard. General Greene took pains to collect the best information relative to the circumstances of the late campaign, and his communications finally determined Congress to restore him to his command in the northern army."

Says Paul Allen: "That the conduct of General Gates previous to the fatal battle of the 16th was full of blame, will hardly be denied. He trusted too much to himself, and too easily spurned the advice of those who merited his attention; but here the blame stops. His conduct in the battle was worthy the hero of Saratoga, and his efforts to retrieve his original errors were unceasing; but it was too late, and hard as was his fate in the result, it was perhaps not worse than his unadvised rashness merited."

It was a matter for congratulation to General Gates that he had secured as aid and member of his military family so high and heroic a character as Gen. Thomas Pinckney, who, while struggling to rally the militia, was severely wounded. We are informed* that he wrote a pamphlet in mitigation of the popular clamor against General Gates, wherein, "while he admitted his sad error on that occasion, recalled his valuable services at Saratoga. He advocated the justice of striking a balance between failure and success. Washington took a similar view, and never withheld his confidence from the defeated general."

Judge James, himself a Revolutionary veteran, in his life of Marion, says: "Had General Gates reached the important pass of Gum Swamp and occupied it properly, the fortune of war might have been different. It is a miry creek, impassable for many miles except at the road. He missed it only by a few minutes. And his popularity, though gained by much merit, was lost by no greater crime than that of trusting too much to militia."

*See Rev. C. C. Pinckney's Life of Gen. Thomas Pinckney.

Finally we quote the charitable judgment of Miss Mercy Warren, of Plymouth, Mass., who, in her History of the American Revolution (1805), writes: "Yet neither the courage nor the fidelity of the bold and long-tried veteran could be called in question. The strongest human fortitude has frequently suffered a momentary eclipse from that panic-struck influence under which the mind of man sometimes unaccountably falls. This has been exemplified in the greatest military characters. Even the celebrated royal hero of Prussia has retreated before it, as in a fright, but recovered himself, defied and conquered his enemies. General Gates, though he lost the day in the unfortunate accident at Camden, lost no part of his courage, vigilance, or firmness."

After the lapse of a hundred years the character of General Gates still rests under a cloud of disfavor. Later authors seem more disposed to ignore or discredit him than those of his own day, and less reserved in charging to him cowardice, presumption, malice, and incompetence. There seems actually more readiness to make allowances for Benedict Arnold, of whom a formal biography has been written, while of Gates there is none.

Has the final estimate of posterity been made up, to exclude his portrait from the gallery of American worthies, and to deny all homage to his memory? Would a more thorough and fairer inquiry into the facts of his life than any heretofore made, result in any revision of judgment, or be viewed as but a fantastic effort to reverse the verdict of a century and to regild a tarnished character?

Yet his career is full of picturesque interest, woven into the brightest and darkest threads of American history, and for all time associated with Camden. Winner of the brightest triumph, victim in the direst defeat of the Revolution, comrade of the great men of that great era, is contempt only to be allotted his name? Is it impossible now to restore him to the place in that goodly company he once occupied? We shall attempt here but a brief outline of his career, from limited sources of information.

At the outset we are faced with contradictions. The facts of his nativity are not free from mystery. He was born in England in 1728, at Malden, on the Blackwater River, Essex County. One author* says he was "the son of a clergyman; another† that he was "the son of a respectable victualer of Kensington." Irving‡ says that he was the son of a captain in the British army. Again we read§ that his parents were servants to a noble English family, at whose residence the Walpoles visited. A rumor got abroad that he was the illegitimate son of Sir Robert Walpole, originating, it is said, from the fact that Horace Walpole officiated as godfather at his christening.

Horace Walpole himself writes that Gates "was the son of a housekeeper of the second Duke of Leeds, who, marrying a young husband when very old, had this son by him."¶ In a letter to George Montagu, March 22, 1762, Walpole writes: "Perhaps you may think me proud, but you don't know that I had some share in the reduction of Martinico; the express was brought by my godson, Mr. Horatio Gates."

Thus his very birth rests under a stigma, probably unjust, perhaps now impossible to remove. The same fatality of doubt and discredit seems to have pursued him through life. Amid the conflicting statements

---

*Wyatt's Generals, etc., p. 59.
†Sargent's History of Braddock's Defeat, p. 106.
‡Life of Washington, Vol. 1, p. 385.
§National Cyclopaedia of American Biography. New York, 1892, James T. White & Co.
¶Journal of the Reign of George III, p. 200.

concerning his early life it is difficult to select. His father died when he was very young.* At the age of twelve he determined on a military career, from which his guardian could not dissuade him,† and at seventeen was an ensign under General Monkton. He received a liberal education.‡ At twenty-one he volunteered under General Edward Cornwallis (not the famous Charles, by whom he was defeated), with whom he was stationed for some time in Nova Scotia.

He joined General Braddock's fatal Indian campaign of 1755, in which he commanded, as captain, the advance, consisting of parts of two New York companies. In the surprise and massacre he was severely wounded through the body. It has been stated that he was rescued from the field by Washington.§ Another writer attributes this rescue to a soldier, to whom, in his old days, Gates wrote: "Come rest your firelock in my chimney corner and partake with me."¶ After Braddock's defeat he remained in western New York two or three years.‖

In 1762 he served as aide-de-camp to General Monkton in the attack upon the Island of Martinique, and for gallantry in this service was promoted to Major in the Royal Americans.** He aspired, however, to higher position and more lucrative service, and Irving states that he engaged in a long course of solicitation, haunting of public offices and antechambers, and "knocking about town," wherein he learned to wheedle and flatter. Not attaining his objects, he sold his commission, and in 1772 migrated to Berkeley County, Virginia, where he

*Wyatt's Generals, etc., p. 59.
†*Ibid.*
‡Irving's Life of Washington, Vol. 1, p. 385.
§Cyclopaedia of American Biography. New York, 1892.
¶Principles and Acts of the Revolution, p. 276.
‖Irving's Life of Washington.
**Irving, *ibid.*

purchased an estate on the Potomac which he named "Travelers' Rest."

It has been stated that he married a lady of rank in England, the daughter of James Valence of Liverpool,* from whom he inherited a half million dollars. This fortune enabled him to dispense a liberal hospitality on the Virginia plantation.

In the contentions leading to Revolution, Gates enlisted heartily in the cause of the colonies. He spent three days with Washington at Mount Vernon just before the meeting of the Continental Congress. A cordial attachment up to this time existed between them. Washington writes, May 19, 1776, of Gates's "military experience, zeal and attachment to the cause of America." To Washington Gates proclaims the "greatest respect for your character and sincerest attachment to your person." Richard Henry Lee writes to Washington, June 13, 1776: "It is more than probable Congress will order our friend Gates to Canada. His great ability and virtue will be absolutely necessary to restore things there." John Adams writes to Gerry, about this time: "Lee [Charles] and Gates are officers of such great experience and confessed abilities that I thought their advice in a council of officers might be of great advantage."

With such opinions in vogue as to his fitness, he accompanied Washington to Massachusetts, and was appointed chief of staff, and adjutant-general of the American army. It is said that he desired to be a major-general with an active command, and became piqued at Washington's failure or refusal to secure him the position. He managed to obtain independent command of the troops for Canada, and later superseded General

---

*Cyclopaedia of American Biography.

Schuyler in New York, and by good fortune gained the glittering prize of Saratoga.

The glamor of this victory, contrasting with Washington's reverses in New Jersey, produced an intrigue on the part of certain officers and members of Congress to elevate Gates to the chief command. This is known as the "Conway Cabal," of which General Conway was the most active and unscrupulous spirit. Gates, dazzled by his success, was not averse to receipt of letters flattering him and condemning Washington. He probably encouraged these suggestions, which a lofty principle would have caused him to repudiate. His aide, Wilkinson, indiscreetly exposed the contents of a letter of Conway to Gates reflecting on Washington, to whom it was reported. This led to a correspondence between Gates and Washington, in which the former was decidedly worsted.*

Under influence of the Cabal, Congress created a Board of War, and elected Gates president. This Board had power to direct the military policy of the war, and being composed of Washington's opponents, proved a thorn in his side. In a letter to Henry Laurens, President of Congress, he passes the most caustic strictures upon Gates, and alleges against him "an air of design, a want of candor, and in many instances even of politeness—little underhand intrigues which he

---

*This letter of Conway's came also near to causing a duel between Wilkinson and Gates, who, in his explanatory letter to Washington, had said that his private papers had been "stealingly copied." This hinted at Wilkinson, who challenged Gates. A meeting with pistols was arranged. Before the time arrived Gates sent for Wilkinson, then a young man, and the issue is told in Wilkinson's memoirs as follows: "I found General Gates alone, and was received with tenderness, but manifest embarrassment. He asked me to walk. We turned into a back street and proceeded in silence, when he burst into tears, took me by the hand and asked me 'how I could think he wished to injure me.' I was too deeply affected to speak. He continued: 'I should as soon think of injuring my own child.' I was flattered and pleased, and if a third person had doubted the sincerity of the explanation I would have insulted him."

is frequently practicing," and terms his attitude towards himself as "malignant." With due allowance for irritation, these charges will stand as the most serious reproach upon the memory of Gates.

But ever after the awful humiliation of his rival at Camden, Washington displayed towards him only a magnanimous grandeur of spirit. When in October, 1780, Congress directed a court of inquiry as to Gates's conduct at the Battle of Camden, Washington, who was authorized to name the members, ordered that only those officers should sit who were not present at the battle, or such as were unobjectionable to General Gates.

The court of inquiry never sat, so great was the urgency of the war. Indeed, there seems not to have been any serious purpose to hold it. On May 22, 1781, Congress resolved that the order of inquiry was not intended as a suspension and that General Gates was at liberty to report to headquarters and take such command as the Commander-in-Chief should direct. Washington was ready to assign him to command of his right wing. But Gates declined to serve until a formal exoneration by the court or by Congress.

After General Greene, on December 3, 1780, relieved him of the command at Charlotte, he set out for "Traveler's Rest," his Virginia home. Says Col. Henry Lee: "On his route no countenance shed the balm of condolence, all were gloomy and scowling until he reached Richmond. Great and good men then governed the State. They appointed a committee of their body to wait upon the vanquished general and to assure him of their esteem, that the remembrance of his former glorious services was never to be obliterated by any reverse of fortune, but ever mindful of his great merit, they would omit no opportunity of testifying to the world the gratitude which Virginia owed him." These resolutions were presented by Patrick Henry. Colonel Lee compares this act of the Virginia Assembly to that of the Roman Senate of old, when they tendered thanks to the fugitive Varro after the destruction of his army by Hannibal at Cannae.

The court of inquiry was dispensed with by Congress on August 14, 1782, and, with only three dissenting votes, General Gates was exonerated and restored to his rank. As senior officer he was placed by Washington in command of his right wing. But hostilities were now well-nigh over. In place arose an ominous mutiny of the army, threatening forcible redress for arrears of pay. It has been charged, how truly cannot here be considered, that Gates fostered the spirit of discontent out of "impotent malice" still rankling in his breast towards Washington, who, as on all occasions, was equal to emergencies. He assembled the officers at Newburgh. Gates was chosen to preside. Washington addressed the meeting in one of his grandest efforts, allayed the storm, and thus ended the Revolution.

Gates lived at his Virginia home till 1790, in which year he freed his slaves and moved to New York. Here he was received with honors and presented with the freedom of the city. Here he died, April 18, 1806, at the age of seventy-eight.

What an example of capricious fortune his career exhibits! The zenith of fame, the depths of despair! His character presents equal contrasts, in appearance at least. On the one hand his gallantry at Martinique, and at Braddock's defeat; his services in organizing the army; his generous treatment of Burgoyne and the British at Saratoga; his fortitude and manly bearing under disgrace after the Camden disaster. These are conceded merits. On the other, a spurious ambition, a mean jealousy, a pompous vanity, a ludicrous flight. Upon such a medley it is difficult to pass judgment. There is little doubt that he has suffered much from calumny, and indiscriminate censure, based on erroneous premises, and partisan prejudice. Here lies a rich and inviting field for a quest after historic truth.*

Another reflection occurs. Could this man, well known to them, have secured the confidence and esteem of the Adamses, the Lees, of Henry, even of Washington, and be indeed the veritable sham as represented by some authors? For the present we should prefer to cherish the sentiments of Paulding, the biographer of Washington: "His name is embodied in history; it occupies an honorable station among the heroes of the Revolution; it has become a part of the inheritance of national pride; it belongs to the people of the United States; and I would not, if I could, throw any additional shade over its brightness."

As stated in the preceding chapter, after the battle the wounded of both sides were gathered in wagons and taken to Camden. The fight being ended probably by sunrise, the whole day was before them for this gruesome journey. Among their number were Baron DeKalb, Chevalier DuBuysson, Maj. Thomas Pinckney, Colonel Porterfield, Colonel Webster, General Rutherford, many other minor officers, and hundreds of privates.

The conduct and death of Baron DeKalb, affording one of the most illustrious examples of constancy and

---

*Colonel Henry Lee, writing to Gen. Anthony Wayne, January 7, 1781, from the camp on the Peedee River, says of General Gates: "This unfortunate General has been most insidiously, most cruelly traduced. Happy on all occasions to support the injured, I feel it my duty as an honest soldier to give you an account of that action. The impartial and sensible part of the army here are the persons from whom I have my communications." General Greene also invariably defended the reputation of General Gates whenever he heard it aspersed.

courage in American history, demand the most particular and authentic account attainable. As is almost invariably the case, the testimony of eyewitnesses is irreconcilable. Humphrey Hunter, afterwards a distinguished divine of North Carolina, was in the battle, probably one of Dixon's Regiment, which, as stated, stood its ground with DeKalb. Hunter was captured and taken to Camden with the other prisoners.* In his memoirs he gives this observation: "Soon after he (Hunter) surrendered, he witnessed the painful incidents of the battle resulting in the death of Baron DeKalb. He saw the Baron, without *suite or aid,* and without manifesting the design of his movements, galloping down the line. He was soon descried by the enemy, who, clapping their hands on their shoulders, in reference to his epaulettes, exclaimed, 'a general, a rebel general!' Immediately a man on horseback (not Tarleton) met him, and demanded his sword. The Baron reluctantly presented the handle towards him, saying in French: *'Etes-vous un officier, monsieur?'* ('Are you an officer, sir?') His antagonist not understanding the language, with an oath, more sternly demanded his sword.† The Baron then, not understanding him perfectly, with all possible speed rode on, disdaining to surrender to any but an officer.

"The cry 'a rebel general' sounded along the line. The musketeers immediately, by platoons, fired upon him. He proceeded about twenty-five rods, when he fell from his horse, mortally wounded. Soon afterwards he was raised to his feet, and stripped of his hat, coat and neck-cloth, and placed with his hands resting on a

---

*He tells us how they were confined in a stockade. He was without a hat for some months. He managed to escape by knocking down the British officer with a lightwood knot.

†Silas Deane says DeKalb spoke English. Wharton's Dip. Cor., Vol. 2, p. 200.

Baron DeKalb.

ILLUSTRATION G.

wagon. His body was found upon examination to have been pierced with seven musket balls. Whilst standing in this position, and the blood streaming through his shirt, Cornwallis and his suite rode up. Being informed that the wounded man was Baron DeKalb, he addressed him, saying: 'I am sorry, sir, to see you, not sorry that you are vanquished, but sorry to see you so badly wounded.' Having given orders to an officer to administer to the wants of the Baron, the British general rode on to secure the results of his victory."

The above is given in Wheeler's History of North Carolina, as a quotation from Hunter's manuscript. In the *Camden Journal* of June 19, 1830, we find a reproduction, professedly verbatim, of Hunter's narrative, which tallies with that given in Wheeler, up to the point where the wounded Baron is lifted from the ground, and here a strange divergence appears. In the Wheeler extract, the Baron is placed against a wagon. In the newspaper quotation no reference is made to the wagon, but instead it is stated: "He was placed against a pine post"; and continues: "He died that evening. His remains were carried to Camden and there interred with the honors of war."

The version which mentions the "pine post" corresponds with local tradition, which identifies the spot, and the very pine where the wounded DeKalb lay. The elders tell us, that it has been handed down to them, that the "pine post" beside which he was laid, was a young pine, whose top had been cut off by a cannon shot. It grew later to a stocky, but sturdy tree, and stood until 1884, in which year it fell victim to a forest fire. Portions of the charred trunk are still to be seen, and lie a few feet to the east of the highway.* See diagram No. 13.

---

*Colonel Shannon, in his sketches of "Old Times in Camden," says: "The

The Rev. Hunter, as we shall see, is certainly mistaken in his statement that the Baron died upon the battlefield, and that his *remains* were carried to Camden that evening. Equally astray, no doubt, is a local tradition to the effect that he expired at a point on DeKalb street (not then laid out), just east of the corner of Broad and DeKalb streets, where he was taken immediately upon his arrival at Camden, to refresh his fainting condition at the waters of a pump said to have been there located. It is stated as a well-known fact in the *Camden Journal* of July 31, 1830, that: "DeKalb died in what was called the 'Blue House' in this town, a day or two after the battle."

This statement of the *Journal* may be accepted as the best authority as to the spot where DeKalb breathed his last, for there then still survived in or near Camden some veterans of the battle: Col. Richard Anderson of Stateburg, who was living in 1832; Lewis Cook, who died at the age of ninety-two, on Twenty-five-Mile Creek; Adam Team, who died June 12, 1844, at the age of eighty-five; Capt. Benjamin Carter, died January 20, 1830; and Maj. Samuel Jones, who died on Lynches Creek, January 20, 1847, at the age of ninety-one, buried with military honors. He was the father of those well-known old citizens, Burwell and Seaborn Jones.

The Blue House was situated at or near the corner of Broad and Meeting streets, due east of the old Presby-

---

battle was fought mostly on the west side of the road. When a boy we have stood at the head of a little bay, in the deep shades of the forest, and had pointed out to us by an aged man, who knew of what he spoke, the spot where DeKalb fell and where the gallant and devoted DuBuysson intervened his body between the thirsting bayonets and the fallen hero, and stayed their onslaught with the earnest appeal: 'Save the Baron DeKalb!' This old man, our guide, who had been during a long life, a mighty hunter, assured us that the lead for his rifle had always been supplied from the great old pines of that battlefield. The cut and hacked condition of the trees well indicated that he and many another 'deerslayer' had drawn their bullets from the same storehouse."

terian Church and Cemetery, and a few yards only from the spot where DeKalb was first interred. The lot upon which it stood was originally the property of William Ancrum, of Charleston. By him in 1798 it was deeded for £300 to Gayetan Aiguier, of Charleston, who seems then to have become a resident of Camden. It next passed to Mrs. Margaret Adamson Alexander, wife of Dr. Isaac Alexander, who by her will, dated 1802, leaves it to her son-in-law, Henry Dana Ward, in trust for her grandson, Henry Dana Artemas Ward. In 1807 it passed to Zebulon Rudolph,* a partner of Thomas Broom in the milling business. In 1818 Royal Bullard became purchaser, and beyond that we have no trace of it.

But most, if not all, of the doubt and contradictions surrounding the death of DeKalb have been officially dispelled by the discovery of two letters of his faithful aide, the Chevalier DuBuysson, which are here reproduced in full. That from Hillsboro has but recently been resurrected by Wharton (Diplomatic Correspondence) from the archives in Washington:

Charlotte Aug 26th 1780.
To Generals Smallwood and Gist:

Having received several wounds in the action of the sixteenth instant, I was made prisoner with the honorable Major-General the Baron de Kalb, with whom I served as aide-de-camp and friend, and had an opportunity of attending that great and good officer, during the short time he languished with eleven wounds, which proved mortal *on the third day.*

---

*This Zebulon Rudolph was the grand-uncle of Mrs. Lucretia R. Garfield, the widow of President Garfield, a fact confirmed by a letter from Mrs. Garfield, in reply to an inquiry. Zebulon Rudolph left Camden for Alabama, where he died in the year 1855, at the advanced age of eighty-six.

It is with pleasure I obey the Baron's last commands, in presenting his most affectionate compliments to all the officers and men of his division; he expressed the greatest satisfaction in the testimony given by the British army of the bravery of his troops, and he was charmed with the firm opposition they made to superior force when abandoned by the rest of the army. The gallant behaviour of the Delaware regiment and the companies of artillery attached to the brigade, afforded him infinite pleasure, and the exemplary conduct of the whole division gave him an endearing sense of the merit of the troops he had the honor to command.

    I am dear generals
   Your most obedient humble servant
      LE CHEVALIER DUBUYSSON.

It does not appear to whom the following is addressed:

      Hillsboro Sept. 2nd 1780.

SIR: The Baron DeKalb, taken by the British and mortally wounded, desired me to repair immediately to Philadelphia, to give, in his name, to Congress, a full account of his transactions relative to his command of the Maryland and Delaware line, since his departure from Pennsylvania, to clear his memory of every false or malignant insinuation, which might have been made by some invidious persons, but as my wounds do not permit me to travel as fast as I could desire, I thought it convenient to acquaint you, sir, of my repairing to Congress with all the baron's papers and accounts, that no measure be taken towards this affair before my arrival in Philadelphia, which will be as speedily as possible.

The Baron DeKalb, deserted by all the militia, who fled at the first fire, withstood with the greatest bravery, coolness and intrepidity, with the brave Marylanders alone, the furious charge of the whole British army; but superior bravery was obliged at length to yield to superior numbers, and the baron, *having had his horse killed under him,* fell into the hands of the enemy, pierced with eight wounds of bayonets and three musket balls. I stood by the baron during the action and shared his fate,* being taken by his side, wounded in both arms and hands. Lord Cornwallis and Rawdon treated us with the greatest civility. The baron, dying of his wounds two days after the action, was buried with all the honors of war, and his funeral attended by all the officers of the British army. The doctor having reported to Lord Cornwallis the impossibility of curing my wounds in that part of the continent, he admitted me to my parole, to go to Philadelphia for effecting an exchange between me and Lieut.-Col. Hamilton &c.

LE CHEVALIER DUBUYSSON.

The surgeon who attended upon Baron DeKalb was Dr. Isaac Alexander,† ancestor of the Camden family of that name. He was with the American forces at the Battle of Camden, and was probably there taken by the British. It was his wife who became owner of the Blue House in which DeKalb died.

John Kalb was the son of a German peasant, born 1721, in Alsace, previously a German province, then subject to France. He entered the French army at an early age. He *assumed* the title of Baron, adding "*de*" to his name. This was done to make promotion possible, for all military rank in the French army depended on social

---

*Comparing this with Hunter's account, we must conclude that he saw the Baron fall when his horse was killed, and that the wounds were received later, while the Baron was "fighting afoot," as stated by Tarleton.

†This statement is made upon authority of the *Southern Home*, a journal published in Charlotte, N. C., 1875, by Gen. D. H. Hill.

rank, and titles were jealously scanned. Yet he maintained his pretension, and rose to some distinction in the service. In 1768 he was sent on a secret mission to the American colonies to observe their attitude towards the mother country. He reported that they would certainly in time strike for independence, but advised against interference by France then, as likely to cause a reaction of feeling.

In November, 1776, Silas Deane, on behalf of the colonists, accepted his services as a "gentleman, zealous friend of liberty, civil and religious." On April 25, 1777, he and Lafayette set sail for America in the "Victoire," which they chartered, and landed on the coast of South Carolina. It has been stated that all during his American service, he remained in the pay of France, as secret agent, and made cipher reports to his government.

Colonel Lee says of him that he was of stout frame, excellent health, and abstemious to excess. He lived on bread, water and sometimes a little soup, rose habitually at five, "lit candle, and devoted himself to writing, which was never intermitted during the day, but when interrupted by his short meals, or by official duty. He wrote in hieroglyphics, in large folio books, which he carefully preserved. He betrayed unceasing jealousy lest his journals and mystic documents might be perused, and great dread of losing his baggage, which was very trifling, except for those valuable writings. It is not known what became of his journals, but supposed that he did not bring them to South Carolina."

As to his age there is conflict. Indeed, few alleged historic facts are free of debate. Col. H. Lee says: "Though nearer seventy than sixty, his good habits and health gave him the appearance of being so much younger, that his age is inscribed on the monument to him at Annapolis, Md., as 48." The date, 1721, assigned to his birth by Kapp, is no doubt correct, which would make his age fifty-nine at his death.*

To DuBuysson, Washington wrote: "The manner in which he died fully justified the opinion which I ever entertained of him, and will endear his memory to the country."

To the inimitable Weems we are indebted for this depiction of DeKalb's tomb not long after the Revolution, and probably before the erection of the first tablet to his memory: "I have seen the place of his rest, in the lowest spot of the plain. No sculptured warrior mourned at his head, no cypress decked his heel. But the tall corn stood in darkening ranks around him, and seemed to shake their green leaves with joy over his narrow dwelling.

> "Fair Camden's plains his glorious dust inhume,
> Where annual Ceres shades her hero's tomb."

Since then, as set forth in another chapter, Camden has fully redeemed herself from any reproach for neglect of "her hero's tomb."

In our soil also doubtless repose the remains of the gallant Colonel Porterfield, of Virginia, who is said to have died of his wounds in October, 1780. Whether he was taken to Camden or to his Virginia home has nowhere been stated. General Gregory, of the North Carolina troops, was bayoneted and died of his wounds, and is probably buried here. Gen. Thomas Pinckney remained an invalid in Camden for some time, but finally recovered. His wife, a daughter of Rebecca Motte, came here to nurse him. It is related that he reached Camden with the wounded at night and was laid on the porch of the house of the Clay family, then residing in Camden.

---

*Kapp's Life of Kalb.

Here he was found the next morning, having received no attention all night. Colonel Webster, who commanded the British right wing in attacking the militia and Maryland reserve, recovered, only to perish in the sanguinary Battle of Guilford the following March.

There is room for but a few words about some of the other distinguished officers who figured in the battle General Stevens* fought again at Guilford, where his Virginians redeemed themselves for their dastardly flight at Camden. General Caswell, who had received a medal from Congress for bravery, was Gates's companion in his attempts to reform the militia, and in his escape to Charlotte. He suffered no diminution of esteem with his North Carolina compatriots, for after his exploits at Camden, a counterpart of those of Gates, he received every honor in the gift of his State. Of him Nathaniel Macon, colleague of Adams, Jefferson, Madison and Monroe, has said: "Governor Caswell was one of the most powerful men that ever lived in this or any other country."

Bannastre Tarleton, "bloody Tarleton," the hated scourge of Carolina, was a young man on the day of the battle, lacking five days of being twenty-six. With the face of a girl, the heart of a tiger, swift, daring and cruel, he was certainly, to quote Weems, a very "thunderbolt of war." He had butchered Buford's regiment, and slaughtered the people of Waxhaw, annihilated the militia at Camden, chased Gates, routed the Continentals, and a few days later by a splendid stroke crushed Sumter at Fishing Creek. No wonder Cornwallis intrusted to him the flower of his troops to dispose of the patriot bands gathered at Cowpens. But here

---

*It was he who at the midnight council of war proposed to fight. After the battle he tersely remarked: "The defeat was due to the damn'd cowardly militia."

Lord Cornwallis.

ILLUSTRATION H.

Morgan plucked out his plumes, and destroyed his force, horse and foot. To this reverse Stedman, Cornwallis's quartermaster, attributed the loss of America. He reasons that with the men, his best, there lost, Cornwallis would easily have disposed of Greene. But the brilliant and daring deeds of Tarleton were highly appreciated in England, where on his return after the war he was immensely popular. He was son of a Liverpool merchant, rose to rank of general, served in Parliament, and died in 1833 at the age of seventy-nine.

The career of Charles, Marquis of Cornwallis, is familiar to all, standing as he does well-nigh in the class of Marlborough and Wellington. He certainly rendered to his country arduous service. Born in 1738, he was nine years younger than Gates. After the Revolution, he served as Lord-Lieutenant of Ireland. As Governor-General of India he achieved a great military success at Seringapatam, and died at Ghazepoor, in Benares, 1804, at the age of sixty-six. Of him Napoleon said: "I do not believe he was a man of first-rate abilities, but he had talent, great probity and sincerity—*un tres brave homme.* He never broke his word."

But our local characters must not be forgotten, and one at least shall receive mention. Capt. Benjamin Carter, for fifty years a resident of Camden, a gallant soldier of the Revolution, was in the Battle of Camden. He had been at Brandywine, Germantown, and Valley Forge. A native of Salem, Sumter District, he was a student at an academy in Charlotte, N. C., in 1776, and enlisted for the war. He died in Camden January 20, 1830, at the age of seventy-four. Judge O'Neall has related for us this anecdote, one of the few local traditions of this battle that have survived: "This old soldier (Captain Carter) said that he commanded a company on the extreme left of Gates's line, at the battle of Gum

Swamp, near Camden, and at the first fire all his men fled. Left alone he went to the captain next to him, whose men had also abandoned him, and asked what was to be done. He received no satisfactory answer. Whereupon he said to his neighbor: 'I'll be d—d if I am here to be shot down.' He jumped on his pony, which he had fastened in the bushes, left the field, and said he: 'I suppose I was the first man out of the reach of danger.'"

[Quite a year after the above chapter had been prepared and laid aside, and all hope abandoned of finding any utterance of Gen. Thomas Pinckney, the best qualified of all witnesses, in reference to the conduct of General Gates in the Battle of Camden, the original of the following letter, through the kindness of Mrs. Ravenel, a descendant of General Pinckney, came to our hands. It proves that General Pinckney did remonstrate against the severe criticism of General Gates, to whom he had been aide in the battle. The lofty character and conservatism of General Pinckney would render any statement or opinion from him well-nigh conclusive. His letter to Judge Johnson, written forty years after the events, when ambitions and prejudices had disappeared, could it be discovered, would be a document of inestimable value.]

Clermont, Sat'y 27 July 1822.

My dear Cotesworth:

I have just received your letter of the 23rd, covering the half of a bill for $100.

I send in this and another similar package a long letter which I have written to Judge Johnson—on perusing his account of the transactions of General Gates while in command of the Southern army—it appeared to me that it was so much more unfavorable to the character of that officer than the facts warranted, that I thought it right in me, who was his aide, and who probably am the only person in this State and (perhaps now living) who was a witness to the scenes described, and at the same time from situation acquainted with the General's views, to undertake his defense.

Another part of the Judge's work, throwing in my opinion unmerited censure on the American army which attacked Savannah in conjunction with the French under Destang and a third, which does not give the true representation of Genl. Lincoln's retirement from the army, I have also thought right to notice. Be so good before you send the letter to the Judge to request the favor of your Uncle to peruse it with attention for the purpose of making any alterations he may suggest, and as he was present at Savannah his memory is so accurate that he can decide whether what little I have said on that subject be correct. He will possibly think I have been too civil to the Judge for an officer concerned in that assault—but I believe he did not advert to the serious imputation cast by his expressions:—and old age and calamity have blunted those feelings which would have dictated a more indignant refutation of the calumny. The concluding paragraph of my letter to the Judge will shew what I wish to be your agency in this business.

I would write more at length on this subject, but we are all here in the utmost anxiety for poor little Harriott who was taken with a violent fever the day before yesterday, which has increased, rather than diminished, notwithstanding she has taken much medicine. She has been delirious since yesterday and the doctors think her in imminent danger, and this morning Arrabella has been seized with a fever apparently of the same type— you can easily imagine my poor Lucy's distress—

Sunday Morn'g: Poor little Harriott Horry is no more. We have great hope of Arrabella's recovery. Lucy bears this with her accustomed resignation.

     Your truly affec. father,
         T. PINCKNEY.

CHAPTER VIII.

INTERIM.

The distressing disaster of August 16th was followed, two days later, by another almost equally appalling.

Mention has been made of the capture by Sumter, on August 15th, of Carey's Fort, and of the convoy of more than forty wagons loaded with rum and other provisions for the Camden garrison. This occurred about one mile from the town, on the other side of the Wateree, near where the old bridge stood. Thence Sumter proceeded with his prizes up the west bank of the river, with all possible expedition. En route, he met the messengers sent by Colonel Davie to warn him of the flight of Gates and to urge him to hasten to Charlotte, as a rallying point for what was left of the American army.

No rest was taken on the night of the 16th, and on the evening of the 17th Rocky Mount, about thirty miles north of Camden, was reached. Impeded with baggage and prisoners, and exhausted by the intense heat, the Americans here made a halt for the night.

Meantime that vigilant commander, Cornwallis, had been promptly informed of Sumter's success, and, upon the fresh-won field of Gum Swamp, took immediate measures to recover the losses at Wateree Ferry. Colonels Turnbull and Ferguson, stationed on Little River, were ordered to head Sumter off, while, early on the morning of the 17th, Colonel Tarleton was hurried forward with his legion and some mounted infantry— a total force of 350 men—to overtake him.

Sumter eluded Ferguson and Turnbull, but was in apparent ignorance of Tarleton's movement. The Bloody

Dragoon had, with his usual celerity, covered the distance of nearly thirty miles from Gum Swamp to Rocky Mount ford by evening, whence, about a mile away, could be seen the smoke from Sumter's camp. Next morning, it was discovered that the Americans had moved onward.

Eight miles further north, unable to cover any more ground, Sumter once more halted to rest, on the north bank of Fishing Creek. His position seemed well taken, between the creek and the river, with ravines on the north and south.*

Here, in a strange fancied sense of security, his men either sleeping, cooking, or bathing in the stream, he was taken completely by surprise, about 2 p. m., August 18th. Tarleton had pushed on from Rocky Mount. His men were as exhausted as Sumter's, but he picked out one hundred dragoons and sixty infantrymen† of greatest endurance, and, leaving the others, with the three-pounder, to guard his retreat if necessary, rushed forward to the attack.

Sumter's videttes fired on the advance guard. No notice was taken of this, however, by the men in camp, who imagined it was some one shooting at bears;‡ in a moment, before the guns could be reached except by a few, the shouting troopers were upon them. A feeble resistance was attempted by those with arms, from behind the baggage wagons, but the panic quickly became a rout.

General Sumter himself barely escaped. He was sleeping in his tent when one of his captains, John

---

*According to McCrady, Sumter's troops "occupied in line of march a bridge contiguous to the north side of the creek, at which place his rear-guard was stationed, and two videttes were posted at a small distance in its front."

†Stedman.

‡Mrs. Ellet's "Women of the Revolution."

Steele,* picked him up bodily, carried him out, hatless, coatless, bootless, and set him upon his horse, before the gallant general had quite waked up.† Two days later he reached Charlotte, without a single attendant.

Fishing Creek, in actual losses, and much more in its discouraging moral effect, was almost as disastrous a field as Gum Swamp. Few comparatively of Sumter's men escaped either the sword, or, perhaps worse, the prison.

The British and Tory captives—nearly three hundred in number‡—were liberated; two pieces of cannon and one thousand stands of arms were taken, together with the whole British baggage train, recently captured. One hundred and fifty men were killed or wounded, and considerably more than three hundred were made prisoners—more than half the entire American force, which Stedman says was one hundred Continentals and seven hundred militia. The same authority says that Tarleton's loss was six wounded and nine killed, among the latter one officer. The American prisoners were bound with cords and marched off to Camden.

A cloud of despondency now hung over the land. The "Hero of Saratoga," on whom such high hopes had been set, had ignominiously fallen, and the little patriot band of Carolinians that had been constantly growing around Sumter's standard had been completely destroyed or dispersed.

With characteristic arrogance, the British now deemed the rebellion crushed and began a policy of vindictiveness, contempt, and cruelty that led in a short while to their own undoing.§

---

*John Steele had lands in this county, on Beaver Creek. He was a dashing officer, winning from his admirers the sobriquet of the "Murat of the Catawba River," says Mrs. Ellet.

†Mrs. Ellet's "Women of the Revolution."

‡Ramsay.

§*Ibid.*

From Camden, a few days after Fishing Creek, emanated the infamous order of Lord Cornwallis to the commandants at Ninety-Six and other posts:

"I have given orders that all the inhabitants of this province who have subscribed and have taken part in this revolt should be punished with the greatest rigour; and all those who will not turn out that they may be imprisoned and their whole property taken from them. I have likewise ordered that compensation should be made out of their estates to the persons who have been injured or oppressed by them. I have ordered in the most positive manner that every militiaman who has borne arms with us and afterwards joined the enemy shall be immediately hanged."

In justification of this order, Cornwallis wrote General Greene, who protested against its enforcement: "I can with truth assure you that no man abhors acts of cruelty more than myself or would more reluctantly adopt measures of severity; the proving to the suffering Loyalists that I am in earnest to protect them and to retaliate on their inhuman oppressors is a duty which I owe to my country.

"You have been greatly misinformed if you have ever been told that any inhabitant of this country has been punished by us for observing a neutrality; but you will find instances enough of the most inhuman persecutions and even tortures inflicted on those who refuse to take arms on your side."

Doubtless Cornwallis was right in believing that the Tories, during the long period of Whig ascendancy in the province, had suffered many wrongs, but the effect of his unwise manifesto was both to revoke all paroles and to make neutrality impossible. As a consequence, many who had taken British protection, now finding that, in utter breach of faith, they were compelled to take arms either with or against their fellow Americans, naturally took the former course.

Some—not many—whether sincere Loyalists, or from the base motive of self-interest, hastened to renew their allegiance to the Crown of England. For instance, there were one hundred and sixty-four signers, among them prominent names, to an obsequious address of congratulation to my lord Cornwallis on his splendid victory at Camden, which had "redeemed" the colony.

Only men of the stoutest heart, or who had nothing to hope from submission, were now so bold as to raise their heads in defiance. The heel of the invader was no more severe than the ruthless hand of the Tory, who sought retaliation for bitter grievances long harbored.

For about one year the sway of the enemy was marked by murder and rapine, by burning mills and homes, by sequestration of estates, by war against helpless women and children.* No section of the State suffered more than Camden District.

Men were deported on prison-ships to St. Augustine or the West Indies simply because they would not use their influence against their own side. The British historian, Stedman, says that the reason for these expatriations was that letters were found on some of Gates's officers taken at Camden which proved that men in high places in Charleston had been holding secret communication with the rebels. Among those exiled from Camden were Col. Joseph Kershaw, who was detained for about a year and a half in British Honduras and Bermuda, and his brother, Eli, who died en route to Bermuda, December, 1780.

At Camden was one of the five principal garrisons maintained by the British for the policing of the interior of South Carolina. The others, making a semicircle

*Ramsay.

around Charleston as a center, were at Georgetown, Winnsboro, Ninety-Six and Augusta. Smaller posts and depots of supplies were established at Fort Watson, Motte's House, Granby, Dorchester, Orangeburg, Monks Corner, and at one or two other points, forming in all a complete chain.

Camden, as strategically the most important of these posts, was well fortified. There were four redoubts at the four corners of the village, and a large stockade, surrounded by high wooden walls, in the center, probably taking in the entire space occupied by the old Public Square about which the town was built. A fifth fortification, a little north of the others, on the Salisbury road,* protected the jail, and some sort of works were thrown up around the British headquarters.† A glance at Diagram No. 14 will show them all. That on the southwest guarded the road from Wateree Ferry (the old River Road). That on the southeast protected the Magazine and commanded the road from Charleston. The northernmost one guarded not only the jail but the roads from Charlotte and Cheraw. On the northeast and northwest, about the junction of King street, then the upper limit of the town, with Market and Campbell streets, respectively, were two others.

The southeastern, or "Star" redoubt, so called from its shape, is the only one of which there are any remains. A description of this work, which had the Magazine in its center, has been given in another chapter.

Lord Rawdon was in command at Camden. The regular garrison consisted of the Twenty-third and Thirty-third Regiments Volunteers of Ireland, recruited

---
*Now Broad street.
†The "Cornwallis House."
‡McCrady.

in Philadelphia‡ and New York by Rawdon himself; a legion of cavalry; a detachment of artillery; and Brown's and Hamilton's corps of provincials.*

This force, of course, varied, as detachments were sent out or reinforcements came in. For instance, Cornwallis's entire command was here until September 8th.

To house the garrison, rude huts were made out of the stores† and churches‡ of the village. Miss Mary Kershaw§ remembered seeing a row of these cabins on Meeting street between the Presbyterian Churchyard and the Quaker Cemetery.

To Camden were brought all the prisoners and wounded from the many fights in the vicinity; and here executions are said to have taken place so often that, as Garden graphically expresses it, "they were regarded with mute astonishment. If words found utterance, the inquiry was not 'who' but 'how many' are to be hanged today?"

Rawdon had his headquarters in the large new residence of Col. Joseph Kershaw.¶ Here, in his absence and that of Lord Cornwallis, Major Doyle acted as commandant.

Ramsay gives us the names of five men who were unceremoniously hanged here just after Gates's defeat, to wit: Samuel Andrews, Richard Tucker, John Miles, Josiah Gayle and Eleazer Smith. He says there were others whose names are unknown. Some were allowed a court-martial, but witnesses were not put upon oath, and slaves were encouraged to accuse their masters.

Cornwallis, in a letter to General Smallwood, November 10, 1780, attempts to justify his action in these

---
*Stedman.
†Tarleton.
‡Records of Grace Episcopal Church, Camden. See Part II.
§*Ibid.* Miss Kershaw, a daughter of Colonel Joseph, lived until 1848.
¶See "Cornwallis House."

cases: "I am not conscious that any persons have been executed by us, unless for bearing arms after giving a military parole to remain quietly at home; or for enrolling themselves voluntarily in our militia, receiving arms and ammunition from the King's store, and taking the first opportunity of joining our enemies. The only persons hanged at Camden, after the actions of the 16th and 18th, except some deserters from our army, were two or three of the latter description, who were picked out of about thirty convicted for the like offense, on account of some particularly aggravating circumstances which attended their cases."*

Stedman asserts that these hardened men had arms in their hands and protections in their pockets.

The unhappy American soldiers captured at Camden were the first to feel the effects of British oppression. Many of them were hurried on foot to Charleston in the burning heat of August, a distance of about one hundred and thirty miles. Here, we are told by Dr. Peter Fassoux, director-general of the American hospitals in Charleston at the time,† they were fed on salt provisions, and no proper medical aid or nourishment was allowed them. The ships, too, aboard which they were crowded, were infected with the germs of smallpox. Many succumbed to this loathsome disease, and others to a putrid dysentery. At least one hundred and fifty died like cattle aboard the filthy vessels.

We are indebted to Mrs. Ellett's "Women of the Revolution" for the following anecdotes, vouched for on the authority of Revolutionary veterans, or their sons, living along the Catawba River, from whom Mrs. Ellet personally got them.

Among the many prisoners that Tarleton was bring-

*Johnson's Life of Greene, Appendix D.
†Ibid.

ing from Fishing Creek to Camden were Col. Thomas Taylor and Capt. John Taylor. These gentlemen, having taken British protection and, like hosts of others, afterwards rejoined the rebels, realized that there was naught in store for them but the gibbet. They therefore resolved to take any chances of escape, however desperate. So, when camp was pitched for the night on Wateree Creek, they waited until all was quiet, then rolled down the steep twenty-foot embankment into the water and swam to safety, though injured by the fire of the awakened guards.

Another captive taken at the same time was one Thomas McCalla. His wife was a cousin of Gen. Anthony Wayne. This good lady rode on horseback from her home on the Catawba to visit her husband in Camden jail. She was conducted by Major Doyle into the presence of Lord Rawdon, who, she said, was a fine-looking young man of prepossessing countenance. To her entreaty for her husband's liberation, Rawdon replied: "I would rather hang such a d—d rebel than eat my breakfast." The sight of the prison-pen sickened her. It was an inclosure like those for cows or pigs, and within, sitting or stretched on the bare earth, with no protection from the ardent September sun, were hundreds of unhappy prisoners, some of them with smallpox.

On a subsequent visit, she was present when eleven of these poor wretches were finally exchanged for two British officers. She found them chained to the floor, with handcuffs on. Besides her husband, she recognized John Adair, Thomas Gill, William Wylie, Joseph Wade, and Nicholas Bishop.

As these liberated men marched out through the streets of Camden, they sang at the top of their voices the songs of the Liberty-men.

Bishop was eighty years old and perfectly deaf; his crime was that he had eight or nine sons fighting on the American side.

Joseph Wade had been caught in arms after taking British protection. For this he first received one thousand lashes on his bare back. Having tried to break jail, an iron was about to be put on one of his feet, when he facetiously asked that he be allowed a pair of stockings. Being accommodated, he created amusement by playing Yankee Doodle with his fetters.

Lieut. John Adair, who spent seven months in prison here, taught his companions how to play cards. He had had smallpox and was unable for a while to walk, but Joseph Wade would obligingly carry him around on his back, with the remark that Adair was not so heavy as a thousand lashes. After the war, Adair* became a noted Indian fighter, a major under St. Clair and Wilkinson. He was born on Catawba River, but Kentucky was the home of his manhood. He was Governor of his adopted State, United States Senator, and Brigadier-General in command of the Kentucky forces at the battle of New Orleans. Here, strange to say, he served under another famous son of the Waxhaws, a fellow-sufferer in Camden jail, Andrew Jackson.

Jackson and his brother were both prisoners at Camden. Here is said to have occurred the incident of his refusal to blacken the boots of a British officer and the consequent saber stroke that left its mark for life—a badge of honor to that great man.

One of his biographers asserts that Jackson, through a hole that he cut in the high wall of the stockade, witnessed the fight on Hobkirk Hill. It is true that the woods then were all cut down from the village a little be-

---

*Adair is represented in Camden by a collateral descendant, Dr. Albertus Adair Moore.

yond Log Town,* but the growth above was dense, and, from the very topography of the ground, one can scarcely believe such a thing possible. Still there is other testimony to the same effect. Mr. John Rosser, a resident of Camden in 1826, writes to Col. William Shannon in 1876:† "When young I frequently met with old Revolutionary soldiers. One of them, W. McCain, from the Waxhaws, told me he was in jail at Camden when Rawdon and Greene had the fight on Hobkirk Hill. He said they were in the second story and could see the battle going on—that they were all greatly excited in the hope that Greene would release them, and that, of course, they were greatly disappointed at his failure. He said that the British soldiers were terribly mad when they got back to Camden, and the prisoners expected to be slain right there. Mr. McCain and others have told me that the old jail stood at the corner of Broad and King streets, where the market house of my day stood."

Mr. Rosser added that Elder O'Cain, a tailor by trade, who was living in Camden, a good-sized boy, in 1780, informed him that the British and Tories would bring men into the town, torture them with pain and insult, and then hang them by the neck till they were dead—as it seemed to him, just for their amusement.

George Weir, another inmate of the jail, was, strange to say, an acquaintance and playmate of Lord Rawdon, as a boy, in Ireland.

William Wylie was of powerful physique, and somewhat of a wit and poet. He and Robert Gill, who later died in the jail, on one occasion escaped, by removing iron bars and overpowering the guards, but they were recaptured.

---

*See Chapter IX. Log Town itself may not have been standing at that date. The Vallancey map shows that it was "destroyed" during the British occupancy.
†Old Times in Camden.

Robert Wilson, the father of eleven sons in the patriot army, was being carried, with ten others, from Camden to Charleston. Near Fort Watson he and his companions managed by bribes to get some rum. Feigning drunkenness themselves, they induced their guards to drink with them. This they did, as expected, to excess, when the prisoners seized the guns, captured the whole convoy, paroled them, and escaped in the face of some British dragoons who came to the rescue.

One of the most pathetic cases on record was that of Peter Yarnall,* a poor Quaker living near this place. From religious convictions he was a noncombatant, yet he was so unwise as to oblige a friend, whom he was casually visiting in Sumter's camp, by holding a gun for him a few moments over some Tory prisoners. These informed on him, after Fishing Creek, and in consequence Yarnall was cast into a dreary dungeon here. His wife and daughter daily rode in, in their "chair," to bring him milk and fruit. One morning, when they came as usual, Miss Charlton,† a friendly young lady living near the jail, knowing that good, obliging Peter had been executed the night before, tried to dissuade the ladies from visiting the prison. They insisted, however, and were conducted, without preparation, to where the husband and father was hanging dead on a beam from an upper window. Mrs. Yarnall lost her reason at the gruesome sight.

Rev. Humphrey Hunter, who gives, in "Wheeler's History of North Carolina," so interesting an account of DeKalb's death, was one of the notables that languished behind bars in Camden; and it would seem, from the following newspaper report, that Col. William Thompson, commander of the celebrated "Rangers," was an-

*Weems's Life of Marion.
†Doubtless a daughter of Thomas Charlton.

other. *The South Carolina and American General Gazette*, a Loyalist sheet published in Charleston, says, July 26, 1780: "Lieut. James Campbell, of the Royal No. Ca. Volunteers, has lately taken the infamous Thompson and part of his rascally gang, while plundering some houses of persons well-affected to government and committed them safe to Camden Gaol."

Gregg* tells of the escape of Samuel Bacot† and thirty others, who had been in jail here, while being taken to Charleston. After a weary day's march, they had camped for the night in a little log cabin, their guns being stacked outside. The prisoners occupied one room, separated by a thin partition from the guards. Having carefully laid their plans, Bacot, in the middle of the night, pretended to be sick, and, knocking at the door between, begged for a little whiskey. This gave him an opportunity of seeing that all the British soldiers were sleeping soundly, so, when the stimulant was brought him, he dashed it in the officer's face, a signal for his men to rush through the open door, overpower the convoy and seize the guns. The entire scheme worked well and the quondam captives made quick tracks for home.

* * * * * * * * *

We are able to give merely a running survey of the principal military movements connecting the two battles of Camden.

For three months after the first engagement there was no Continental army in South Carolina, the spirit of opposition being kept alive solely by those indomitable partisan leaders, Marion, Sumter, Pickens and Davie.

Marion was operating in the swamps of the eastern

---

*History of the Old Cheraws.
†Bacot was one of the early settlers on the western side of the Wateree.

counties. We hear of his capturing, with sixteen men, near Nelson's Ferry, a convoy taking about one hundred and fifty prisoners from Camden to Charleston; this occurred a few days after Gum Swamp.

Colonel Ferguson, during the summer months, had been busy enlisting the Tory young men of the western parts of the State. These licentious fellows, by their maraudings, so alarmed the people west of the Alleghenies that, gathering in little separate bands, under Cleveland, Sevier, Shelby, and Williams, though without a recognized leader, they trapped Ferguson on the summit of Kings Mountain, killed him, and destroyed or captured his whole command. This great victory, October 7, 1780, marks the beginning of the downfall of British power in the southern country. Ten prisoners were hanged at Kings Mountain in retaliation for the execution of patriots at Camden and other places.

On September 8th Cornwallis moved up to the Waxhaws, sending Tarleton in the same general direction along the west bank of the Wateree, and leaving Rawdon at Camden. He camped about forty miles from Charlotte in order that he might keep an eye on Gates.

That most unfortunate and disheartened general in October sent Morgan from Hillsboro, N. C., with three hundred Maryland and Delaware troops, to aid the Whigs in Mecklenburg and Rowan Counties. From this section Col. William Washington made his famous little incursion to the vicinity of Camden, where, by a clever ruse, he captured Rugeley's Fort.

Col. Henry Rugeley was one of the leading Tories of South Carolina. He held office under the King, and his brother, Rowland Rugeley, was appointed a member of the Royal Council, 1769. It is not unnatural that both should have become Royalists.

Colonel Henry must have bestirred himself in that cause. His name has been embedded in a stanza of the burlesque upon the duel between Generals Howe and Gadsden, by the sportive pen of the ill-starred Major Andre. It runs thus:

> "It was on Mr. Percy's land,
>   At Squire Rugeley's corner,
> Great H. and G. met sword in hand,
>   Upon a point of honor."

Squire Rugeley, prior to the Revolution, conducted a mercantile business in Charleston, with country branches. One of these was on his estate in the fork of Flat Rock and Grannys Quarter Creeks, about thirteen miles above Camden. This spot he called "Clermont." Here the British established a military post, and here the Squire, risen to Colonel, was placed in command of one hundred and odd fellow Tories. His heavy log barn had been fortified and well protected by abattis. Here he lay after the Battle of Camden.

Cornwallis only awaited a trial of the Colonel's soldiery to make him a brigadier. The test came. Col. William Washington, as said, was with Morgan just across the line in North Carolina, and, noting the exposure of Rugeley's post, he obtained permission to make a dash upon it. With his horsemen he made a quick march from Charlotte and suddenly appeared before the fort, which was impregnable to cavalry.

But Colonel Washington had sized up the garrison! Mounting a pine log upon its branches (some authorities say upon cartwheels), he planted it in full view, trained upon the barn. It really did, we hope, resemble a cannon. The spectacle was too much for the inmates. They surrendered at discretion.

Cornwallis in disgust laconically tells of the incident in this note to Tarleton:

Wynnesboro, Dec. 4th, 1780.

Rugeley will not be made a Brigadier. He surrendered without firing a shot, himself and 103 rank and file, to the cavalry only. A deserter of Morgan assures us that the infantry never came within three miles of the house. CORNWALLIS.

Alas, Major André had met his sad fate a few months before! How he would have reveled in recording this bloodless incident that immortalized Rugeley the Dupe!

The following letter from Rawdon was found in Colonel Rugeley's house by General Gates when occupied by him the preceding August 13th:*

Headquarters, Camden, 1 July, 1780.

SIR: So many deserters from the army have passed with impunity through the districts which are under your direction that I must necessarily suspect the inhabitants to have connived at it, if not facilitated their escape. * * * I will give the inhabitants ten guineas for the head of any deserter belonging to the Volunteers of Ireland; and five guineas only if they bring him in alive. They shall be rewarded, though not to that amount, for such deserters as they may secure belonging to any other regiment. RAWDON.

After the Revolution, Colonel Rugeley seems to have occupied a respectable position among his neighbors.†

His name appears signed to an important presentment

---

*Sparks's Life of Washington.

†He was on the list of the proscribed by the Jacksonboro Assembly, 1782, but, with the general amnesty, the stigma of Toryism attaching to his name doubtless lost its force.

Gen. Nathaniel Greene.

ILLUSTRATION I.

of the Grand Jury at Camden in 1788. From data in our Courthouse, it is inferred that he died about 1799.

Henry Rugeley.

The old ledger containing accounts of his Clermont store, from 1776 to 1780, is in existence. It shows dealings with such familiar names as Trantham, Drakeford, Hilton, Russel, Mickle, Vaughan, Saunders, Duren, Dixon, Kirkland, Fletcher and many others, showing them to have been settlers in that vicinity prior to the Revolution.

In 1820 the heirs of Henry Rugeley conveyed "Clermont" to Daniel DeSaussure, who resided there with his family a number of years. No descendants of Colonel Rugeley now live in this county.*

On November 20th, about the time of the comedy at Clermont, Sumter, who like Marion, had just been made a Brigadier-General by Governor Rutledge, won a signal victory over Tarleton at Blackstocks. He was himself, however, so badly wounded that he was forced to retire from active service for several months.

The Continental army moved from Hillsboro to Charlotte during the last days of November, and there, on December 4th, Gen. Nathaniel Greene of Rhode Island superseded General Gates in command.

We learn from Colonel Lee† that Greene was then decidedly corpulent, complexion fair, with a coun-

---

*Colonel Rugeley's son, Edward, married Ellen, daughter of John Blair, Clerk of Court of Kershaw County, who removed, with his family, to Mobile, Ala., in the '30's. Edward Rugeley was killed in the Civil War, leaving several daughters.

†"Campaigns in the Carolinas."

tenance serene and mild that softened the fire and greatness of his expression. His age was thirty-eight years, and his health, naturally delicate, was maintained by systematic temperance in all things. His manner was genial and he soon won the ardent attachment of his troops.

Greene came south with a reputation for great military talents. Especially his soundness of judgment and his enterprise and decision were admired. He was a prime favorite with Washington, who had selected him for this very important mission.

His army consisted of nine hundred and seventy Continentals and one thousand and thirteen militia,* ragged and for a long time without pay. The flower of it was the Maryland and Delaware regiments, which had already served four years.

That all might have a chance to enlist, General Greene divided his force—a part being sent under Morgan to the western part of South Carolina, while he himself, on December 20th, with the main body moved to the Peedee near Cheraw and went into camp.

The first notable event of the campaign of 1781 was the collision between Morgan and Tarleton at the Cowpens, where the latter lost his prestige in a signal defeat. Here Capt. Robert Kirkwood won new laurels and Congress awarded medals to Morgan, William Washington, Howard, and Pickens for their conspicuous success. This was the scene of the hand-to-hand conflict between Tarleton and Washington, in which the former was severely wounded and the latter had his sword broken.

In the hope of recapturing the five hundred prisoners taken by Morgan at the Cowpens, Cornwallis hastened northward from Winnsboro. General Greene, fearing

---

*Otho Williams states that, at the reorganization at Hillsboro, 1,241 Continentals, escaped from the Battle of Camden, were reenrolled.

lest the two wings of his army might thus be entirely cut apart, marched rapidly from Cheraw to the Catawba, a distance of one hundred and fifty miles, to try to effect a reunion with Morgan. His men are said to have left a track of blood across the frozen ground, many of them being shoeless. Heavy rains had swollen the creeks and made the roads almost impassable; so, despite almost superhuman efforts, he did not then join Morgan, who was being closely pursued by Cornwallis.

It was a most exciting chase. The floods in the Catawba, the Yadkin and other rivers, seemed to come just after the passage of the Americans and in time to check the British. This created in the minds of the superstitious the idea that God was working miracles of intervention in the patriot cause, and inspired many with new hope.

After much skilful maneuvering, Morgan finally succeeded in joining General Greene, at Guilford Courthouse, N. C., on February 7, 1781, with the enemy close behind him. Too weak to risk an engagement, Greene fell back to the Dan, which was barely crossed before Cornwallis came up. Believing that North Carolina was now rid of the rebels, and his baggage having been left far behind in the swift pursuit, Cornwallis retreated to Hillsboro and later to Guilford.

Greene at once recrossed the Dan, and, reinforced by some Virginia and North Carolina troops, proceeded to offer battle to the British at Guilford. The engagement came on March 15th. The American army was the larger, but was composed of raw militia, who gave way, after a most obstinate contest, before the well-trained British regulars. It was, however, a success so dearly bought that Fox was moved to exclaim in the House of Commons, "Another such victory would destroy the British army!"

Indeed, three days later, Cornwallis hastened towards Wilmington, leaving his wounded behind him. He realized that the British interests, if not ruined, were in great danger in North Carolina, and he was sorely puzzled whether to go on to Virginia or back to South Carolina. Tarleton censures him for not adopting the latter course, but Stedman thinks the step a wise one, and accuses Tarleton, who, in his opinion, was "without any extraordinary degree of merit," of ingratitude to his commander-in-chief. The withdrawal of the enemy was justly regarded by the Americans as a retreat, so Greene, though too much battered to renew hostilities at once, followed closely on their heels. His men had nothing to eat on this march but the refuse of the British camps.

At Ramsay's Mill, on Deep River, he halted, and the idea, whether original or suggested by Colonel Lee, of making a sudden descent upon the garrisons in South Carolina now took definite form. His subsequent movements are told in our next chapter.

We must now make a brief retrospect. The temporary absence of both main armies left our partisan chieftains in this State free to renew their activities with redoubled energy. The American successes at Kings Mountain and the Cowpens had brought daily increasing additions to their ranks.

Early in February, Sumter, having sufficiently recovered his health as well as his command, laid siege to Fort Granby, on the Congaree. It was saved by the timely arrival from Camden of Lord Rawdon with a superior force. Sumter then retreated to the Santee, near Colonel Thompson's, where he was so lucky as to fall in with and capture a train of bountiful supplies on the way to Camden. Thirteen of the British escort were killed and sixty-six made prisoners.

Swimming the river with three hundred and fifty

horse, Sumter now suddenly assailed Fort Watson, but his plans were again frustrated by Rawdon's coming up. He then withdrew to the swamps of Black River.

After remaining there a short while in concealment, he came out and moved toward North Carolina. Near Lynches Creek, not far from the present town of Bishopville,* he was overtaken by Major Fraser, who had been dispatched from Camden for that purpose. According to all American authorities, Fraser was no match for Sumter and lost twenty men in the sharp little brush that followed. Sumter retired in safety beyond the State lines. The British version of the fight may best be given in a letter from Rawdon to Colonel Watson,† which was intercepted by the patriots:

Camden, March 7, 1781.

SIR: I arrived here about noon on the 5th, and, on the same evening, detached Major Frazer with the South Carolina Regiment to Radcliffe's Bridge. The cavalry were to have accompanied him, but, just as they were to march, the report of a body of the enemy being within a few miles of us, occasioned my detaching them another way, ordering them, however, to join Major Frazer after they had fulfilled their first object. Frazer yesterday fell in with Sumpter (who was advancing this way), between Scape Hoar and Radcliffe's Bridge. A smart action ensued, in which the enemy were completely routed, leaving 10 dead on the field and about 40 wounded. Unfortunately none of our Dragoons had joined Frazer, so that he could not pursue his victory. Sumpter fled across Lynch's Creek and continued his retreat northward; he has his family with him, so that

---

*From note made by Judge Brevard on his copy of Mills's Statistics. The spot was formerly in Kershaw County.
†Gibbes's Documentary History of South Carolina.

I think he has entirely abandoned the lower country. * * * By the account of the prisoners, Marion has but a very trifling force and is not likely to increase it.

I have the honor to be, sir,

Your most obedient
R.

Colonels Watson and Doyle, with 500 men, had recently been sent from Camden to seize Marion in his famous retreat on Snow's Island, Peedee. The former was to move down the Santee, and the latter down the eastern bank of Lynches Creek, and "the Swamp Fox" was to be caught in a trap. But he was too old and wary for that.

His enemy were met in detail. Doyle was defeated in a single action and driven back into Camden; Watson came nearer succeeding, but was foiled by the intrepid stand of Marion's men, who burned the bridge over Black River near Kingstree and compelled him to hasten by forced marches into Georgetown.

Affairs were in this condition when General Greene reentered South Carolina.

HOBKIRK HILL.

Waxhaw Road, through center of Field, looking North. (The British line was extended on both sides of road, in foreground of picture. Two of Greene's cannon were planted in middle of road on summit of the Hill).

CHAPTER IX.

The Battle of Hobkirk Hill.

Though of questioned wisdom at the moment, General Greene's determination to turn from his pursuit of Cornwallis and make a sudden dash into South Carolina proved, in the event, most fortunate, and has been reckoned one of his finest military maneuvers, whether or not, as claimed, the suggestion came from Col. Henry Lee.

The prevailing argument seems to have been that, if Cornwallis followed, both Virginia and North Carolina would be relieved, and, if not, the South Carolina posts might be captured before succor could reach them.

None but Greene's officers were informed of the purpose of the movement, and the British learned of it too late to prevent its accomplishment. Therefore, after mature consideration fraught with perplexity, Lord Cornwallis decided to let his South Carolina garrisons look out for themselves, and followed the direction pointed by the finger of Fate to his doom at Yorktown. From Wilmington he sent word to Rawdon* of Greene's approach, but the message never reached its destination.

The American army had halted a few days on Deep River to rest and collect provisions, as well as to allow the enemy to get well away. The men were half starved and nearly destitute of clothing. On the morning of April 7th they were again set in motion. After proceeding one day's march in pretense of following Cornwallis, Greene turned his columns abruptly to the right and headed direct for Camden.

---

*Stedman, "History of the American War."

Before leaving Ramsay's, the heavy baggage and all stores not in immediate demand had been sent under General Davie to Oliphant's Mills at the headwaters of the Catawba, where supplies were to be collected in case of retreat. Orders at the same time had been dispatched to General Pickens to keep an eye on the posts at Ninety-Six and Augusta, and to General Sumter, who had been recruiting three militia regiments in North Carolina, to join General Greene at Camden. Colonel Lee, too, on April 6th, had been sent with his partisan legion and a part of the Second Maryland infantry—three hundred men—to cooperate with Marion, on the Peedee, against Watson and Doyle.

Greene's route* lay through a sterile pine barren, a sandy desert with few oases. The distance from Ramsay's to Camden was one hundred and thirty miles. The country had few inhabitants and a majority of them were King's friends, who not only kept Rawdon well-posted as to every move of the Americans, but rendered it as difficult for them to get supplies as if in a foreign territory.

The Peedee was crossed below the mouth of Rocky River. The line of march ran thence through Anson County, N. C., and the eastern section of Lancaster County, S. C. Both branches of Lynches Creek were passed some distance above their confluence. A delay of four days had been necessitated at the Peedee for want of boats.

Judge James† asserts that, a few miles out from Camden on the Cheraw road, Greene was met by Dr. Matthew Irvine, who had been sent by Colonel Lee to act as a guide. Within a mile of the town, after descending

---

*Almost identically the same as that followed by Gates the preceding August, with similar sufferings.

†Life of Marion.

a sandy ridge between Big and Little Pine Tree Creeks,* Irvine led the army southward, crossing the former stream at what was a little later called McRae's millpond. Four miles further south, English's old mill on Town Creek was reached. The troops were almost starving. Here, for some reason, Irvine left; but fortunately young Zach. Cantey,† who had been General Greene's assistant commissary on the Dan, came just then upon the scene. From his father's nearby plantation, the famished troops were supplied with bacon and corn that had been hid in the swamps. A few lean beeves, too, were brought in and butchered, but at that season this was nauseating food. The usually fertile region below Camden had been swept clean of provisions; Cantey therefore advised General Greene to move to the north side of the town, where the militia might aid him and food be more attainable. But for this, Judge James thinks the position below Camden had better been maintained. Cantey was then sent to General Sumter, one hundred miles off, to solicit his aid. General Greene was greatly exasperated, says the narrator, by Sumter's refusal to comply.

McCrady seems to verify this situation of the Americans on their first appearance before Camden. He cites a letter, written on April 19th to Sumter by Greene, who states that he had then taken a position *three miles* from the town; that the country was barren of all supplies; that he depended on Sumter for corn, meat, and other necessary provisions, without which he could no longer

---

*Probably Meroney's Hill. An old road leading to Camden from the northeast, crossing Saunders Creek at Tryon's Bridge and entering the extension of Lyttleton street in Kirkwood, is said traditionally to have been Greene's route, and is known in the section through which it passes as Greene's Road. It does not, however, pass between the creeks, and hence does not fit in with James's account.

†Cantey himself gave Judge James this information (1821).

keep his station; and that he would like to know Sumter's position and how he proposed cooperating with him.

It is rather strange that General Greene does not say something specific of this in his official reports to Congress. He tells us only that he arrived "in the neighborhood"* of Camden on April 19th and that, on reaching the village, he pitched his camp at Log Town, on a rising ground within a half mile of the enemy's works and, from that point of vantage, surveyed the situation.

As said in our last chapter, the British were strongly intrenched in Camden. Nature afforded additional protection in the dense swamps of Pine Tree Creek on the east and south, and of the river, not far to the west.

The vigilance of Pickens and Sumter had not prevented Colonel Fraser's bringing reinforcements into the town from the region between Broad and Saluda Rivers. These had offset the reduction of the garrison by the dispatch of Doyle and Watson into the lowcountry.

Without Sumter's aid, Greene saw that it was impracticable to attempt an assault on the fortifications of Camden, so, on the 20th, he withdrew one mile northward from Log Town to the slightly higher ridge known as Hobkirk Hill—a much stronger position.

Here he remained until the 22d, when, learning that Colonel Watson was returning toward Camden, he decided to move his army to the southeast of the village, for the double purpose of cutting off that command and of preventing Rawdon's sending relief to Fort Watson on the Santee, then beseiged by the combined forces of Marion and Lee.

---

*Letter to President of Congress, of April 22d.—Johnson's Life of Greene.

To make this movement, it was necessary to cross the swamps of both Little and Big Pine Tree Creeks, where there were no roads or bridges. Greene had lost all of his artillery at Guilford, but two cannon had recently been forwarded to him from Oliphant's Mills, where they had been repaired. It was out of the question to take such impedimenta in a quick march across practically pathless swamps, so they were sent for safety with the baggage, under Colonel Carrington, to Lynches Creek, twenty miles to the northeast.

A corduroy road was made, and a bridge thrown across Big Pine Tree Creek, known thenceforth as "Greene's Bridge."* The passage was accomplished during the night.

For two days Greene encamped at what he called the "South Quarter"; tradition says this was on the brow of Paint Hill. Then, being short of supplies and learning of Watson's retreat to Georgetown, he dispatched orders to Carrington to rejoin him immediately, and, on the 24th, repassed the creeks and resumed his station on Hobkirk Hill. Here he had expected to be joined by both Sumter and Carrington, but neither had arrived. Carrington, it seems, had gone to Upton Mills, eight miles further than intended, which had delayed his return. He had sent one of his cannon to Marion and Lee, under orders from General Greene, who was unaware that Fort Watson had already fallen (April 23d).

Hobkirk Hill,† on the crest of which the Americans took post, is a narrow sandy ridge of about eighty feet

---

*The last bridge on this site, at McRae's Pond, was removed in 1897, when the course of the stream that it spanned was changed.

†It is a matter of tradition that Hobkirk Hill derived its name from an old man by the name of Hobkirk, who lived on the ridge prior to the date of the battle. In confirmation of this, an old grant has been found (State Archives, Plat Book 11, p. 179,) of one hundred acres to Thomas Hobkirk, in Fredricksburg Township, "near Pine Tree," dated September 8, 1769, which locates him near Camden.

elevation above the plain whereon lay the village of Camden. The southern slope is somewhat abrupt near the summit, but very gradual towards its base. The northern declivity is so slight as to be scarcely noticeable, owing to the greater general elevation of the land on that side. From east to west the ridge is not more than a half-mile in length. Beltons Branch, an inconsiderable stream, has its origin from the southwestern base, and Mount Creek* waters the extreme western slope.

From a cup in the eastern side of the hill gush many bold founts, that, at successive periods, have been designated Mortimer, Kirkwood, and Johnson Springs. They now afford the water supply of Camden. These uniting form a stream, called, on the Johnson map, "Miry" Branch, later Martins, now Kirkwood Branch, which flows eastward for less than a half-mile, emptying into Little Pine Tree Creek.

A dense growth of pine and shrubbery covered the land for a mile southward to the upper edge of the Log Town plateau, from which point on to the fortifications, a mile below, the forests had been felled and left lying on the ground. This exposed the approaches to the town to the guns of the redoubts, and, except by the roads, rendered them impracticable for foot or horse.†

The Americans were encamped in order of battle on both sides of what is now known as the Kirkwood extension of Broad street. On the military maps of the period it is variously named the Salisbury, Charlotte, and Waxhaws road.

General Greene was in hourly expectation of an attack, which, said he in a letter to Colonel Lee, was an

---

*So named from the fact that it enters the river near the Indian Mound. Later it was known as Nixons Branch.
†Johnson's Life of Greene.

event devoutly to be wished for, both from the "superiority of (his) force and the advantage of the ground."

On his extreme left, facing Camden, lay the Second Maryland Regiment under Lieutenant-Colonel Ford; this line extended to the swamps of Kirkwood Branch.

On his extreme right, stretching into the woods, which, on this side, had been cut to the foot of the hill as a protection, lay the First Virginia Regiment under Lieutenant-Colonel Campbell.*

In the center, on the left of the road, were the First Marylanders under Colonel Gunby, and, on the right, the Second Virginians under Lieutenant-Colonel Hawes.

John Eager Howard was lieutenant-colonel of the First Maryland Regiment, General Huger was in command of the Virginia brigade, and Colonel Otho Williams, of the Maryland line.

A picked troop of light infantry, all Irishmen under thirty years of age, had been drafted from the Maryland brigade and, under command of Capt. John Smith, was in reserve, a few hundred yards in the rear.

Washington with his cavalry was still a little farther back,† and near him were the North Carolina militia under Colonel Reid, which, by the way, seem never to have come into the action.

Two strong companies of pickets, under Captains Morgan of Virginia and Benson of Maryland, were stationed at the point where the "Bye Road"‡ crossed the highway from Camden to Cheraw. General Greene

---

*About the situation of the modern Kirkwood Heights Hotel.

†In a marginal note to James's Life of Marion, Judge Brevard states that, at the beginning of the engagement, Washington's Troop of Horse was at "Mrs. Reid's plantation on the river, now Mr. Adamson's"—the present "Springdale" plantation.

‡So called on the map in Johnson's Life of Greene—probably the most eastern street of the village, now named Mills street. The point of intersection would seem to have been near "Saarsfield."

evidently expected an assault from that quarter, for he had stationed Captain Kirkwood, with the remnant of his veteran Delawares, in the woods between the main army and the pickets, about a half-mile from each.

Patrols, both British and American, paced the ground, within earshot of each other, along the line where the trees fringed the open.

To guard against a surprise, as well as against desertions from his ranks, General Greene had issued the following order:

"Camp before Camden, North Quarter, Tuesday, 24th April.

"The general orders respecting passes are punctually to be observed. None are to be granted but by commandants of corps. The rolls are to be called at least three times a day and all absentees reported and punished. Officers of every rank are to confine themselves to their respective duties. And every part of the army must be in readiness to stand at arms at a moment's warning."

Despite all these precautions, during the night of the 24th, a drummer* from the Maryland line, whose fidelity had for some time been questioned, deserted, made his way into Camden, and informed Rawdon that the Americans were without cannon or provisions, and that Sumter had not yet come up. This information, together with the knowledge that Fort Watson had fallen

---

*Gordon says his name was Jones. Lee asserts that he had come into Greene's camp on the 24th, with a number of prisoners from Fort Watson, all of whom claimed that they were patriots at heart and had enlisted in the British ranks as the best chance of escaping to their friends. Greene received them into his army, with the above result. The perfidy of this wretched drummer recoiled upon his own head, for, after the battle, Lord Rawdon, believing he had tried to lure the British to their destruction by false representations about the artillery and supplies, had him hanged in Camden.

and that Marion was on his way to Camden, determined the British commandant to strike at once.

Early next morning, April 25th, both the hostile camps, almost within hailing distance of each other, were the scenes of unwonted activity, though of very different character.

The Americans were rejoicing at the most timely arrival, between nine and ten o'clock, of Carrington, bringing with him, in addition to baggage and provisions, two extra pieces of artillery just brought by Colonel Harrison from Prince Edward Courthouse, Va.

These cannon were at once placed in the middle of the line, pointing down the Waxhaws road, which was not sunken then as now at that spot; while the third piece was stationed between the two Maryland regiments.

After the morning's exercises, arms were stacked in ranks, and the troops with delight hastened to appease the cravings of an appetite whetted by many fatigues and two long days of fasting. A gill each of rum—a luxury long denied them—was allowed. General Greene, with his officers, was reveling in a dish of coffee.[*] Pots were boiling merrily, and the "feasting"— not Lucullan, one imagines—was at its height. Some soldiers were bathing, or washing their clothes, in the neighboring brooks.[†] The horses were tethered nearby to graze, with saddles, as a precaution, not removed.

Let us peep behind the curtain of woods that screened Lord Rawdon's encampment and see what was happening there that same eventful April morning. At earliest break of day, the following announcement[‡] was made to the little garrison:

---

[*] Johnson's Life of Greene.
[†] Kirkwood and Mount Branches.
[‡] From the *Royal Gazette*, Charleston, May 5-9, 1781.

Headquarters, Camden, 25th April, 1781.
Morning Orders.

The Troops will march at 9 o'clock to attack the enemy in their camp. It is proposed to gain the enemy's left flank.

The following to be the Order of Battle:

† Cannon †

King's Amer. Regt.	New York Inf.	63d Regt.
Capt. Robinson's Regt.		Volrs of Ireland.
	So. Carolina Regt.	
Cavalry.		Cavalry.

Order of March.

Light company of the Volunteers of Ireland formed to the right. Sixty-third Regiment and Volunteers of Ireland in columns, four in front, each regiment marching from its right.

The Guns.

Infantry of the New York Volunteers, King's American Regiment and South Carolina Regiment, in columns like the Sixty-third and Volunteers of Ireland.

The Cavalry.

Flanked on the left by Captain Robinson's detachment.

A British officer who was present writes to the Charleston paper:[*] "Nothing could exceed the joy manifested by the whole garrison on these orders being made known. Every arrangement was made; but part of the cavalry being then out aforaging, prevented the march of the troops at the hour appointed."

[*] *Royal Gazette,* May 5-9, 1781.

Every man capable of bearing arms, even the musicians and drummers, were enlisted in the ranks. Leaving the sick and helpless to guard the works, out sallied the gallant band at ten o'clock. They were but nine hundred, all told. Marching forth to assail an enemy stronger both in numbers and in position, staking all on this one stroke, we can but applaud the pluck and spirit of both leader and men.

No drum was beat. In dead silence the garrison left the common in front of Headquarters and, descending the hill to Little Pine Tree Creek, followed closely its meanders northward.*

They were concealed by the bluffs and woods on their left from the view of the villagers, and, as the correspondent above quoted expressed it, "always avoiding the publick road," they passed undetected until their advanced guard, the Volunteers of Ireland, were fired upon by the American pickets, at the crossing of the Cheraw road.

It was this startling discharge of musketry that gave the Americans on the Hill the first intimation of the approach of the foe. Instantly there was a transformation of scene. Men rushed to arms, some barefoot, most, we are told, without coats; the baggage was hurried off to Saunders Creek. It required but a few moments to reform the lines of battle, as the camp had been pitched in that order, and both commander and troops, confident of victory, awaited the assault.

The pickets under Benson and Morgan contested every foot of ground with the utmost courage and steadiness, but were driven back upon Kirkwood, with his thinned line of Delawares. Nobly did these veterans of many fights live up to their high fame. Had it not been

---

*The line of march corresponded closely with the present track of the Southern Railway, including the spur back of Magazine Hill.

for the check which they gave to Rawdon's advance, it is questionable whether Greene would have had time to establish any sort of order, and Fishing Creek might have been repeated. But Kirkwood, too, must slowly fall back, and soon the British column, having crossed in a diagonal line from the intersection of the roads towards the northwest,* displayed itself on the Waxhaws road at the foot of Hobkirk Hill. Here an unpleasant surprise awaited them. Lord Rawdon, on the information that Greene was without artillery, had, despite his morning orders, not impeded himself with cannon in this sortie. What was his amazement therefore when Greene's two pieces, planted in the middle of the big road, and hitherto masked by the two central regiments, greeted him with a deadly shower of grape and canister! For a moment his ranks, in consternation, staggered and threatened to break.

At the same time, perceiving the narrow front with which the British had advanced, as well as the dismay created by the discharge of the guns, General Greene conceived a maneuver that, had it properly carried, would have crushed Rawdon beyond recovery. The regiments of Campbell and Ford, on the ends, were ordered to descend the Hill and close in upon the enemy's flanks, the two regiments of Gunby and Hawes, in the middle, to advance "with trailed arms" and charge bayonets, without firing a shot,† while Colonel Washington with his cavalry was directed to make a detour to the right and, falling in their rear, prevent the escape of a single redcoat into the town.

These orders were perfectly executed at first and success seemed almost assured. But, alas for General

*From about the site of the present DeKalb Cotton Mills. It is singular that neither Greene's nor the Vallancey map shows the Factory Pond, close by, though it was there from 1760.
†Johnson's Life of Greene.

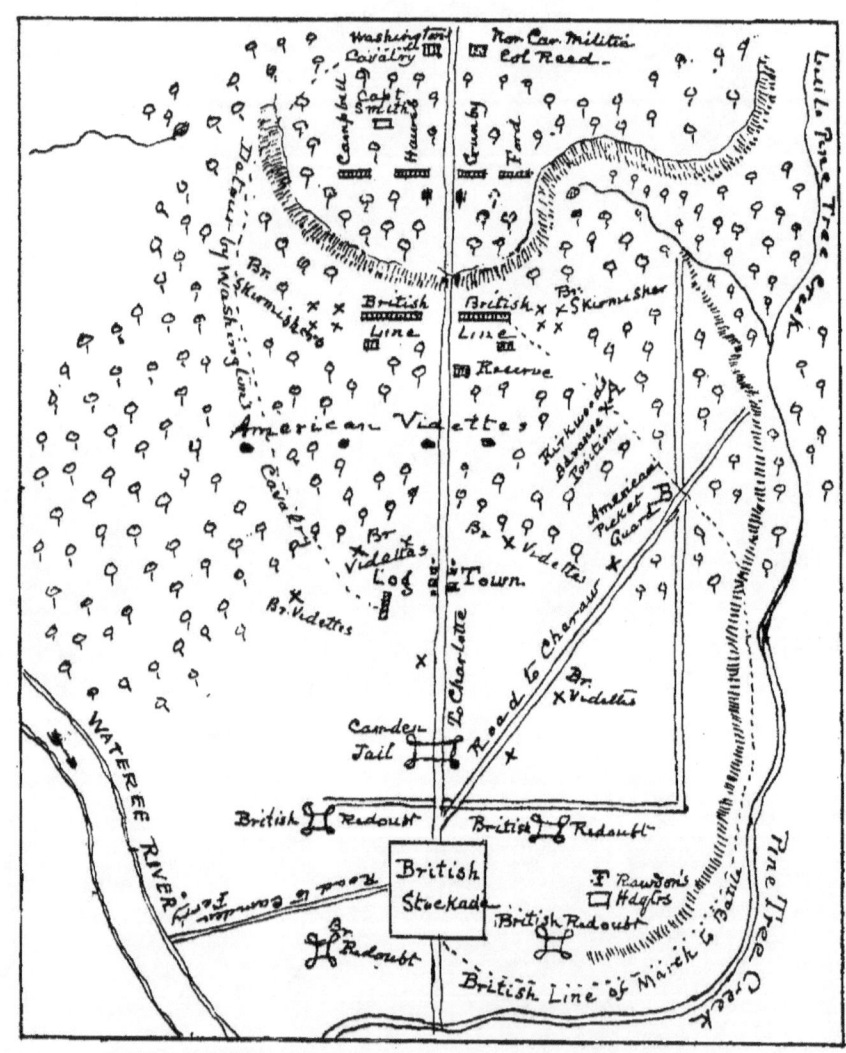

Battle of Hobkirk Hill. (Plan in Johnson's Life of Greene.)

DIAGRAM No. 14.

Greene, he was facing a bold and most ingenious foe, whose quick eye detected at once both Greene's intention and his own imminent danger. With a coolness born of a fertile and decided mind, he instantly brought up his reserves, Captain Robinson on the left of the King's American Regiment and the Volunteers of Ireland on the right of the Sixty-third Regiment.

Thus the Americans, by this counter flank movement, found themselves caught at their own game. Still, though disconcerted, they continued advancing and the enemy were actually giving way before them on all sides,* when a most unexpected and unaccountable panic seized the veteran regiment of Gunby, which had covered itself with glory at Cowpens and Guilford Courthouse, and was considered by Greene himself the very bulwark of his army. This panic may be only partially explained by the fall of Captain Beatty, of the company nearest the road, as the first advance was made. The loss of this young officer, who was much beloved by his men and, in General Greene's own opinion, was an ornament to his profession, seemed to create confusion in his ranks. Contrary to orders, his men began firing, and the disorder communicated itself to the next company; both now broke and fell back. In this way, the other companies of the regiment passed beyond them. In order to restore his original line, Colonel Gunby now made the fatal mistake, as the event proved, of ordering the forward companies to fall back upon the other two, which were rallying a few yards in the rear. This retrograde movement was mistaken for an order to retreat, and created a consternation of mind which rapidly spread to the Second Marylanders, new troops, whose colonel, Ford, had just been mortally

---

*General Greene's official report, published by order of Congress.

wounded. The entire Maryland brigade now retired in great confusion, despite the desperate efforts of Williams, Howard and Gunby. They were partially rallied and reformed a few hundred yards to the rear, but it was too late, for, by this time, the British had returned to the charge and were now appearing over the brow of the hill, with shouts of victory.

On the extreme right, Campbell's regiment, which also was composed of raw militia, had become somewhat disordered. The command of Colonel Hawes, which is said to have suffered more than all the rest in this battle, was alone advancing steadily and had come within forty yards of the enemy. General Greene, who was himself with this regiment, seeing that its left flank was entirely exposed by the retiring of the Marylanders and the consequent advance of the enemy, gave orders for the whole Virginia line to retreat.

He, in person, summoning to his aid the Light Infantry, under Captain Smith, hitherto not in action, hastened to the rescue of the artillery, which was in imminent danger of being captured.

Johnson's account of this incident is perhaps somewhat fanciful, no corroboration being found in any other reports considered authentic. Still, being traditional, it is worthy of preservation. General Greene is described as dashing up alone, amid a perfect hailstorm of deadly missiles, to the precious guns which were about being deserted by the last matrosses. Dismounting in haste, he himself seized a rope and dragged with all his might. Such an example could not be withstood. The gunners returned, and Captain Smith also, with his company of forty-five men, came to the rescue, just in time, for Coffin's cavalry were now descending upon them from the woods. Into the midst of these Smith's little band poured such a destructive fire that they re-

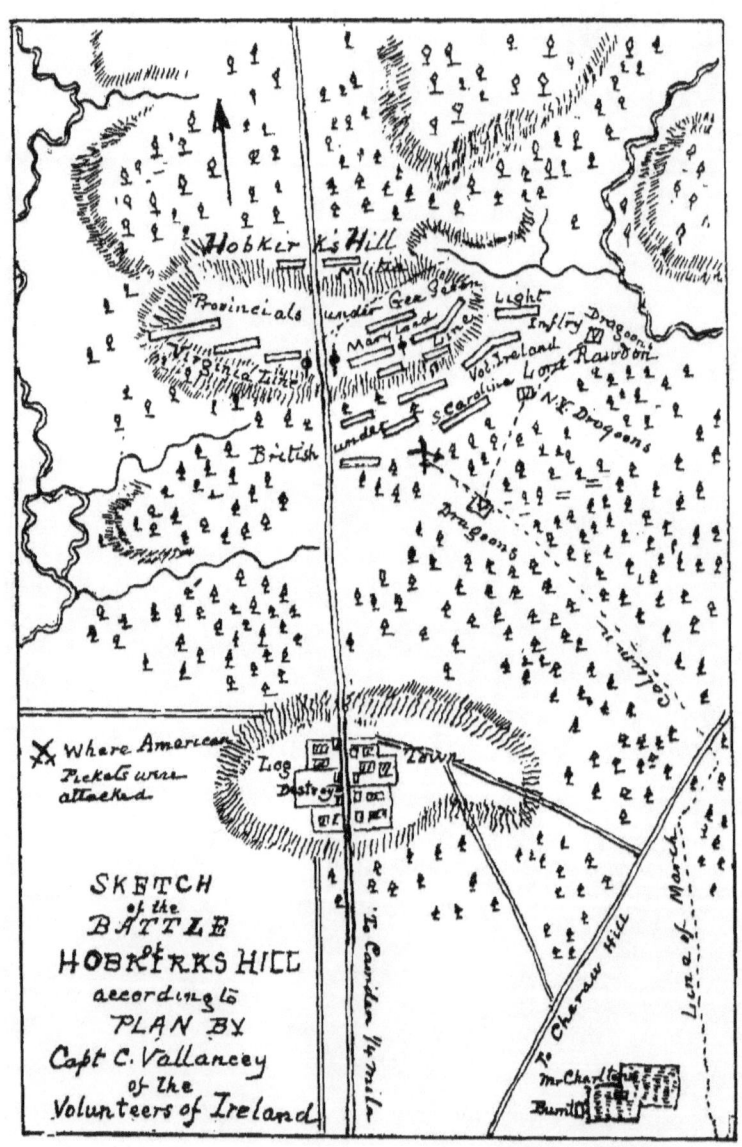

Captain Vallancey's Map, 1783.

DIAGRAM No. 15.

coiled, thus rendering it possible to drag the cannon a little further. Several similar attempts were made by Coffin, but each was met in the same way. The devoted American guard had now dwindled to fourteen. The British infantry coming up at this time, the artillery seemed doomed, for every man in Smith's company had now been either killed or taken; among the latter was Captain Smith himself.

It was just at this most auspicious moment that Colonel Washington's cavalry came dashing down the road, drove back the British, mounted the cannon upon the limbers discovered in the bushes nearby, and bore them off in triumph. Washington then protected the retreat of the Americans, which thus was accomplished in admirable order. The broken regiments partially reformed and retired under cover of the cavalry and of Colonel Hawes's troops, who fell back deliberately.

Garden, in his "Anecdotes," tells of Greene's helping to draw off the artillery, but does not mention the parts played by Smith or Washington.

The correspondent from Camden of *The Royal Gazette*,* describing the action, says that the cannon were either hid in the bushes and overlooked by the British in their "pursuit of the flying rebels," or that they were taken off the carriages and hauled off in wagons early in the fight.

Tarleton credits the former supposition, adding that, before the return of the British from the pursuit, the guns had been carried off by Washington's cavalry.

The Vallancey map (Diagram No. 15) indicates that the pieces were concealed in the hollow at Kirkwood Springs, but there is no other evidence to that effect.

General Greene himself, in all his private and official

---

*May 5-9, 1781.

letters on the battle, never even suggests so dramatic an episode as that narrated by Johnson. He says simply that he had "suffered no loss of artillery, wagons or stores of any kind, except a few of the soldiers' knapsacks and blankets," and that Colonel Washington had "made good his retreat out of the enemy's rear."

We feel disposed therefore to agree with Henry Lee* that this story of Judge Johnson's is a "piece of frothy heroics."

Colonel Washington, at the beginning of the engagement, did make, as ordered, a detour to the right through the woods, coming out on the Waxhaws road in the open between Camden and Logtown. Here he found a number of the enemy in retreat towards the town, believing at that moment, it is said, that the field was lost. Of these he made upwards of 200 prisoners,† among them fifteen or twenty officers, most of whom he mercifully paroled upon the spot rather than put them to the sword, as the strict rules of war perhaps, under the circumstances, demanded. When compelled to retire, by news of Greene's repulse, he mounted fifty prisoners, one behind each of his troopers, and bore them off the field.

It is probable that Washington's appearance put a stop to the further pursuit of the Americans, and that, either then or later in the evening, he did bring off the cannon.

General Greene, in his report, thus gracefully acknowledges the gallant conduct of his cavalry leader: "Colonel Washington never shone upon any occasion more than this."

It is true that Lord Rawdon gained possession of the

---

*"Campaign of '81 in the Carolinas." The author was a son of Col. H. Lee.

†Some historians say that they were mostly noncombatants.

battlefield, but the serious losses that he had himself sustained, and the steady conduct of the Americans in retiring, prevented anything like a rout. At a distance of only two and a half miles* the British turned back, and General Greene halted to refresh his troops and collect his stragglers. In the afternoon, unmolested, he proceeded to the other side of Saunders Creek, two miles further on, and there stopped for the night.

In the dusk of the evening, Colonel Washington, being sent back to reconnoiter, adopted another of those stratagems for which he was famous.† It seems that Colonel Coffin, with his cavalry and a detachment of mounted infantry, had been left for the night as a guard on Hobkirk Hill, the main body with Rawdon having withdrawn into Camden. Washington concealed the greater part of his men in the thickets on either side of the road, and dispatched the rest, as a decoy, nearly to the Hill. The ruse worked well. Coffin pursued, with forty Irish Volunteers, and dashed into the ambuscade, where they were fallen upon and driven precipitately back into the town, with a loss of twenty men killed. The battleground remained that evening in the hands of the Americans—a fact that was very encouraging to them.

Moultrie‡ tells us that General Greene sent in to Lord Rawdon the eleven surgeons captured by Colonel Washington, knowing that they would be needed to attend the wounded. This gracious act of humanity so pleased the British officer that he at once asked the commandant at Charleston to allow General Moultrie to exchange the like number of his medical line.

During the whole of the 26th and part of the 27th General Greene remained at Saunders Creek. He then

---

*Probably at Cool Spring.
†Johnson's Life of Greene.
‡Revolution in South Carolina and Georgia.

fell back four miles to Rugeley's Mills. On the 26th he had written General Marion:

"We are now within five miles of Camden and shall closely invest it in a day or two again. That we may be enabled to operate with more certainty against this post, I should be glad if you would move up immediately to our assistance and take post on the north side of the town. I have detached a fieldpiece to your assistance, with an escort of a few Continental troops under the command of Major Eaton."

Again, in his official report to Samuel Huntingdon, President of Congress, he says: "Our army is full of spirits and this little check will not by any means derange or alter our general plan of operations."

General Greene realized that Rawdon had been too badly crippled to pursue his advantage. Still, despite this brave show in his public letters, he was then in a far from cheerful frame of mind, as his private correspondence will prove. He had seen a victory that seemed secured torn from his grasp by, as he thought, the blunder of a trusted lieutenant and the consequent bad conduct of a favorite brigade. He never hesitated to assert that Colonel Gunby had been the sole cause of the misfortune. This opinion was acquiesced in by the Court of Inquiry, composed of General Huger, Colonel Harrison and Lieutenant-Colonel Washington, which, at Colonel Gunby's request, was immediately convened on the subject, during the halt at Rugeley's. The findings of the court concluded as follows: "It appears, from the above report, that Colonel Gunby's spirit and activity were unexceptionable. But his order for the regiment to retire, which broke the line, was extremely improper and unmilitary, and, in all probability, the only cause why we did not obtain a complete victory."

Several points in controversy as to this battle will be

discussed more fully in our next chapter—among them this, of Gunby's sole responsibility for the disaster.

According to Tarleton, the British loss at Hobkirk Hill was 258 killed, wounded, and missing. Only one officer was slain; eleven were wounded.

Lee says that Tarleton's figures include those paroled by Washington. Stedman* states that thirty-eight men were killed on the field.

The casualties on the American side were almost the same, in all 270, as appears by the following official report:

"Lieut.-Col. Ford, Maryland, dangerously wounded in the elbow; Lieut.-Col. Campbell, Virginia, a slight contusion on the thigh; Capt. William Beatty, Maryland, killed; Capt. J. Smith, 3rd Maryland, taken prisoner; Captain Dunholm, Virginia, slight contusion; Capt. Lieut. Bruff, Maryland, wounded in both ancles, and prisoner on his parole; Lieut. M. Galloway, Maryland, wounded slightly; Lieut. Ball, Virginia, ditto dangerously in the leg. Non-commissioned officers and soldiers killed, wounded and missing:

    1 sergeant, 17 rank and file, killed.

    7 sergeants, 101 rank and file, wounded.

    3 sergeants, 133 rank and file, missing.

"The greatest part of those who are missing had not well understood the order to rally at Saunders Creek; some were killed; 47 of them were wounded and are in the enemy's hospital; we have tidings of about one-third of the remaining number and hope they will be able to join us.

"(Signed)   O. H. WILLIAMS,
"Deputy Ad.-General."

---

*American War.

The strength of the American army at Hobkirk Hill has been variously estimated and much disputed.

Ramsay, Moultrie, and other historians state that Greene had 700 Continentals, and say nothing of any other troops.

General Greene himself frequently said that his army was nearly equal to that of Rawdon, which was only 900;* still, in his letter to Colonel Lee, he spoke, as we have seen, of the superiority of his forces.

Marshall† thinks that the field returns made the day after the battle (April 26th), would make it appear that the number of effective rank and file of the "Continental" troops engaged at Hobkirk rather exceeded 1,200 men, of whom 130 were cavalry and artillery. He says that the figures in Ramsay and other authorities were only of the "fit for duty" the day after the action. Marshall, it appears, does not include the militia in his estimate.

Lee, in his Memoirs, declares that, by the last return made before Greene left Ramsay's, the regular force of every sort might be put down at 1,800 effectives. Deducting the 300 horse and foot detached under Colonel Lee, the army, when arrived before Camden, was not more than 1,500, "exclusive of a small body of North Carolina militia."‡

McCrady, in the midst of such wide discrepancies, prefers to adopt the carefully detailed estimate made by Johnson, in his "Life of Greene."

To begin with, Johnson states that, the return of April 25th having, by some accident, escaped from his files, he took the numbers given by Gordon, because he knew

---

*From Stedman we learn that some Tory militia, who offered their services to Rawdon a little prior to the action of April 25th, were "necessarily, though reluctantly, dismissed, on account of a scarcity of provisions."

†Life of Washington.

‡As these numbered 254 men, Lee's total would approximate 1,750.

that Gordon had them from the Adjutant-General, Colonel Williams. This would seem authoritative.

He asserts that only 843 "regular" infantry were fit for duty, the ranks having been much depleted by sickness, recent desertions, and the expiration of the terms of enlistment of some of the Maryland and Virginia lines.

The cavalry, which consisted nominally of two regiments, White's and Washington's, numbered really only eighty-seven men, of whom but thirty-one were mounted.*

There were only forty men to handle the three pieces of artillery.

Colonel Reid's North Carolina regiment of militia consisted of 254 men. Of these, 150 had been with Greene since he left the Dan; the rest had come down, with the supplies, under Colonel Davie, from Oliphant's Mills.

Captain Smith's company, the "Camp Guards," cannot be added to this estimate, as they were detailed from the Maryland line. Half of Washington's cavalry, too, was drawn from the Virginia brigade.

According to Johnson, therefore, the entire American force numbered about 1,200 men, if by "regulars" he meant, as generally understood, Continentals.

Two rather singular facts may be noted about this second battle of Camden. First: The only South Carolinians in the fight, as an organized body, were the Tory regiment enlisted under Rawdon's banner.†

Second: The only British force was the Sixty-third regiment. Of Rawdon's other troops, the Volunteers of Ireland were enlisted in Philadelphia; the King's American Regiment, in or around New York; Turnbull's

---

*McCrady, "1780-1783," p. 240.
†McCrady, "1780-1783."

Volunteers (the "New York Infantry") and Coffin's Dragoons, also in the Empire State.* Captain Robinson's regiment, too, were Tories.

Perhaps in no other battle of the Revolution were the forces engaged so largely composed of Americans on each side.

*McCrady, "1780-1783."

CHAPTER X.

GLEANINGS FROM HOBKIRK.

No other of General Greene's battles has been so often refought, by critics, as that on Hobkirk Hill. We have noted the wide discrepancies of opinion as to the numbers engaged, the rescue of the cannon, and the reasons for the change of position to the east of Camden. More detailed attention must be given the two most mooted points—whether or not the Americans were "surprised," and, next, the true causes of the repulse.

Tarleton says that General Greene was shamefully remiss and inattentive in not discovering Rawdon's sortie until the pickets were fired on.

Stedman (British) remarks: "The enemy, though apparently surprised and at first in some confusion, formed with great expedition and met the attack with resolution and bravery."

Colonel Howard, who was with the Maryland line, wrote, in 1809, to Henry Lee:[*] "Our men were never properly formed." Again: "Certainly the sudden manner in which the enemy came upon us had the effect of a surprise."

Moultrie[†] adopts the same view. General Huger told him that, so little were the Americans expecting an attack, he and other officers were washing their feet, and a number of soldiers were scouring their kettles, when the British engaged the pickets, and that, but for the fact that Washington's cavalry horses were already saddled, the "surprise" would have been attended with more disastrous results.

---

[*] "Campaign of '81 in the Carolinas."
[†] American Revolution in Carolina and Georgia.

Washington, on the occasion of his visit to Camden in 1791, made the following entry in his diary: "I examined the ground on which General Greene and Lord Rawdon had their action. The ground had but just been taken by the former—was well-chosen—but he had not well established in it before he was attacked, which, by capturing a videt, was in some measure by surprise." Strange it is that no other writer on the battle mentions the capture of a vidette.

Henry Lee* says: "Marshall and Lee both allege that the object of Greene was to draw Lord Rawdon out to attack him, and they only infer, as every one else of common sense must, that, had his attack been apprehended at the moment it was made, he would not have found the American troops washing, cooking, and dramming, nor their gallant general over his tea-things."

On the other hand, General Davie, a most reliable witness of the battle, declares: "There is not one single circumstance attending this affair that marks it as a surprise; the position was taken for the express purpose of forcing Lord Rawdon to fight. The men had been under arms from daylight, and only dismissed for the express purpose of cooking, about one hour and a half before the attack on the picket. Men must cook and eat, and, when they can, will be washing and mending their clothes—this is all of course. Every battalion was even resting in the line; the artillery in battery; and all the baggage moved off, before the enemy presented themselves before our line of battle; all was cheerfulness, confidence and tranquillity; no confusion or noise, and the whole line resembled a common parade."

In this opinion, such writers as Ramsay, Marshall, Simms, and Johnson concur, more or less fully.

*"Campaign of '81 in the Carolinas."

The dispute really seems to be a quibble as to the idea of a surprise. General Greene had certainly taken every necessary precaution, in anticipation of an attack from the very quarter whence it came, as we saw in the disposition of his troops. He himself wrote the President of Congress: "In this situation we remained constantly on the watch and ready for action at a moment's notice." And yet he was not informed of Lord Rawdon's movement from the fortifications until the enemy had advanced quite a mile and suddenly fell upon his pickets, which gave the American commander scarcely time enough to form his ranks, despite his seemingly complete preparations for such an emergency. There may be some foundation for Washington's comment on the capture of an outpost—probably another case of a sentinel caught napping. The time of the assault and the swiftness of Rawdon's movement could not, of course, be foreseen; but General Greene's military genius had led him to station his pickets in the very places they were most needed to give him due warning, and he was, to all intents and purposes, quite prepared to give his adversaries a warm reception by the time they reached the foot of the hill. It would be absurd to liken this affair to a real surprise, such as Sumter's at Fishing Creek, or even Buford's, in the Waxhaws.

As to the cause, or causes, of the failure of the Americans in the engagement, justice to Colonel Gunby, whose illustrious war record is entitled to all honor, demands that the severe verdict of the Court of Inquiry be at least modified. It was made in a moment of discouragement and may have been inspired, as some think, by the disappointed ambition of General Greene, who was quite willing to shift his own responsibility on any scapegoat. On August 6, 1781, he wrote Governor Read: "The troops were not to blame in the Camden affair; Gunby was the *sole cause* of the defeat, and I found him much more blamable afterward than I represented him in my public letters. * * * We should have had Lord Rawdon and his whole command prisoners in three minutes, if Colonel Gunby had not ordered his regiment to retire; the greater part of which were advancing rapidly at the time they were ordered off. I was almost frantic with vexation at the disappointment. Fortune has not been much our friend."

Admitting, without argument, that Colonel Gunby's unfortunate order, at a crucial point in the conflict, was the main factor in the resulting disaster, historians are by no means willing to accept General Greene's dictum that it was the sole cause, nor does that officer himself escape a full share of censure.

Lossing[*] tells us that, when Beatty fell, pierced through the forehead by a bullet, several officers, not knowing he was dead, rushed forward to pick him up. This gave rise to some halting and confusion, taking advantage of which the British pushed forward, causing the Marylanders to break. This, he thinks, caused the subsequent misfortune.

Tarleton says of Greene's change of position just prior to the battle: "Such irresolution or indecision of mind, under the eye of a vigilant enemy, can never be displayed without great, if not certain, danger."

Lee[†] thinks that the usually prudent General Greene was overconfident in detaching Washington at the very beginning of the engagement. The American cavalry could not accomplish much in the rear of the enemy, owing to felled trees and dense undergrowth. Further, the rallying of Gunby's regiment would have been facilitated, and the advance of the enemy checked, had Wash-

[*]American Revolution and War of 1812.
[†]Memoirs.

ington been on hand to support them, at the proper moment.

Johnson* is of opinion that Washington's movement was a loss of valuable time.

General Davie declares that Washington charged a mixed multitude of doctors, surgeons, waiters, and the loose trumpery of an army, and that, in stopping to parole 150 and carry off fifty of these noncombatants, he missed the chance to charge Rawdon's fighting line, which might have been done with the happiest results just prior to the breaking of the Maryland line.

Bancroft, too, believes that Greene weakened himself irretrievably in sending off his cavalry when he did.

McCrady says that the British were never in such confusion as Greene imagined them, and that it was their steady advance up the hill that so disconcerted the Americans.

Besides, it must be remembered that the regiments of Campbell and Ford were raw recruits, and that they gave way about the same time as the First Marylanders. The retreat of Campbell's Virginians certainly was not affected by the panic on the other side of the road, of which they were unaware.

A very able defense† of Colonel Gunby's conduct at Hobkirk has recently issued from the pen of his grandson, A. A. Gunby, Esq., of the Louisiana bar. To rebut the verdict of the Court of Inquiry, that Gunby's order was extremely improper and unmilitary, he sets forth:

1. That similar orders had been executed with entire success by the same troops at the Cowpens and at Guilford; by Washington's command at Monmouth, and, in more recent times, by General Bee at First Manassas. The maneuver was therefore not unmilitary.

*Life of Greene.
†"Col. John Gunby of the Maryland Line."

2. That the breaking of the two right companies on the death of Beatty, and of the Second Marylanders on the fall of Ford, would have left the remaining troops under Gunby exposed to an attack on their left flank from a party of the enemy that had nearly reached the top of the hill.

3. That the order was not to retreat or retire, but to "fall back and form on the colors." If there was misunderstanding, it was blamable on Colonel Howard, who delivered the order.

4. That Gunby's veterans reformed sixty yards in the rear, and, by their steadiness, saved General Greene a rout worse than that of Gates at Gum Swamp.

In conclusion, this author, after giving, in his judgment, the real causes of the catastrophe (most of which correspond to those we have enumerated), ventures the very extreme opinion that, had Greene himself been absent from the field at Hobkirk, as he was at the Cowpens, the fight might have been won by Gunby and William Washington alone.

General Greene's culpability in this affair may perhaps be summed up in the one fault of overconfidence.

Of his personal gallantry, General Davie says that he exposed himself in the engagement so much as to elicit the remark from one of his officers that his conduct was more like that of a captain of grenadiers than that of a major-general.

* * * * * * * * *

Few traditions bear the searchlight of investigation. Such is doubtless the case with the two local versions of the beginning of this battle.

One of these* has it, that Rawdon moved up the Wax-

---

*This account was transmitted to Maj. E. B. Cantey from his grandfather, James Cantey, a Revolutionary soldier, said to have been in the engagement.

haw road with his main force, while a flanking column was sent around by the swamps of Pine Tree Creek to strike the Americans in the rear. The deserter had told Rawdon that, to execute this flank movement, two small streams must be crossed, Kirkwood and Horse Branches. Mistaking the rill known as Nettles Branch for number one, the British came out just beyond Kirkwood Branch, on the Common, where they surprised the pickets at the spring, where they were cooking and washing.

Though at variance with all the military charts and reports, this testimony seems to find some corroboration in the story told by an aged negro slave. We quote the words of the late Dr. E. M. Boykin: "Old Abram, who had been Col. Eli Kershaw's body-servant and was, when we knew him, Colonel Chesnut's carriage driver, has told us that he went out of Camden with Rawdon's army, with the best Whig intentions, we presume, but which would not prevent his embracing whichever side might win; and that they were to cross two branches before they made the attack, so as to get into Greene's rear; but made the mistake of considering a small branch head that rather made out of the main creek than into it as one of those landmarks of the topography of the march, when it was not to have been so held; and so turned to the left and marched up the right after crossing the spring branch, sixty years after a dense thicket, as we well remember, for we built a house* upon the very spot where Rawdon crossed the branch and turned the head of his column to the left to fall upon Greene, who, sitting in his tent door, a quarter of a mile off, was looking for him down the big road."

Contemporary accounts of great events by eyewitnesses or participants, even if prejudiced, are usually

---

*"Millbank," on the old Factory Pond, now owned by John Boykin, Esq.

valuable and always interesting. Without doubt the very first published news of Hobkirk was given in the *Royal Gazette* (Loyalist), of Charleston, May 5-8, 1781, Allowing for the colored spectacles through which the battle was viewed, the report is probably nearly correct. We copy it in full from the files in the Charleston Library:

"By an officer who left Camden the 2nd instant,* we are favored with the following:

"Lord Rawdon having received information, by a deserter from Greene's camp, early in the morning of the 25th of last month, that a part of the Rebel army with some artillery had been detached to Lynch's Creek for provisions, gave orders for his troops to hold themselves in readiness to march at half past 9 a. m. to attack the enemy in their camp at Hobkirk's Hill, near two miles from Camden. Nothing could exceed the joy manifested by the whole garrison on these orders being made known; every arrangement was made; but, part of the cavalry being then out aforaging, prevented the march of the troops at the hour appointed.

"A sufficient body of men being reserved to take charge of the works, our little army marched at 10 o'clock, taking a circuitous rout through the woods, and always avoiding the publick road. At 5 minutes past 11, the rebel picket fired on the light company of the Volunteers of Ireland, who formed the advanced party. In an instant, the whole pickets were driven in, and carried to their astonished brethren in camp the first intelligence of our army's approach. The Rebels had been without provisions the two preceding days. Their party had returned from Lynch's Creek that morning, and a number of them were then busily employed in cooking.

*One week after the action.

In their hurry and surprise, they flew to their arms, most without their coats, and a considerable body had formed when Lord Rawdon came up; they gave our troops a very heavy fire of musketry and grape shot, but could not check their ardour. The fire was immediately returned, the Rebels were charged and driven from their advantageous situation. In 15 minutes the rout was general. Several attempts were made by Greene to rally his dismayed tattered companions, but the keenness of the pursuers rendered them totally ineffectual. The pursuit was continued to Sandy Creek, six miles from the field of battle.

"The loss of the Rebels on the field and in the pursuit was upwards of 500 killed and wounded. Our loss in killed, wounded and missing, was 151. Not a man deserted from Camden from the day the first accounts of Greene's approach were received.

"Seventy deserters, amongst whom were several of Lee's dragoons, with their horses and accoutrements, came into Camden in the course of three days after the action. They all agreed in saying there were in Greene's hospital from 200 to 300 men dangerously wounded, besides those who could walk about.

"The Rebels saved their cannon by taking them off the carriages and putting them in waggons, which were drove off early in the action. At least 700 stands of their arms were taken and destroyed.

"On the 1st inst., Greene's camp was two miles beyond Rugeley's Mills, on the north side of the creek. He was then employed in sending off his wounded, and it was reported he had sent off his cannon.

"The gallantry and good conduct displayed by Lord Rawdon on this occasion are spoken of in the highest terms by the whole army, and particularly entitle him to the grateful acknowledgments of every loyal inhabitant in this province. His Lordship enjoys good health, the troops under his command are in high spirits and amply supplied with provisions."

It will be noted that the entire time of the action is here given as fifteen minutes—an incredibly short while, one would think; yet, hear the verification from the Diary of Samuel Mathis:*

"Wednesday, April 25th (1781)—Between 11 and 12 o'clock heard a very heavy fire of cannon and musketry lasting 15 minutes towards C. No news all Day what it was. Afternoon hard rain.

"Thursday, 26th. Understood ye firing we heard was an engagement above Camden."

*   *   *   *   *   *   *   *   *

At this point, the reader is advised to glance at the entries in Mathis's Diary, from April 16-25, 1781, for some entertaining personal notes.

It will be seen that on April 17th some Americans came by "Burndale" in the early morning, and that they were pursued by the New York Volunteers, who later, on returning, reported the killing of Major Downs. Confirmation of this incident is to be found, strangely enough, in the autobiography of Rev. James Jenkins,† a pioneer in Methodism, who labored for many years in Camden and rests in our Quaker Cemetery. We give his words:

"When the British were in possession of Camden under Lord Rawdon, Marion sent a small company to make observations. The British had charge also of the mills near Camden (now belonging to Col. Chesnut), where they got grinding done for their army, and had stationed a company of men to defend it. This scout of Marion's

---

*See Appendix A.
†Mr. Jenkins has many descendants in Camden, through the marriage of his daughter to William C. Workman, Esq.

approached in the night, and my brother, with one or two more, was in the act of setting fire to the building, when M'Pherson, contrary to orders, shot down their centry. This roused the men in the house, who came swarming down like bees; and alarmed the horse in Camden, whose feet roared like thunder, as they came to their relief; so the scout had to retreat.

"After they left Camden, they came upon a party of Tories, dancing, and ordered them to surrender; they did so; but when Maj. Downs,* their leader, came out and saw so few, not knowing that there were more just behind, he ran back, shut the doors, and commanded his men to fire. Here the brave M'Donald was shot down in the yard. By this time the balance of the squad came up, rushed in, and killed every man. Downs was shot last, under the bed. His daughter was wounded, and remained a cripple near Camden, until she died a few years ago. After M'Donald fell, he begged not to be left; but the Camden horse were pursuing; hence they had to escape for their lives."

* * * * * * * * *

From a hymeneal notice in the *Royal Gazette* of June 8, 1782, it appears that the relict of the lamented Downs did not long remain inconsolable:

"Marriage—Maj. Gibbes of the Royal Ninety Six militia to Mrs. Jane Downs, widow of the deceased Maj. Downs, of the Royal Camden militia."

* * * * * * * * *

In regard to the attack on the mill† by Marion's men, above alluded to, it will be noticed that Mathis, too, speaks of a heavy cannonading about 3 P. M., April 23d,

---

*The Mouzon map of 1775 shows that Downs lived on the Wateree River, about the mouth of Cornal Creek, about fifteen miles below Camden.
†Probably one of Kershaw's mills on Pine Tree Creek.

"supposed to be at the mill." The authors have an old flintlock, picked up, during some excavations, in 1903, at the site of the mill burned by Rawdon; the flint is still in position and perfect.

Tarleton, in his Memoirs, says, in this connection: "The efforts made by the enemy to examine the British works, and particularly, an attempt to destroy their mill, necessarily brought on some skirmishes. By the prisoners taken in these excursions, Lord Rawdon had the satisfaction to learn that Gen. Greene's army was not by any means so numerous as he had apprehended."

* * * * * * * * *

Some waggish officer of the British garrison at Charleston was inspired to satirical doggerel by the request of General Greene for a return of the casualties at Hobkirk, that he might submit them to the public:*

"To Camden, so fatal to Rebels, we're told
That Greene with his forces, and forces so bold,
Of success so secure, advanc'd, that the Tanner
Promis'd laurels to each who fought under his banner.
On the 25th ult., fatal day! what a hardship!
Without the least warning, out sallied his Lordship:
Killed, wounded and took, alas! my poor Tanner,
How many of those who fought under your banner?"

* * * * * * * * *

Among the nursery legends of the battle, preserved for years in the vivid imagination of superstitious old maumas, is the following gruesome one: The trunk of a soldier, whose head had been completely cut off on the Hill, by a cannon ball, was carried by his horse in a mad gallop down to the creek below the town, before losing its balance. On peculiarly black nights the decapitated ghost of this poor fellow, mounted on a skele-

---

*Royal Gazette.

ton steed, may be seen emerging from the swamps of the creek and riding cautiously, by unfrequented paths, to the battlefield, where, till the cocks crow for day, he vainly gropes in search of the missing member.

The spot on the Hill where General Greene is said to have pitched his tent was marked, until about 1885, by a large flat-top pine. In that year this old tree was struck by lightning and died, leaving in evidence only a fat stump. It stood nearly in front of the present residence of George T. Little, Esq., about 150 feet from the Lancaster road and 200 yards from the brow of the hill. Not thirty feet away now flourishes a fine post oak that, as a sapling, may have witnessed the camp and the battle, a century and a quarter ago.

* * * * * * * * *

Until quite recently the field of Hobkirk was a fertile one for the relic-hunter. Dr. E. M. Boykin, writing in 1876, of the engagement, says:

"Time went on; the war was over, and nothing marked the scene of the fierce battle we have spoken of except two mounds where the dead men lay; one on the top of the hill* immediately on the roadside, about two hundred yards in front of where General Greene's tent was pitched; the other deeper in the woods, near the edge of the ravine where the spring makes out. When we first remember, they could be recognized by a luxuriant growth of the largest kind of whortleberry bushes. Relics of all kinds accumulated—grapeshot, small arms, etc. We had a beautiful pocket pistol with a golden falcon sitting on a globe inlaid upon the barrel. The larger mound upon the roadside caved into the road and exhumed whole skeletons, with numbers of flat brass

---

*On the east side of the Lancaster road, in the front grounds of C. C. Moore, Esq. The spot is now marked by a cluster of small cedars.

buttons of the Eighty-third* Regiment, British, proving that the poor fellows who came so far to get their bullets had been buried with their martial cloaks around them, not stripped, at least, on the battlefield."

Gen. James W. Cantey built, in 1835, a handsome residence on the position occupied by Hawes's Virginians, where, as we have stated, the fight raged thickest. Bayonets, gunbarrels and locks, cannon balls and quantities of bullets were picked up on his grounds and given to his friends. His son, Maj. E. B. Cantey, the present owner of the place, has an old sword, discovered by a little boy in the vegetable garden, in 1900. The point was noticed sticking out of the ground. It is evidently a Revolutionary officer's side-arm, though there is nothink to indicate on which side its owner fought—and, perhaps, died. Who knows but that it belonged to the sole British officer that fell in the action! The blade is three-edged, like a bayonet. The basket work of the hilt is of allegorical figures and was handsome, the gilt still bright. Silver wire is braided around the wooden hand-grasp. The weapon is too light to have been of actual service.

In 1786, Elkanah Watson visited the fields of Gum Swamp and Hobkirk and wrote in his Memoirs: "No vestiges of these sanguinary battles remained upon their theaters but shattered trees and the unburied bones of men and horses." This shocking state of affairs, five years after the latter of these conflicts, seems almost past belief; and yet Mr. Watson is a reliable witness—himself a veteran.

Col. William Shannon informs us† that, when clearing the grounds of his Kirkwood residence, "Pine Flat,"

---

*More likely the Sixty-third.
†Old Times in Camden.

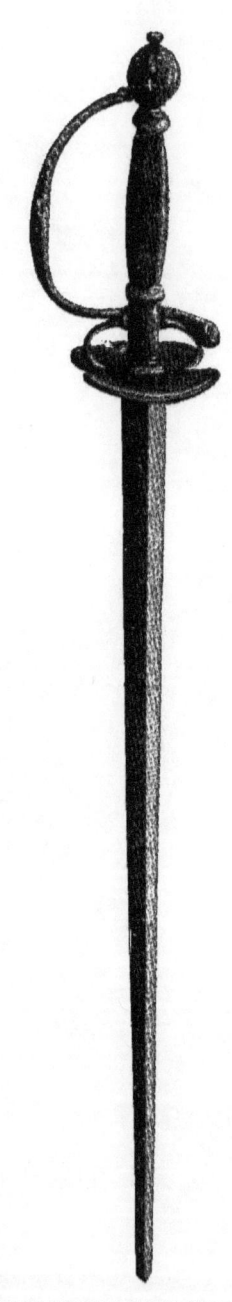

REVOLUTIONARY SWORD.

Unearthed on the Field of Hobkirk in the Year 1900.

ILLUSTRATION K.

now the "Hobkirk Inn," he found bullets imbedded in nearly every old tree.

Mrs. Anne Royall,* on her memorable visitation in 1830, says of Hobkirk: "The remains of several redoubts are still to be seen, and the graves, mostly Americans, are visible. These are on each side of the road, and though on a high, barren soil, are overgrown with flowers and a rich coating of fine grass, the only grass which I saw in the State, and mark the dimensions of the graves precisely."

In the field near the old Presbyterian burying-ground, DeKalb was interred between two British officers. May they have been "Captain Peacock and Captain Harrison, of the Seventh Regiment (British)," whose deaths at Camden are reported in the *Royal Gazette* of November 1, 1780?

Alas, how many "unknown dead" will rise, at the last trump, from the soil that we daily tread in Camden! Many dead and fatally wounded, on both sides, were brought into the village from the various engagements in this vicinity, and doubtless scores perished in the crowded, pestilential prison-pens, of which Mrs. Ellet gives us so vivid a picture.

Had the beautiful custom of observing a "Memorial Day," and the patriotic societies of Sons and Daughters of the Revolution, originated half a century earlier, the names and graves of these men who gave their lives for right and country might not now be forgotten.

* * * * * * * * *

Brief personal mention may be made of the opposing leaders in the Battle of Hobkirk Hill.

---

*"Mrs. Royall's Southern Tour." She refers to the redoubts in the lower part of the town.

Lord Rawdon was born in Ireland in 1754. He was therefore only twenty-seven years old at the time of the engagement here. He served throughout the entire American war, being made a general in 1780. In August, 1781, just after the atrocious execution of Col. Isaac Hayne, for which he was partly responsible, he sailed for England, from Charleston. For his services in America, he was made Baron Rawdon and aide-de-camp to the King. By the death of his father, in 1793, he became Earl of Moira. His rise in both military and political life was rapid. After serving as Lord Lieutenant of Ireland, he was made Governor-General of India, where he personally conducted the Nepaul, Pindaree and Mahratta wars. In 1816, he was created Knight of the Garter and Marquis of Hastings. After ten years in India, he was transferred to Malta, as Governor. In this office he died, in 1826.

Lord Rawdon differed with Cornwallis as to the importance of Camden from the military point of view. In a letter, to Col. Henry Lee,[*] after explaining that Cornwallis had allotted to him the management of Camden and of the troops on the frontier and to Colonel Balfour the whole tract within the Santee, Congaree and Saluda Rivers, he says: "Camden had always been reprobated by me as a station; not merely from the extraordinary disadvantages which attended it, as an individual position; but from its being on the wrong side of the river, and covering nothing; while it was constantly liable to have its communication with the interior district cut off. Lord Cornwallis did not consider how much he augmented this objection, often urged by me to him, by an arrangement whence I was

---

[*] "Memoirs of the War," edited by Gen. R. E. Lee (1869). Rawdon attempts, in this communication of June 24, 1813, a justification of the murder of Hayne.

Lord Rawdon.

ILLUSTRATION L.

debarred from any interference with the district from which alone I could be fed: the country in front of Camden, as well as that between the Wateree and Broad Rivers, being so wasted as to afford nothing beyond precarious and incidental supplies. Fixed at Camden, with seven hundred men (Lieutenant-Colonel Watson's corps never having formed part of my garrison, and the residue of the force with which I encountered General Greene having been introduced by me into Camden three days after he sat down before it), I was completely dependent on Lieutenant-Colonel Balfour for subsistence, for military stores, for horses, for arms, and for those reinforcements which were indispensable from the expenditure of men, in the unceasing activity of our service."

Nathaniel Greene's brilliant and inspiring career is, or should be, familiar to every reader. Space forbids its rehearsal here. For his services to the State, South Carolina gave him a fine plantation on the Edisto, known as "Boone's Barony"; and Georgia presented to him "Mulberry Grove," a splendid estate near Savannah, where he spent his last years.

Be it ever recorded to his honor, that, when urged to abandon South Carolina, after his repulse at Ninety-Six, he exclaimed: "I will recover the country or die in the attempt." From Colonels Creek, near Camden, he wrote General Marion, May 9, 1781: "It is now going on seven years since the commencement of this war. I have never had leave of absence an hour nor paid the least attention to my own private affairs." His was a spirit deeply consecrated to his country's cause.

Alexander Hamilton pronounced General Greene's qualifications for statesmanship little less remarkable than his military ability, which was of the highest order.

Col. John Gunby was born in Somerset County, Eastern Shore, Maryland, in 1745. He was a farmer and was also engaged in the carrying trade on Chesapeake Bay. He volunteered as a minuteman in 1775, and, from 1776 to 1780, as Colonel of the Second, later of the First, Maryland Regiments, he served with distinction in the Northern campaigns. Transferred to the South, in 1780, his troops became the mainstay of the patriot army, winning a glowing tribute, at Gum Swamp, from the lips of the dying DeKalb, carrying the day at the Cowpens, and performing prodigies of valor at Guilford. Mortified by the censure of the Board of Inquiry, after Hobkirk, yet too patriotic to resign from the service of his country, Colonel Gunby volunteered to return to Maryland and endeavor to enlist recruits for the Southern army. In this laudable work he was engaged until the end of the war.

Some years later he passed through Camden, and was given a reception at the Cornwallis House. On this occasion, touched doubtless by the manifestations of affection and respect on this, the scene of his reputed bad conduct, he is said to have made his first and only speech, in vindication of his much-condemned order. How regrettable it is that there is no record of this noteworthy address!

His last days were spent on his farm near Snow Hill, Maryland. Political honors were neither sought nor desired. In the journals of the Order of the Cincinnati, of which he was an original member, he is invariably spoken of as "Brigadier-General" Gunby, which would seem to indicate that this rank had been conferred upon him before the end of the war.

His death occurred in 1807, and he is buried in a private inclosure on his farm.

William Augustine Washington, the dashing cavalry leader, was born in Stafford County, Va., in 1752. He was a son of Bailey Washington, who was second cousin to our first President. Every schoolboy knows of the exploits of this picturesque figure in South Carolina—for instance, his personal combat with Tarleton at Rantowles Bridge, in which the British officer lost several fingers by the sword; his comic capture of Rugeley's; his second duel with Tarleton at the Cowpens, in which, this time, he came near losing his life; the blowing off of his hat at Guilford, which is said to have changed the fate of the day; his charge at Hobkirk; and, finally, his capture at Eutaw, after his horse had been shot under him. He remained a prisoner until the end of the war, when he married Miss Eliot, and settled in Charleston, S. C., though passing much of his time at "Sandy Hill," his wife's plantation, thirty miles distant. He declined to accept a nomination, which meant practically an election, as Governor, on the ground that he was not a native South Carolinian and, furthermore, that he could not make a speech.

Washington died in 1810. Historians style him "the modern Marcellus, the sword of his country."

Isaac Huger, second in command at the battle of Hobkirk Hill, was the only South Carolina officer, in fact, perhaps, the only South Carolinian, on the American side, in that engagement. There were a great many fighting under Rawdon. General Huger was born on Cooper River, in 1742. His education was received in Europe. At the outbreak of the Revolution he was made Colonel of the Fifth South Carolina Regiment in the Continental army. Three years later he was promoted to the rank of Brigadier-General, and took part in every battle of consequence fought by the Southern army. He led the unsuccessful attack made by the South Carolina and Georgia troops on Savannah, and served gallantly in the siege of Charleston. At Guilford and Hobkirk he commanded the Virginia troops. After the war, he lived in retirement on his plantation, until his death in 1797. General Huger was the first Vice-President of the Order of the Cincinnati in South Carolina.

John Eager Howard, who succeeded to the command of the Second Maryland Regiment, upon the fall of Colonel Ford, at Hobkirk, was born in Maryland in 1752. His war record was conspicuous. He was with Gates at Camden. His splendid cavalry charge is said to have gained the victory at Cowpens; here seven British officers surrendered their swords to him in person. At Eutaw, he was severely wounded; his command at that time was reduced to thirty men, he the sole surviving officer. Howard's subsequent political career was brilliant. He was Governor, and, later United States Senator, of Maryland. In 1796, he declined a place in Washington's cabinet, and, in 1816, was a candidate for the Vice-Presidency. His beautiful country seat, "Belvidere," was visited by Lafayette in 1825. Howard died two years later.

Richard Campbell was born in the beautiful Shenandoah Valley. He commanded the First Virginia Regiment at Guilford, Hobkirk (where he was wounded), Ninety-Six and Eutaw. In this last battle, while leading the charge that drove the enemy from the field, he was mortally wounded, September 8, 1781. His last words, on hearing of the success of the Americans, were: "I die contented."

Of *Colonels Ford and Hawes* we can find no biographies. Ford, who was killed at Hobkirk, was presumably a Marylander. Samuel Hawes, of Virginia, entered the service in 1776, and served until 1783. His troops played a gallant part in our Second Battle of Camden.

William Richardson Davie, one of the ablest of our partisan leaders, is somewhat identified with our local history by virtue of the facts that his home was in Camden District, and that his blood courses in the veins of some of our most estimable people.

He was born in England, 1756, but, as a boy of eight, came to South Carolina, as the adopted son of an uncle, Rev. William Richardson, a noted Presbyterian divine of the Waxhaw country. After graduating at Princeton, he practiced law in Salisbury, N. C., until 1779, when he enlisted as a major of dragoons under Count Pulaski. Next year, he expended the entire estate left him by his uncle in raising a cavalry troop. His career, with this little band that was never captured or conquered, adorns the pages of the Revolutionary history of the Carolinas.

At General Greene's urgent request, Davie acted as Commissary-General of the Southern army. He was full of zeal, had great influence, and was familiar with the country. The brilliant war record of this, our Bayard, needs no repetition here.

He was strikingly handsome, graceful, and of wonderful physical strength. Indeed he is said to have overcome more men in personal encounter than any other man in the army; and his voice was so commanding that, like Roland's, it could be heard at an almost incredible distance.

It is not surprising that a man of such rare endowments should attain high political preferment. After the war, he served many years in the legislature of North Carolina, was a member of the convention that framed the Constitution of the United States, and was the father of the University of North Carolina. In 1794 he was made a Brigadier-General, U. S. A., and, five years later, became Governor of his adopted State. The same year he was intrusted by President Adams with a special mission to the Court of France; here his tact, dignity, and elegance caused him to attract much personal attention from the great Napoleon.

In 1803 he retired to Landsford, his plantation on the Catawba, about thirty miles above Camden, where he spent his declining years. He died in 1820.

General Davie's wife was a daughter of Gen. Allen Jones, of Northampton, N. C. His daughter, Sarah, married William F. DeSaussure, Esq., of Columbia, S. C., whose daughter, Sarah, married A. Hamilton Boykin, Esq., of Camden. The descendants of this last union are numerous in Kershaw County.

Captain John Smith, of the Third Maryland Regiment, is famous for the desperate personal encounter he had, at Guilford, with Colonel Stuart of the Guards. They had clashed in a previous combat, and had each been biding his time. Smith is said to have laid out several men in order to reach Stuart, whom he killed with one mighty stroke of his heavy saber. At the same moment, a ball grazed Smith's head, causing him to fall upon the lifeless form of his late antagonist.

When taken prisoner at Hobkirk, Captain Smith was refused a parole and was cast into the common prison on the baseless charge that he had inhumanly put to death an officer and three private men of the Guards,* who were prisoners and defenseless, after the action at

---

*See letter to General Greene from Rawdon's Brigade Major.

Guilford. Greene, Washington, and Howard vigorously protested against this procedure, in consequence of which Smith was released on parole and sent to Charleston. A few miles out of Camden, however, he was set upon by a party of men, probably Tories, who stripped, bound, and mercilessly flogged him upon his bare back. This dastardly outrage went unavenged.*

From James's "Marion," we learn that the lieutenant, to whom Smith surrendered his sword at Hobkirk, contemptuously struck him with the broad side of it. To their honor, be it said, the other British officers of the garrison did not approve such conduct, as they recognized Smith's courage; so they arranged a little dinner, in Camden, to which both he and the lieutenant were invited. It was agreed that Captain Smith might treat as he chose the man who had insulted him, so, with this permission, he promptly proceeded to kick the fellow downstairs, as soon as he showed his face in the room. The lieutenant did not resent this indignity, and was soon after cashiered.

Smith settled in this State after the war, and was long and most favorably known as Capt. John Smith of Darlington.†

Capt. Robert Kirkwood's name must ever excite the liveliest interest in the mind of a Camdonian, for it has attached itself to the scene of his valor here—that broad southern slope of Hobkirk Hill, on which now rest in smiling beauty many of the finest residences and gardens in the community.

Robert Kirkwood was born in Mill Creek Hundred, Delaware. The date of his birth is unknown. In 1771,

*Johnson's Life of Greene.
†James's Life of Marion.

we hear of him as a lieutenant in Col. John Haslet's militia regiment. He was then living with a married sister in Newark, Del., and was merchandising. His business interests, however, were laid aside after the Declaration of Independence, and he hastened with his regiment to New York, where it was mustered into service. In his first fight, on Long Island, he displayed that conspicuous gallantry which characterized his entire career. After participating in the battles of White Plains, Trenton, and Princeton, Haslet's regiment disbanded, and, in the new regiment formed, Kirkwood was made a captain, December 1, 1776.

Joining Washington's army, his regiment was engaged at Brandywine, Germantown, and Monmouth, indeed in all the principal actions during the years 1777-79.

In April, 1780, the Delaware and Maryland troops, as we have seen, were ordered south under Baron DeKalb. At Gum Swamp, Kirkwood's Regiment went in 500 strong and came out with only 188 men. They were in the front line and did not break in the shameful panic. Both his colonel and major were taken prisoner, and after the battle the regiment, reduced to two companies, was put under the command of Robert Kirkwood as senior captain. With no increase of rank, he thus served during the rest of the war. His splendid services at Hobkirk and Eutaw drew from General Greene unstinted praise. In 1781, a resolution of thanks was passed by Congress, in which the Delaware battalion was especially mentioned, and, in 1783, Kirkwood was given a commission as brevet-major.

It is pleasant to record that the State of Virginia, in recognition of his eminent labors, gave him, in 1787, two thousand acres of land in Ohio, then the Northwest Territory. About this period, he married a Miss England, of New Castle County, Del., and resumed his mercantile pursuits at Cantwells Bridge, in that State. In 1785 he removed to St. Georges, Newcastle County, one mile south of the present station of Kirkwood. Soon afterwards we find him farming on his western lands in Belmont County, Ohio, on the other side of the river from what is now the city of Wheeling, W. Va.

On the outbreak of Indian hostilities, in 1791, he could not repress the old war fever, and enlisted as a captain under St. Clair. The little army was cut to pieces, on the night of November 2d, at the Great Miami Village, and among the dead was our hero, Robert Kirkwood. Of his regiment of 258, there were but 111 survivors, of whom 42 were wounded.

It seemed the irony of fate that this knightly soul that had passed unscathed through thirty-two battles of the Revolution should perish in a midnight massacre during days of peace only temporarily disturbed.

Many towns throughout the United States bear his chivalrous name, among them our beautiful suburb.

Captain Kirkwood left two children, a son who settled on his father's western lands, and a daughter who married Arthur Whiteley of Delaware and became the mother of General Whiteley, U. S. A.*

* * * * * * * * *

Rawdon's victory at Hobkirk was really fruitless. His adversary was driven scarcely out of his sight, and yet he himself had suffered too severely to renew operations. He was afraid to attack Greene at Rugeley's, not only because of his own weakness, but for fear lest the Americans might slip by him into Camden. His

---

*For the facts of Robert Kirkwood's career, the authors are indebted to a sketch contributed to the *West Virginia Historical Magazine*, October, 1901, by Judge G. L. Cranmer.

sole hope was that Watson would come to his rescue. This General Greene set himself to prevent, if possible. With the reinforcements expected from Virginia, he believed that Rawdon might either be starved into submission or his works taken by storm.

Having had much trouble by desertions from the militia, particularly on the eve of battle or after a repulse, Greene had five (Gordon says eight) deserters hanged at Rugeley's. These executions came near causing a mutiny in his camp, the militia being unused to rigid discipline.

Major Eaton, who had been sent with a piece of artillery to General Marion on April 24th, had turned back on hearing of the reduction of Fort Watson. On April 28th Captain Conyers, with a few Continentals, was dispatched to reconvey the cannon to Marion at the High Hills of Santee, and instructions were sent that general and Colonel Lee to cut off all supplies from the low-country, and to intercept Colonel Watson. For the same purpose, on May 3d*, Greene himself crossed the Wateree at Chesnut's Ferry, and took position on Twenty-five Mile Creek, commanding the communication by Camden Ferry.

Despite the vigilance of Marion, Lee, and Sumter, Watson passed the Wateree, opposite Stateburg, and, on May 7th, brought his command, estimated at 600 men and four pieces of artillery, into Camden. Rawdon, however, in a letter to Cornwallis, says that Watson's force had been greatly reduced by sickness and casualties, and that a part had been left in Georgetown.

Alarmed by this dreaded increase of the British garrison, General Greene, on that same evening, withdrew to the high bluff on the north side of Sawney's Creek,

---

*Gordon.

but, being afraid to risk an action even there, he left the horse, light infantry, and pickets at that encampment, and on May 8th retired, with his main body, behind Colonels Creek.*

On the 8th, Rawdon moved out from Camden and crossed the river, expecting to find the Americans on Twenty-five Mile Creek. He advanced as far as Sawney's, when, finding their position practically impregnable, and afraid, as at Rugeley's, to attempt getting in their rear, he retired into the town.

We find, on May 9th, the remarkable situation of the two opposing generals, each fearful of the other, and of the ground on which he himself stood, making ready to run from each other at the same time. On that date General Greene unbosomed himself of his sad forebodings to General Davie: "Lord Rawdon has now a decided superiority of force. * * * He will strike at Lee and Marion, reinforce himself by all the troops that can be spared from the several garrisons and push me back to the mountains. * * * You observe our dangerous and critical situation. * * * Congress seems to have lost sight of the Southern States and to have abandoned them to their fate; so much so that I am even as much distressed for ammunition as for men. We must always calculate on the maxim that your enemy will do what he ought to do. We will dispute every inch of ground in the best manner we can; but Rawdon will push me back to the mountains. Lord Cornwallis will establish a chain of posts along James River, and the Southern States, thus cut off, will die like the tail of a snake."

The reinforcements from Virginia had not come in, and there were rumors that Cornwallis was on his way

---

*Letter of Greene to Marion, May 9th.—Gibbes's Documentary History.

southward. Greene, therefore, gave orders for his army to move, on May 11th, towards Friday's Ferry.*

At the very moment that the American commander was bewailing his fate to Davie, Rawdon was hastening his arrangements to evacuate Camden. He was suffering for provisions, of which he was cut off on all sides; Fort Motte was about to fall into Marion's hands; Sumter and Lee were threatening Orangeburg and Granby. He therefore realized the necessity of getting once more in touch with his base of supplies at Charleston.

About daylight on May 10th, General Davie tells us he was again summoned to the tent of General Greene, who, with a countenance expressing the liveliest satisfaction, informed him that Rawdon was leaving Camden, and that, as that place was the key of the army's line of posts, all would soon fall, and things would henceforth go well.

We shall let the now jubilant American commander continue the narrative for us, in his letter of May 14th to Samuel Huntingdon:

"Sir: * * * on the 8th† the place was evacuated by the enemy with the utmost precipitation. Lord Rawdon burnt the greatest part of his baggage, stores and even the effects belonging to the inhabitants; he set fire also to the prison, mill, and several other buildings, and left the town little better than a heap of ruins. He left behind him our people who had been wounded in the action of the 25th of April, and had been taken prisoners; they are 31 in number. His Lordship left also 58 of his own people, with 3 officers, who were so badly wounded that they could not bear a carriage. Several of the inhabitants assert it as a fact that in the

---

*Pendleton's letter to Marion.—Gibbes's Documentary History.

†It was the night of the 9th, as Rawdon and others tell us. See Diary of Samuel Mathis.

last action the loss of the enemy in killed and wounded was not less than 300 men.

"As soon as the enemy left Camden, we took possession of it, and are now employed in razing all the works—a plan of which I inclose for your excellency. Had the Virginia militia joined us in time, the garrison must have fallen into our hands, as we should then have been able to invest the town on all sides; and the garrison was in too great want of provisions and military stores to be able to stand a siege. The detachments under Genl. Marion and Lieut.-Col. Lee, in the lower districts of the country, had cut off the enemy's provisions, and particularly salt, with which they were totally unprovided. On the 9th, our army began their march towards this place," etc. This communication was sent from McCord's Ferry on the Congaree. General Greene seems to have been confused on the dates.

Lord Rawdon reported the evacuation to Earl Cornwallis, from Monks Corner, on May 24th. He states that he destroyed all the works, and sent his baggage out of Camden, under a heavy escort, on the night of May 9th; that he himself remained in the town until ten the next morning, in order to cover the march. He reached Nelson's Ferry on the night of the 13th, and, by the evening of the 14th, everything was safely across. His rear-guard had been harassed by some mounted militia, but a part of these had been ambuscaded and the rest gave him no trouble. Continuing, he says: "We brought off all the sick and wounded, excepting about 30, who were too ill to be moved, and for them I left an equal number of Continental prisoners in exchange. We brought off all the stores of any kind of value, destroying the rest; and we brought off not only the militia who had been with us at Camden, but also all the well-affected neighbors on our route, together with the wives, children, negroes and baggage of almost all of them."

There is a sad sequel to this migration of the poorer class of Tories from this vicinity. Fearful of the vengeance that they believed would surely be wreaked upon them, did they remain at home, the miserable refugees followed Rawdon to Charleston. There they built a village of rude huts outside the city's walls and named it "Rawdontown," and, there, despised by patriots and totally neglected by their so-called protectors, they lived in misery and squalor and were scourged by death-dealing disease until the wretched little colony was extinct.

Thus ends the highly dramatic act of the Revolution whose scene was laid in or about Camden. As General Greene predicted, the fall of this post was quickly followed by the evacuation of the other less important ones. After the unsuccessful siege of Ninety-Six, which was relieved by Rawdon, Greene rested his soldiers during the dog-days of 1781 in what he called his "Camp of Repose," at the High Hills of Santee, below Camden. Rawdon meantime had abandoned Ninety-Six and fallen back to Orangeburg.

On September 8th was fought the action at Eutaw Springs, said by Greene to have been the bloodiest and most obstinate in which he had ever engaged. Though a drawn battle, it was really an American victory, the enemy retiring to Charleston, where for fourteen months they were practically shut up, protected solely by their fleet. On December 14, 1782, a month after the independence of the colonies had been acknowledged by the mother country, the last British soldier withdrew from the soil of South Carolina, whose people were at length free to enjoy that liberty for which they had suffered far more than was their share.

Within a radius of thirty miles from Camden, as a military and geographical center, fourteen engagements had been fought during the war; to wit: Buford's Massacre, May 29, 1780; Flat Rock,* July 20th; Rocky Mount, August 1st; First Hanging Rock, August 1st; Second Hanging Rock, August 6th; Wateree Ferry,* August 15th; Camden,* August 16th; Fishing Creek, August 18th; Rugeley's Mill,* December 4th; Lynches Creek* (Radcliffe's Bridge), March 6, 1781; Waxhaw's Church, April 9th; Hobkirk Hill,* April 25th; Friday's Ferry, May 1st; Granby, May 15th.

*Of these, six, marked above with an asterisk, took place within the present confines of Kershaw County. Radcliffe's Bridge may have been in the present county of Lee, recently created.

CHAPTER XI.

THE CORNWALLIS HOUSE.

The historic residence of Col. Joseph Kershaw, known as the Cornwallis House because it served as British Headquarters during their eleven months' occupancy of Camden, stood at the extreme southern end of Lyttleton street, facing west, upon Magazine Hill, a gentle eminence rising from the swamps of Pine Tree Creek.

It was a large, and, for the times, very elegant, mansion of many rooms and passages, three stories high, with spacious attics. The materials of which it was constructed are said to have been imported, but were more probably of native timbers sawn at Colonel Kershaw's own mills, the so-called "English" brick being made perhaps on the place, the soil of which is peculiarly well adapted to that use.*

Tall poplars and other handsome trees and shrubs adorned the surrounding grounds, which were extensive and beautiful.

The house was never completed, the railings not having been put upon the hall stairways and the ballroom being still unfinished, when Lord Cornwallis entered the town in June, 1780, and took possession of it for his quarters.

Colonel Kershaw was then taken prisoner and soon after deported to Bermuda. His wife and children were, for a short while, allowed to occupy an upper room of their home. Here, from a window, they witnessed, with sad hearts, the spectacle of the return of the vic-

---

*Mr. E. Von Tresckow found, several years ago, in the ruins of an outhouse on the premises (formerly) of Dr. L. H. Deas, now of Mr. C. J. Shannon Jr., an old brick stamped with the name of Joseph Kershaw.

Cornwallis House. (From an Old Painting.)

ILLUSTRATION M.

torious British army from the field of Gum Swamp. Miss Mary Kershaw, one of these children, herself then seven years of age, lived until 1848, with unimpaired memory. Many romantic stories of her early youth did she tell to a wondering little great-niece, now quite an old lady,* from whom, fortunately, the authors obtained them.

August 16th, said she, was a sultry day. The American prisoners were driven like sheep into Colonel Kershaw's backyard, where barrels of water were brought in and dipped out to them in tin cups. Not till long after midnight did they quiet down.

The house was filled with the wounded on both sides. One of these, an American, was a good fiddler, who managed by merry tunes to enliven the dreary tedium of illness and captivity. The guards were suffered to listen outside the door, but, if one of them dared show his face inside, he was met with a volley of brickbats, which had been supplied the lamed musician by the little rebel Kershaw children.

Many a poor soldier did the young girl see laid to rest in long trenches near the house, and she was also a witness to the interment of Baron DeKalb, who, said she, was buried, with his sword beside him, between two British officers.

When Lord Rawdon took command at Camden, Mrs. Kershaw and her young family were forced to leave their home and occupy an outhouse on the premises that had been infected with smallpox. Later they were permitted to retire to Burndale, a farm a little below the Hermitage. Here they suffered many indignities, and, tradition says, were saved from starvation only by the exertions of faithful slaves, notably one, Guinea

---

*Miss Mary Young, of Decatur, Ala.

Cato, who hid cattle and other provisions for them out in the swamps.

Regardless, too, of the good lady's wishes and entreaties, liquors and other requisites for Bacchanalian festivities were sent to her retreat, and there dances, doubtless riotous carousals, were frequently given by young officers.

On one occasion, her residence was searched at midnight to find Col. Wade Hampton, whom she was suspected of harboring. Miss Hettie Cummings, a Royalist young lady, who was then living with Mrs. Kershaw,* indignantly resented the suggestion that a man was in hiding in her room, but, despite her protests and well-known loyalty, the British troopers were not satisfied until they had thrust their bayonets through the mattresses on her bed.†

Another time, we are told, Hampton had really taken refuge at Burndale, and barely escaped through the back door as Tarleton galloped into the front yard in pursuit of him.

The two oldest sons of Colonel Kershaw, John and James, were then lads at school in England, but the brave wife and mother was fortunate in enjoying such protection as could be afforded by the presence of a brother, Samuel Mathis, a prisoner on parole, whose Diary, given entire in the Appendix, furnishes an interesting insight into the social conditions of that period in Camden.

Meantime tragic scenes were being enacted at Headquarters on Magazine Hill, giving to the house in its old age a ghostly reputation that caused many a childish heart to flutter in climbing, on a "dare," to the bullseye

---

*Miss Cummings, for many years after Mrs. Kershaw's death, lived with Mrs. Benjamin Perkins.
†Johnson's Traditions.

in the attic. Here, in the long dining-room, Cornwallis, Rawdon, and Tarleton discussed, over their grog, their wicked schemes of oppression and revenge. Here their bloody fingers signed orders for needless executions in the nearby prison pens.

In the southeastern room a stain of blood, long visible, marked the spot where a British officer fell, shot, through the open window, by some reckless patriot lurking in the neighboring swamp.

From the second-story windows, in the northwest room, American prisoners were hung on beams—so old-timers said.

The spot was reported to be haunted.

On the great common in front of the mansion reviews of the red-coated troops of King George were held. Says Mrs. Royall,* writing of the place in 1830:

"One of the trees, which they planted as a stake merely to direct their center-march, is now green and flourishing." Mr. Daniels† confirms this: "The very hawthorn trees‡ by which Lord Rawdon and Colonel Balfour§ ranged their scarlet lines of war are yet among us."

After the evacuation of the town, May 10, 1780, Mrs. Kershaw returned to her dismantled home, which, for some unaccountable reason, had escaped the general conflagration that had left almost every other building of consequence a heap of ashes. Her furniture had been pitched out of the windows by the retiring vandals and broken into pieces. The few articles saved had previously been buried, among them a grandfather's clock,

---

*"Southern Tour."
†*Camden Journal*, 1830: Editorial on Cornwallis House.
‡Unfortunately the Common is now a plowed field and these historic trees have long since fallen by the ax, to make way for a few stalks of corn or cotton.
§Colonel Balfour, so far as known, was never stationed in Camden.

still doing service. Family tradition has it that these household goods, including the punch bowl out of which Lord Cornwallis drank and the fine crockery imported direct from China, were destroyed, after Rawdon left, by a party of Tories from the Waxhaws; but, as the Americans almost immediately occupied the town, this seems improbable.

The wife of General Greene was a guest of Mrs. Kershaw at the mansion for several days at this time. She is described as a very handsome woman, of elegant manners and person. Clad in a rich military costume, she was traveling on horseback, with an escort of cavalry and a considerable retinue.*

At the end of the war, Colonel Kershaw returned to his family, and for some years the house was the scene of much hospitality and gayety. But earnest work was now necessary to resuscitate his crippled fortunes, and Colonel Kershaw set about this task with characteristic pluck and energy. One mark of his enterprise, about this period, was the cutting of a private canal† to connect his town residence with the Hermitage.

Joseph Kershaw died at the Cornwallis House in 1791. A few years later the mansion passed out of the hands of the family. From 1805 to 1822 it was the home of the Camden Orphan Society, having been purchased from Mr. James English, who probably bought it in at the sale of Colonel Kershaw's property. Subsequently it was owned, successively, by Mr. John Workman, Mr. James C. Doby, and Mr. John Meroney.

On the verdant Common‡ that it faced, most of the civic and military gatherings were held, prior to the

---

*Johnson's Traditions.

†Though abandoned for perhaps a century, this old canal is still well defined. It may be seen from the trestle of the Southern Railway over Pine Tree Creek. See Diagram No. 11.

‡Called, for many years, Orphan House Square.

Civil War, and the fine spring at the foot of the hill was the scene of many a big barbecue.

Lafayette reviewed the troops on this green in 1825, and here were mustered in the soldiers that left for Mexico in 1848 and for Virginia in 1861.

Several Revolutionary cannon mounted in front of the house were used for firing salutes on holidays and other notable occasions. These were not removed until in the '80s. Two of them now guard the entrance to the Hobkirk Inn: on one are the fleurs-de-lis of France; this gun, it is said, was taken by the British at the capture of Louisburg.

It seems the irony of fate that the Cornwallis House, one of the chief glories of Camden and a landmark of American history, after passing through more than eight decades of storm and stress, should at last have fallen by the incendiary torch of one of our own people. Yet such are the exigencies of war. Mr. John Meroney, who owned the building, had allowed its use as a storehouse for the Confederate service. The supplies there collected caused its destruction. In a letter to the authors, of November 21, 1901, Rev. John Kershaw writes: "Capt. John H. Devereux of this city (Charleston) told me that he had set fire to the Cornwallis House on the day in February, 1865, that Sherman's men entered Camden. In the basement were stored many barrels and hogsheads of sugar belonging to the Confederate government. Devereux was there as commissary and under orders not to let the stores fall into the hands of the enemy. He was run out by Sherman, but in going he stopped long enough to fire the sugar, and the old relic went up in smoke and flames."

This settles the point; but, strange to say, the local tradition that the house was destroyed by Sherman's troops finds seeming confirmation in the testimony of one E. P. Burton, a surgeon, who was with the Union party that raided Camden. Says he:* "The old house, once the headquarters of Cornwallis, was standing, but used as a warehouse. I did not see it. It was fired and burned by order of the commander"—meaning evidently his own commander.

A young elm, the last scion of the noble monarchs of the forest that used to dignify the spacious grounds, stands a lone sentinel to guard the spot where the famous house stood, and molten glass and scattered brick are all that remain to tell the tale of its stately halls, once so replete with human interest.

*In a letter to the *Camden Journal,* dated New York, Iowa, February 24, 1890.

CHAPTER XII.

AN HONORED TORY.

Mrs. Martha Bratton of York was one of the heroines of the Revolution. The incident of her narrow escape from decapitation with a reaping-hook, on the eve of the action known as "Huck's Defeat," July 12, 1780, is familiar to all, but it is not so generally known that the young Tory officer who gallantly saved her life was John Adamson, of Camden, whose ashes lie in the Quaker section of our cemetery, and whose descendants are numerous in our midst.

The story of Adamson's chivalrous part in that tragic affair has never, we believe, been so vividly told as in the narrative of Col. William Bratton,* a son of the heroine, who, as a child of six years, was an eyewitness of the scene.

Says he: "We were duly warned of the approach of the Redcoats and were on the lookout for them. At last they were seen coming up the road, a long line of Redcoats, followed by a great crowd of Tories. A small squad first reached the house and my mother met them in the piazza and asked what they wanted. They wished to see her husband and were told that he was not at home. She was asked where he was and replied that she did not know; when a red-headed ruffian swore that he would make her know, and, seizing a sickle (an implement used in those days for harvesting grain) that was hanging on a peg in the piazza, placed it in position

---

*This circumstantial account was transmitted by the author to his son, Gen. John Bratton, who inclosed it in a letter (April 18, 1876,) to Dr. E. M. Boykin.

around her neck and, drawing his sword, swore that, if she did not immediately tell where her husband was, he would cut her head off and split it.

"I, a little chap clinging to my mother's dress, was transfixed with horror and fright, could not even scream, could only clutch the dress with a tighter grip and watch the countenance of the monster.

"My mother did not move but spoke in deliberate and measured tones to this effect: 'I told the simple truth and could not tell if I would; but I now add, that I would not if I could.' The villain's face grew pale, but was the most horrible countenance that I ever beheld, and, just when I expected the blow to fall, the sword and sickle fell to the floor and the wretch crouched, a pitiable beggar for his life. I was so paralyzed with horror that, although I saw the change in his countenance and attitude, I could not at once take in the scene. He was pleading for life to an officer who stood over him with a drawn sword. The officer did not slay him, but beat him out of the piazza with the flat of his sword and kicked him headlong down the steps. He then turned to my mother, and, expressing regret at the occurrence, gave her assurance of protection. My mother said not a word, but turned and went into the house, and I with her, still clinging to the skirts of her dress."

Dr. Bratton then tells of Colonel Huck's coming up and of his vain attempts to induce Mrs. Bratton to use her influence towards winning her husband over to the Royal cause. As night came on, supper was ordered, and then Mrs. Bratton and her family were locked up in the garret. Through cracks in the wall, and by the light of a vivid aurora-borealis, she witnessed the sanguinary attack upon the house made by her husband with a band of patriots. About daylight, after the firing had ceased, a young man by the name of Adair called to her to come down, as her husband wished to see her. Thinking, naturally, that he was perhaps dying, she hastily picked her way through the masses of dead and mortally wounded that literally covered the floor, and reached the yard. We shall let Colonel Bratton continue the story: "We passed out and saw at a short distance my father and old Captain Chambers standing with drawn swords over a prostrate Redcoat. On our approach, my mother was asked if she recognized this man. He was so pale and changed in appearance by his wound that she did not recognize him. Indeed she was lost in a sort of maze of relief from the fearful anticipations with which she left the house and could not take in the situation or recognize the officer until he addressed her, saying: 'Madam, you were sent for at my request, more to save your husband from a cruel injustice to himself than from any service that you may be able to render me. He has heard that it was I who threatened your life.'

"He spoke with difficulty, but my mother recognized him and at once comprehended the whole scene. (My father had heard of the dastardly assault, but, as might easily happen under the circumstances, was misinformed as to the perpetrator of it, and he and old Captain Chambers were about to hack him to pieces with their swords, although he was apparently dying. He, of course, denied the charge, but was not believed; so far from it, was taunted with his cowardly capacity for lying to save his dastardly life, while they drew their swords to cut him into mincemeat. My father says that his sword was raised to strike, when he was checked as much by the countenance of the man as his words, which were: 'It is of little consequence to me, sir, for you can only hasten the end, which, I feel, is fast approaching, but I beg of you to consult Mrs. Bratton before you perpetrate so great a wrong.' Then it was that young Adair was sent for my mother, and the scene which he left behind him accounts for the stern brevity with which he performed his mission and excited such alarming anticipations in my mother's breast.)

"When my mother gave the true statement of his part in the attack upon her, all of their savage fierceness changed into tender care. My father and old Captain Chambers were kneeling on either side of him, administering rum, the panacea of our Revolutionary Fathers, when my mother with Adair and some others went to the house to prepare a place for him. I remember well how Adair and another man took up Redcoats, one by the head and the other by the heels, and threw them out of the house like dead hogs, and laughed at my mother when she remonstrated with them. A room was cleared of dead and wounded, of whom the whole house was full, and a bed was prepared, when the British officer, Captain Adamson, was brought in. My mother, who possessed some skill in concocting healing salves and poultices, dressed his wound, and he was made as comfortable as the circumstances would admit of.

"He was not touched by ball or saber, but was thrown from his horse and impaled on a pine sapling stump about the size of a candle. It penetrated his chest. The wound was a terrible one, and little or no hope was entertained of his recovery, but all that could be done was done for him and he got well.

"The attack was a complete surprise, but Huck and Adamson displayed splendid pluck and courage, rallying their men and returning to the charge only to be broken and repulsed by the sure aim and deadly fire of our men who were fighting for their very firesides. Huck was killed in the second or third charge, when the command devolved on Adamson, who rallied his men and fell, leading the last charge that was made. After his fall, the enemy never rallied again, but fled in confusion."

* * * * * * * * *

John Adamson was a nephew of James Adamson, who was massacred by Indians at Fort Loudoun. He came to this country, after the death of his uncle, with Joshua and Robert English, all of the same county in Ireland and probably related.* Whether he, like the Englishes, was a Quaker, is uncertain, but seems probable. These three young men became the husbands, respectively, of the three daughters left by Lieut. James Adamson, and, with Jonathan Belton, who married a sister of the two Englishes, all espoused the Royal cause after the apparent subjection of the colony, just subsequent to the fall of Charleston, accepting commissions in the British army. They are types of the better-class Tories in Carolina.

* * * * * * * * *

Governor Rutledge, who, since its evacuation by Rawdon, had chiefly made Camden his headquarters, issued, in the last days of 1781, writs of election for a session of the Legislature to be held at this place. Later, for greater protection from General Greene's army, he changed the place of meeting to Jacksonboro, a little village on the west bank of the Edisto, about thirty miles from Charleston. None who had given aid and comfort to the enemy, or who had taken British protection, of course, were eligible. From the diary of Josiah Smith Jr.,† one of the exiles from Charleston to St. Augustine, we learn that the following persons were elected to this legislature, "to be convened at Cambden, the — Jany, 1782," from Camden District:

---

*On authority of Dr. E. M. Boykin.
†Records of South Carolina Historical Society.

Senator, General Sumpter.

Representatives: James Bradley, Samuel Dunlap, Wood Furman, Captain Gordon, John Gamble, Col. John James, Joseph Kershaw (recently back from Bermuda), Joseph Lee, Richard Richardson, Wm. Welch.

This famous Jacksonboro Assembly was in session from January to March, 1782. The war being practically at an end, rather drastic measures, later repealed or modified, were passed, looking mainly to the punishment of those who had been disloyal to the State in her hour of need. Among those whose estates were ordered confiscated and themselves "forever banished" from South Carolina were the following, in whom we are locally interested: Class II (those who presented a congratulatory address to Sir Henry Clinton and Admiral Arbuthnot on the capitulation of Charleston)—William Ancrum, Aaron Loocock. Class V (those who bore commissions, civil or military, under the British government, since the conquest of this province)—John Adamson, Jonathan Belton, John Downey (Camden), Robert English, William Valentine (Camden), Henry Rugeley.

A fine tribute to the character of the Tory, John Adamson, is that paid by his late enemies—personally they must have continued throughout his friends—who, the next year, prayed the Legislature for a remission of the penalty pronounced against him:

To the Honble the Senate and House of Representatives.
    The Petition of a number of the Inhabitants
        of the District of Camden and others
Sheweth

That Mr. John Adamson late of said District is Banished by the late Confiscation Act, that many of your Petitioners impressed with Gratitude for his Humanity to them, when they Laboured under the severe Treatment of the British officers, during their Domination, Beg leave to lay before you some facts which they presume were not Known, to the late Honble Senate and House of Representatives.

Mr. Adamson, altho' he took part with the British Government, we are led to believe was not an Enemy to the freedom of America, because whilst he had any Influence he ever exerted that Influence in behalf of Distressed Americans by getting them Released from loathsome Jails where they must have perished had not his Influence saved them.

In getting the property of all those who were obnoxious to the then Reigning Power restored to them, and even Excusing those from military Duty who oppenly Avowed their Attachment to the American Cause. The Widow, Orphan & Distressed wife and children of a Banished American were sure of his Protection to the utmost extent of his Influence. These are Facts which your Petitioners well Know and therefore Pray that, in Consideration of them, that you will Permit the said Mr. John Adamson to return to this State & Grant to his wife and children (now with us) such Indulgence & Support as in your Wisdom may be thought fit.

    Joseph Hill, Capt.   John Dinkins
    Wm Richardson   Richard Singleton
    Jno. Singleton, Senr   Coleman Leonard
    Mattw Singleton   Thos. Lenoir
    Nathan Pace   Caleb Gayle
    John James   Thos Andrews
    Wm Brummitt   John Harvin
    Spencer Brummitt   William Lang
    Jno. Boykin   Wm Wyly
    William Boykin   John Martin
    Huberd Rees   J. Galbraith
    Samuel Dinkins

Indorsed on back: "Confiscation, 6th Class ——— 1783."

Mr. Adamson seems to have spent the period of his banishment in Florida. His letters at this time are full of interest; for example:

To Mr. Joshua English, near Camden.
>On Board a Schooner in the Harbour*
>July 22d, 1783.

Dr. Joshua,

I still Remain on Board in the Harbour, and not permitted on shore—however there is some hopes as I think they will make a House. I am one of those recommended favourably. Still wou'd be dubious of going into the Country as I understand I am threatned by people whom I never in the least injured, but its too often the Case. I understand they are endeavouring to make you pay for some of their losses, however cant say how far the law will Extend. But upon the whole I think it wld be better for us to go to some New Country (say Georgia) if we are permitted to sell our property; I long to have the pleasure of Seeing you; at which time we shall know more of our Concerns. Am with love to Sally and children—

>Your affectionate Brother,
>JOHN ADAMSON.

My compliments to
John Belton† and family

---

*Of Charleston.

†John Belton was also compelled to leave the State for a while. D. Hart, writing to Joshua English from Bellville, August 24, 1783, speaks of Belton's being then in St. Augustine. He refers to him as "Major" Belton. Joshua English seems, for some reason, to have escaped punishment under the Confiscation Act.

In a subsequent letter to Mr. English from Charleston, February 7, 1784, Mr. Adamson states that he had been permitted to return on as good terms as he could possibly expect. He continues:

"Your brother Robert I left in Augustine about ten days ago, all his family in tolerable good health, but he is not determined where to go as yet. But your brother John came over the Bar of Augustine in another Vessell at the same time I did, altho' he is not arrived as yet but Expected hourly."

Robert English never returned to Carolina from the British West Indies, whither he went. One of his daughters, Amelia, was married to Isaac Lenoir of Camden, and their daughter, Louisa, became the wife of Benjamin Haile Jr.

John Adamson was a merchant in Camden from before the war until his death. In 1782, he was a copartner with John Chesnut and Duncan McRa, as we learn from an affidavit made by Jonathan Belton and Henry Rugeley at Charleston *in re* the debts due the firm (Adamson & Co.) by the Volunteers of Ireland. Herein it is stated that, "As Mr. John Chesnut and Mr. Duncan McRa, two of the Partners, are now with the Americans and are looked upon in this garrison as Enemies to the British Government, said John Adamson declared before these deponents that he is under the absolute necessity of taking their Bonds in his own name, but that it is his Intent and meaning that the said Bonds so given by the Officers in his Majesty's different Regiments shall be looked upon and are to all intents and purposes the same in respect to the Copartnership concern as if they were taken in the firm, &c."*

---

*The originals of these Adamson papers are in the collection of the late Dr. E. M. Boykin.

John Adamson's plantation home, "The Retreat," on the river near the Indian Mound, was a center of hospitality. He died in 1816, after a long and useful life.

His oldest daughter, Margaret, married, in 1791, Edward Mortimer, of the low-country, who was in business in Camden for some time. Their one child, Charlotte, became the wife of John Boykin, Esq. She was the mother of Mrs. Savage Heyward, of Charleston, and of the late lamented Dr. Edward Mortimer Boykin.

Of his other daughters, Eliza married William Rees, of Stateburg; Amelia became the wife of Francis A. Deliesseline, a lawyer practicing in Camden; Sarah married Lewis Ciples, a planter. None left descendants.

John Adamson's only son, William, married Amelia, daughter of Dr. Isaac Alexander. William predeceased his father, leaving three sons, John, Alexander and William. John, who lost his mind, was killed in an unfortunate difficulty by Lewis Ciples, acting in self-defense. Neither he nor his brother, Alexander, married. William married a Miss Carmichael, of New Jersey. Of this union there were three children: Amelia, who became the wife of Maj. Zach. Cantey; Lewis C., who died young; and Edward, who moved to Florida, after the Civil War; he married Sallie, a daughter of Christopher Matheson, of Camden.

In John Adamson's will, made in 1814, he leaves a bequest to a nephew, Jonathan Belton Adamson, son of his brother James.

The Grave of Agnes of Glasgow.

ILLUSTRATION N.

CHAPTER XIII.

AGNES OF GLASGOW.

A low headstone to a sunken grave in the old Presbyterian Churchyard, just back of the grim Nixon inclosure of tragic memories, bears the following quaint inscription, rudely cut:

> Here Lies
> The Body
> of Agnes of
> Glasgow, who
> departed this life
> Feb. 12, 1780. Aged 20.

It is a desolate spot, overgrown with tall grasses and matted myrtle, and almost hidden from view by overhanging vines and drooping boughs of cedar. A fitting sepulcher, you will say, for a broken heart! Aye so, for thus the pretty old legend has it; and many a pilgrim finds his way to the ancient tomb, with its queer epitaph, and pauses there in a sort of fascination born of mystery.

Agnes, a winsome Scotch lassie, had given her heart to a brave young soldier who had embarked with the British army for the American war. Tidings from her betrothed came seldom and finally ceased altogether. This the true-hearted girl could not endure, so, without the consent or knowledge of her family, she set out to find him, taking passage in a sailing vessel that, weathering many storms, brought her safely over.

But here her sufferings had but begun. The British

camps were scattered all along the Atlantic coast and his command was unknown to her. A second Evangeline she wandered, until, almost in despair, from fatigues and disappointments, she learned that he was with Rawdon at Camden. From Georgetown, friendly Indians brought her, in a birch canoe, up the winding waters to this point. With hope renewed, she rushed to Headquarters and called her lover's name. A rough soldier brusquely informed her that he was dead—there, pointing through the open window, was his new-made grave.

The curtain soon fell upon the little tragedy. A low fever seized her and, in a few days, her sweet spirit was freed to join her Gabriel in the land where partings are not.

Lord Cornwallis, touched with pity, had her laid to rest, near his intrenchments, by the side of her lover, and, by his command, the little memorial was erected. The inscription gives all that she had told of her name, which has led to the speculation that she was of noble birth.

Another tradition, believed by many to be the true account, holds that poor Agnes was but a social pariah, a favorite of my Lord Cornwallis, to whose suite she was attached. This has been so delicately elaborated by a quondam northern visitor to Camden that we may be pardoned for letting him tell the painful story for us:*

"In 1780 an incident had occurred at this house (the Cornwallis House), which would not have been remembered but for a monument that records it.

"A young and pretty Scotch girl had accompanied Lord Cornwallis's command to this country. She had

---

*In a letter to the Columbia *State* from Stamford, Conn., April 24, 1893, unsigned.

followed and shared the fortunes of the camp, but at this house she had given up in despair. All efforts of the women in the neighborhood were unavailing, and she died, away from home and country. But she must have had some one to feel for her and respect her grave. I can imagine now a procession slowly moving from the house, across the fields, to a small graveyard—a God's Acre occupied by the bones of some early Scotch settlers. At the head rode Lord Cornwallis and Rawdon and the wicked Tarleton. Then followed the body of the poor girl, laid upon a stretcher, and that borne on muskets, in the hands of the soldiers; others followed, all with military precision. Slowly and quietly they approached the burial ground. The silence was broken by a single mockingbird, who sang a requiem in the bare limbs, the bud and blossom as lifeless as the poor girl. Arriving at the resting-place, a detachment of soldiers were ordered to loosen the soil with their bayonets, while another scooped out the earth with a dish from the mess-chest. The fair, frail girl was laid in her narrow, shallow bed. A soldier stepped into the grave and, filling the dish, carefully sifted the earth about the pale face that had been protected by her luxuriant hair. Finally the grave was filled and all marched as quietly to camp. But her resting-place was not forgotten. A rough stone having been selected, a rude inscription was cut by the sculptor—probably with a broken bayonet in the left hand and a fragment of rock for a hammer.

"It had now been there 112 years, and I knelt and deciphered the inscription, and this is it: 'Here lies the body of Agnes of Glasgow, who departed this life February 12, 1780, aged 20.'

"The grave had sunken as the body returned to earth, the stone had partially fallen, and part of the lettering was beneath the soil.

"It was now high spring here—the 10th of April, 1893. The young foliage shielded our party from the hot sun: the Cherokee rose and the yellow jessamine gave us their odor; a mockingbird whistled as his ancestor had done when the poor girl was buried, and our party then and there resolved that her rude monument should be recut and reset. And so it has been laid in brick that we gathered from the ruins of the Cornwallis House—brick that were pressed and burned in England before the poor girl was born. These laid in cement will secure the stone in its place for another century; then perhaps another Old Mortality will recut it."

Questioned as to the age of these legends, Rev. John Kershaw writes* that his father, General Kershaw, said he had heard them when a boy, as coming down from Revolutionary days; further, that the peculiar way in which the grave lies—not towards any particular point of the compass, had led to the belief that it pointed to buried treasure, and, some coins having been plowed up nearby, crowds had flocked to the spot and dug holes in many directions, seeking for the supposed treasure, which they never found.

G. G. Alexander, Esq., grandson of Dr. I. Alexander, DeKalb's surgeon at Camden, adds this interesting bit of information. He was told by his father, also by Messrs. James Cureton and David Kennedy, all old citizens and sons of men who had lived during the Revolution, that Agnes had followed her lover—no less a personage than Lord Cornwallis—to Camden; that here she had died of malarial fever; that the stone which now stands at the head of her grave was sent from Glasgow, but, before it could be placed in position, the British

*May 21, 1901.

evacuated the town; that it remained in an old warehouse in the lower part of Camden until long after the Revolution. One day the matter was spoken of in the presence of some prominent citizens, and one of them suggested that a collection be taken up to have the monument placed over the grave. This met with a prompt response, and the spot was soon marked as it now is.

* * * * * * * * *

It is almost an act of iconoclasm to cast a doubt upon these romantic legends, nor should we assume so ungracious and thankless a role save in the interest of truth. We must, however, submit a few unpleasant facts.

On February 12, 1780, the date of Agnes's untimely death, not a single Redcoat, so far as known, had penetrated into the interior of South Carolina. Charleston fell three months later. Tarleton, in pursuit of Buford, passed through Camden on May 27th, the very first appearance of the British here; and Cornwallis did not enter the village until June 1st.

The surname Glasgow was not uncommon in this section of colonial Carolina. McCrady mentions a family of that name among those that moved from the Waxhaws to other parts of the State, about the beginning of the Revolution, and we have seen that one Samuel Glasgow signed the petition to General Lincoln, with the other "country militia," May 11, 1780.

The Probate Court Records of Charleston County, Book 1771-75, contain the following entry:*

"Citation granted to Agnes Glasgow, widow, and James Lindsay, both of Prince Frederick's Parish, to administer on the estate of Robert Glasgow, late of the

---

*For this curious find we are indebted to Mr. A. S. Salley, the able Secretary of the South Carolina Historical Society and author of "A History of Orangeburg County."

parish aforesaid, Dec'd, as next of kin. To be read in the parish church aforesaid and ret'd certified, Oct. 8, 1773."*

This parish, St. Mark's, was cut off from Prince Frederick's in 1757.

But, enough—why pursue the subject to distasteful conclusions! These old stories, originating when the memories of the great Revolution were still fresh, must have had some solid base. The erroneous association with the British occupation of the town is a mere excrescence—and of this one can feel little regret, removing, as it does, all stigma attaching to the young sleeper's fair name.

Certain facts seem apparent, and to these we may pin our faith. The girl was young, and rarely sweet and comely, of course; and she died of a stricken heart for some gallant patriot boy that had laid his budding life upon his country's altar; and who knows but that Cornwallis, a man of refined sensibilities, moved by the sad recital of her woes, had the spot marked as a tribute to woman's surpassing love.

So may the pitying tear ever fall on the humble mound, in its picturesque isolation amid entangled wildwood, and may the little feathered choristers never cease wailing their dirges over the unknown but not neglected dead.

"Long, long be my heart with such memories filled!
Like the vase in which roses have once been distilled—
You may break, you may shatter the vase if you will,
But the scent of the roses will hang round it still."

*After all, one can only speculate as to the queer expression "Agnes of Glasgow." Is it possible that the original was "Agnes O Glasgow"?

CHAPTER XIV.

DANIEL McGIRTT.

"I grant him brave,
But wild as Bracklinn's thundering wave;
And generous—save vindictive mood,
Or jealous transport, chafe his blood.

* * * * * * * * *

I grant him liberal, to fling
Among his clan the wealth they bring,
When back by lake and glen they wind,
And in the Lowlands leave behind,
Where once some pleasant hamlet stood,
A mass of ashes slaked with blood.

* * * * * * * * *

No! Wildly while his virtues gleam,
They make his passions darker seem,
And flash along his spirit high,
Like lightning o'er the midnight sky."
—*Lady of the Lake.*

Within the present limits of Kershaw County was born, about the middle of the eighteenth century, a doubtful hero, Daniel McGirtt,* one of the most picturesque figures of the Revolution. He was a savage Tory outlaw, another "Terror of Loch Lomond's side," whose career might well adorn a highly-colored page of Scottish Border fiction.

Daniel was of good stock. His father, James, had a grant of land on the Wateree of 400 acres, five miles

---

*Or McGirth. The name is spelled both ways in the old deeds and papers.

below Camden, at the horseshoe in the river then called the "Great Neck," near Mulberry. Here probably Daniel first saw the light, though the bulk of his father's estates seem to have been lower down the stream. In 1753, James and his wife, Priscilla, conveyed this land in the Neck to Robert Milhouse. They also sold some of the "Hermitage" lands to Joseph Kershaw.

James McGirtt is said to have been a man of considerable culture. From "Wells' Register and Almanac," for 1775, we learn that he filled places of trust and confidence, being lieutenant-colonel in Richard Richardson's regiment of Provincial militia. It was probably he, and not his son Daniel (as stated in the *South Carolina Gazette* of April, 1769), who, with Colonels Richardson and William Thompson, behaved with such "great spirit, discretion and success" in suppressing the Schofield (or Coffil) trouble on Saluda River. The *Gazette* characterizes the three colonels as "gentlemen of great reputation and highly esteemed by the whole body of backsettlers."

One of James McGirtt's daughters married Captain John Cantey, the founder of the Camden branch of that family.

Johnson* says that the elder McGirtt was firmly attached to the American cause throughout the war, but there is no evidence to confirm this, and we incline to the opinion that he remained true to the Crown, and with his family retired to East Florida about the beginning of the struggle. Certainly this might be inferred from the following letter written by William Ancrum, a Charlestonian by residence but one of our first and largest landowners, who knew all the families hereabouts. It is directed to his agent at the Congarees, on

---

*Traditions.

May 9, 1778, and relates to the recent stealing of three negro slaves from his plantation at that point. He says:

"It is suspected that some of the McGirts who were formerly settled near Camden and some time ago retired to East Florida and who, it seems, have given themselves up to these scandalous practices are the perpetrators of this villany, who have also taken off with them a great many horses from the settlements on the Wateree River."

From the reputed high character of the man, it is impossible to believe that James McGirtt, the father, is to be included in this grave charge of Mr. Ancrum. There may have been other misguided sons besides Daniel who had abandoned themselves to such nefarious businesses, all too common, alas, in the unsettled times of war and the unprotected condition of the up-country.

Among Dr. Johnson's interesting traditions is one purporting to explain the reason of young Daniel McGirtt's desertion of the patriot cause. As a young man, says he, Daniel was a noted hunter and rider, thoroughly familiar with the woods and paths from Santee River to the Catawba Nation. As a scout, he was invaluable to the Americans, as well for his daring courage as for his accurate knowledge of the countryside.

His favorite mount was a magnificent mare that he called "Grey Goose." His devotion to this animal led to his ultimate ruin. At Satilla, Georgia, a superior officer coveted the steed, and, not being able to get her by other means, swore that he would have her by force. This threat led to a personal difficulty in which the high-spirited Daniel felled the officer to the ground. For this he was court-martialed, found guilty of a serious violation of the rules of war, and publicly whipped at the post. By the terms of his sentence, a second whipping was subsequently to be inflicted. Stung to madness by this disgrace, Daniel determined to escape, in which, perhaps by the connivance of his guards, he succeeded. Mounting beautiful "Grey Goose," who happened to be tethered near, he made a wild dash for liberty, turning however, in his saddle, to hurl back at his former comrades anathemas and threats of revenge. The latter he vindictively fulfilled.

Dr. Johnson represents this as having taken place, evidently, after the British had overrun the province, for he adds that, "When the State was again recovered by the American army," McGirtt retired to East Florida. As a matter of fact,* however, he had withdrawn to Florida and been made a lieutenant-colonel in the (Tory) Florida Rangers as early as 1775, just after the "Snow Campaign."

Dr. E. M. Boykin says of Daniel that his ruling passion seems to have been for horses. Indeed that he loved a horse so well that "he did not always stop to examine his title to it, but was in the saddle and 'over the hills and far away,' taking, it is said, from the Whigs to sell to the British and vice versa."†

Daniel McGirtt was attached to Prevost's army on its devastating raid through lower Carolina. It will be recalled that plantations were laid waste and robbed of all their valuables—live stock, silver plate, provisions, even negroes.

Commenting on this, the *Gazette* of July 7, 1779, says that with Prevost was "a large body of the most infamous banditti and horsethieves that perhaps ever were collected together anywhere, under the direction of McGirt (dignified with the title of colonel), a corps of

---

*McCrady's "South Carolina in the Revolution," p. 201.
†Records of the Boykin Family.

Indians, with negro and white savages disguised like them, and about 1,500 of the most savage disaffected poor people, seduced from the back settlements of this State and North Carolina."

Again, on July 28, 1779, the same journal remarks: "A report prevailed that Brig.-Gen. Prevost was ordered to New York under an arrest for not having done more mischief in this State than he did. But, if it be true that he was in copartnership to share all plunder, whether in plate, horses, or negroes, with the famous McGirt (as was confidently affirmed by most of the British officers while they were in this neighborhood), the general will have no cause to regret even a dismissal from their service, for McGirt himself has declared that his own share of what he has stolen amounting to his weight in gold, he is now satisfied and will immediately quit his thieving and settle in West Florida."

Let us now turn from this sinister side of the man's nature and consider one or two instances of his generosity and courage.

Lieut. James Cantey of Camden, with a small escort, was once convoying a large amount of money from Augusta, Ga., to Charleston. The wife of General Wilkinson was with the party. McGirtt, with a much larger force, hung upon the flanks of the convoy, and would occasionally call out: "James Cantey, get out of that party, or I will pounce down on you and wipe the last one of you off the earth. I have need of that money and am going to have it." To this Cantey defiantly replied that he could get it only by walking over his dead body. Finally, seeing that his game of bluff would not work, McGirtt withdrew, when nearing the city, yelling out, as a farewell: "You confounded, hardheaded fool! You had better thank your stars that you happen to be my nephew!"

On another occasion, while Capt. John Boykin, of Hampton's Cavalry, and a party of Whigs were on a scouting expedition about the Santee Ferries, they encamped, one night, in a bend of Jacks Creek, near Vance. When all was silent, a voice was heard from the other side of the stream, "Hello! Is there a Boykin, or an Irvin, or a Whitaker in camp? If so, tell him to come where I may speak to him." One of the gentlemen named at once responded, with the inquiry, "Well, who are you and what do you want?" "Never mind who I am," said the voice, which was at once recognized as McGirtt's, "but take my advice and break this camp. Tarleton knows where you are and will be on you by daylight." Needless to say, the advice was heeded, and, leaving their fires brightly burning, the party escaped to the other side of the stream, barely in time, and witnessed, from a place of safety, the Bloody Dragoon's furious overhaul of their abandoned camp. This story was told Dr. E. M. Boykin by Mr. Stephen Boykin, who, then an aged man, could distinctly remember the days of the Revolution.

One of Daniel McGirtt's acts of daring is commonly believed to have given a name to a locality in this county. With a single companion he once ventured to make a secret reconnaissance in the swamps on the western side of the Wateree. Some patriots of the neighborhood, learning of his presence, determined to entrap him. Suspecting that he would wish to cross a creek with very high banks, on the Bettyneck plantation, ten miles below Camden, they removed the only bridge at that point and concealed themselves on either side of the way. McGirtt and his comrade rode blindly into the ambuscade, but, putting spurs to their horses, passed unscathed by the fire of musketry until they reached the yawning chasm. Retreat was impossible, so both urged their horses to the leap. The distance from bank to bank was quite twenty feet. McGirtt, as by a miracle, passed safely over, but his unfortunate attendant perished in the attempt. The stream has since been known as "Jumping Gully."*

After the war, McGirtt took his band of desperadoes to Florida, where they seem to have maintained themselves for a while by their wits and their good right arms, after the manner of medieval robber knights.

The contemporary Charleston papers afford occasional glimpses of our border hero and his band.

The *Gazette*† of April 3, 1784, says: "By a gentleman arrived this week from St. Augustine, we learn that the notorious McGirth, who came into this State with Prevost's army in 1779 and committed numberless depredations on the inhabitants, is confined in the castle of that place for several robberies committed by him and his party in that province."

Ramsay thus summarizes his career:

"Mr. Tonyn, governor of the last-mentioned loyal province (East Florida), granted a commission to a horse-thief of the name of McGirth, who, at the head of a party, had for several years harassed the inhabitants of South Carolina and Georgia. By his frequent incursions, he had amassed a large property which he deposited in the vicinity of St. Augustine. After peace was proclaimed, he carried on the same practices against his former protectors in East Florida, until they were obliged, in self-defense, to raise the royal militia of the province to oppose him."

---

*It is almost cruel to question these cherished traditions, but a recently discovered plat of James McGirtt's lands in the Fork of the Wateree, made May 4, 1756, shows that this stream was, even at that early date, known as "Jumping Gully."

†*South Carolina Gazette and Public Advertiser.*

The journals of the day carry on the romantic story for us. The *Gazette,* on May 12, 1784, contains this item:

"The noted McGirth, who, we mentioned some time past, was confined in the castle of St. Augustine for stealing, lately made his escape, assisted by two others, from the place of his confinement, and in the face of the guard."

Again, on June 12th of the same year:

"Letters from St. Augustine inform us that, on the 27th of last month, a party of about thirty men, under the famous Col. McGirth, met with a party of men under the command of Col. Young, some little distance from St. Augustine, which he immediately attacked, and killed Col. Young and his servant and took eight or nine of his men, which he disarmed and let go."

But the damp dungeons of St. Augustine, though they had little tamed this truly dauntless spirit, had wrecked the physical man.

Abandoning his life of adventure and outlawry, he sought an asylum at the home of his brother-in-law, Col. John James, of Sumter District, in this State. Here his wife, a sister of Colonel James, had lived in seclusion during the war. With woman's poetic devotion, she had never lost faith in him, and, in her society, he peacefully passed the evening of his life. His identity was, of course, carefully concealed.

A part of the time was passed under the generous protection of his nephews, Zach. and James Cantey, in Camden. Here occurred the following incident, which we give on the authority of Dr. Boykin:

Years after the war, Anthony Hampton paid a visit to Col. James Chesnut at Mulberry. The conversation turned, one evening, on the redoubtable McGirtt, and Mr. Hampton told how, during the Revolutionary struggle, his life had been saved by McGirtt, who had secretly cut the cords that bound his limbs, while he was being carried, a prisoner, to Charleston, thus enabling him to escape in the darkness. To his guest's inquiry as to the ultimate fate of McGirtt, Colonel Chesnut replied, "If you would very much like to know, I shall let you ask him personally"; and that evening the astonished Hampton was conducted into the presence of his former liberator, at his secluded cottage in Gen. Zach. Cantey's yard. The two men had been friends as boys, and, despite the fact that both were now bent with age, the meeting was cordial and pleasant. Among the many reminiscences that such occasions are wont to evoke, was that of the escape of Hampton above related. "Well, come now, Anthony," said McGirtt, "suppose we had been in each other's shoes that night, what would you have done?" "Let you go on and be hanged, by George," said Hampton; "it would have been a great pity, I know now, since you have turned out such a clever fellow, but the truth must be told."

Johnson, so frequently quoted, gives us the information that Daniel McGirtt ended his checkered career at the home of Colonel James, in misery but not in want, and that his widow long survived him.

CHAPTER XV.

Washington's Visit.

In the second year of his Presidency, Washington made a tour of the South, that he might see this section of the new nation, make the personal acquaintance of the leading citizens, and inspect some of the notable battlefields of the recent war.

It is not surprising that, among interesting places, he elected to visit Camden, in whose soil many heroes of that great conflict were sleeping and where two of his best generals had suffered severe repulses.

A visit from the great and beloved "Father of his Country," at the zenith of his glory, was indeed an honor to any community, and we are glad, from the contemporary Charleston papers, and from other sources, to be able to give an authentic account of so momentous an occasion.

The President set out from Philadelphia in March, 1791, making stops at Fredericksburg, Richmond, Wilmington, and Savannah—the southernmost point reached.

On the return trip, he passed through Augusta, Ga., coming thence to the pretty little Carolina capital on the Congaree. At Granby he was met, on May 23d, by a number of gentlemen on horseback and a troop of cavalry from Camden commanded by "Captain Kershaw" (presumably John). Crossing the Ferry, he was conducted, by way of the State House, to his quarters, where, next day, he was introduced to the prominent citizens of Columbia, as well as to a great many visitors from the neighboring villages of Granby, Winnsboro,

Camden, Stateburg, Bellville and Orangeburg. The attentions shown him, both social and official, were of an elaborate character.

At four o'clock on the morning of the 25th, accompanied by his suite and his secretary, Major Jackson, he started for Camden.

His retinue was stately, as befitted so august a personage. First came the great white chariot in which His Excellency rode, drawn by four stalwart horses—the same that served him, without change, throughout the entire journey. Next was a two-horse baggage wagon, followed by two mounted servants, leading an extra saddle horse. Captain Kershaw's Troop of Light Horse, as an escort, with a number of mounted men from the adjacent country, brought up the rear.

From Washington's famous Diary of this tour, we learn that one of the horses had foundered, and so the trip was rendered even more than usually tedious. The following entry will appeal to those who have passed over the same route in more recent years:

"Breakfasted at an indifferent house 22 miles from the town*—the first we came to. * * * The Road from Columbia to Camden, excepting a mile or two at each place, goes over the most miserable pine barren I ever saw, being quite a white sand and very hilly.

"On the Wateree, within a mile and a half of which the town (Camden) stands, the lands are very good; they culture Corn, Tobacco, & Indigo. Vessels carrying 50 or 60 Hhds. of Tobo. come up to the Ferry at this place, at which there is a Tobacco Ware-House."

The river was reached at midday. Here an expectant throng, including almost the entire population of

---

*Columbia.

Camden, were assembled to greet the distinguished guest, and the plaudits with which he was hailed, as his boat drew across the stream, were as hearty as they were vociferous.

The largely augmented train now proceeded into the town, where a halt was made in the central public square and the following address of welcome was delivered by the Intendant of the town and chairman of the reception committee, Col. Joseph Kershaw:

"Sir: Impressed with every sentiment of friendship, esteem and gratitude which can actuate the human heart, and amid the congratulations and voluntary homage of freemen and fellow-citizens that accompany your progress in the Southern States, the citizens of Camden and its vicinity, in whose country the ravages and distresses of war were once as severely and painfully felt, as the blessings of peace and good government are now gratefully cherished, yielding to the universal sentiment, but more to the impulse of our own hearts, beg leave to express the satisfaction and happiness we feel, at seeing among us our great deliverer—the venerated chief, who heretofore under the standard of liberty, defended the invaded rights of America, and led her troops with success through all the doubtful changes of a perilous war; now our first civil magistrate, under whose administration we forget our dangers and perilous past, and rest in the perfect enjoyment of those invaluable rights secured to us by his labours.

"We congratulate you, Sir, on your return thus far; and we hail your arrival in this town with a welcome, though less splendid, yet not less sincere, than what you have anywhere received.

"And now, Sir, permit us to bring to your recollection that noble foreigner, the Baron deKalb, whose dust, with that of many other brave officers, is entombed on the plains of Camden; to him we owe this grateful mention, who, despising ease and inaction, when the liberties of his fellow-creatures (however distant) were threatened, entered the lists in our late contest, and fell bravely fighting for the rights of mankind.

"May Almighty God long preserve a life so beloved, and make the future as happy as the past has been illustrious; and at the close of a life rendered thus illustrious, may you greet on the happy shores of blissful immortality, the kindred spirits of those heroes and patriots, who have in all past ages been distinguished as the guardians of liberty and the fathers of their country.

"Signed by order of the inhabitants of Camden and its vicinity:

> "Joseph Kershaw
> "John Chesnut
> "William Lang
> "Isaac DuBose
> "Adam F. Brisbane
> "James Kershaw
> "Joseph Brevard
> "Isaac Alexander
> "Samuel Boykin
> "D. Starke."

To this the President responded:

"Gentlemen: The acknowledgments which your respectful and affectionate address demand, I offer to you with unfeigned sincerity. I receive your congratulations with pleasure, and estimating your welcome of me to Camden by a conviction of its cordiality, I render those thanks to your polite and hospitable attentions to which they are so justly entitled.

"Your grateful remembrance of that excellent friend and gallant officer, the Baron deKalb, does honor to the goodness of your hearts; with your regrets I mingle mine for his loss, and to your praise I join the tribute of my esteem for his memory.

"May you largely participate the national advantages, and may your past sufferings and dangers, endured and braved in the cause of freedom, be long contrasted with your future safety and happiness.

"(Signed) G. Washington."

After this stately function, the committee "shewed the President to the house especially prepared for him."* Tradition says that this was the residence of Mrs. Brisbane,† near the southeast corner of Fair and York streets, then presumably untenanted. It was Washington's invariable rule, on this trip, not to accept invitations to private houses; this left him, to quote his own words, "unincumbered by any engagements, and, by a uniform adherence to it, I shall avoid giving umbrage."

That evening, he was entertained at a great public dinner, at which were present a large number of ladies and gentlemen, including many visitors. This was probably given at the home of Col. John Chesnut, a large frame building still standing on the northwest corner of King and Fair streets, as Miss Mary Kershaw told her nephew, Judge Kershaw, that she attended a reception to General Washington in that house.

The published report of the affair states that the Chief Magistrate graciously sought an introduction to each of the ladies and that "every one took delight in contemplating this dignified personage, whose presence inspired and animated every social and convivial breast."

---

*Charlestown *City Gazette and Daily Advertiser,* June 6, 1791.
†The site of the present Brasington house.

The banquet lasted until the "wee sma' hours" and doubtless lost some of its stateliness before the seventeenth toast was drunk. The ladies wisely retired after the third, and the President withdrew about midnight. The quaint old sentiments responded to may interest some readers:

"1. The united states* of America. May they rival in the arts and sciences, as they have already equalled in arms and excelled in the mild arts of peace and government, the polished and enlightened nations of Europe.

"2. The Congress. May wisdom inspire, virtue direct, and unanimity inform, their councils.

"3. (By the President.) The Governor and state of South Carolina.

"4. Louis the 16th and the French Nation, the noble and generous allies of America. May a true spirit of freedom, tempered with moderation and generous politeness, prevail in the constitutional reform.

"5. The Vice-President of the united states. May he long bless his country with the ability and integrity that has hitherto characterized him.

"6. The memory of General Greene. May his name inspire us with gratitude so long as his military atchievements excite our applause.

"7. The memory of the brave Baron deKalb. May every generous American mix the tributary tear of grateful remembrance with the dust that covers over his grave.

"8. General Lincoln. May a generous country never forget his steady virtue, patriotism and services.

"9. The memory of the brave martyrs in the cause of American liberty. May their names ever be grateful

---

*Note throughout the significant absence of capitals in the spelling of United States. This is from the *City Gazette and Daily Advertiser*.

to our memories; and may their fates animate posterity with the love of freedom and their country.

"10. The brave seamen of America, who fought and died in the glorious cause.

"11. The agricultural and commercial interests of the united states. May they advance hand in hand, and reciprocally support each other.

"12. The manufactories of the United States. May they rapidly improve; and may fashion favor their growth.

"13. The fair of America. May wisdom with modesty, beauty with prudence, and every virtuous attraction, always distinguish them.

"14. True religion, unmixed with hypocricy and intoleration; but distinguished for charity and benevolence.

"15. (By the President.) The town of Camden, and prosperity to it.

(And, after the President retired)

"16. The President of the united states.
"17. Lady Washington."

Early next morning, Washington rode on horseback to the grave of DeKalb,* where he reverently paused for a few moments, then on to the remains of the "works and redoubts erected by the British,"† all of which he carefully inspected.

---

*Near the old Presbyterian Cemetery.

†This mention, in the paper of 1791, of other "works," besides the redoubts, brings up a mooted question as to the age and purpose of the embankment extending on the south side of Meeting street, from the Presbyterian Cemetery to the Quaker burying-ground. Tradition says it was an earthwork thrown up by the British, presumably as a shield to the line of soldiers' huts, which extended along its northern side. Certainly the huge pines that grow thickly, almost in a row, on its top and sides, would indicate that it had not been put there within the past century. One of

His northward journey was then resumed, with a number of mounted citizens in attendance. Halts were made at both the fields of Hobkirk and Gum Swamp, and notes of his observations carefully entered in his Diary.

At the latter battleground, he "very affectionately" took leave of his Camden friends. To their urgent invitation to prolong his stay, he replied that he had already been several days longer on his tour than he had intended and that public business demanded his immediate return.

Fourteen miles above Camden, he records in the Diary, that he stopped at "one Sutton's," and, twelve miles farther on, at James Ingram's.

Thence his route lay through Charlotte, Salisbury, Salem, Guilford, and other towns—at each of which he received almost regal honors—until he finally reached his beautiful estate on the Potomac, Mount Vernon, where he enjoyed a much needed rest.

Irving, in his Life of Washington, says that the whole journey of eighteen hundred and eighty-seven miles had been accomplished without any interruption from sickness, bad weather, or any untoward accident.

our oldest citizens, however, states positively that, as a boy, he was told that this bank was built about 1830 by Col. William Nixon along the northern edge of a then open field that belonged to him, for the purpose of forcing travel to keep to the proper route which ran close by the inclosures of the Presbyterian churchyard, turning at right angles on Wateree street to enter the old Ferry road. The same venerable witness says, further, that, within his memory, the present road, cutting through the embankment, was made by John McKain, owner of the stage-coach line from Raleigh to Augusta, because his stage had upset by the Nixon inclosure, breaking the leg of one of his passengers. Diligent effort has failed to establish which of these theories, or traditions, as to the picturesque old embankment, is correct; but we incline strongly to a belief in its Revolutionary origin, even though it is not indicated on the supposedly authentic map of the fortifications of Camden, which we have elsewhere copied from Johnson's "Life of Greene."

CHAPTER XVI.
Citizen-Minister Genêt.

At the outbreak of the French Revolution, all classes and parties in the young Republic of the West accorded the most enthusiastic sympathy and moral support to the fierce democracy of France. This was due partly to a belief in the doctrine of the rights of man, but even more, perhaps, to a still violent antipathy towards Great Britain and to a sense of gratitude for the aid France had, but a few years before, given America.

Typical expression of this popular sentiment may be found in the many pro-French meetings held at Camden at the time, of which the old papers tell us, and especially in the cordial reception tendered the first Minister of France to the United States when he passed through Camden.

At the earliest recorded celebration here of the Fourth of July,* which was in 1792, we find the assemblage drinking "Success to the Reformation of the French Nation. May all arbitrary governments experience like changes."

This was but a month before the slaughter of the Swiss

---

*In the *South Carolina Gazette* of July 5, 1792, its Camden correspondent says of this celebration:

"The anniversary of our independence was welcomed with the usual demonstrations of joy by our citizens. The Camden company of light horse, and the militia of the village and its vicinity, assembled in the morning. After having performed their respective evolutions, they marched to the remains of a British fort, where some pieces of ordnance had been erected; the American colours were flying, and fifteen rounds were fired in honour of our glorious emancipation—striking contrast to what might have been seen on the same spot twelve years ago. A well-served dinner was prepared at the court-house, at which a very numerous and respectable company were present. The following toasts (each accompanied with a fire from the cannon) were drank after dinner, etc."

The British fort referred to was probably the Star Redoubt.

Guard at the Tuilleries, which was the end of the monarchy. The following September, the First Republic was declared, and, three months later, Edmond Charles Genêt was appointed "Citizen-Minister" to the United States. It proved an unfortunate selection.

He did not set out on his important mission until March, about the period of that frightful political nightmare, the Reign of Terror. Poor Louis had recently bowed before the Widow Guillotine, and his unhappy Queen was soon to follow. Such excesses had somewhat alienated the more conservative Federalists in this country, but the Republicans, led by Jefferson, continued their support; and so, when M. Genêt landed, April 17, 1793, at Charleston, S. C., he was received with every manifestation of delight. After accepting (and abusing) the hospitality of that generous city for a few days, he proceeded on his journey to Philadelphia, there to present his credentials to President Washington.

His route, by stage, brought him through Camden, which was reached on April 25th. Our good townspeople, learning of his approach and charmed to do honor to the infant French Republic in the person of her distinguished ambassador, had prepared to receive him in a style befitting his lofty office. Had they then known his conduct in Charleston and been able to foresee his subsequent notorious career in this country, their welcome might not have been so cordial.

At Town Creek he was met by the Camden Troop of Horse, and, under their escort, conducted to the residence, which, after the custom of the period, was placed at the disposal of the honored guest.

Here the Intendant, Isaac Dubose, delivered the following address:

"Citizen Minister: The citizens of the town and district of Camden wait on you to congratulate you on your arrival in this country, and to express the pleasure and satisfaction they feel in seeing among them the representative of the republic of France.

"Your nation has a just claim to our gratitude, for the services rendered us in the hour of our distress, whilst we contended against tyranny and oppression.

"But, independent of this tie, we feel ourselves warmly and generously attached to her, for the noble example which she now gives to the world, of hatred to tyrants and abhorrence of oppression; and the ardent desire which she manifests of making man *happy,* by making him *free.* May success ensue her endeavors, and may present and future generations have cause to venerate and honour the name of Frenchmen for ever.

"Science and knowledge have not yet enlightened sufficiently any other nation in Europe to emulate her glorious example; she stands *alone* in the noble contest, and bids defiance to the united despots of the world, who have combined against her; and we trust the invincible spirit of liberty will carry her through all her difficulties with honor and glory, to the confusion of her foes.

"We wish you much satisfaction, with the blessing of health, as you travel to Philadelphia; and may our fellow-citizens evince, by their attention and respect to you, their attachment and their esteem for your republic."

In reply, the minister thus expressed himself:

"The citizen-minister plenipotentiary of France to the United States, to the citizens of the town and district of Camden, April 26, 1793, 2nd year of the French Republic.

"Citizens: I receive with the greatest pleasure, in the name of the nation I have the honor to represent, the expression of your gratitude and of your friendship for her. It will be extremely agreeable to the French Republic to know that you appreciate her glorious labours, and that, in following the virtuous example given by the United States, in embracing the principles which they supported with so much courage, she has merited your applause and your most sincere wishes for the accomplishment of her extended task.

"Since my arrival in America, citizens, I have not enjoyed so much satisfaction as I do today; and I see that the more I penetrate into the interior parts of your happy country, and communicate with those generous veterans who enjoy now the blessings of a rural life, after having fought so bravely for the cause of their country and liberty, the more I shall find that my fellow-citizens have friends and brothers in this continent.

"I thank you, citizens, for the obliging wishes you have formed for the success of my journey to Philadelphia. I will never forget your kind and brotherly reception, and desire you to be convinced of my utmost regard and unbounded esteem. GENÊT."

That evening a sumptuous dinner was tendered the minister and his suite. The musty chronicle* from which we obtain our account of the reception states that the utmost harmony and brotherly love prevailed. The Marseillaise and other songs of both nations were sung standing, and the following sentiments, among many others, were proposed:

"The Republic of France—May her success induce mankind to be free." (By the Intendant.)

---

*Charleston *City Gazette and Daily Advertiser*, May 4, 1793.

"Everlasting friendship and amity between the republic of France and the United States of America." (By the Minister.)

"The author of the Rights of Man and Common Sense." (By Dr. Alexander.)

"Liberty and no King." (By Capt. Joseph Brevard.)

The next morning the distinguished visitor departed northward.

Acting under instructions from his government, M. Genêt had no sooner set foot in Charleston, before presenting his credentials to the President, than he began enlisting American sailors to man privateers, which, in utter defiance of our neutrality and treaty laws, preyed upon British ships even in American waters.

The attitude of the National Assembly of France towards the United States at this period was singularly arrogant.

Encouraged by such attentions as had been showered upon him in Charleston, Camden and other places, the head of the poor citizen-minister seems to have been completely turned. Congress, the Cabinet, even the President himself, were to be browbeat into active aid of the French Revolutionists. His insolence reached its climax when he threatened to appeal from Washington to the people of the States. The placid Father of his Country was then aroused to a white heat of indignation, and the recall of the objectionable diplomat was peremptorily demanded.

The disgraced minister did not return to France, where his popularity had vanished, but settled in New York, married a daughter of Governor Clinton, and died at his home on the Hudson in 1834.

That this unfortunate experience with M. Genêt did not dampen the ardor of the people of this section for the French patriots may be inferred from the following account* of a grand rally in Camden on July 14, 1794, in memory of the fall of the Bastile:

"Yesterday (July 14) was celebrated here as the anniversary of a great revolution. The American and French flags were displayed in the morning, and at two o'clock the citizens of the town and vicinity assembled at Dinkins' Tavern,† inspired with those sentiments which arise from the contemplation of a political change which has restored to freedom 25 millions of people and opens a prospect of liberty diffused over the globe. * * *

"The company dined together in great good humor, and the evening was concluded with a ball, where there was a brilliant assemblage of ladies."

A few of the toasts responded to were:

"The French Republic, one and indivisible, pure and permanent."

"The Rights of the injured—satisfaction or vengeance. May British insolence and knavery soon be taught humility and honesty by free republicans."

"Universal liberty founded on the rights of man."

"The people of Great Britain and Ireland. May they soon adopt French fashions in politics."

"A scarcity of kings and increase of republics throughout the globe."

"The fair Sans-Culottes of America!"‡

"King Prow—may all kings who will not follow his example follow that of Louis XVI."

The significance of this sentiment is explained in a note attached to the *Gazette's* report:

*Charleston *City Gazette*, etc., August 14, 1794.
†A large two-storied inn on the northwest corner of Broad and Meeting streets. Here M. Genêt had been banqueted.
‡One would like to know the author of this strictly original tribute to the fair sex.

"[Prow was the last king of the Catawba nation, a fellow of mean capacity and incapable of governing his reduced tribe. They had sense enough to see that he did them no other service than to eat their homminy, and determined to dethrone him. To prevent his subjects shedding each other's blood, he voluntarily resigned his crown,* and they chose a general for his talents who has ever since presided over them very happily. What a pity certain people on a certain island have not as good optics as the Catawbas!]"

This spirit of hatred for Great Britain, intensified by the War of 1812, was strong within the memory of men now living.

A highly respected Scotch merchant who settled in Camden about 1845 has told us that, even then, the Englishman was looked upon in this country with dislike and suspicion and that goods of British style or manufacture had absolutely no sale here, French goods and fashions controlling the market.

*Cornshucks, possibly, as symbolic of his capacity for corn meal.

Joseph Brevard.

ILLUSTRATION O.

CHAPTER XVII.

JOSEPH BREVARD.

The career of none of her citizens affords to Camden more just cause for pride than that of Joseph Brevard. Upright, unostentatious, industrious, he performed a deal of excellent and valuable work. As soldier, statesman, lawyer and jurist he may be cited for imitation.

The first known ancestor of the Brevard family was a French Huguenot, who refugeed among the Scotch-Irish of North Ireland, where he fell in with the McKnitts, with whom he emigrated to America, settling on Elk River in Maryland. A daughter of that family became his wife. Their children were six, of whom John Brevard, with three others, between 1740 and 1750, came to North Carolina. In Maryland John had married Miss McWhorter, whose brother, Doctor McWhorter, came also to North Carolina and founded the noted Queen Museum at Charlotte.

John located in Iredell County, N. C. At the outbreak of the Revolution, his children numbered twelve, eight sons and four daughters. Joseph, our subject, the youngest son and tenth child, was born July 19, 1766.

An incident is related of Joseph's mother, showing her to have been a Spartan matron. When some of Cornwallis's troops came upon her house, they found her alone at home. Having heard of their approach, she had hidden her daughters in a swamp. The officer in command ordered the house to be fired, which was promptly done. The old lady strove to save the furniture, but the soldiers tossed it back into the flames. The ruffians tore her clothing, but she escaped personal injury. They justified themselves by saying she had "eight d——d rebel sons in the army."

Joseph entered the Revolutionary service a mere boy, and in 1782, at the age of sixteen, was commissioned as lieutenant in the North Carolina line, filling this position till the end of the war. His brother Alexander said of him that he was so small and delicate that he felt sorry for him when his turn came to mount guard. According to Wheeler (History of North Carolina) he served for a time as Secretary to General ———— (name not given, Arnold probably), who was in command of Philadelphia and who had discovered that young Joseph could write a fine hand. From all which we may well infer that he was an exceedingly manly, precocious and accomplished youth.

Immediately after the war he settled in Camden, which seems to have attracted so many of the Revolutionary soldiers who had come within its influence during military operations. In 1789, at the age of twenty-three, he was elected by the Legislature to the responsible position of Sheriff of Camden District, then covering the wide extent of seven counties, and an arduous post in those unsettled times. The returns on some of his old writs are still in our court records, showing a very neat, artistic hand. In 1792 he was admitted to practice of law, and March 17, 1793, he married Rebecca, daughter of Col. Eli Kershaw.

It requires only an inspection of our earlier court records to show that his success at the bar was eminent. William Falconer, that strong, rugged old Scotchman of Chesterfield, was for a time his associate. It is an interesting fact that the gifted and erratic Charles Motte Lide, of Cheraw, read law in Brevard's Camden office. Of Lide, Hugh S. Legare, Attorney-General in Jackson's cabinet, declared that he was the greatest natural genius he had ever known. For the graphic story of his eccentric course, reference is made to Bishop Gregg's History of the Cheraws, wherein he depicts Lide's vagaries through law, poetry, planting and back to law, and his final argument, pursuing some chimera, before a legislative committee, who were moved to tears at his haggard, pitiful appearance.

In 1793 Brevard began the compilation of the law reports which bear his name, continued down to 1815. In December, 1801, he was elected one of the Judges of the highest State Court. The following year he lost his wife and was left with a helpless family. He continued, however, to serve on the Bench, how well is thus testified by Judge O'Neall: "No Judge had a better reputation or was looked to with more confidence. Judge Brevard's opinions and notes, scattered all through the three volumes of his reports, show that he was a man of untiring industry, learning and taste. They, with his admirable Digest of the State Law to 1814, now and forever constitute a better memorial of him than anything which now can be offered." This work was accomplished under the burden of ill health, which caused him to resign in 1815.

After release from taxing labor his health improved, and in 1818 he contested with James C. Postell, of Sumter, the seat in Congress from this district, and was elected. From a letter of his written from Washington, January, 1820, relating to the great Missouri question, the following extracts are taken, as illustrating the times and his style of composition:

"The principal question whether Missouri shall be admitted unconditionally is yet to be debated and settled. The crisis is awful and big with consequences fatal to the peace and safety of the Southern States. Authors by trade and scribblers of every size and degree have been busy and eager to distinguish themselves by some literary achievement in the crusade against modern Saracens, the holders of slaves.

"This apple of discord thrown amongst the States, is intended doubtless to produce division, hostility and finally disunion of the States, unless a certain political party can again become dominant and again sway the scepter which has been so long departed from Judah. The public mind of the North and East has been so charged with the electric spirit of reform and regeneration, that it really seems as if the salvation of their souls and bodies both depended on the renunciation of the right of claiming any property in slaves by their brethren of the South, and a practice which has existed for more than a century, and rights which have been constantly claimed and exercised, and which have never been till of late disputed, must all at once be yielded up and forever renounced, without hesitation and without any regard to consequences.

"Those who calculate on emerging to honor and power amidst the tumult and confusion which is expected to ensue, may find themselves wofully deceived. I have been led to these reflections from a persuasion that the fixed object of the advocates for the power claimed of imposing conditions upon their admission into the Union, and of the doctrines avowed in support of such claim, is a general and complete emancipation in all the States.

"A man must have very slight acquaintance with the world, and very little knowledge of the men in it, especially those who do the business of it in public life, who would much credit those who profess to be actuated in this question by the canting, hypocritical and puritanical motives which are often assigned as the ruling principle by which they are governed. The most mischievous and dangerous designs are sometimes disguised under the specious cloak of sanctity and a scrupulous adherence to conscientious punctilios. These scruples easily relax when a question of interest affects themselves; not so when it affects others.

"I sincerely deprecate the discord and hostile feelings which this controversy has engendered and will give birth to, and am not without apprehensions that it may rend in pieces the bands of federal union, and tumble down the firmest fabric of government that has ever yet been raised on earth."

Here we have a most impressive and prophetic forecast of the "Irrepressible Conflict" and its results. No public utterance of the day was more discerning, comprehensive or typical of Southern sentiment.

In the *Camden Gazette* of August 10, 1820, Judge Brevard announces that his private affairs would not longer admit of his serving in Congress, and that he would decline reelection. That he would have been returned, it has been said, was not a matter of doubt. To succeed him Judge John S. Richardson, of Sumter, was elected in October, 1820, without any opposition and without any solicitation on his part, a well-nigh unprecedented compliment in the political annals of this State. Judge Richardson declined to accept the tendered honor. Another election was ordered for February, 1821. By this time Judge Brevard had reconsidered his previous decision, and authorized the announcement that if elected he would serve. However, James C. Postell, his old antagonist, and General James Blair, then a new star, entered the lists. Blair was elected. In October following, 1821, at the age of fifty-five, Judge Brevard passed away at Camden. He lies interred, probably in the Quaker Cemetery, without a stone to mark his honored grave.

No worthier comment may be passed upon him than that of Judge O'Neall:

"In every situation and office of life he did his duty. What more can or ought to be said, unless it be to say that he feared God and kept his commandments, which is declared in the inspired volume to be 'the whole duty of man.'"

The mother of Judge Brevard's wife was Mary, a daughter of Capt. John Cantey. Thus the descendants of Judge Brevard trace also to Cantey ancestry.

Judge Brevard left four children: Dr. Alfred Brevard. who married Harriet Chesnut McRae, daughter of Duncan McRae, leaving at his death, in 1836, two children, Alfred and Harriet, both now living in this community; Edward and Eugene, who died childless, and a daughter, Sarah Aurora, who married Benjamin T. Elmore.

A brother of Judge Brevard, Ephraim, was the author of the famous Mecklenburg Declaration of Independence. Another, Alexander, after serving with distinction in the Northern campaigns under Washington, was acting as quartermaster under General Gates at the disastrous battle of Camden. Others of his brethren showed great activity and talent, and no family of the South or North performed more distinguished or patriotic service in the Revolution.

CHAPTER XVIII.

MINTON'S MILL.

About twenty-five miles northeast of Camden, in a valley of that sandy region, the public road leading to Cheraw crosses a clear, brisk stream,* near the site of an old mill, traces of which are still visible. The surroundings are waste and desolate. The old field on the nearby hill has long been abandoned to broom-sedge, fennel and life-everlasting, badges of poverty and desertion. Here a century ago was David Minton's mill and home.

David, whose father, Jesse Minton, had lived here before him, was a millwright, and by diligence had acquired some means out of his trade and these poor lands. Life in those parts and in those days must have been decidedly rough and hardy. Churches and schools were scarce, but the country tavern of the roadside, where the traveler could find board and grog and the neighbors grog without board, was not so rare. This old institution, scene of many an ancient brawl, has long been a thing of the past. We may well suppose it to have been a source of incorrigible evil to the forefathers. It may be sufficiently curious to note some of their regulations on the subject.

On the first pages of the record book of the County Court, at its opening in Camden, February 28, 1791, Adam F. Brisband,† Samuel Boykin and John Kershaw presiding, the following entry catches the eye:

---

*"Jumping Gully" Creek, not to be confused with the stream of that name in West Wateree.

†This was the way he repeatedly signed his surname, which later members of the family converted into *Brisbane*.

"Ordered that the following Rates be established in the County of Kershaw for the ensuing year for Tavern Keepers:

"Jamaica Rum, when drunk in Tavern per Quart 4/, pr pint 2/, ½ pint 1/2, p. Gill 7d.

"Grog of ditto pr Quart 1/, 1 pint 7d.

"Punch of Ditto 1/8 pr Quart, with Loaf Sugar and Fresh fruit; 1 pint Do 1/

"French Brandy and Gin at the Same Rates as above

"Good West India Rum pr Quart 3/ per pint 1/6, ½ pint 9d.

"Grog of Do. pr Quart 1/, pint 6d.

"Northward Rum pr Quart 2/. pr pint 1/. ½ pint 7d.

"Grog of Do. p. Quart 7d. p. pint 4d.

"Best Madeira Wine pr Bottle 6/, p. pint 3/

"Good Port Do.

"Fayall & Clarett pr Bottle 2/4

"Lisbon & Teneriffe 4/ p Bottle

"Good London Bottle Porter 2/4.

"Bristol Cyder 2/ p. Bottle. Country Do. 9d.

"Peach Brandy the same as West Ind. Rum

"Whiskey the same as Northward Rum

"For Tody instead of Grog made of Loaf Sugar add 3d. p Quart & 2d. pr pint

"Wine and Sagaree add 7d. more to Bottle

"Breackfast or Supper with Tea or Coffee 1/

"Dinner with Grog or Other Liquors 1/6, without 1/.

"Horse Keeping 24 Hours with Plenty of Good Hay or Blades & 6 Quarts of Corn or Oats 2/ the first Night, 1/6 Every 24 Hours after. Corn or Oats Extra p. Quart 2d.

"Lodging pr Night 6d. on Good Feather bed, with Linen, Mattrass 4d.

"All Entertainment bespoke where a bill of fare is Given in the Price to be agreed by the parties."

We may imagine with what gusto that judicial trio concerted this unique schedule of toddies and grogs, for the construction of which they were doubtless eminently qualified, and with what zest and diligence they tested its merits. The powers and privileges of a modern Dispensary "Board of Control" pale into insignificance before theirs.

Down stream from David Minton, a mile or two, resided Lovick* Rochell, on the fertile lands of Lynches Creek, of which he owned a wide extent. In their day they had doubtless been chums at Danzy's tavern; but David was prudent, and Lovick reckless. A matter of money caused a deadly breach between them.

Lovick had purchased several slaves from Jesse Minton, David's father, giving a mortgage of the slaves to secure the price. Upon the death of Jesse a difference arose between David and Lovick over this mortgage, the one demanding payment or the slaves, the other claiming it had been paid. In the midst of the contention the slaves disappeared from Lovick's possession. Perhaps, not knowing to whom they belonged, they may have run away.

Lovick doubtless believed that David was privy to their departure, and, in the April Court, A. D. 1800, at Camden, indicted David Minton upon the charge "that the said David on Dec. 8th 1799, at the house of the said Lovick, three negro slaves, Nat, Cele, and Joe, proper goods and chattels of the said Lovick, did feloniously aid and assist in running away and departing from the service of the said Lovick." Among the papers in the case is an affidavit of Joshua and Ruth Lisenbe,† stating that they had heard Jesse Minton, in March, 1796, acknowledge to Lodowick Rochell, at his house, that the

---
*Contraction for Lodowick.
†Lizenby, now Bethune, derived its name from this old family.

slaves had been paid for. However, the jury, Duncan McRae foreman, found "no bill," and threw out the indictment.

This failure caused Lovick the sharpest chagrin, and whetted his animosity. In the heart of Lovick's plantation lay a tract of 300 acres, partly on each side of Lynches Creek, which divides Kershaw and Chesterfield Counties. This land he had purchased at a judgment sale against James Holmes. In 1802, a year or so after the indictment against David, suit is brought against Lovick by James Holmes, son and heir of the former owner, to recover this land, on the ground that it had been illegally sold by the Coroner of Chesterfield County. Holmes, who won the case, was represented by Abram Blanding and Joseph Brevard of Camden, and Rochell by Falconer, a notable attorney of Chesterfield. When the suit was brought young Holmes was living in Georgia, but David Minton was his agent on the spot, and was viewed by Rochell, with feelings other than complacent, as the instigator and real author of this, his second discomfiture.

The turning question of fact in the case had been as to young Holmes's age. If he was over twenty-six, Rochell, by having held the land in possession for five years after his majority, under the law of that day, had acquired title. After the verdict against him Rochell brought a suit in equity to prevent its enforcement, alleging that in the former trial David Minton, agent of Holmes, or Blanding, his attorney, had fraudulently suppressed the family Bible and other testimony which would have proven that Holmes was over twenty-six. This injunction suit, or some phase of it, was pending in Charleston Court, where in January, 1805, all parties were in attendance. The termination seems to have been in favor of Rochell, but this in no wise ended the retaliation between him and Minton, which developed into a veritable *cause celebre*. Its outlines have floated as a picturesque local tradition, which we are enabled to recount with some authentic detail by reference to the old record, which seems to have been undisturbed since tied in its original tape. Thus the sequel may be told in the words of the witnesses.

Thomas Minton states that his brother David had a law suit with Rochell depending in Charleston January last (1805); that he was with his brother; that Rochell there abused said David and seemed to bear great malice towards him, and signified by his language that he wished him out of the way.

Charles Evans tells that on the 26th of February last at Danzy's tavern, in Kershaw District, he was present when Lovick Rochell and David Minton were also present. That said Rochell, without reasonable cause or provocation, used very abusive language towards Minton, spit in his face, drew his knife and attempted to stab said Minton, but was prevented by the company present.

For this assault Minton entered an indictment against Rochell, for which he was arrested. This added fresh fuel to Rochell's frenzy. He swaggered the more, and in his drinking bouts tried the harder to drive Minton to a personal encounter. Drink had raised his hatred to mania.

Edward C. DeBruhl declared that on April 9th he slept in Camden at Caston's tavern with Lovick Rochell. In the night he talked very much, being intoxicated, and seemed to be addressing one Kemp, saying: "G— d— him, I'll kill him. He shall not enjoy any of my property," and deponent believes he meant David Minton.

Ambrose Bryant states that on Monday, April 8th, he

met with Lovick Rochell in Camden, who took him aside and asked him whether he could not prove that David Minton had stolen a horse from him, the said Rochell. Bryant denied that he could prove any such thing, and advised Rochell to make up his dispute with Minton, or he would be a ruined man. Whereupon Rochell declared that before Minton should have any of his property, one of them should lose their lives.

Then comes another prosecution in Court, in the files of which is to be found entry of the following *writ*:

    David Minton ⎫
         vs.   ⎬ Slander. April, 1805.
    Lovick Rochell ⎭

This wrought the morbid Rochell to the last degree of desperation. His bluster changed to calm. The rod of open rage turned into the venomous serpent.

On Saturday, April 13, 1805, Rochell was journeying homewards from Camden. With him rode Isaiah Jenkins, Jesse Fley, Joel Bliss and James Perkins, the latter his nephew. They no doubt stopped more than once at the wayside taverns. The event shows that mischief was brewing in that company. On reaching home that evening Rochell *slept,* so his daughter states, a mark of hardihood beyond a Macbeth.

That day David Minton had been busy rebuilding the mill above mentioned, known by his name. At evening he sat with his family at the fireside of their log house, taking tea, the beverage which cheers and civilizes the world. David was just raising the cup to his lips when a deadly volley was discharged through the very chimney nook upon this quiet group. David fell sprawling, and feet were heard shuffling on the outside and scurrying away.

The report of the gun, which was heavily charged,

traveled down the valley until it reached the intent ears of Lovick Rochell, who had for some time risen from his nap, and sat listening on his porch. He rose and went into the house, exclaiming, "the work is done." Young Webb, a schoolboy staying in the house, heard the words and had also heard the report of the gun.

The next morning David died. The inquest fixed suspicion upon Lovick Rochell, Isaiah Jenkins, Jesse Fley and James Perkins. Jenkins could not be found. He had immediately disappeared and was never after heard of—or rather not until lately, as explained hereafter. There is a tradition that Rochell defied arrest and had to be taken by a strong posse, but no record confirms this. Fley was taken. Judge Brevard refused them bail, but released Perkins.

For some reason the prosecution was long delayed, wisely it turned out, for in time suspicion ripened into proof. After a term or two, Rochell was released on bail. Fley broke jail in 1806. In 1807 he was recaptured by Fletcher of Flat Rock, leader of a wagon party on its way to Charleston, thereby earning three hundred dollars reward.

Four years had passed, but in that time, Blanding, acting State's attorney, had completed the chain of evidence. On Thursday, April 20, 1809, the prisoners, Rochell and Fley, were brought to trial, defended by Messrs. Witherspoon and Richardson. The stout old Falconer, Rochell's former attorney, had died in 1805, in consequence of a forced trip from Cheraw to Camden and back, in one day, sixty miles each way. He had hurried over at Rochell's urgent call on his arrest for Minton's murder. Judge William Smith (afterwards Senator from South Carolina) presided at the trial, and as Judge O'Neall relates, reported all the evidence in the case minutely, from memory, to the appeal Court.

The indictment, with much of the elaborate verbiage of those times omitted, ran to the effect:

"That Isaiah Jenkins, laborer, moved and seduced by the instigation of the Devil, on the 13th April, 1805, with force and arms at Minton's Mill, of his malice aforethought, upon one David Minton, in the peace of God and of the State then and there being, a certain gun loaded and charged with gunpowder and divers leaden bullets, against and upon the said David Minton did shoot and discharge, giving the said David Minton two mortal wounds of which the said David Minton on the fourteenth of April died.

"That Jesse Fley, laborer, was present aiding and abetting.

"That Lovick Rochell, planter, instigated by the Devil, the said Isaiah Jenkins and Jesse Fley, the felony and murder aforesaid to be done and committed, of his malice aforethought, did incite, counsel and procure."

Some of the evidence survives with the record.

Francis Robertson testified that he was present when David Minton was killed. Said Minton was shot with two balls through his back. It appeared the gun rested in an aperture between the logs of the house at the chimney. One ball passed through his body and lodged in the forefinger of the right hand. Minton fell back exclaiming: "Lord have mercy, they have done it at last." Two persons were heard to run from the chimney, and two tracks plain to be seen next morning. Minton retained his senses to the last moment, and when asked whom he suspected said: "Fley."

About eight days previous Fley came to the house where witness and Minton were at dinner with the hands who were raising the mill. They invited Fley to join them at dinner, but he declined, and sat with his eyes direct to where the opening was at the chimney. Minton remarked after he had gone, "He is after no good."

Elizabeth Minton testified that as David Minton, her husband, was drinking tea, about two hours after dark, a gun was discharged through the logs of the chimney, near where Minton sat. That upon being shot Minton cried out: "I am killed. They have done it at last. It was what I expected. Rochell has done it, or had it done by Fley."

Lovick Rochell made oath "that he is not guilty of the crime whereof he is charged. That on the morning of the 13th of April he left Camden and returned home, where he arrived at half-past three o'clock, and remained an hour in the house walking about and afterwards went to bed and slept until after sunset, and afterwards remained in the house all night. *That he has no knowledge of who were concerned in the murder of said David Minton.*" This statement he made on applying for bail.

Charlotte Rochell said that her father, Lovick Rochell, arrived at his home on the evening of the murder of David Minton before night, and remained at home without being absent therefrom all night, as she believes, as she saw him at dark and afterwards till ten o'clock, and again early in the morning. And the same statement was made by Elizabeth Rochell, wife of Lovick, and by Barsheba Clanton, his niece.

Jesse Fley saith he is innocent of the death of David Minton, and ignorant of the person or persons concerned. That he never had any personal quarrel with him. That on the evening of the night on which the murder happened, he went to the mill where Minton was, before sundown to see Moore, with whom he had business; that he left there before dark, and did not return again that night.

Thomas Havis said that he was employed as assistant to his brother John Havis, keeper of the common jail. That he happened to be in company with Jesse Fley in the room where he is kept confined, when Fley said that one Jenkins committed the murder; that Rochell had offered him, Fley, three hundred dollars to murder Minton, and counted out the money; that he refused to take it; that then Rochell offered him fifty dollars to bring Jenkins to him; that he procured a meeting; that Jenkins agreed to commit the murder for seven hundred dollars.

That afterwards a rifle was loaded with three bullets, which were patched or covered with homespun. Fley remarked that the cloth might lead to detection, whereupon the gun was discharged and reloaded with bullets covered with tow.

That he, Fley, went two or three times to the mill to ascertain when Minton was there; the last time he went Minton was there, whereupon he returned and informed Rochell and Jenkins *that Minton was at the mill;* that then Jenkins set out, but that he did not go himself.

Havis was brought back from Tennessee in order to give this testimony.

Mary Groves related that she lived with Mr. Havis at the jail. That she overheard James Perkins and Lovick Rochell conversing. Perkins said, "Uncle Lovick, G— d— you, you know you had the murder done, and I must suffer for it here in jail. Jesse Fley and Jenkins were the men that did it, and that night I lay innocent in my bed." Rochell made no denial, but desired he would hush, being apprehensive that she had heard what they said.

Rochell and Fley told her that if she would say nothing about what she had heard, they would give her a negro girl. They called up the girl, placed her hand in that of witness and gave her their writing thereon. Rochell said that Minton ought to have been killed long ago.

Mary Crane also testified to a conversation, overheard by her, between Fley and his brother-in-law, John Moore, after Fley had escaped and was at large. Fley said that he and Jenkins had divided the money paid by Rochell for killing Minton, and that Fley was to have two negroes besides.

On Saturday, the third day of trial, the jury found a verdict of guilty.

An appeal was made, one of our earliest reported cases. The ground taken was that accessories could not be convicted before trial of the principal. But the Court held that in murder, accessories were principals. The prisoners were sentenced to be hung on "Friday the ninth day of June 1809."

That day came. Tradition says that Rochell, some say his daughter, offered the jailer, John Havis, twenty thousand dollars (this may be an overestimate) in crisp bank bills, to allow an escape. To the honor of the jailer, tradition says also that he refused. We note that in the *Camden Gazette* of 1816 John Havis advertises as keeper of the "Eagle Tavern."

The hour arrived—Rochell to the last hard and defiant. The morning he spent playing cards in his cell with Fley.

In those days a certain tree, a gum, served as gallows. It stood in the hollow just east of Fair street, about the middle of the area inclosed by Laurens, Mill, Boundary and Fair streets.

The moment had arrived, the throng expectant, the cart with one of the condemned was at the spot. Rochell alighted and drew forth a decanter of choice whiskey, with which he had armed himself. The glass stopper stuck fast, so that he could not twist it out. He struck the neck off upon the wheel of the vehicle, and swallowed the contents, remarking, "I took breakfast in Camden today. I will take dinner in hell with David Minton." And so he went to the halter. One month later Jesse Fley swung from the same limb. The Camden gum bore, like ripe fruit, the felons of Minton's Mill.

What of Jenkins? As aforesaid, he escaped, and was never heard of again—until the year of grace 1901.

Coincidences are curious. A letter was lately received in Camden from one N., official in another State, a man of credit and repute, inquiring whether any record could be found here of the Rochell murder trial. The records of this case, undisturbed for near a century, had just been explored for the purposes of this sketch. The letter was duly answered and we were further informed by N. that his uncle, who had once lived in Kershaw District, about the year 1820 went on a visit to that other State. There he recognized Jenkins, who under the assumed name of "B." had married respectably, become the father of a family and was prospering. He had no heart to break up that family. He told the secret only to N.'s father. The descendants of Jenkins, or B., have been of good standing in that State, but the male members have all met violent deaths, the last of them having come to a tragic end shortly before N.'s letter of inquiry. N. writes to us: "Facts are sometimes stranger than fiction. I presume that I am the only person to whom my father told it, and you are the only one to whom I have ever communicated it. Secrecy is no longer necessary except in this: for the sake of the family, who are highly respectable people, I shall never tell who B. was."

At the summit of a steep bluff, on the western bank of Lynches Creek, near its confluence with Jumping Gully, a sequestered, overgrown place, an explorer may find an inclosure, some fifty feet square, surrounded by brick walls higher than a man's head. The lands once belonged to James Holmes. The center of the inclosure is marked by a large stone slab, bearing the following inscription:

MUTATIS MUTANDIS

Here rests the earthly remains
of
Mr. Lovick Rochell, Senr.
who was born in the year of
our Lord 1754, and departed
this life in the fifty-fifth year
of his age, leaving a disconsolate
wife, son and daughter to lament
their irreparable loss.
"An honest man's the noblest
work of God."

CHAPTER XIX.

EARLY REPRESENTATIVE FAMILIES.

[This chapter is devoted to brief genealogies of those families only whose ancestors settled at or near Camden prior to the year 1800. The various descents have not been brought further down than the past generation, from which point the living may carry out the connections for themselves. Nor could we include all those families worthy of mention which may come within that category, for it is evident that to have done justice to all would have required unlimited time and space.

Some families have been treated more fully than others for the reason that they branched more widely, or had preserved more particulars, or were more prominent in public affairs. In regard to some notable families it was found that only meager and general information could be procured, and that to obtain dates and details would involve endless labor and delay.

In the second volume, which we hope to accomplish, some of these deficiencies may be supplied, and due attention will be given to those individuals of the families herein listed, who attained distinction, but who figured in a later period than is covered by this volume; also to many families whose connection with Camden began later than 1800. In every classification a border line is reached where it is hard to determine on which side to place some of the subjects. So we were in much doubt whether or not the founders of such families as Cureton, Doby, Douglas, Lee, McCaa, McKain, Deas, Salmond, Thornton, and others reached Camden or Kershaw County prior to 1800. From search of the records, how-

EARLY REPRESENTATIVE FAMILIES. 341

ever, they appear to have come a little after that date, so they are left for the subsequent part.

Of others still, once prominent in the early period of this community, not a single representative could be found or traced. Just here we shall name some of these, and insert a few fragmentary data concerning them, gathered from one source and another.

BALLARD. Lewis Ballard, who died 1817, age 55, patriot in Revolution, for 20 years resident of Camden; mercantile partner of C. J. Shannon in 1816. Thomas Ballard, planter, probably brother of Lewis, Justice of Peace 1791, Major Kershaw County Regiment 1794, surviving Revolutionary veteran in Kershaw County in 1841. John Ballard was living on White Oak Creek 1793.

BROWN. Daniel and Jacob Brown, attorneys at law in Camden prior to 1790. The former married Mary Polk. Jacob engaged in a noted duel with Thomas Baker, in corporate limits of Camden, both principals killed. This incident will be fully related in Volume II. John Brown, also a lawyer at Camden, married Rebecca, daughter of Joseph Kershaw, 1798. James Brown imprisoned in Camden by British 1780.

COOK. James Cook, Provincial Surveyor, one of Commissioners who ran boundary line between North and South Carolina 1772, married Sarah Milhouse at Camden, October, 1768. Cook's Mount on Wateree River named for him. Polly Cook, daughter of Capt. John Cook, married at Camden 1773 to John August, both of Camden. Lewis Cook, a soldier at Battle of Camden, died 1846, age 92, at his residence on Twenty-Five Mile Creek.

HUNTER. Henry Hunter, on grand jury at Camden, 1772, capitulated with militia at Charleston 1780, Sheriff Camden District 1783. His will, 1783, leaves property to two sons, Henry and Henry Starke Hunter. Close connection between families of Hunter and Starke. In 1806 Starke Hunter married Elizabeth, daughter of Burwell Boykin. His old house still stands on the State farm at Boykin.

MARTIN. John Martin receives grant of lands in Kershaw County 1761; Captain in Second Regiment Continentals 1775; conveys message from General Davie to General Sumter of Gates's defeat. John Martin, probably son of above, married Rachel Burns, daughter of John Burns, who settled in West Wateree, said to have been a relative of the poet Robert Burns. In 1753 John and Isabella Martin appear as witnesses to a deed executed in Fredricksburg Township.

ROSS. Isaac Ross, member of Continental Association, 1775. He, his son Isaac, Ely Ross, Arthur Brown Ross, Samuel Ross, sign as inhabitants of Camden and neighborhood a petition in 1788 to Legislature in regard to McCord's Ferry. George Ross, member of House of Representatives, Kershaw County, 1794. A signer of Declaration of Independence, from Georgia, named George Ross.

STARKE. Douglas Starke, planter, Revolutionary soldier, at fall of Charleston 1780, Justice Peace 1787. Reuben Starke, probably son of Douglas, State Senator from Kershaw County 1812. Wyatt W. Starke, son of Reuben, attorney at law Camden, member Legislature 1816, died about that time, a young man. Turner Starke, Sheriff of Kershaw County 1810.]

ADAMSON.

See Chapter XII.

ALEXANDER.

Dr. Isaac Alexander was of a distinguished North Carolina family. His father, Abraham Alexander, enjoyed the honor of presiding over the famous Mecklenburg Convention of 1775, at Charlotte. The family had migrated to North Carolina from Cecil County, Md., in the early part of the 18th century. Dr. Isaac Alexander graduated from Princeton College in 1772, in the same class with James Madison and Aaron Burr. On his return to Charlotte, he entered upon the practice of medicine, and served for one year as first President of Queen's Museum. He removed to Camden about 1784, where, for nearly 30 years, he was a leading physician and citizen. He had been a surgeon in the American army during the Revolution, and was a participant in the disastrous defeat of Gates at Camden, rendering important aid to the wounded and attending the Baron DeKalb in his mortal illness. Although not an office-seeker, Dr. Alexander was called upon to do public service. He represented the county in the Legislature in 1786, was Intendant of Camden, and served as one of the first Trustees of the South Carolina College. He was also for many years an elder in the Presbyterian Church. He died in 1812, and is buried in the Presbyterian graveyard.

Dr. Alexander's first wife was Margaret, daughter of Dr. William Brisbane, of Charleston. This excellent woman, one of the builders of the first Presbyterian Church erected in Camden after the Revolution, died in 1801, at the age of 44. She left one child, Amelia, who married Wm. Adamson, Esq.

His second wife was Sarah Thornton, of New York, a sister of Phineas Thornton. This marriage took place in 1807. Of it there were two children, Isaac B. Alexander, who died in 1885, at the age of 73, leaving a large family; and Henry Dana Ward Alexander, who married his cousin, Mary Alexander, of North Carolina, removed to Georgia, served in the western army, C. S. A., and lost his life in a steamer burned on the Savannah River in 1865.

Isaac B. Alexander married Miss Gilman of Camden. He is remembered as an excellent citizen, of considerable talent as a painter of miniatures on ivory, and interested in scientific investigations, though his business was that of a jeweler.

ANCRUM.

The Ancrum family is identified by property rights, as we have seen, with the earliest history of Camden; by residence it dates from the first years of the 19th century.

William Ancrum (I), of the wealthy firm of Ancrum, Lance & Loocock, probably never set foot in Camden, his extensive business interests here being looked after by such competent agents or partners as the two Kershaws. He was a native of the County of Northumberland, England. On his tombstone in the old Scotch Churchyard, Charleston, it is written that he was "for many years, a respectable merchant of this city, and an elder of the Scotch Church of Charleston for nearly half a century. Through a long life of integrity and honor, he performed the duties of a man and Christian, and died, esteemed and regretted, on the 24 Feby, 1808, in the 86th year of his age."

Mr. Ancrum was unmarried. The bulk of his landed estate in this section, including the plantations of Red Bank and Good Hope, he left to his nephew and namesake, William Ancrum, son of his brother George, by his wife Katherine, daughter of Isaac Porcher, of St. John's, Berkeley.

William (II) had been sent by his uncle to school in England. Here, at a Fourth of July celebration, gotten up by some Americans of the vicinity, he joined in so enthusiastically as to cause his expulsion. On his way home, he stopped with a friend in Jamaica, where he was so pleased with the style of residential architecture that he modeled after it the house, still standing, which he later built as his summer home, on Fair street, Camden.

In 1802, Mr. Ancrum married Elizabeth, daughter of Adam F. Brisbane, and settled in Camden. Col. Shannon* says that he was a man of "high character, eminent social qualities and scholarly attainments." His aspirations did not lead him to seek public position, the easy plantation life being more to his taste. To him

---

*"Old Times in Camden."

partly is due the erection of the handsome Presbyterian church on DeKalb street. His death occurred in Stokes Co., N. C., in 1831, at the age of 60, and he is buried in the old Presbyterian Cemetery, at Camden.

He left three sons: Adam Brisbane, who died at the age of 21; William Alexander (1815-1862), and Thomas James (1817-1887).

William (III) graduated from Princeton College in 1836. The next year he married Charlotte, daughter of James K. Douglas, Esq.

Thomas married Margaret Douglas, sister to Charlotte.

The plantations of these gentlemen were in the fertile lower part of the county, near the river. Their town houses were in Kirkwood; William built that so long occupied by Dr. Edward Boykin, which was burnt about 1890, and Thomas that next to it, now the property of Mrs. John D. Kennedy. Both families are widely connected here.

BELTON.

See Chapter III.

BLANDING.

Will be treated in Volume II, under sketch of Abram Blanding.

BOYKIN.

The Boykin ancestry traces back to the early colonial period of Virginia and South Carolina, and its descendants are widely disseminated throughout the Southern States. As to the origin and most other data in regard to this family we draw from the record compiled by the late Dr. Ed. M. Boykin, a most readable pamphlet published by him in 1876. The subject ramifies into such innumerable branches that economy of space will permit here only a meager outline.

EDWARD BOYKIN came from Caernarvonshire, Wales, to Virginia, and a grant to him of 525 acres, in Southampton County, of that State, is found of record, dated Apr. 20, 1685, and other grants on down to 1725, about the date of his death. At the same period grants of lands in the same locality were also obtained by

WILLIAM BOYKIN (I), whose death is attributed to the year 1731. It is not pointed out whether William was the son, brother, or what relation of Edward, but it is stated that he had a brother Thomas, and that his wife was named Margaret. His children were William, John, Thomas, Simon and Martha.

WILLIAM BOYKIN (II), son of William (I), about 1755 or 1756 established himself in South Carolina, some six miles south of Camden. The date of his coming doubtless nearly corresponds with a conveyance made to him by Ann Sinnexon, formerly Ann Duyett, dated Mar. 26, 1756, of 300 acres in Fredricksburg Township, adjoining lands of Benj. McKinnie, near Town Creek. In the same year he purchased other neighboring lands, in the locality known as Stockton. This estate devolved, under the law of primogeniture, to his eldest son Samuel; to Samuel's granddaughter Sally Cantey; from her to her husband Philip Stockton (hence the local name), from whom it was purchased by Col. Wm. Jesse Taylor, who sold to Joseph Cunningham, who devised to his daughter, wife of Gen. J. D. Kennedy. On this tract is located the early burial place of the family. The wife of this William was a Bryant. Their children were Samuel, Burwell, Francis, William, Amelia and John. These were all, it is said, except John, born in Virginia before their parents' emigration to Carolina.

Although no mention is made by Dr. Ed. M. Boykin in his history of the family, of any pioneer of the name in South Carolina other than William, there are to be found in the State records two early grants, each dated Oct., 1755, one to Henry Boykin of 100 acres on the south fork of Lynches Creek, the other of 100 acres to Edward Boykin on Jeffreys Creek, in the present County of Florence. Whether any such settlers ever established families in this State or have any descendants we have not been able to ascertain.

SAMUEL BOYKIN, eldest son of William (II), was a man of notable strength and energy, both physical and mental, a sterling character. Six feet tall, 225 pounds weight, and strenuous in proportion, he was well equipped for subduing the wild. In days prior to the

Revolution, when there were no courts outside of Charleston, and the interior was driven by necessity to the summary process of "regulation," Samuel Boykin was a leading regulator. A circumstantial story is told of how he with two companions, Shiver and Arthur, applied 39 lashes to one Timothy Dozier, whom they had bound to a blackjack, for ill treatment of his family, which correction, unusual instance, reformed the said Dozier and made a man of him.

With Joseph Kershaw and John Chesnut, he was a delegate to the Provincial Congress of 1775. It is told in a preceding chapter how he bestirred himself in the Revolution, especially with his Indian troops on Sullivans Island. He was active as a partisan throughout the struggle under Taylor and Sumter.

While still in the prime of his strength he came to a violent end at the hands of certain ruffian wagoners who had camped upon his land and were committing depredations. He went alone to rebuke them, whereupon they set upon him and broke several of his ribs. He managed to remount his horse and brought back some friends, administered a severe "regulation" to his assailants and burnt their wagons. But inflammation resulted from his hurts, and his death occurred shortly after, in Dec., 1791.

His wife was Elizabeth Brown, who after his death married Thomas Broom.

His children were four, viz.:

Burwell, died unmarried, age 18.

Mary, died single.

Elizabeth, who married John Witherspoon.

    Children of Elizabeth: Mrs. Sally Williams, S. C.; Mrs. DuBose, Ala.; Boykin Witherspoon, La.; Mrs. Wallace, S. C.; John Witherspoon, S. C.; Mrs. Evans, S. C.

Sally, who married Zach. Cantey.

BURWELL BOYKIN, second son of William (II), was born in 1752, and possessed in a high degree the family qualities of enterprise and sturdy manhood. He too was a militant patriot of the Revolution, ever ready to respond to the call of Marion, Sumter and other leaders.

He was an eminently successful planter, and acquired a great area of choice land, surrounding his father's settlement, extending from Town Creek to the lower side of Swift Creek, including the mill on latter stream, now the property of his grandson, Burwell H. Boykin. He left to each of his seventeen children a considerable estate. In 1790 he was member of the Legislature from Kershaw County. His portrait, in the possession of his grandson, A. Hamilton Boykin, at The Terraces, shows an intellectual and resolute face. The name Burwell is derived from that of a well-known Virginia family, with which some early Boykin intermarried.

In 1812 he built, at Pleasant Hill, the house occupied by his grandson, Thomas L. Boykin* (near The Terraces). He died in 1817 at the age of 65. His first wife was Elizabeth Whitaker, by whom he had three children, Elizabeth, Francis, and Burwell. Elizabeth married Starke Hunter, of Camden, and with him removed to Conecuh County, Ala., in 1818. They had no children. Francis, born in 1785, married Mary James, and also moved to Alabama with Starke Hunter. There are descendants of his in that State. Of Burwell nothing is recorded.

After death of his first wife he married her sister, Mary Whitaker. Upon his death she was left with the care of their fourteen children—most of them young— a charge to which she was fully equal, for she is noted in the family tradition as a woman

> "Planned
> To warn, to comfort and command."

Dr. Boykin draws a graphic picture of the life of that large household at Pleasant Hill. The country behind it for sixty miles was a forest of primeval pine and oak, abounding with deer and other game. The horse, horn, hound and chase held sway as at an Osbaldistone Hall, without its rude revelry. Neighboring were other lordly estates, such as those of Chesnut, Cantey, English, Ancrum. Those were as feudal times touched with chivalry and romance.

*Alas! recently deceased.

Children of Burwell Boykin's second marriage:
  Katherine, who married W. W. Lang.
  Samuel, who married Miss Ross.
  John, whom he married, not recorded.
  Amelia, who married Dr. John McCaa.*
  Lemuel, who married Mary E. Hopkins.
  Mary, who married Hon. S. D. Miller.
  Thomas, who married Eliza Boykin of Va.
  Elizabeth, who married Hon. T. J. Withers.
  Sally, who married W. C. Clifton.
  Burwell, who married Sally W. Lang.
  William, who married Martha Rives.
  A. Hamilton,† who married Sarah J. DeSaussure.
  Charlotte, who married James Taylor.
  Stephen H., who married Miss Addirton, of Md.

FRANCIS BOYKIN, third son of William (II), was a zealous soldier in the Revolution. According to Moultrie, he was 1st Lieut. of Mounted Rangers in one of the first three Provincial regiments of 1775, in which Eli Kershaw was Captain and Wm. Thompson Colonel. Maj. Saml. Wise (Gregg's Old Cheraws, p. 272) writes of his intrepid conduct at Sullivans Island. He rose to rank of Major in Middleton's infantry regiment. He was accounted one of the handsomest men in the service.

His wife was Katherine Whitaker. Subsequent to the Revolution he lived in Camden and served for years as Clerk of Court. Our earliest recorded deeds in Book "A" are in his handwriting. About the year 1800 he moved to Georgia, settling where Milledgeville stands, engaged in planting, and died in 1821. His children were William, Samuel, James, Mary and Eliza, of whom there are many descendants in Georgia.

Eliza, born in 1788, married Wm. Rutherford, died in Milledgeville, Ga., 1837, leaving three sons.

Samuel, born 1790, practiced medicine with success in Milledgeville, removing to Columbus, Ga. He was twice married. Of his first marriage there was one son, of his second four sons and four daughters. He was a man of scientific acquirements, a specialist in botany.

*Son of that John McCaa naturalized at Camden in 1804.
†His home at "The Terraces." Here also was the residence of Gov. S. D. Miller, in 1830, then known as Plane Hill.

A genus of plants has been named in his honor "Boykinia."

James Boykin, born 1792, served in the war of 1812, died in 1846, and left two sons and three daughters.

WILLIAM BOYKIN (III), fourth son of William (II), lived and died a bachelor, and of him nothing memorable has been recorded.

AMELIA BOYKIN, only daughter of William (II), married Thomas Pace, who moved to Georgia with Francis Boykin in 1800. She died in 1835 at an advanced age, having survived all her brothers. The names of her children, so far as ascertainable, were William, Samuel, Thomas, Nathaniel, and Harriet, who married a McArthur. Probably not a few of her descendants may be located in Georgia and beyond.

JOHN BOYKIN, youngest child of William (II), at his father's death was adopted by his eldest brother, Samuel, who donated to him, on his coming of age, a plantation in the Boykin neighborhood. He, like all his brethren, embarked in the Revolutionary cause, and was commissioned Captain in Col. Wade Hampton's cavalry regiment. He was among those patriots whom the British distinguished by incarceration in the Camden prison. He rode as a Regulator under his brother Samuel. His home on Swift Creek was burnt in 1794, with a crop of indigo in the garret. He then sold the place and located across the Kershaw County line in Fairfield County, at or near Longtown. He died in Columbia, 1798, while attending the Legislature, of which he was a member from Fairfield, leaving a considerable estate of land and negroes. He possessed the family strong physique, and a prepossessing address. He was twice married, first to Miss Starke, sister of Reuben Starke. She died a year after marriage without issue. His second wife was Frances Brown, sister of his brother Samuel's wife. Of this second marriage there were three children, John, William and a daughter Frances.

William died in 1812, a student at S. C. College, and Frances died at an early age.

John, born 1790, married Charlotte A. Mortimer (granddaughter of John Adamson). He was a man of great personal charm and popularity. He took an interest in public affairs and was in the exciting political contest of 1832 as a candidate on the Nullification ticket for the Legislature. A part of his life was spent in New Jersey, but he returned to South Carolina. His summer home was at Cool Spring, where his neighbors were John Chesnut and Benj. T. Elmore. He died in 1840. His children were a son and daughter, Dr. Edward M. Boykin, who married Mary C. Lang, and whose descendants all reside at or near Camden, and Mrs. Kate L. Heyward, who married Savage Heyward, both deceased.

The Boykin family has ever evinced a strong attachment to the soil. It has produced a race of planters, types of staunch and steady citizenship, seldom aspirant for public honors, but ever responsive to the calls of public duty, civic or military, displaying that prime qualification of Horace's *"Beatus ille"* in the culture of the *"Paterna rura."*

BREVARD.

See Chapter XVII.

BRISBANE.

Adam Fowler Brisbane was a man who figured prominently in the early annals of Camden. He was the son of William Brisbane of Charleston and Margaret Stuart, his wife, of Beaufort, and was born in the former city in 1754.

At the age of 21, he married Mary Camber, of Georgia, and settled in Camden, certainly as early as 1780, as the Courthouse records prove. Four years later he was elected to the Legislature from this District, and, in 1790, was a member of the Constitutional Convention of the State. He was chosen first President of the Camden Orphan Society, in 1787, and, in 1791, was appointed one of the first Judges of the County Court of Kershaw. His death occurred in 1797.

His residence stood on the east side of Fair street, near the corner of King. This house, furnished, was placed at the disposal of Washington on his visit to Camden in 1791. It was subsequently burned, as was a second one on the same site, built by Col. James S. Deas.

Mr. Brisbane left three children:

1. Adam Fowler (II), who married Margaret Irvin. With the death of this gentleman, in 1806, without issue, the name became extinct in the community. His widow became the wife of Thomas Salmond, Esq.

2. Elizabeth Dale, who married Wm. Ancrum (II).

3. Mary Camber, who married Reuben Arthur, once Sheriff of this county and its representative in the Legislature in 1808. Mr. Arthur later removed to Cahaba, Ala., where the family is still largely represented.

BROOM—MURRAY—RUDULPH—ARRANTS.

A few years prior to A. D. 1800, this group of families, connected by blood or marriage, came to Camden from Elkton, Md. Thomas Broom came in Oct., 1794, a widower, with a daughter, Frances, then a child of six or seven. It has been stated that he had been at Camden previously as a Revolutionary soldier with Lee's legion, or perhaps with Col. Washington. He brought with him on his return a stock of goods worth £1,600, and established a mercantile business in Camden in partnership with Zach. Cantey and Duncan McRae.* He also purchased the mills on Pine Tree Creek just south of the town limits (now Carrison's) and here did considerable business. Some old records show that the sales of flour from this mill (presumably the 1-10 toll for grinding) amounted annually to six or seven thousand dollars, which indicates an output of sixty or seventy thousand dollars value.

In Dec., 1795, he married the widow of Samuel Boykin. There were two children of this marriage, Thomas, who died an infant, and Martha Rebecca, of whom nothing is known. His daughter Frances became the wife of Francis Stephen Lee, and from them descended the

---

*Robert Henry, another of the names of old Camden leaving no trace, was for a time a partner with Cantey, McRae and Broom. He was one of the assignees of Joseph Kershaw, 1790. We only know that about 1800 he moved to Kingston, Jamaica. An old manuscript of his is indicative of culture.

numerous Lee and Bonney families, long residents of Camden, but now unrepresented here. Thomas Broom died suddenly on a visit to Charleston in Oct., 1799, probably of yellow fever, which about the same time carried off young John Chesnut (II). His short career in Camden manifested an enterprising and progressive spirit.

ZEBULON RUDULPH, a half brother of Thomas Broom, accompanied him to Camden, and was associated with him in the milling business here and at Beards Mill on the Saluda River. He administered upon Broom's estate, and became engaged in heavy suits for its settlement, with the executors of Samuel Boykin and with McRae, Cantey and Robert Henry. The papers in these old proceedings of a century ago, form ponderous packages, filled with the grievances and cross-complaints of the parties.

The name of Rudulph was prominent among the Revolutionary patriots of Maryland, the devoted band who, with the Delawares, redeemed the Carolinas under Greene. Zebulon was a citizen of Camden for over twenty years, an accomplished man to judge by traces of his writing. In 1807 he purchased from Henry Dana Ward, the executor of Margaret Alexander's will, the "Blue House," in which DeKalb died, situated on lot 65, near corner of Broad and Meeting streets. Here was his residence in 1816, that of Robert Mickle on the opposite side east, they being then the most southern residents of Camden. In that day the elite of Camden dwelt between Meeting and King streets, where now not an edifice, save a few shanties on the upper edge, remains, amid fields of cotton and corn. Thus completely has the old order passed.

Among the achievements of Rudulph was the successful cultivation of the castor bean—as much as fifty acres in a field, according to an authority. In the *Camden Gazette* of 1818 are advertisements by druggists of "Rudulph's cold drawn castor-oil." About that period he departed from Camden (*eheu fugaces!*) to Columbia, and later to Edgefield County, for the reason, in the words of the *Camden Journal*, "to enable him to attend to the religious education of his negroes." Later he removed to Lowndes County, Ala., where he died at the ripe age of 86, in March, 1855. Of his descendants, if any, we know nothing. His wife's name was Abby. From his brother is descended Mrs. Lucretia R. (Rudulph) Garfield, the widow of President Garfield.

JAMES SYNG MURRAY, another of the Maryland colony, was born at Elkton in Feb., 1777, and came to Camden about 1798. During his residence here of thirty-six years he was highly esteemed for his worth and pious character. In 1805 he was elected an elder of the Presbyterian Church. His first wife was Sarah Barry Willett, daughter of Capt. John Willett, of Philadelphia, Revolutionary stock. Her brother, John S. Willett, came to Camden, where he practiced law, and died in 1818 at the age of 30, as his gravestone in our cemetery records. Here also lies his sister, Mrs. Murray, who died in 1822. Through marriage, in some way, Jas. S. Murray was a brother, by affinity, of Zebulon Rudulph. In 1834 he, too, left Camden, and died at Ottawa, Ill., at the age of 78, in Feb., 1855, leaving a large family by a second marriage. His eldest son (by first marriage), Maj. John D. Murray, so well known to the elder people of this community, remained in Camden until about 1850, when he left for Florida, where he soon after died, a bachelor, age about 50.

Harmon and Johannes ARRANTS, two brothers, were in some manner, not now clear, connected in business and by family with Thomas Broom and Rudulph, coming to Camden with them, or near the same time. They acquired lands just across the creek south of Camden, and about the year 1800 conveyed them to Zeb. Rudulph and Jas. S. Murray. Harmon is said to have been drowned in the Potomac on the retreat of Americans from Washington in War of 1812, and left no descendants. Through Nathan Broom Arrants, son of Johannes, the present members of the family in Camden are descended.

CANTEY.

Ancestors of the Cantey family came to South Carolina in its earliest colonial period. Two brothers, JOHN CANTEY (I) and WILLIAM CANTEY, were the first of the name to settle in America, it being uncertain, it seems, whether they were from Wales or Ireland. Of these brothers nothing is related beyond the fact of their emigration. For such imperfect account of their descendants as is here presented, we have followed a paper prepared by Gen. J. B. Kershaw and data furnished by the Camden branch of the family, and errors and deficiencies must be attributed to the sources of information.

JOHN CANTEY (II), son of John (I), referred to in the records as Capt. Cantey, comes to notice for his conduct in defense of Charleston against the attack of French and Spaniards under LeFeboure in 1704, during the administration of Sir Nathaniel Johnson. He was a resident of Goose Creek, above Charleston, and we may read in Carroll's Hist. Collections, Vol. I, p. 161, how Captains Cantey, Lynch and others brought companies to the relief of the city. The enemy landed a party on Wando Neck, and Carroll relates how Capt. Cantey was sent to watch them with a hundred chosen men. He not only saw, but conquered, for he surprised the party at their camp-fires, and captured those who were not killed, drowned or wounded. He maintained a post successfully and gallantly against Indians on one occasion, probably the Yemassee war. In 1712 he commanded forty-one Catawbas in Barnwell's arduous expedition against the powerful tribe of Tuscaroras, which was completely subdued.

The Captain was also a prominent churchman, and in those days the parish church practically governed the State, for there all elections of officers by the people were held by the vestrymen. At his death, the date of which was not ascertainable, he left a family, several members of whom were settled in Clarendon, a part of St. Mark's Parish, and in 1757 his sons, Joseph, William and John, were appointed by the Commons to establish a church in that parish, which also included the present County of Kershaw.

According to Gen. Kershaw's paper, a daughter of this John Cantey (II) was the first wife of Gen. Richardson of the Revolution, and among their children can be mentioned the gallant Col. Richard Richardson, Edward Richardson, Mrs. John Singleton, Mrs. McDonald, Mrs. Manning, wife of the Col. Lawrence Manning of Lee's Legion, "who made a shield of the British officer at the battle of Eutaw."

JOHN CANTEY (III), son of John (II), came up from the lower section of the State to Fredricksburg Township about 1752, if we may judge from an early grant to him, Oct. 6, 1752, of 150 acres on Town Creek, in the Mulberry neighborhood. There is also a conveyance to him dated May 12, 1753, of 50 acres in the same locality, by Robert Milhouse, being part of a tract which Milhouse on same day had received from James McGirtt. It seems that about this time he settled on this land, and married a daughter of James McGirtt and sister of the famous Daniel. Jan., 1764, he is living at Pine Tree Hill, where Samuel Wyly conveys to him, for love and affection, four acres. In 1765 Joseph Kershaw, also for love and affection, gives him six acres cornering on said John Cantey's dwelling, located near the intersection of Broad and Meeting streets, east side. Adjoining was the lot of Eli Kershaw. No incidents of his career have been recorded (except that his wife had to light his pipe), nor can we give the dates of his birth or death. Grants to him are found as late as 1772. His children were Zach., James, Sarah (wife of John Chesnut), Mary (wife of Eli Kershaw).

ZACH. CANTEY, son of John (III), married Sally, daughter of Samuel Boykin. He enlisted in the Revolutionary militia.

"No braver youth * * appeared in arms,
When Gideon blew the trumpet."

He was one of those paroled from Charleston in 1780. In a preceding chapter it is told how he scorned threat and bribe to pilot Tarleton in pursuit of Buford. He returned to the service and acted with Gen. Greene as quartermaster. After the war he engaged in a successful mercantile and milling business as partner of Duncan McRae. He was State Senator in 1804 from this county, and held the rank of general of militia.

The children of Zach. Cantey were four sons, Zach.,

Edward, Samuel and Henry, none of whom left descendants, and two daughters: Elizabeth, who married an Edwards, no issue; and Sally, who, while a schoolgirl at Philadelphia, contracted a romantic clandestine marriage with Philip Stockton. It is related that at a ball given to her on her return home, Stockton appeared, and to the amazement of her family, claimed her as his wife. Their children were Philip A. and Edward C. Stockton. Philip married a Miss Cunningham, of the North. He and she lived in Camden at time of Civil War, at corner Boundary and Lyttleton (lot 897). Here his wife died, and is buried in the Camden cemetery. These Stocktons are the only descendants of Gen. Zach. Cantey.

JAMES CANTEY (I), son of John (III), married Martha, daughter of James Whitaker. He was named doubtless for that Capt. James Cantey, probably an uncle, who is mentioned in the State records as commanding a scouting party against the Indians in 1733. True to the family martial instinct, he took up arms in the Revolutionary cause, and was surrendered at Charleston with his brother Zach. and a Capt. Philip Cantey, in 1780. He was a Lieutenant under Col. Richardson in the "Snow Campaign," and commanded an outpost on Sullivans Island. He was active in the operations preceding the fall of Charleston, and at this time commanded an escort conducting Mrs. Gen. Williamson to Augusta. An episode of the route (be it legend or not, yet upon the authority of Gen. Kershaw's paper,) was an attack upon the escort by a party under Cantey's inveterate Uncle Daniel McGirtt, whom he managed to repulse. When paroled from Charleston, he went to his mother's retreat at Knight's Hill. But, as did all the discharged militia, he construed the British cruelties, and Cornwallis's extreme orders, as a release of their parole obligation, and so he entered the field again. It is said he guided Col. Washington to Rugeley's Fort. After the war he would take no other office than that of Captain of militia. In 1798 he sold his Town Creek lands to John Chesnut, and moved to the vicinity of Milledgeville, Ga., where he resided till his death in 1817. His children were James Willis, John, Mary, who married (Willis) Whitaker, and Sarah, who married Henry Crowell.

JAMES WILLIS CANTEY (II), son of James (I), was born Nov. 30, 1794, on Town Creek, below Camden. He was taken to Georgia with his father. He was in the Creek Indian hostilities of 1813, as sergeant of his company commanded by Capt. John Irwin, son of Gov. Irwin of Ga. In his certificate of discharge he was specially commended for gallantry. A mere reference can be here made to his hand-to-hand encounters with Indian warriors, one of whom he shot twice through the body. Another of Cantey's party came along and duly scalped the brave, who was left for dead. Years after this Indian presented himself to Col. Crowell, Cantey's brother-in-law, and gave proof of his identity.

James Cantey returned to Camden in 1814, where he resided to the end of his life. In 1821 he was Sheriff of the District. In 1833 he was elected Brig.-General, and in 1843 Adjt.- and Inspector-General of the State. He served two terms in the Legislature, 1846-48. He was recognized as an exemplary soldier and citizen. He married Miss Camilla F. Richardson, daughter of John P. Richardson. Of their nine children the eldest, JAMES WILLIS CANTEY (III), an officer in the Palmetto Regt., fell heroically in Mexico. We hope to do justice to him and others of his brethren, in Volume II.

MAJ. JOHN CANTEY (IV), son of James Cantey (II), married Miss Emma Richardson. He served as brigade Major in the War of 1812 with the State troops at Charleston. He was prominent in political movements, an ardent Nullifier and advocate of separate secession in 1851. His children were:

Gen. James Cantey, of Alabama, officer in Palmetto Regt. in Mexico, and General in Confederate service.

Capt. John Cantey, of Camden, who married Miss Camilla Richardson.

Mary, who married Brown Manning.

JOSIAH CANTEY was probably a descendant of that William Cantey who emigrated with his brother John to this country. He married a Miss Vine.

The earliest indication of his presence at Camden or vicinity is about 1786, as appears from some old land surveys executed by him, his calling being that of a surveyor.

His daughter, Ann, married Henry R. Cook, and their only child, Ann C. Cook, married Dr. E. A. Salmond.

Another daughter married David Schrock, from whom Joel A. Schrock and others of the Schrock family of Camden descend.

The Cantey lineage in all of its branches has been conspicuous for its chivalrous, military spirit. It has produced many superb soldiers, and of three noted Confederate Generals two, James Chesnut and Zach. Cantey Deas, were grandsons, and another, James Cantey, of Ala., a great-grandson, of the John Cantey who settled on Town Creek in 1752.

CARTER—BYNUM.

The Carter family is one of the many once prominent in Camden, now utterly vanished. Their early location was at Carter's Crossing, in old Salem County, now part of Lee County. Few facts concerning this family can now be recovered. In our Probate Court is an old will of Henry Carter, leaving property to his sons, John, Benjamin, George, Robert, to his wife, Barbara, and daughter, Rachel. In 1784 Joseph Kershaw conveys Camden lots 635 and 636 to "Robert Carter of Salem." On lot 635 still stands an old house, probably one of the oldest in Camden, where once lived Benjamin Carter, son of Robert. It will only be added here concerning Benjamin, the old Revolutionary hero, of whom a short sketch will be found at the end of Chapter VII, that he acquired wealth in the business of tanning, producing fine leathers and moroccos. His vats were near the creek swamp at east terminus of York street.

John C. Carter practiced law in Camden. He died Apr., 1828. Graduate of S. C. College.

JOHN CARTER, known to his familiar friends as "Black John" to distinguish him from John C. Carter, was, it is said, a nephew of Benjamin. He was born on Black River, in Salem County, Sept. 10, 1792, and was a graduate of the South Carolina College. As one of the notable men of Camden his career deserves a fuller notice than can be given here. At the bar he attained excellence, and the records kept by him as Commissioner in Equity show him to have been a masterly scribe. In 1822 he was elected to Congress at the early age of 30 and served four successive terms. In 1829 he announced his retirement, and the esteem in which he was held may be gathered from the account of a public celebration held in Camden that year, it would appear, in his honor. On that occasion a salute was fired by McWillie's Artillery at the old Arsenal (corner of Fair and Bull streets), and the national flag was displayed from Jackson's Hotel (corner Broad and King streets), where a convivial party met. Among the toasts was the following:

"John Carter: The representative of Kershaw in Congress—we feel grateful for his past services and regret to lose his support in the councils of the country, but trust to receive a good citizen while we lose an able advocate."

At the time of Lafayette's visit to Camden in 1825, Carter's residence was at the handsome edifice on lots 729-730 (alas, this year destroyed by fire), known to us as "Lafayette Hall" from the fact that it had been placed at the disposal of the Marquis. This property John Carter purchased in 1823 from Henry R. Cook, by whom it was built about the year 1821—a prosperous year in Camden's annals and noted for erection of good buildings. In 1836 he departed from Camden and took up his residence in Georgetown, D. C., where he died June 20, 1850. His wife, Elizabeth Haslett Carter, died 1820, according to her gravestone in our cemetery. She was a daughter of Maj. McClelland by his first marriage. Her only daughter, Ann, married an Englishman of Bermuda, and beyond this we lose all trace of the Carters.

The names of BENJAMIN BYNUM and Benjamin Carter are as naturally associated in the memories and traditions of Camden, as those of Castor and Pollux or Romulus and Remus in legend. Their only link, however, seems to have been that they were two congenial old bachelor chums, long notable figures and companions in this community. Both were active and successful in business, men of substance and influence. They were indeed a rare old pair, according to the few very elderly citizens who can recall them.

Benjamin Bynum (who, by the way, in many instruments of his on record, signed himself, in elegant chirography, Bineham) was born in Surrey, now Stokes County, N. C., Jan. 2, 1772, and came to Camden about 1794, where possibly he may have had some relatives. In 1800 and again in 1814 he was elected Sheriff of Kershaw County. He long served faithfully as the executor of the extensive estate of Richard Lloyd Champion. His residence, partly brick, was that now occupied by Dr. A. A. Moore on lot 726, built by him, it is said. It seems that he imbued the edifice with an invincibly masculine quality, for the record is that only sons are born there, and the very poultry on those premises never produce pullets.

Benjamin Bynum died July 9, 1836. He lies in the Quaker Cemetery beside his friend, Benjamin Carter, who preceded him in 1830. The stones above each are duplicates. From the inscription on that of Bynum, we learn that he was the son of Gray and Margaret Bynum, that he was "the friend of man, lover of country and father of the poor." That "as the executor of a departed friend he managed his estate for twenty years with spotless purity."* This brief sketch of the two Benjamins we close with a quotation from Col. Shannon: "The former (Bynum), bland, smooth, soft, and winning; the latter (Carter) with all his kindness of disposition, and warmth of heart, was rough and brusque, and in many things like an old bachelor. Each kept open, hospitable parlors and dining-rooms, where whist and loo parties made attempt to compensate for the absence of domestic ties. Excess never characterized their meetings, however, and we never heard of evil attributed to their examples."

---

*It is interesting to learn that a nephew of Benjamin Bynum resides in Charlotte, N. C., now advanced in years—that venerable and distinguished jurist of the Old North State, Judge William Preston Bynum.

CHAMPION.

In our peaceful God's Acre sleeps Richard Champion, one of the eminent English potters of the 18th century. The simple headstone, among the oldest in the cemetery, would little indicate that it marks the last resting-place of a gifted man, scarcely known in this country, whose life and works are treated at length in every standard book on British ceramics.

Mr. Champion was born in Bristol, in 1743. His youth was spent with his father in London, but, in his twentieth year, he returned to his native town and entered the office of his uncle, Richard Champion, merchant. Four years later, he married Julia,* daughter of Judith Lloyd, widow. In 1768, he formed a copartnership with William Cookworthy, the first maker of true porcelain, or hard china, in England. Five years afterwards he bought out Cookworthy, who retained, for himself and heirs, a royalty for ninety-nine years. Here for eight years he conducted the Castle Green Pottery, where the famous, and, at the time, unique "Bristol Ware" was manufactured. Jewis, an authority on ceramics, says of his work: "The most characteristic productions of the Bristol Factory are white china biscuit placques, decorated with flowers and foliage in relief. One has on it a bas-relief bust of Franklin. These flowers were of exquisite tenuity and delicacy and were marvels of ceramic skill, and were far finer than those made at Derby. Statuettes were also largely made, and also a fine series of hexagonal vases painted with foliage and exotic birds. Sumptuous table services were also produced, with grounds of lapis lazuli blue and elaborately gilded surrounding panels of painted flowers."

Richard Champion was an active participant in the politics of his city. His affiliations were, naturally, with the Liberals, of whom his kinsman, the great Fox, was then a leader. He nominated Edmund Burke as member of Parliament from Bristol, and, on the occa-

---

*This is the name upon her tombstone. Family records say her name was Judith.

sion of that divine orator's visit to the city in 1774, he presented to Mrs. Burke a magnificent Bristol china service. In later years, the teapot alone of this set was sold for $1,050, and the milk jug for nearly $600.

His cordial sympathy for the American colonies was evidenced by his presentation to Washington and Franklin of busts of themselves, which he had caused to be cast in his pottery. That of the former is now owned by a gentleman in Baltimore; Franklin's is said to be in Philadelphia.

In 1775, Champion's petition to Parliament for an extension of the Cookworthy patent was granted, though strenuously opposed by Josiah Wedgwood and other distinguished ceramists. After this, however, for some unexplained reason, Mr. Champion's financial affairs became entangled, and, in 1781, he disposed of his patent rights to some Staffordshire potters, who continued the making of hard porcelain at New Hall, Shelton. The last product of the Bristol factory is now owned by Mr. Henry Davis, of Atlanta, a descendant of the maker, and is, at present, in Camden. It is a statuette, over a foot high, of Grief, and is dedicated to the memory of a young daughter, recently deceased, whom he pathetically names, in the inscription, "Dear Eliza." It is a beautiful and valuable specimen of his work.

In 1782, when Burke was made Paymaster-General of his Majesty's forces, he appointed Richard Champion a deputy paymaster, at a salary of £500, conjointly with his own son, Richard Burke. Two years later, however, because of his extreme political views, Mr. Champion resigned. His eyes had long been set upon the "Land of Liberty," with whose people, in their war for independence, he had, as we have said, strongly sympathized. Indeed he had given our patriot leaders valuable information through his brother-in-law, John Lloyd, who had lived in Charleston since 1777. This Mr. Lloyd had been sent over as the agent of the British government, but, revolting at the inhuman execution of Col. Isaac Hayne, had gone over to the American side.

Accordingly, in 1784, Richard Champion emigrated to South Carolina with his entire family. Mr. Lloyd had purchased lands for him in the present counties of Kershaw, Sumter and Beaufort. For his residence, he chose a site on Rocky Branch, a tributary of Grannys Quarter, about ten miles north of Camden. What especially attracted him here is unknown, but he may have had some idea of testing the clays along our river, which, even at that early date, are said to have been known to the English potters as of a fine quality. It is certain, however, that he did not attempt the establishment of a pottery here.

Mr. Champion was a political pamphleteer of ability. His "Comparative Reflections on the past and present Political, Commercial and Civil State of Great Britain, with some Thoughts concerning Emigration" was published anonymously, on the eve of his departure for America, but a second edition, in 1787, had his name attached. That on "America" was issued also in 1784.

His naturalization papers, made out in 1787, are in our Courthouse. The only office that he is known to have held in this State was that of delegate to the Constitutional Convention of 1790.

His death occurred the next year, at his secluded country retreat. His wife had died the year before. They were buried, first, in the old Episcopal cemetery in Camden, but, in recent years, owing to depredations upon the family inclosure, all the bodies therein were removed to the Quaker burying-ground.

To John Lloyd Champion, probably his eldest son, Mr. Champion leased, in January, 1791, his place on Rocky Branch; it is described as containing 1,000 acres, bounded by the lands of Chesnut, Kirkland, Milhouse, Watkins, Dixon, and others. John died in 1793.

George, another son, who never married, was considered somewhat daft because, as early as 1820, he plied *The American Farmer* and other journals with articles in enthusiastic advocacy of railroads. He was one of those sanguine spirits, says Col. Shannon, who predicted that "cars could be propelled with reasonable safety as fast as eight miles an hour, and that, if a railroad were built from Charleston to Camden, Columbia and Hamburg, it could transport per annum fifty thousand bales of cotton and a corresponding amount of up-freight."

A daughter of Richard Champion, Sarah, born in 1774, became the wife of WILIE VAUGHAN, a Virginian, who, from 1818 until 1820 (the date of his death), was the proprietor of *The Camden Gazette and Mercantile Advertiser*. This unfortunate lady and her daughter, Virginia, were victims of that horrible catastrophe on the Alabama River, the burning of the steamer "Orleans St. John," March 5, 1850, in which also two other esteemed citizens of Camden, James R. McKain, then Intendant, and his venerable mother, Mrs. Wm. McKain, lost their lives. John Champion Vaughan, a son of the above marriage, practiced law in Camden, in partnership with Thomas B. Lee, Esq. His residence, on the S. E. corner of King and Market streets, is still standing. About 1834, he removed to Cincinnati, where he attained great success in his profession. One of his sons, Champion Vaughan, was a distinguished officer in the Regular Army, serving under Custer in the Indian campaigns, and rising, we are told, to the rank of general.

The most prominent of the sons of Richard Champion was RICHARD LLOYD CHAMPION, who was born in Bristol in 1771, and died in Camden in 1813. He was a gentleman of culture as well as of business acumen, acquiring a very large property, both around and in the heart of the town. Among other offices of trust in the county, he held the position of Clerk of Court from about 1790 until 1808, when superseded by Thomas Salmond, Esq. In our Courthouse may be seen a plat of that part of Camden owned by Richard Lloyd Champion, some ninety acres in the center. It bears date 1808, and is executed with exquisite art, in coloring, lettering and decorations. Doubtless it was the work of Mr. Champion himself, an evidence of inherited artistic talent.

In 1810, Richard L. Champion married Mary, daughter of Capt. Isaac Dubose, and widow of Dr. John Trent. Of this union there was but one issue, Eliza, who became the wife of Major John M. DeSaussure. Her descendants, once numerous in the community, are now widely scattered over the Southern States. It is sad to relate that not a single representative of the Champion blood, or of this branch of the DeSaussure family—once so conspicuous an element in the society of Camden—is now left in the county.

CHESNUT.

This sketch has been composed from such authentic materials as the Registry in the family Bible and notes accompanying same, supposed to have been dictated by Col. James Chesnut, of Mulberry, to his daughter, Sarah; from old deeds and public records, together with such other gleanings as seemed reliable.

JOHN CHESNUT (I) was born on the Shenandoah River, Virginia, June 18, 1743. His parents came as children with their parents from Ireland, settling on the frontiers of Virginia, where they endured all the exposure and dangers of the pioneers, by no means conducive to longevity. His father died or was killed when quite a young man, and left his widow with three young children. His mother married again, Jasper Sutton, who was member of a company of frontier rangers. After Braddock's defeat in 1755 the Indians devastated Virginia. Mr. Sutton, with his wife and Chesnut stepchildren, retired, as did many other families, to the protection of the fort at the new town of Winchester. As soon as lines of regular troops had been posted so as to check the savages, most of these families, among them that of Jasper Sutton, moved South. John Chesnut was then about 13 years of age, making the date of their removal 1756.

This family halted a year or two on Fifers Creek, in North Carolina, between Salisbury and Charlotte, and then came on down and located on Grannys Quarter Creek, in Kershaw County, the Clermont or Rugeley neighborhood. A year or so after this John Chesnut entered upon an apprenticeship in Joseph Kershaw's store at the then Pine Tree Hill. The first record proof of his presence here is found in his signature as witness to an old land deed of Gover Black (son and heir of John Black) to Samuel Wyly, dated Jan. 8, 1763. In the year 1767 is another deed of Ancrum, Loocock & Kershaw, conveying to Eli Kershaw and John Chesnut a considerable amount of land in and around the site of Camden, among others the 150 acres which was Pine Tree Hill, and Pine Tree Mill—now the Carrison Mill just below Camden. He had thus rapidly risen to an independent merchant and landholder.

In the year 1766 we find grants of land, in various parts of Kershaw County, to James Chesnut, a brother of John, and also of land (adjoining James), in the same year to one Samuel Chesnut, of whom there is no mention in the family record. In the year 1774 Joseph Kershaw conveys to Jasper Sutton lots 334 and 335 in the Town of Camden.

John Chesnut was a staunch Whig in the Revolution. He was paymaster in the third of the first three regiments, with the rank of Captain. After the battle of Purrysburg he resigned, being rendered unfit for service by rheumatism, which kept him abed for six months. On recovery he entered the militia and served in the Georgia campaign, commanded the Camden militia in Charleston when that city was besieged and captured in 1780, and was paroled to his plantation. When the British occupied Camden they took possession of his home, drove his family to Knights Hill and put him in the Camden prison. He was chained closely to the floor and bore the marks of iron on his ankles to his death, and likewise the resentment, for in his will he makes a bequest to his grandson, John Chesnut, of "two pair of old mahogony" (word missing) "much injured with the Royal stains of Lord Cornwallis and other inveterate enemies of that period."

He accumulated a great extent of land immediately north and south of Camden, by original grants and by purchase from estates of Kershaw, Cantey and others. He seems to have resided much of his life in Camden. His family being at Knights Hill during the Revolution, his wife's mother, Mrs. Cantey, also being with them, died and was buried there, at the spot where the family cemetery is located. Mrs. McGirtt, the mother of Mrs. Cantey, is buried at Mulberry.

He possessed the confidence of the people, as indicated by his frequent election to office. He was a delegate to the State Convention which ratified the Federal Constitution. He was elected to the State Senate in 1793 and 1796. His portrait, executed by Gilbert Stewart, manifests a decided likeness to that of George Washington, and is marked by strong features. An original of Washington by this noted artist used to hang on the walls at Mulberry until purchased some years ago for the Corcoran Gallery.

John Chesnut married Sarah Cantey, daughter of John Cantey of Town Creek, and granddaughter of James McGirtt. She was born Feb. 15, 1753. John Chesnut died April 1, 1818, age 61.

JAMES CHESNUT (I), brother of John (I). died while quite a young man, unmarried, and is buried in the old Presbyterian Church Cemetery at Camden. He owned the land on which Mulberry is built, and intended it for James, the son of his brother; but dying without a will, it was inherited by his brother, who, however, effectuated that intention by deeding it to his son, James.

MARGARET CHESNUT, full sister of John (I) and James (I), married Mr. Irwin. Her granddaughter married Thomas Salmond, ancestor of the Salmond family of Camden.

Sally Sutton, a half-sister of John, James and Margaret Chesnut, married a Ross; and Richard Sutton, a half-brother, settled in Florida.

Children of John Chesnut (I).

MARY CHESNUT, born Jan 20, 1771, died Camden Jan., 1843. Married Duncan McRae. They had eight children. She is buried in Quaker Cemetery.

SARAH CHESNUT, born Dec. 12, 1774, died June, 1851. Married Gov. John Taylor, of Columbia. They had twelve children.

HARRIET CHESNUT, born Dec. 19, 1776, died Camden Sept., 1831, unmarried. She resided in the large house which still stands at corner King and Fair streets (lot 537). Tradition says she lived there as a recluse, because prevented by some barrier from requiting a true love.

MARGARET REBECCA CHESNUT, born Jan. 24, 1786, married Col. J. S. Deas, of Camden. Moved with him to Alabama in 1835. She died 1874. Their children were: (1) Alan (Mrs. Huger). (2) Sallie, married Dr. Knott, a distinguished physician of Mobile, later of New York. (3) Margaret (Mrs. Auzé).* (4) Mary (Mrs. Brown). (5) Serena (Mrs. Murphy). (6) Zach. Cantey Deas, the Confederate General. (7) John. (8) Henry.

JOHN CHESNUT (II), born Jan. 3, 1783. Died in Charleston of yellow fever, Aug. 16, 1799. Remains removed seven months later from St. Michael's Church to Knights Hill.

JAMES CHESNUT (II), born Feb. 19, 1773, died at Bloomsbury, 1866, age 93. As a boy of seven he rode horseback to Charleston with his father, who was sent there a prisoner by the British. He acquired Belmont, Town Creek and Mulberry lands through his father's will. To these he added acres until he became the owner of the entire territory, some five miles square, extending from the southern edge of Camden down to Daniels Branch, and bounding on the river all the way. His slaves numbered several hundred. His vast interests he managed ably and was also active in public matters. In 1802, 1804, and 1808 he was elected to Legislature. In 1806-07 he was Intendant of Camden, and in 1832, after a bitter contest, was elected to State Senate, by the Union party, over his brother-in-law, Jas. S. Deas, the candidate of Nullifiers.

His residence was in Camden till 1820, in which year he built Mulberry house, two miles south, a four-story brick and stone mansion, slate roof, of plain exterior, but handsome interior. Here he spent the winters, but the situation being near the low river swamps, in summer he would remove the family to his Sandy Hill place, three miles east on the uplands. The road between these two residences was a bee line, kept in perfect order.

---

*One of the victims in the burning of a great hotel in New York City of recent years. She was then an old lady.

When his coach traveled over this road or to Camden, outriders went ahead to see that the way was clear. The Sandy Hill home was burned some twenty years ago. Mulberry, though unoccupied, still stands intact, an old manorial hall, with its noble oaks, avenues and lawns, suggesting, as no words can, the state and style of the ante-bellum Southern landlord.

He married Mary Cox, of Philadelphia, Sept. 20, 1796. She was the daughter of Col. John Cox, of Revolutionary note, who, before coming to Philadelphia, had lived at a country seat near Trenton, N. J., on the Delaware, called "Bloomsbury." Here Count de Rochambeau was entertained, the house being given up to him by Col. Cox, as was the courteous custom of the time.

Mary Cox was one of the six girls who strewed flowers before Gen. Washington at Trenton Bridge, N. J., just before he was made President. She was highly educated and attended Washington's receptions. She was the first Vice-Regent, for South Carolina, of the Mt. Vernon Association, in April, 1860. She was then 85 years of age, and her daughter, Sallie Chesnut, attended to the clerical work. The gentleness and sweetness of her character has been the theme of a writer who had means of personal knowledge. At the Mulberry premises, in a long brick outbuilding, it is said she taught the slaves to spin, weave, and other useful arts. Though delicate and nurtured like a house plant she attained the age of 89, and was the mother of thirteen children. She died, March 13, 1864, at the Bloomsbury home, just beyond the northern boundary of Camden, which was built by Col. James Chesnut for their daughter, Sally, and named for the Cox place on the Delaware. Here, too, James Chesnut died two years later, in 1866.

Children of James Chesnut (II).

ESTHER SERENA CHESNUT, born in Camden 1797. Married 1820 to Nicholas Williams, of Society Hill, son of Gen. D. R. Williams. She died in 1822.

JOHN CHESNUT (III), born 1799. Married Ellen Whitaker. Died 1839. State Senator 1836. Descendants in Florida. More fully mentioned in second volume.

MARY COX CHESNUT, born 1802. Married Dr. Geo. Reynolds 1834. Died 1899. Her handsome residence in Camden, on Laurens, Lyttleton and Fair streets, built by Dr. Reynolds.

HARRIET SERENA CHESNUT, born 1809. Married Wm. J. Grant. Died Dec. 2, 1835. Buried at Knights Hill.

EMMA CHESNUT, born 1812. Died, unmarried, 1847.

SARAH CHESNUT, born 1813. Died, unmarried, 1889, at "Bloomsbury."

JAMES CHESNUT (III), born in Camden Jan. 18, 1815, died Feb. 4, 1885. Married Mary Miller, daughter of S. D. Miller. No children. His distinguished career will be fully treated in Volume II.

Six other children of James Chesnut (II) died in infancy.

The Chesnut family has been marked by distinct political abilities, and during three generations appears perhaps oftener than any other Camden name in the list of public representatives. It is sad to reflect that, like so many another distinguished surname, it no longer survives in our community.

CUNNINGHAM.

Will be treated in Volume II under head of Liberty Hill.

DUBOSE.

Capt. Isaac Dubose removed to Camden, from Chesterfield County, soon after the Revolution. He had served, with distinction, in the war as Lieutenant in the 2d Regiment of Foot, organized in 1775. He was one of the officers stationed in Fort Moultrie at the time of the British attack on Sullivans Island.

His father, John Dubose, of the old Huguenot family, had settled, about the middle of the 18th century, on Lynches River, in the Old Cheraws.

Isaac Dubose was highly honored by our people. He was sent to the Constitutional Convention (1790), was Intendant of Camden (1792), and was elected to the Legislature in 1796, 1800 and 1806. His first wife, who was a Serrée or a Dutarque (the family records are not clear on the point), died in 1793.

Of his children, by this union, Mary was married, in 1799, to DR. JOHN TRENT, a native of Trenton, N. J., who was for sixteen years a prominent physician in Camden. Of this marriage, there was one son, Isaac, who died in early manhood, and two daughters, Mary and Martha, who lived, unmarried, to quite old age, with their half-sister, Mrs. John M. DeSaussure. Dr. Trent died in 1809, and is interred in the Presbyterian burying-ground.

A year later, his widow became the wife of Richard Lloyd Champion, Esq., by whom she had one child, Mrs. DeSaussure. After Mr. Champion's death, in 1813, she married MAJOR JOHN MCCLELLAND, who was born in Ireland in 1768, settling, as a young man, in North Carolina. He served gallantly as Captain of the 3d Regiment, U. S. A., in the war of 1812. Before the close of the war, he was promoted to the rank of Major, but resigned his commission after peace was proclaimed, and settled in Camden. He and his wife are still remembered by aged residents as a most charming old couple. Their house, one of the oldest in Camden, stands on the west side of Broad street, just north of Lafayette Hall. Maj. McClelland was a typical gentleman of the old school. His death occurred in 1853. Mrs. McClelland died the next year and is buried by the side of her first husband, Dr. Trent.

Harriet, a second daughter of Capt. Dubose, married, in 1812, Hon. John Kershaw.

Isaac Dubose had a son named Serrée, but it is not known what became of him.

From a notice in the Charleston papers, we learn that Capt. Dubose was again married, in 1797, to Miss Catherine Dubose "of Camden." This lady was doubtless a daughter of Sam'l Dubose, Esq., then temporarily a resident of the town.

The John Dubose "of Camden,"* who married Miss Ann S. Cantey, of St. Stephen's Parish, in 1804, may have been a son of either Isaac or Samuel, or, probably,

---

*Charleston Gazette.

he was the son of Elias Dubose, of Chesterfield, a brother of Isaac.* From Elias, who married Lydia Cassels, of Sumter District, are descended the present Dubose and Blakeney families of Kershaw County.

Isaac Dubose died in 1816. His Camden home stood at the corner of King and Market streets.

DUNLAP.

Among the many sturdy Scotch-Irish settlers from the north of Ireland who found homes in America shortly after the Revolution was Robert Dunlap. With his young wife, whom he had married in the old country, he located on Grannys Quarter Creek, about ten miles north of Camden. They reared a family of two daughters and several sons. All of the sons went west, except the youngest, James, who came to Camden and was, for many years, prominent in business affairs. He married Elizabeth, a daughter of John Doby, Esq., and was the founder of a large and once influential family, now, like so many others, without a representative in the community. Their home, for half a century, was "Lafayette Hall." Here Mr. Dunlap died in 1874.

The oldest daughter of Robert Dunlap, Nancy, was married three times—to her cousin, Robert Dunlap, John Trantham, and John McDowell, in the order named. She raised seven sons, but no daughter.

This branch of the Dunlap family is related to the Dunlaps of the northern and western parts of the State.

ENGLISH.

See Chapter III.

HAILE.

Benjamin Haile was born in 1768 near Fredericksburg, Va. As a young man, he moved to South Carolina, settling on Lynches Creek, Lancaster County. At this time, his worldly possessions are said to have been one negro and one horse. The story is told that, in building a log cabin on his farm, gold was discovered in the mud with which the interstices were filled. Investigation proved the existence there of an abundant vein

---

*Gregg names John among the children of Elias.

of the precious metal, and, though his mining operations were crude, Mr. Haile soon became a rich man. The mine that he discovered, still known as the Haile mine, is now operated, with improved machinery, at a handsome profit, and is rated the largest in the south.

Col. Shannon,* who knew some of the men of that early period, says: "Capt. Benj. Haile was a remarkable man in his day; rough, self-willed, yet of the most sterling integrity; devoted to principle, of sturdy and earnest attachments, frank, honest and true, he possessed the confidence and esteem of all. He amassed one of the largest fortunes ever built up in our district."

His plantations were on Lynches Creek, in West Wateree, and lower Kershaw, among them the present State Farm, near Boykin.

Mr. Haile represented the county in the Legislature in 1792. Among other offices that he filled with credit was that of Trustee of the South Carolina College (1809).

About the beginning of the 19th century, he purchased the Ben Bineham house on Broad street, Camden, at present the property of J. B. Wallace, and here he reared his large family of thirteen children, now scattered from Virginia to Florida. He died in 1842.

His first wife was Mary Cureton, a sister of Everard Cureton. Of this union were born:

1. James, who married Miss Truesdale, and was the father of the late lamented Capt. Columbus Haile.

2. Benjamin, who married Louisa, daughter of Isaac Lenoir.

3. Catherine, who became the wife of Christopher Matheson.

4. Susan, afterwards wife of Dr. Thomas Lanier, of Lancaster.

5. Sarah, who married a Mr. Knox, and lived out West.

The second wife of Benj. Haile was Amelia Evans, of Chesterfield. By this marriage his children were:

6. Mary, who married William Kennedy.

7. Caroline.

*Old Times in Camden.

8. Rebecca, who became Mrs. Farquhar Matheson.

9. Columbus, who married Louisa, daughter of Dr. John McCaa.

10. Elizabeth, who married Thomas E. Shannon, Esq.

11. Thomas, who married Serena, daughter of Capt. John Chesnut.

12. Edward, twice married; first to Mary Chesnut, sister to Serena; second to Miss Chapman.

13. William, accidentally killed at the University of Virginia, while target practicing with a pistol.

14. Charles, who married Elise McCaa, sister to Mrs. Columbus Haile.

Wm. Kennedy and both the Mathesons were merchants and landowners in Camden.

Columbus Haile removed to Staunton, Va., where he engaged in business. Thomas, Edward, and Charles made their homes in Florida. Benjamin (II) and James were large planters in Kershaw, and their descendants are the sole bearers of the name left among us.

Charles and Elizabeth (Mrs. Shannon) are the only surviving children of the first Benjamin Haile.

KERSHAW.

The Kershaw family, by reason of its great services to this community and to the State, deserves first consideration in the history of a town to which it gave the founder and of a county to which it gave its name. In each of four successive generations it has maintained its prestige of usefulness and honor.

Of such a family it is lamentable that we have so few personal data concerning the early members. The letters and other papers of both Joseph and Eli Kershaw were, by request, intrusted to the gifted Henry G. Nixon,* doubtless for some historic compilation, about 1820, but, by a curious stroke of misfortune, Nixon's house was burglarized and the valuable documents were lost. Thus, of necessity, must our sketches of these two notable characters be brief and unsatisfactory, and to be considered only as supplementary to what has been said of them in other connections.

*Johnson's Traditions.

Three brothers, Joseph, Eli, and William, sons of Joseph Kershaw, of Sowerby, in the West Riding of Yorkshire, England, came to seek their fortunes in America about the middle of the 18th century. They seem to have first settled in Charleston. There WILLIAM lived, a prosperous merchant, until his death in 1785. Heitman's Historical Register of officers of the Continental Army states that he was a Brigade Major of South Carolina troops from 1776 to ———. However this may be, it is certain that he welcomed the opportunity to return to his allegiance to the King, after Charleston fell. A letter of his to this effect is among the family relics.

No biography would excite greater interest locally than that of JOSEPH KERSHAW, the recognized "father" of Camden and the patriot in honor of whom the county of which Camden is the capital was named. Of him we first hear as a clerk in the store of James Laurens & Co., Charleston. His initial advertisement in his own name, offering for sale "Exceeding good Bohea Tea, Bristol Beer, &c.," appears in the *Gazette* of May 6, 1756. As elsewhere said, he came to Pine Tree Hill (Camden) about 1758, as the agent of Ancrum, Lance & Loocock. Two years later, this firm advertises "Fine Carolina Flour fresh from Pinetree Hill," in the making of which they were "concerned." This would indicate that Kershaw, who probably had learned all about flour milling in the Old Country, had been sent to establish mills on Pine Tree Creek, and we are of opinion that he was a pioneer in this industry in South Carolina.

Certainly his flour became famous, and was probably the foundation of his fortune. In a few years, by dint of fine executive ability, he had acquired lands, built saw, grist and flouring mills, indigo works, a tobacco warehouse, a brewery* and a distillery,† and established large mercantile businesses at both Camden and Cheraw. In short, by the Revolution, he had become, both

---

*Probably stood on the southwest corner of Meeting and Broad streets, that lot being spoken of in John Adamson's will as "Brew House Squ·.·e." In the Brew House our first County Court sat (1791).
†All specified in his last will.

in wealth and influence, the leading man of the district. We have seen how, under his direction mainly, the wilderness about Pine Tree Hill was converted into the well-planned and prosperous town of Camden.

Catholic in spirit, he gave lands for the erection of places of worship, not only to his own church, the English, but also to the Presbyterians, to the Baptists, and to "God's Antient people, the Jews."*

The ferry across the river, at the site of the old bridge, was chartered by him and Samuel Wyly, prior to the Revolution. Upon his plantation on the other side, near the Ferry (now the Savage lands), he attempted to found another town, which he named "Westerham." Streets were laid out and some lots were sold, but not a trace of this projected city, except the title applied to the plantation, now is left.

His career, as legislator, soldier, administrator of state affairs in Camden District, has been told, however inadequately, in other connections.

As chairman of a committee in the Assembly of 1768, he recommended the division of St. Mark's into several parishes, the building of convenient churches and schools, and the payment of schoolmasters out of public funds, on condition of their giving free instruction to a certain number of indigent children—a suggestion of our modern free school system. Later, in 1787, we hear of him as a charter member of the Camden Orphan Society, whose object, in part, was to provide such free education.

In 1772, he was appointed Sheriff of Camden District, in place of Roger-Peter Handasyde Hatley, Esq., who died in Camden, at Mr. Kershaw's house.

Johnson says that Col. Kershaw's Orderly-book, containing accounts with each officer serving in his regiment during the Revolution, was, in 1851, in the hands of the late Judge J. B. Kershaw. It is now lost, and with it, forever, perhaps, definite information about Kershaw's troops.

A thorough patriot, he suffered much during the war,

---

*His will.

sacrificing time, talents, wealth, even liberty, for his adopted country.

We have seen that he was captured, at the fall of Camden, cast into prison, loaded with irons, and later, with Eli, banished to British Honduras, being afterwards permitted, on account of Eli's health, to go to Bermuda. Here, for fifteen months, he lived in exile, until exchanged about the end of the war.

While in Bermuda, Col. Kershaw conceived the idea of furnishing the colonies with much-needed supplies. To accomplish this enterprise, which had to be undertaken at his own risk, his estates around Camden were mortgaged to the Bermuda merchants to the sum of £9,000. A shipload of clothing and other military stores was sent out, but was captured and confiscated by the British. In later years, Congress was petitioned for some redress, but, the enterprise not having been official, all in vain. The merchants in Bermuda instituted proceedings to recover their advances, and thus Col. Kershaw's possessions, or what remained of them after the war, were sold out by degrees until there was little left.

His son, John, as the agent of the creditors, spent a good part of his life closing up these matters.

Efforts were also made to have the State reimburse Col. Kershaw, even partially, for the ruinous losses that had fallen upon him in his patriotic service. His appeals for justice, which we subjoin, met with a seemingly poor response, as great perhaps, however, as the duresse of the times would allow.

1.

Joseph Kershaw to Gov. John Rutledge:*

Charleston, Tuesday Morn.
24 Feby, 1784.

Sr: I waited on your brother, Mr. E. Rutledge, agreeable to your desire, but found him too much engaged to examine the papers of Mr Thos. Rutledge, in order to enable me to make out a fair state of my accounts settled with him in Sept, '79, the duplicates of which was,

*From State House (Rubbish Room).

with my other papers, destroyed by Lord Rawdon, 22nd June, 1780. Fortunately for me, I had sent my principal Books of accounts & Land Titles to the mountains of Virginia & my Bonds & Notes into the hands of Mr Hillegas, Philadelphia, which is nearly the whole property I saved except my dwelling House, the British having destroyed not less than from 17 to £20,000 of my rich property, besides cutting me out of an Income of at least £2000 sterling per annum, which my Mills, Brewery and distillery and Farms yielded me, so that I am very near, if not entirely ruined.

I find I am likely to be put under many difficultys in getting my accounts settled with the auditor, tho' there is not a shilling charged but what I honestly furnished, besides dedicating my whole time and riding many thousand miles at my own expense on the public service from October 75 to 27 May 1780,* for which I never charged one farthing, except when out on two or three Commands which never indemnified me for one quarter the expense I was at in providing extra supplies to the men under my Command. I have just taken the liberty of laying these facts before you, as the supplys was chiefly furnished by orders from you when you presided as Govr, and which you assured me the Public would reimburse. I am, with great esteem, Sir, Your most obt svt, JO. KERSHAW.

2.

Kershaw to Rutledge:†

Charleston, 25th Feby, 1784.

Sir: As you was so obliging as to promise your assistance in getting my public accounts adjusted so as to enable me to get Indents for the same, I have taken the liberty to enclose you a state of my request, which I hope will not be thought unreasonable—A great proportion was the produce of my Mills, Farms & Stock or taken for old debts as Specie Currency. My Brew House & Out Houses were much Injured, as was several of the Stores belonging to my Brother's Est., and the old

---

*Evidently the date of his capture by the enemy.
†From State House.

store burnt to the ground, by being made use of as Barracks &c. All I wish is to be repaid the Carpenter Bill for the repairs, no compensation as Rent or any other thing having ever been received.

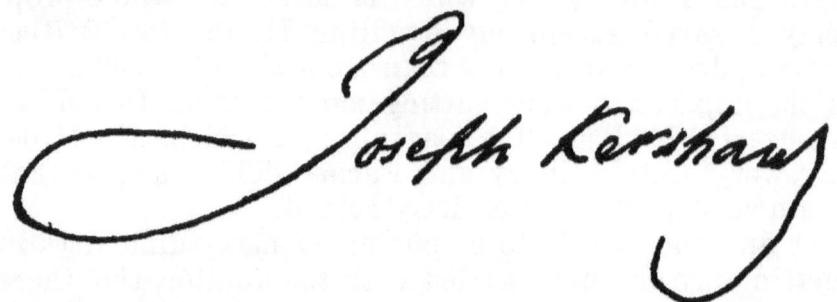

A memorandum indorsed on this paper states that Council approved Kershaw's claims for £3593-11-4, and for this amount he receipted on April 11, 1784. His claim of £406-8-8 for damages to buildings was not allowed.

His last will and testament, executed June 1, 1788, shows that, even then, he had large estates. This will, however, was superseded by an assignment made by him Feb. 4, 1790, to five of his principal creditors, William Ancrum, Edward Darrell, James Fisher, Robert Henry, and James Kershaw.*

Joseph Kershaw was married, about 1763, to Sarah, daughter of Daniel and Sophia Mathis, early Quaker settlers. The issue of this union were:

1. James—Born 1764. Married, first (1798), Sarah, daughter of Joshua English; second (1813), Mrs. Lydia Ann Vaughan. For an acquaintance with James Kershaw, read the extracts from his Diary, Appendix B.
2. John (1765-1829).
3. Joseph (1769-1798). Married Miss S. Hutchins.
4. Mary (1771-1848). Unmarried.
5. George (1773-1803). Married Miss Ann Hutchins.
6. Sarah (1775-1824). Married Benj. Perkins, Esq.†
7. Rebecca (1779-1811). Married John Brown, Esq., an attorney at law in Camden.
8. Samuel Geoffrey (1782-1812). Unmarried.

*Recorded in Lancaster Courthouse.
†See sketch of Perkins family.

JOHN KERSHAW was a member of the Constitutional Convention, 1790; a Judge of the County Court of Kershaw, when first established, in 1791; a member of the Legislature in 1792 and again in 1800, and a Representative of this District in the Congress of 1812. The same year, he married Harriet, daughter of Capt. Isaac Dubose, who long survived him. To them were born one daughter, Mary, who became the wife of Robert Young, Esq., of Camden, and one son, that great citizen, soldier, jurist and gentleman, Gen. Joseph Brevard Kershaw, whose life will be given in the history of the Civil War Period (Vol. II). There are worthy descendants of Robert Young in Alabama and in upper Carolina.

A singular fatality has limited the succession of the name in the Kershaw family to one representative in each generation, until the present. John alone of the sons left descendants, and his only son, Joseph, left but one son, John, the present rector of St. Michael's, Charleston.

The death of Mrs. Kershaw occurred in 1789. Her remains are interred, it would appear from the double inscription on the tomb, in the same grave with her mother, Sophia Mathis, in the Quaker Cemetery.

Col. Joseph Kershaw died Dec. 28, 1791, in the 64th year of his age. He is buried in his family inclosure a little below the old Courthouse,* and above the grave rises a modest marble shaft commemorative of his many virtues. A man of mark in his day and generation, of wonderful energy and business capacity, endowed with fine practical sense and an indomitable will, he deserves, both as pioneer and patriot, to be recorded one of the founders of the greatness of South Carolina.

To ELI KERSHAW, in 1766, was granted the land on which the present town of Cheraw is located. Conjointly with his brother Joseph and others, he had the place laid out and called it "Chatham," in honor of the elder Pitt, then championing the cause of the colonies. This title the village bore until its incorporation under the name of Cheraw.

*In the old Episcopal Churchyard.

Here the firm of Eli Kershaw & Co. did a thriving business until dissolved in 1774. We take the following notice from Gregg's History of the Old Cheraws:

"SALE.

"1774. On Wednesday the 16th day of November next and the following days, at the Court House at Long Bluff, will be sold,

"That valuable Plantation, called Liberty Hill, and all their other lands, at and near Cheraw Hill, on Peedee River, together with their Store Houses, Mills, remaining stock of store goods, and about fifty valuable negroes, employed in carrying on their business at Chatham, under the firm of Eli Kershaw & Co. The whole being to be sold in order to make a final settlement of the copartnership which lately subsisted between the subscribers, &c.

"JOSEPH KERSHAW
"JOHN CHESNUT
"ELI KERSHAW
"WILLIAM ANCRUM
"AARON LOOCOCK."

Eli Kershaw gave the land on which was erected the parish church, at Cheraw, and he was for years one of its wardens. As a commissioner, in 1770, to locate the jail and courthouse in Cheraw Precinct, he made a strong effort to have them built at Chatham. In a counter-petition to the Assembly, his opponents made malicious but very effective use of a jocular utterance by Mr. Kershaw that his advocacy of this location was to increase the sale at his store of "grog and osnaburgs"!* The courthouse was built at Long Bluff. It was perhaps partly through chagrin at this that Eli removed to Camden and entered into business with his brother, Joseph (1774). Of his subsequent public career we have elsewhere told. To the end of this sketch we append the roll of his command in the Revolution, which happily has been preserved.

With Joseph, he seems to have been taken prisoner at Camden. En route to Bermuda, to which the two

*Gregg's Old Cheraws.

brothers were expatriated, Eli died of putrid dysentery aboard ship, on the day the vessel arrived in the harbor of St. George, and there his ashes lie. Joseph, himself an exile on that distant isle, had a tablet erected to his brother's memory, which Col. James P. Dickinson said he saw on his visit to Bermuda in 1840.

The *South Carolina Gazette* of Nov. 30, 1769, has this notice: "The 19th instant, Mr. Eli Kershaw, of Rockingham,* was married to Miss Mary Cantey, daughter of Capt. John Cantey of Camden."

Of this marriage there was but one issue, a daughter, Rebecca, who, in 1793, became the wife of Joseph Brevard, later the very distinguished jurist.

Eli Kershaw died in 1780, at the early age of 37. His sword, engraved with his name and the date "1775," is preserved, as a priceless heirloom, by one of his descendants, Miss Harriet Brevard, of Camden.

*Probably near Cheraw. There is a town of the name just over the line in North Carolina.

A General Return of Colo. Thomson's Regiment of Rangers.
Capt. Eli Kershaw's Company.

No. of Privates	Names of Officers, Non-Commissioned Officers and Privates.	Dates of Commissions and Attestations.	Age of Officers, Non-Commissioned Officers & Privates	Country where Born	Size of Men Feet-inchs	Pay to this day
	Captain Eli Kershaw	18th June 1775	30 Years	England	6 x x	332,, 10,,
	Lieuts. { Francis Boykin	18. June "	21 "	North Carolina	5 x 10	213,, 15,,
	Lieuts. { Thomas Charlton	29. June "	29 "	Maryland	5 x 10	189,, 7,,
	Serjts. { Augustine Preestwood	1. July "	26 "	Virginia	6 x 1	66,, 13,, 4
	Serjts. { Thomas Pemble	1. Do "	28 "	..Do	5 x 11	66,, 13,, 4
	Drummer Thomas Wood	1. Do "	26 "	Ireland	5 x 8	53,, 6,, 8
1	Privates—Robt. Martin	1. Do "	28 "	..Do	6 x 2	53,, 6,, 8
2	Newel Bearfoot	1. Do "	24 "	Virginia	5 x 4	53,, 6,, 8
3	James Saxon	1. Do "	20 "	..Do	5 x 10	53,, 6,, 8
4	Uriah Goodwin	1. Do "	25 "	..Do	6 x x	53,, 6,, 8
5	Jacob Cherry	1. Do "	23 "	..Do	5 x 11	53,, 6,, 8
6	James Cook	1. Do "	23 "	England	5 x 3	53,, 6,, 8
7	Peregrine Magness	1. Do "	21 "	Virginia	5 x 9	53,, 6,, 8
8	John Gray	1. Do "	22 "	..Do	5 x 11	53,, 6,, 8
9	Joseph Ferguson	1. Do "	23 "	..Do	5 x 10	53,, 6,, 8
10	Benjamin Ferguson	1. Do "	23 "	..Do	5 x 7	53,, 6,, 8
11	Mordicai McKinney	1. Do "	24 "	Maryland	5 x 9	53,, 6,, 8
12	William French	1. Do "	30 "	Virginia	5 x 10	53,, 6,, 8
13	Richard Nicholls	1. Do "	21 "	North Carolina	5 x 8	53,, 6,, 8
14	Jeremiah Simmons	1. Do "	22 "	Ireland	5 x 9	53,, 6,, 8
15	Thomas Howell	1. Do "	24 "	Maryland	5 x 10	53,, 6,, 8
16	Thomas Coursey	1. Do "	28 "	North Carolina	5 x 8	53,, 6,, 8
17	John Payne	1. Do "	22 "	South Carolina	5 x 9	53,, 6,, 8
18	John Wright	1. Do "	22 "	Maryland	5 x 10	53,, 6,, 8
19	Hugh Gaston	1. Do "	23 "	Ireland	6 x 2	53,, 6,, 8
20	Robert Gaston	1. Do "	25 "	..Do	6 x x	53,, 6,, 8
21	Alexander Gaston	1. Do "	21 "	..Do	6 x 10	53,, 6,, 8
22	George Gray	1. Do "	24 "	Virginia	5 x 9	53,, 6,, 8
23	John Steel	1. Do "	22 "	Ireland	5 x 9	53,, 6,, 8
24	John Swilla	1. Do "	26 "	Virginia	5 x 3	53,, 6,, 8
25	Aaron Alexander	1. Do "	29 "	..Do	6 x 5	53,, 6,, 8
26	Robert White	1. Do "	35 "	Ireland	6 x x	53,, 6,, 8
27	Henry Harmon	1. Do "	30 "	Virginia	5 x 10	53,, 6,, 8
28	William Weatherford	25. Do "	29 "	..Do	6 x x	37,, 3,, 3
29	Samuel Sessions	1 August "	28 "	..Do	6 x 6	33,, 6,, 8
30	John Montgomery	4. Do "	24 "	Ireland	5 x 8	30,, 12,, 8
						£2463.. 5,,

Note.—These pay rolls were Indorsed by John Chesnut, Pay Master of the Regiment; some of them by Joseph Kershaw for Capt. Chesnut. This roll is from the Papers of the First Council of Safety of the Revolutionary Party, in South Carolina—June to November, 1775, and is copied from the *South Carolina Historical and Genealogical Magazine*, July, 1901.

LANG.

WILLIAM LANG (I), son of Obadiah Lang and Elizabeth Wilson, his wife, was born near Wakefield, in Yorkshire, England (the shire whence Joseph Kershaw came), Feb. 16, 1746. He emigrated to the South Carolina colony in 1770, settled at Camden, and in 1775 married Sally Wyly, daughter of Samuel Wyly and Dinah Milhouse, his wife. He died in 1815 and his wife in 1817. A considerable part of the extensive landed estate of Samuel Wyly came to him through his marriage. Their children were:

1. James Wilson Lang, born 1776.
2. Elizabeth Lang, born 1779.
3. Samuel Wyly Lang, born 1782.
4. John Lang, born 1785.
5. Hannah Lang, born 1788.
6. William Wyly Lang, born 1790.
7. Thomas Lang, born 1793.

WILLIAM W. LANG (II) first married Katherine Boykin, daughter of Burwell Boykin. His Camden residence, corner Campbell and DeKalb streets (lot 674), still stands. This lot had been conveyed in 1799 by John Kershaw to the town of Camden as a burial ground for "negroes, slaves, Indians, mulattoes and mestizoes," but had, presumably, never been so used, for in 1814 William W. Lang purchased it from the town and built his home there. This location, the most elevated point in the town, the most desirable and eligible for handsome buildings, has, in the strange mutation of time, become neglected and lost to such purposes.

After occupying a leading position in the affairs of Camden, Mr. Lang left for Alabama about 1845, in the wake of that movement westward which so depopulated the town in that decade. His second wife was Sarah, daughter of Duncan McRae, and their descendants are throughout the South, though none in Camden.

JAMES WILSON LANG married Miss Murray, of Stateburg, S. C. Their children were two daughters, Misses Murray and Susan Lang, who lived together as old maiden ladies, and died unmarried. He was Clerk of Court for Kershaw County in 1836-37.

The Langs now residents of this county are all descendants of THOMAS LANG (No. 7 above), who occupied an important place in the business, social and political affairs of this community. As a planter, on a large scale, he was successful, which of itself bespeaks energy and ability. His residence was in the "Magazine" quarter of old Camden, where he presided with social distinction, and often entertained the military companies at their musters on the green.

In the fierce days of Nullification he came to the front in the politics of the district. To explain his peculiar attitude would require the exploration of the intricacies of the party divisions of the time. His was an example of the adage that extremes meet. Although an ultra believer in State's rights, and the doctrine of paramount allegiance to the State, he would none of the Nullifier's profession of adherence to the Union while repudiating Federal laws. This paradox drove him to the Unionists, who were indeed his opposites in principle, and in the critical contests of 1830 and 1832 he was elected to the Legislature at the head of their ticket.

But when, in 1833, the Nullifiers proposed for enactment the drastic "Test Oath," requiring all State officers, civil and military, to subscribe an oath of paramount State allegiance—when the State, wrought to tension, watched the fate of this measure, which hung in the balance, to the consternation of his Unionist constituents, to his own undoing, he voted for it. Of his conduct Col. Shannon has said: "He in his vote adhered to his principles and took issue with his party, cast his vote sternly, quietly, with calm dignity and gracefully retired, knowing that the act closed his public career. He lived twice over to prove his faith by his works. In 1852 he stood again by the banner of State sovereignty and secession, and in 1860 he gave earnestly of his time and means to the great but now 'lost cause,' and had the satisfaction of greeting as his comrades in that last campaign, every survivor of the 'fifty-seven' "—an allusion doubtless to the number in the Legislature of 1833 who had opposed the "Test Oath." He died May 13,

1861, just as the guns of Sumter proclaimed the principles of the Test Oath.

Thomas Lang married Mary, daughter of Duncan McRae, March 29, 1815. She died Feb. 22, 1848. Their children were: (1) Sally Wyly Lang, who married Burwell Boykin, 1834, died May 17, 1889. (2) Duncan McRae Lang, born 1817, married Mary Honoria Logan, 1853, died 1856. (3) William Lang, born 1818, died 1820. (4) Mary Chesnut Lang, born 1820, married Dr. Ed. M. Boykin, 1841, only survivor of children of Thos. Lang. (5) Thomas Lang, born 1821, married Eliz. Rives, died 1867. (6) William Lang, second son of this name, born 1822, died 1824. (7) Harriet McRae Lang, born 1823, died, unmarried, 1892. (8) John Chesnut Lang, born 1825, died 1889. (9) Ed. Brevard Lang, born 1826, died 1865. (10) Flora McRae Lang, born 1828, died 1832. (11) Septimus Lang, born 1830, died 1831. (12) Theodore Lang, born 1832, died unmarried, at Memphis, Tenn., 1896.

LEVY.

This family will be treated in sketch of Chapman Levy, Volume II.

M'WILLIE.

Will be treated in the sketch of Wm. McWillie, Volume II.

M'RAE.

One of the earliest of the many excellent citizens that Scotland has contributed to Camden was Duncan McRae. He was born at Conchra, Rosshire, in 1754, and came to South Carolina prior to the Revolution. From an entry in the Journals of the Council of Safety, made Feb. 21, 1776, we learn that he served in Col. G. G. Powell's regiment, registering from St. David's Parish. A few years later, he seems to have removed from the Peedee section to this town, where, in 1782, as we have stated,* he was engaged in a mercantile business with John Chesnut and John Adamson.

*See Chapter XII.

In 1785, he married Sarah, daughter of Gabriel Powell, of St. Helena, and widow of the noted royalist, Charles Augustus Steward, of the Cheraws. Bishop Gregg's statement that, in 1789, he was one of the Justices of the County Court of Chesterfield, would indicate that he had returned to the Peedee, or, perhaps, that, up to this time, he had never lived in Camden, being a nonresident member of the firm named above. In 1788, Mrs. McRae died, leaving a son, Powell, who married a Miss Singleton. Of this union sprung one son, Powell (II), who married a Miss May, leaving, at his death, two daughters, one of whom married a scion of the distinguished Livingstone family of New York.

In 1789, Duncan McRae took, as his second wife, Mary, eldest daughter of John Chesnut (I), of Camden. Certainly in 1794 he was established in Camden in business with Gen. Zach. Cantey, under the firm name of McRae & Cantey. Two years later, this firm bought of James Kershaw, as executor of the estate of Joseph Kershaw, 3,203 acres of land, "including the mill," and doubtless the large pond, on Big Pine Tree Creek, now the property of the Camden Cotton Factory. The mill was about the site of old Greene's Bridge. The pond is still known as McRae's. This plant, where a large saw and grist milling business was conducted, was burned, it is said by incendiaries, in 1811. The loss was estimated at $10,000. The year following, Mr. McRae built another merchant mill just across Little Pine Tree Creek, very near the location of the Camden Cotton Mills. The canal which he cut to it from his pond, more than a mile away, is still well defined, running parallel to the larger modern canal.

Duncan McRae closed his energetic career in 1824, and lies in our cemetery. His oldest son, John, married, in 1818, Caroline Jumelle, daughter of the French refugee, Pierre Laurent Jumelle. He was the builder of "Lausanne," for years the residence of John M. DeSaussure, Esq., and later, as "Uphton Court," the home of Mrs. Caroline Jumelle Perkins, a niece of Mrs. McRae.* John McRae left no children. The portrait

*Mrs. McRae exchanged "Lausanne" with Maj. DeSaussure for the Bynum residence (now Dr. Moore's) on Broad street.

of his wife, one of Sully's finest productions, presents a face of exquisite charm; on the death of Mrs. Perkins, it was purchased by a northern collector.

Of Duncan McRae's daughters, Mary married Thomas Lang (1815); Sarah married William W. Lang (1819); Harriet became the wife of Dr. Alfred Brevard (1822), and Margaret, of John Whitaker (1827). Scota (born in 1806), the youngest of the family, married her cousin, John McRa, who, with his brother, Colin, came over from Scotland about 1840. She alone, of the daughters, had no issue. Her home on Jumelle Hill was once one of the "show" places of the town, with its fountains, terraces, and lake from which water was piped to the house. John McRa was a gentleman of scientific attainments and a master mathematician. He was chief engineer, in 1847, of the Columbia and Greenville Railroad, and, in 1849, of the South Carolina Road. He died in 1891, at the age of 82, having survived his wife nine years.

Colin, who, for seven years after his brother's death, lived alone in the big family residence, was one of the most eccentric of characters. Like his brother, he was devoted to mechanical and scientific subjects, and for forty years kept a daily record of Kirkwood weather. Many amusing anecdotes of him are extant. He was at one time presented by a perfect stranger in New York with a button that the donor stated he had promised never to part with until he met a man more homely than himself. We may be pardoned this very personal reference, as Mr. McRa laughingly boasted that the most ferocious canine would quail before one of his grimaces. In old age, as he drove through our streets, with a Scotch plaid shawl about his shoulders and a Scotch cap upon his head, he was a type of the brawny "Hielandman." With his death, a bachelor, in 1898, at the age of 85, the male line of the Camden McRaes came to an end.

MARTIN.

Dr. James Martin was a surgeon of the South Carolina line, Continental Army, in the Revolution. The will of his father, James Martin, "of Wateree," made in

1781 and probated before Patrick Calhoun in 1786, is in our courthouse. By its terms, legacies are left to four sons, William, John, James and Andrew, and to one daughter, Jane. Tradition says that the family came from Maryland.

Dr. James Martin settled, as a young man, in Newberry District, and there married a Miss Caldwell, of Abbeville, by whom he had one child, Sarah, who became the wife of James Calhoun.

After his wife's death, Dr. Martin removed to Camden, where he practiced his profession. His second wife was Sarah, daughter of John Brown and Sarah Davis, his wife, both of Virginia. The following tribute to him is taken from the *Charleston Gazette* of Sept. 27, 1797: "Died at Camden, on the 22nd inst., Doctor James Martin, whose good nature, candour and honesty endeared him to all of his acquaintance. In life he was a good citizen, and in death a man." He was cut off in the 48th year of his age.

By the terms of his will, bequests were left to five daughters, Sarah, "Molsey" (Mary), Elizabeth, Charlotte, Frances. His one son, James, died, unmarried, on the verge of manhood.

Mary was married to James K. Douglas, and Elizabeth to Abram Blanding, on the same day, May 4, 1806.

Frances became the wife of Dr. D. L. DeSaussure, of Charleston, whose son, Dr. Daniel DeSaussure (II), was long an honored physician in Camden.

Many of our largest families trace back to Dr. Martin.

MATHIS.

See Chapter III.

MICKLE.

The founder of this, one of our oldest families, was Joseph Mickle, who was settled on the Wateree as early as 1753. Tradition is silent as to whence he came, indeed concerning his personal history in general. The name is Scotch. As he came about the time of the first Quakers, he may have been of that religious persuasion. An Act of the Assembly, passed April 9, 1778, authorizes the establishment of a ferry over the river "at the plantation of Joseph Mickle," and vests the same in him and his heirs.

The children of this pioneer were:

1. Jane, who married a Saunders, of what is now Sumter County.
2. Jonathan.
3. John, the father of Mrs. Rebecca Mickle Chattan, and of John (II), who married Rebecca, daughter of his cousin, Robert E. Mickle.
4. Robert, who married Katherine Irvin, sister of Mrs. Thomas Salmond. Their offspring were: (a) Robert (II), a Presbyterian minister, who located in Mobile; (b) Rebecca (Mrs. Donovan, of Mobile); (c) Mary; (d) Kitty, who passed her life in Camden.
5. Joseph (II). Major Joseph Mickle was a prominent merchant here for many years, in the first part of the nineteenth century, retiring, in later life, to his plantation across the river, about fifteen miles from the town. His fine country residence and lands, which, in all probability, were his father's, are now in the possession of one of his grandsons. He was an intelligent man of bookish tastes, yet fond of society, in which he freely mingled. Col. Shannon, who admired him, tells the following anecdote of the old gentleman: "We well remember his enthusiasm on the subject of phrenology, and can, in imagination, see him now, with his tall gaunt figure, stalking across our parlor, where he was a frequent guest, and, after examining the developments of three or four boys, gesticulating with his long arms and exclaiming: 'Boys, thank God there is something in the front of your heads; if there were not, the backs of them would carry you all straight to the devil!'"

Major Mickle married Martha, daughter of John Belton and Mary English his wife. The issue of this union were numerous, and still largely represented hereabouts:

(a) John Belton (1812-1864), who married Sarah, daughter of Dr. John Milling. Their old homestead, still occupied by the family, stands just above Saunders Creek.

(b) Joseph (III) 1814-1898, a longtime resident of Camden. He married, first, Nancy Gandy; second, Matilda Whitaker Milling, sister to Mrs. John Mickle.

(c) Martha, who married Rice Dulin, of Fairfield County.

(d) Robert English, whose wife was Mary Pea, of Longtown.

(e) Sally Wyly, who married John J. Nelson, of West Wateree.

(f) Mary, who became the wife of James Lyles, of Fairfield.

Major Mickle died in 1835, from the effects of a fall from an old-fashioned cotton screw.

MILHOUSE, OR MILHOUS.

See Chapter III.

NETTLES.

Capt. William Nettles was born, of Scotch parentage, near Alexandria, Va., in 1734. He came to Camden in the "Fifties" and acquired lands above Gum Swamp, a part of what was afterwards the famous battlefield.

At the beginning of the Revolution, he enlisted and served until the end of the war, most of the time under Gen. Sumter. In one of the battles near Camden, he was severely wounded in the right leg, disabling him for life.

At the Fourth of July celebration in 1832, Maj. John Cantey proposed the health of Capt. Nettles, speaking of him in complimentary terms, as a "crippled patriot of the Revolution, now tottering under a virtuous old age." He had then reached the remarkable age of 98 years and was yet vigorous enough to attend this dinner. His death occurred the same year, closing a long and honorable career, and he lies buried in the old cemetery at Flat Rock.

Capt. Nettles was married three times. His first wife was Amy Alexander; his second, Mary Mathis, a sister of Samuel Mathis; his third, Hester Sanders, widow of Capt. Cook, a fellow veteran. By his second and third unions, he left a number of descendants.

Samuel Nettles, a son of the second wife, operated a tannery in Columbia, where he made a large fortune, removing thence to Montgomery, Ala.

The present representatives of the name in Camden are descended from Jesse S. Nettles, a son by the third marriage, who was sheriff of the county and held other civic positions of trust, besides serving in the War of 1812 and, under Capt. John Chesnut, in the Seminole War.

NIXON.

Treated under sketch of Henry G. Nixon, in Volume II.

PATTERSON.

Treated in Volume II under head of Liberty Hill.

PERKINS.

BENJAMIN PERKINS (I), progenitor of the Camden family, was perhaps the first of that contingent from New England, which soon after the Revolution came to make accessions to the best elements of Camden's citizenship. He was born in Connecticut, 1763. We find him admitted to the Carolina bar in 1787. In the following year he, one H. Beaumont (of whom only the name is known), Daniel and Jacob Brown, were the first attorneys to hang up their shingles in Camden. He appears by the early records in full practice for some years. He married Sarah, daughter of Joseph Kershaw, and through her acquired a considerable area of lands, the Westerham place, across the river from Camden, and a large tract at Hyco, on Pine Tree Creek, where he died in 1841. Some of our older citizens recall the eccentricities of his latter years, and among other things relate how at church he would get up from his seat, stroll about the aisles with hands behind his back, stop and stare at the preacher, sometimes with evident disapproval of his doctrine, go to the door and examine the weather, sit for a while on the pulpit steps, and seemed always unable to keep still.

Of his ten children Charles W., the oldest, died an infant. The second was also named Charles, born 1799, lived as an old bachelor at Hyco, and as such died there 1872. He engaged in farming, milling and cattle raising.

BENJAMIN (II), son of Benjamin (I), was born 1803, died 1868. He lived in or near Camden, his summer residence at "Goodie Castle," now of F. W. Eldredge, in Kirkwood. He married Priscilla Bryan Jumelle, who was born 1819, died 1881. She was a daughter of Pierre Laurent Jumelle, who was one of the wealthy proprietors of Santo Domingo, cast out upon the world by the storm of the French Revolution, and drifted to Camden. Here, driven from affluence to poverty, he resorted to his skill in the polite arts for a living, and taught fashionable French dances to his own music on the violin. "Jumelle Hill" in Kirkwood derives its name from him. The inscription on his grave in our cemetery says that he was born 1768 in the Parish of La Petite Riviere de l'Artibonite, Santo Domingo, and died in Camden 1824. His daughter Caroline married John McRae, son of Duncan McRae, and further reference to her will be found under head of the McRae family.

There were two children of Benjamin and Priscilla Perkins, a son and daughter. Benjamin (III), his middle name Elias, born 1844, died 1867, was a gallant Confederate soldier, married Maria Carter Wormly, of Virginia. Their infant son, Laurence Jumelle, survived his mother, who died in 1873, only a few days. Caroline Jumelle Perkins, born 1843, died Feb. 13, 1898, will be held in remembrance by this community as the accomplished lady of Upton (or Uphton) Court* (now the Court Inn), as one of the pioneers in development of Camden as a winter resort. This old mansion she purchased in 1884, then gone much to wreck, restored and converted into a charming place for guests. It having been originally built for her aunt, Caroline McRae, it seemed the fitness of events that it should become hers. In 1859 she married Roger Griswold Perkins, who died in 1861. They left no descendants.

MARY KERSHAW PERKINS, daughter of Benjamin (I), born 1807, died 1846, married Saml. Wilds DuBose, of Darlington. Messrs. E. C. DuBose and H. K. DuBose,

---

*A tract of land known in 1732 as "Upton Court," is mentioned among the early homesteads of Harford County, Maryland, in Preston's History of Harford County, page 32.

of this county, are their sons, as was also Wilds DuBose, deceased. Thus the DuBose family are the only representatives of the line of Benjamin Perkins in our midst.

THOMPSON.

See Liberty Hill (Vol. II).

TRANTHAM—DRAKEFORD.

The Tranthams, or Trenthams, as the name was written originally, came from Wales about the close of the 17th, or early in the 18th century, and settled in Virginia. In 1702, a German girl, whose maiden name is not now known, came to Virginia and married a German named Eppinger. Upon his death, she married Martin Trantham, and came to South Carolina, prior to the Revolution, and settled in what is now Kershaw County. They reared a large family of sons and daughters, whose descendants may be found in several Southern States.

One of the sons, Martin (II), remained in this county, was a man of means, and had one son, John. Both father and son were patriot soldiers in the war. Martin lived to be a very old man, dying about 1800. John died in 1820, at the age of about fifty-five years. He married Nancy Dunlap, and was the father of Dr. John I. Trantham, born in 1820, who was a highly esteemed physician in the upper part of Kershaw, and was the progenitor of those in our midst now worthily bearing the name.

Dr. Trantham married Elizabeth, daughter of Col. Wm. Drakeford, son of Richard Drakeford. He died in 1881.

Mrs. Elizabeth Trantham, the German girl who came to America in 1702, lived to be considerably over 100 years of age, and died, early in the 19th century, in Lincoln County, Tenn., where there are many of her descendants.

JOHN DRAKEFORD and his brother, RICHARD, came from Fairfax County, Va., and settled on Flat Rock Creek, in the upper part of Kershaw County, about the middle of the 18th century. The old land titles show that John was here as early as 1754. The two brothers were gallant patriot soldiers in the Revolution. Richard was desperately wounded by a sword cut on the head, but he recovered and raised a large family. One of his sons was the Col. William Drakeford mentioned above. Richard died in 1825. John lived to a great age, dying about 1850. The first Drakefords came to this country from England. Many, in this State and Alabama, trace their lineage to the branch of the family that settled here.

WYLY.

See Chapter III.

WHITAKER.

The Whitaker family, both in its own name and by its connections, has played a conspicuous part in the life of Camden from early times.

The first of the name here were James and William, brothers, who left Virginia and, about 1772, obtained grants of land in the vicinity of Camden, besides about 1,200 acres near the old Waxhaws. (Record Land Grants, State House.) They were descended from the famous "Apostle of Virginia," Dr. Alexander Whitaker, by whom Pocahontas was married to John Rolfe.

JAMES WHITAKER'S daughters, Martha and Catherine, became the wives, respectively, of James Cantey and Francis Boykin, both patriot soldiers. His son, Major WILLIS WHITAKER, was a captain in Joseph Kershaw's regiment.* He and John, possibly a brother, were among the country militia paroled at the fall of Charleston.

Major Willis Whitaker was an honored citizen. He served in the Legislature in 1794 and again in 1802, and was one of the veterans selected to act as pallbearers at the reinterment of DeKalb's remains in 1825. He died in Fairfield District in 1832. His son, Capt. Willis Whitaker, in the early years of the 19th century, removed to Texas, where worthy representives of the name are now living. One of the first Willis Whitaker's daughters married Dr. John Milling, and this branch is largely

---

*A memorandum among Kershaw's papers states that there were 48 men in Whitaker's company.

represented here in the families of Lorick and of Belton and Joseph Mickle.

WILLIAM WHITAKER married Mary (or Sarah) Lenoir, and from him is descended the present Camden branch of the family, through his oldest son, Thomas. Two of his daughters, Catherine and Mary, became, successively, the wives of Burwell Boykin, Esq., of Pleasant Hill. Another daughter married Alexander Irvin, of Fairfield, whose mother, Margaret, was the only sister of the first John Chesnut.

THOMAS WHITAKER, as a lad of sixteen, served with gallantry under Capt. Francis Boykin, in the Revolution. It is told of him that he refused to hold an officer's horse, during a battle, saying he had not come out for that purpose; and Marion is said to have expressed a wish to have a whole regiment of such boys as "little Tommie Whitaker."

He married (Mary) Williams, and of this union sprung four sons and one daughter, to wit: John, who married Margaret McRae (1827); Laurence, who married Miss Mure; Ellen, who became the wife of Capt. John Chesnut, of Florida War fame; Thomas and William, who remained bachelors. They have all long since been gathered to their fathers.

The Whitakers were extensive planters and contributed their share to that rare society that was the pride of old Camden. Three living generations are likely to perpetuate the line in the community.

APPENDIX A.

DIARY OF SAMUEL MATHIS.

This fragment is all that survives of a quaint old diary of the Revolutionary days, nowhere revealing, save by internal evidence, its authorship. It was found in possession of Mrs. S. A. Caston, of Cheraw, S. C., who had taken it with her from Camden, where she once resided. She kindly loaned it, with this statement in regard to it: "We lived in Camden in 1850, bought the house now occupied by Mrs. Lyles on Monument Square. The house had been rented for some years, and we found a mass of old letters and papers in an upper room. After calling the attention of former residents to them several times, we did as they suggested with most of them, consigned them to the flames; but this diary and one letter having the name of Maria Edgeworth, and written from England, we preserved as ancient history."

It is printed here in full. Many of its minutiæ may appear too trivial for notice—a veritable "chronicle of small beer." Evidently its entries are by a youthful hand, such for instance as: "N. and me romp'd and smited each other dreadfully." Yet its naive detail of domestic matters gives a graphic picture of the Revolutionary household and hardships under British occupation. It also contains interesting personal references and dots of historic value.

But, apart from any real merit, it seemed the more worthy of preservation after we had become fully satisfied from a close scrutiny of its items, tested by other known facts, that its author was young Samuel Mathis—the first white male born in Camden, and one of its honored names. At the time he was just 21, on parole as one of the S. C. militia captured by the British at Charleston, of whom the records show Samuel Mathis was one. He was in charge of the family of Joseph Kershaw, whom his sister had married. It is written either at the "Burndale" or the "Hermitage" country place, whither they had been forced to retire by the British. He refers to letters from J. K., E. K., and W. K. (Joseph, Eli and William Kershaw), and makes this entry, after the British had left Camden: "Wed. May 23d. I had our family moved into Mr. J. K.'s large new house in Camden." This was the "Cornwallis House" of Joseph Kershaw, then new, in fact not complete. He refers to his "bro. Israel at Natchez on the Mississippi," and Samuel Mathis had a brother Israel. The families among whom he moves are those most likely to be intimate with the Kershaws. The Diary was found on premises (lot 759), once owned by Samuel Mathis and by him in 1816 conveyed to Joshua Reynolds, his son-in-law. From all which, and other coincidences, we became convinced to a certainty that Samuel Mathis was the author.

March, 1781.

Thursday 1st. Sister and me went to Camden and got an Order to take wicked Jin (who had run away from us a few days before). I went to the Genl. Hospital and found her in Mr. French's employ, brot her (to) Mr. Le Conte's. We dined and took our Leave. On our way was overtaken by Rutledge; he saw her safe home while I went to B. Boykins he came with me and attended while I had Jin well whiped.

2nd. Went alone to C. found them alarmed got an order from Maj Frazer to take Punch & (illegible)

4th Went to C. by daybreak, hired two soldiers to help take them sent them before me to the Genl Hospital when I came found Caesar & Punch tied them and came home bringing 100 lb Meal and 100 fresh * * * six sacks & Horse and meat fell all over in Derry's Swamp.

8th—I went with Sister to Camden. She got a genl order to take her negroes. I went to see Mr Postell & Miss P. Morong at Log Town and understood they were to go to Chas Town in a few days.

10th I paid off Murkeson, the Taylor. Got 4 Hogs of B. B., killed and salted them.

11th A Trip to Camden got 1-2 yard Muslin of Charlton.

13—In the morning paid Castelo for a p. shoes. afternoon went to Downs for Rum.

15—I aggreed with O'Quin for 150 B. Corn on Acct of an old Debt due J. K.

16—Went to Whitakers for 2 cows and calves catch'd in the Rain came back without them went home and Dined with Bur. Boykin spoke to him to lett me have some good Bread Corn by and by. Afternoon went with a boy to Marshalls and brot. home some kegs Rum, sugar that W. K. had sent from Town in John Cook's waggon. Sister sett out cale among the Pease no. 1.

Saturday 17th—Took Punch and little Isaac with me to Cam. for Molasses, Butter and Meal. In Camden received Letters from J. K. saw a Mr Reese that had been with bro. Israel at Natchez on Mississippi went to

Cary's for Big Jane had a Divil of a scuffle with her she gives me the slip and I hire her to her husband Ben to be paid monthly. Burl promised to come & Kill Turkey for us. In the evening came home with the Horses loaded. I left some of my cloathes with John Wyly in Camden.

18. A jaunt to Camden. Spoke to Majr Doyle for an order to remove Millstones evasive answer. paid Mrs Dinkins in full for butter.

19. Took little Isaac with me over to Furmans & exchanged him for Jack had a smart scuffle with Peggy was forced to tie her, but let her loose before we left the house and brot her and her two smallest children home and sett her immediately to work.

20. Took Jacob with me up to Martin & brot down a plow.

23. Went down to Murphy's. Paid of Thompson the blk smith for work done for the plantation.

25. Afternoon Saml, W. & B. Boykins came to see us Drank Tea spoke about a School Master Comes up a black blustering windy cloud.

27. Sister went over on foot to Mrs. Whitaker's—Mr. Chesnut dines with us.

28th. First news was that Esther had run off in the night and taken her child & cloathes. I pushed off immediately after her by Cook's to Camden & over the Ferry—overtook Cook's waggon but no news of her. Came back to Cary's Place to get a Bundle that W. K. had sent us, but McKenzie not at home. I cross the river again and by Mrs Belton's up to Nights Hill for a letter from W. K. (On my way tho met with Isaac Pidgeon talked to him about the Millstones. he said he paid Stedman* for them) Dined with Mrs Chesnut & sett out for home but was overtaken by a terrible blustering Rain missed my way and got to Mr Chesnut's Mills staid at Tate's that night. Got a pass over the River. Went on by Furman's, Reynolds and O'Quin's down to H. Hunters. home before night.

30th In the morning had quarrell with Pegg and whiped her. Davison leaves stallions and S. Dinkins came to the House and went to Camden with Sister, Charlotte and Rachel Wade. I went with them as far as Cook's.

31—Took Jacob with me over to Bettie's. got a shoat & 2¾ galls. Rum. Was puzzl'd a good while on coming round Bur. Boykins Field in the Dark.

April, 1781.

2nd. Nothing material only Wooderson's Harry rais'd out of Bed to let me have another Horse Collar.

3rd Went to Camden and waited at Headquarters from 10 till 2 o'clock to speak with Majr Doyle. he sent an Orderly serjt to hunt Esther understood that she was hid in an officer's Room.

4th Up to Camden again. no news of her. bought a knife of Bettie, went up to W. Wyly, S. Boykin and me chases E. K.'s Bett but she gives us the slip.

7th—Hetty returns from Bettie's, brings an old sorrell Horse for Sister to ride to Town. Jas. Rich speaks to me for employment and rode with me to old Bradley's.

Sunday 8th—Sister and me goes to Camden and after waiting a great while she gets a receipt for 3 Head of Cattle & I an Order to receive £ 15 stg for wood cut on J. K.'s lands. Lieut. Willson desires me to call on him next Day for the money. We let Adamson have the Cattle receipt for Goods. Mr LeConte and Mr Whitaker accompanies us part of the way home

9th—Willson paid me for the wood and I got some more from Adamson & Co.

---

*Cornwallis's Commissary—later a historian of the Revolution.

10th—Thos. Lenoir speaks to me for 20 acres Land and is to have it.

11th—Goes to Charlton for a mare and money to carry Sister to Chas Town & got them.

12th Went down to Murphy's to speak with the Boat.

13th Pushed directly over the River. went by Mrs. Bettie's, got to Furman's Bridge after Dark and there finds Reynolds' Horse fell thro'. staid till he was got out. I left my horse with Furman and went home with old Reynolds. N. and me romp'd and smited each other dreadfully.

16th—Came up to Whitaker's and found the Flatt gone. I emptied the corn in Hogshead & left it in John W. care. Came up the River by W. Whitr's up to the Ferry, crossed and came home without going through C. When I got home, understood that all the Nabors went to Camden the night before and that the Y. V.* had been at our House and impressed Aberdeen & took our best spade, the Nabors comes home in the evening. gave Jack money to buy Rice.

17th. A few of the Americans came to the House before I was up and took of Jas. Bettie's Sorrell Horse. they are pursued by the Y. V. who on their return told us the Rebels had kill'd Majr Downs & Jas. Matthews.

21st. Very uneasy to hear from Camden.

22nd. Morning cloudy. Negro Abram tells us that the Americans were camping at Chesnut's Plantation. Afternoon we are visited by Capt Smith, Zach Cantey and several more of the Americans. Capt Smith† drinks tea with us.

23rd—Twelve o'clock comes Cols. Gunby of the 7th, Capt. Smith of the 3rd and Capt Hambleton of another Maryland R. and stays and dines with us about 3 o'clock. Afternoon heard a Cannonade suppos'd at the Mill.

Wednesday, 25th. Set all the negroes except Nutt to making Potatoe Hills. *between 11 and 12 o'clock heard a very heavy fire of Cannon and Musketry lasting 15 minutes towards C. No news all day what it was. Afternoon hard Rain.*‡

26th—Planted Potatoes, finished breaking up Low Grounds. *Understood ye firing we heard was an engagement above Camden.*

27th—Old Bettie went to Camden and seen S. & W. Boykin.

29th—Walked over the Field with B. Boykin. Gave out to be washed 2 shirts, 2 stocks, 2 p. socks, 1 coat, Jacket & Breeches & 1 Handkf.

30th—Mrs Downs went by to Camden.

May 1781.

2nd. Afternoon McGinney & a party of Americans went by the House downwards.

4th Afternoon the Y. Volrs came down with waggons for corn &c, but did not disturb us any way only kill'd a calf in the woods.

5th—Sister went to Camden. Seen Capt. Smith & brot home a Bag of Meal.

Th. 10th—The British left Camden.

Wed. 23. I had our family moved into Mr. J K's large new House§ in Camden.

July.

1st. Joined Genl. Marion at Singleton's Mill.

3rd Marched over the River and down to McCord's Ferry.

4th—Crossed McCord's Ferry and went as far as Brown's Mill.

---

*New York Volunteers.

†See sketch of Capt. John Smith, Chapter VII.

‡The battle on Hobkirk Hill.

§The "Cornwallis House."

5th—Moved down to Sabbs' Place.

6.—I went out on command. We destroy'd a mill & took three waggons near Orangeburgh

7—Sold the Prize we had taken.

8—I went on another command. We took a few Prisoners about half a mile below Orangeburgh & returned to camp, which we found at Holman's.

9—We moved upwards a piece & took across through the woods and encamped about 10 miles above Orangeburgh.

10—We were joined by Gen. Green and Gen. Sumpter.

11. Prepared all matters and marched down within 3 miles of the Post to attack it when it was thought proper to wheel off we marched 8 or 10 miles that night.

12—We parted from Gen. Green & pushed down towards the Corner.

16—About 200 of us destroy Bigham Bridge and two Shooners at the Bridge and came & lay about a mile and a half above the church where as were Resting, Cooking &c, a party of the British Dragoons sally'd out and attack'd us in our Camp but were soon repuls'd and drove quite into their works without any loss on our side.

17—Finding the enemy had left the place & burnt their stores we being join'd by the whole of Sumpter's & Marion's Brigades pursued and overtook them at Shubrick's Bridge, where we had an engagement with them for 40 minutes. I having dismount & joined the Infantry was in the hotest of the action.

18. Poor Bates died of his wounds & was buried on the Road.

19. We got to the River at Cords Plantation.

24. Gen. Marion Discharged our Company & a number more. We crossed the River & came as far as Gen. Richardson's place & staid all night.

25. I got to Sowrby and staid all night.

26. I got safe home to my no small joy, after 26 long and tiresome sultry Days being spent in the utmost hunger and fatigue to man & Horse that ever poor wretches endured.

28. I went up to W. Nettles's with Rutledge. W. N. not being at home I staid at Rutledge's that night.

29. I went to Jesse Minton's & there drank Cyder & eat Peaches all day. Evening went to Watts's.

30. I went home with W. N. & sister.

31. Willm Nettles came down with me went to Sowrby tonight.

August.

1. We went to Jesse Nettles's on Black River.

2. W. N. spent this day among his relatives Staid at Elisha's that night.

3. We start towards home. Went to W. Richardson's & got my Salt being ½ bushel for my Tour of Duty. Came to Sowrby that night.

4. W. N. went home and I came to Camden.

[In preparing the introduction to this diary, and preceding parts of this work, the authors were under the impression that *Burndale* was a little southeast of Camden, but have since discovered from old records that it was located across the Wateree River, some ten miles west of Camden.]

APPENDIX B.

JAMES KERSHAW'S DIARY.

James Kershaw, eldest son of Col. Joseph, was our Pepys. With scrupulous particularity, he recorded his weather observations and the doings of the little world about him from 1791 to 1814. This interesting diary, in five small kid-bound volumes, is now in the possession of a great-niece, Miss Charlotte Kershaw.

What a gay spark the versatile author must have been—and what a universal genius! His pages fairly teem with notes of balls and teafights, of musicales and dramatic performances, in all which he played his part. Now he is mending Miss ——'s spinet; now he commands a military company on dress parade; now he sits as county judge; now he is obligingly painting walls, or flags, or signs!

Each journal is supplemented with miscellaneous matter—copies of legal forms and of sermons; recipes from suet puddings to the most approved methods of "breaking biles" or of removing hairs by the roots; observations on politics, philosophy, science! A fascinating medley!

His familiar mention of people and events makes one almost live again the Camden life of a century ago, in its round of social pleasures, when men wore wigs and knickerbockers, and feminine beauty was enhanced, if possible, by powder and patches, by stiff crinoline and wide spreading hoop-skirts.

We take the liberty—with many apologies to the gallant old gentleman—of reproducing some—about one-third—of his artless memoranda, that were certainly never intended for the public eye. They not only serve as an excellent picture of "a day that is dead," but present, as *en silhouette,* a delightful type of a man of fashion of the period in Camden—the amiable diarist himself.

1791.

April 29—The highest Fresh in the River happend in this month (which was on the 8th day) that has been known for many years & supposed by many equal to the great May Fresh in the year 1771.

Sept. 28—At 10 p. m. was a strange kind of rumbling noise appearantly from distant thunder, but there being no clouds to indicate it—'tis supposed it is the distant explosion of an Earthquake and most probably from the West Indies as the course was nearly from South to North.

1792.

Oct. 11. Dined at Orphan Society.
16. Suped at Lang's.
20. Parade of L. Horse.
24. Thespian Society.*
25. 1st Assembly.†
Dec. 5. Mr Barron's wedding.
14. Acted Busybody & agreeable surprise.

1793.

Jany 1. Fired 3 Rockets at flag staff.
4. Town meeting for clergyman.‡
15. Acted Douglas and Poor Soldier.
22. Sam Mathis married.
Feb. 1. Acted Orphan & Love a la mode.
2. Mrs DuBose died
4. General muster of militia.
12. Rented ye Brew House to Geo. Brown at £15 per annum.
Mch. 15. Acted School for Scandal & Retaliation.
17. Miss R. Kershaw married to Jo. Brevard, & Miss S. Chesnut to John Taylor.
26. St Cecilia Society§ at Dubose's.
April 6. Finished a Batteau.
11. Inoculation of ye Small Pox at ye Hermitage.
19. Camden Court. Judge Burke.
20. This day finished ye Pumping machine
23. French Ambassador Mr Genetz arrived.
the above is a mistake, twas the day after.
May 15. Mr Chas. Croughton & Mr James Abbott arrived.
June 11. Set Hutchins with 3 Brisbane's Negroes to work at Indigo Vats.
15. Raised a bark mill.
17. Dug ye onions 2780.
24. Betsy Hutchins married to Hutchinson.
July 4. Amer. Ind. celebrated at Court House. No. of Ladies.
16. Sat upon the Tryal of Punch for Conjuration.
17. High Fresh in Pinetree Creek—overflow'd all the Bridges and low grounds.
Aug. 22. Ely Ross began to beat indigo.
24. James Hunter went home sick
27. Capt. Dubose & Dan Brown drank tea here—a wonder indeed!
Sept. 12. Mr. John Champion's funeral.
26. Examination of Mr Adam's Academy.

---

*Dramatic Society. Weekly entries of meetings throughout Diary.
†Society Ball. Bi-weekly entries.
‡Rev. Thos. Adams of Mass. elected. See Presbyterian Church, Vol. II.
§Musical Society. Weekly entries.

Oct. 5. Stumpy Jim (shoemaker) began work.
16. Mr Logue* arrived.
17. Rev. Mr. Adams married to Dinah Wyly.
24. Doctor Alexander's Dance.
Nov. 19. Camden Court. Waitles & Bay.

1794.

Jany. 3. Brevard's dance.
6. Sheriff's Sales. Mr Lithgow, for William Ancrum, bot ye Mills at £1520.
9. McRa's dance.
15. Adamson's dance.
20. Miss Moore & Miss Darrington arrived.
26. Entered Geoffrey at Colledge (Winns-borough).†
Feb. 24. Mr Nettles pays visit.
25. Dined with Dr. Trent.
Mch. 6. Patterson fixed ye clock.
10. Played 1st game of Cricket.
18. Drank Tea at Champion's.
20. Subscription ball at Dinkins.
Mch. 19. Attended Cortes Exhibition.
25. Dr. Brownfield paid visit.
June 3. Put off my Flannel jacket; put it on ye next eveng—very cold.
July 4. Election for Col. & 2 Majors in ye Regiment. Cantey elected Col.
14. Anvy. French Revolutn. Raised a flag staff in Camden. Celebration of do. & sundry incidents.
21. Surveyed Mill tract for Mr. Broom.
28. Set fire to ye Magazine (built) by Js. Kershaw, & began to move ye bricks.
30. Bot 7 yds Calimanco from Young.
Aug. 3. Mary started for ye Cataba Springs.
6. Dined at Hermitage—hunting party from Westerham.
14. Sold ye Brewing Impliments to Wm. Mayrant.
Sept. 1. Dined with light Horse at Martin's Spring.‡
15. Meeting of the Town to consider ye removal of ye place of Burial.
17. Mary attended Mrs Lang's Quilting frolic.
Nov. 9. Rev. Mr. Furman preached.§
12. Col. Senf¶ dined here.
Dec. 5. Attended Doty's funeral. Exctn. Gray Briggs.‖
Dec. 29. Dance at McCaa's per subscription.
30. Pd. Stratford £5 for a flatt.
31. Took possession of ye ferry.**

1795.

Jany 2. Bot. a pr. ½ boots frm Broom.
8. Carter's dance.

---

*A Presbyterian minister who held services in Camden prior to the Revolution.

†Mt. Zion Academy.

‡Kirkwood Springs.

§First Baptist services in Camden. See Churches, Vol. II.

¶The noted engineer, of the Revolution. With Gates's army at Battle of Camden. Lived and died at Rocky Mount, Falls of the Catawba.

‖Noted horse thief. See Courthouse, Vol. II.

**In his cash accounts from the Ferry for 1795 is the following curious entry: "Nov. 21. By cash 10 dol. & a french crown—£2-5-11."

23. Paid McWhilly 37/ for surveying.
26. First Camden Lottery drawn
30. Perkins' dance.
31. Parade ye 1st of ys batalion.
Feb. 11. Inspector's Dance.
23. Painted Dr. Alexander's sign.
Apr. 15. Walked into ye Warehouse field.
18. Celebration of ye success of ye French armies in Holand.
29. Attended Anderson's Exhibition & Lecture.
May 5. Gen. Pinkney arrived. Review of Militia
30. Great squabble with Spradley and his family—a premeditated matter!
June 9. Got Kent to shoe my horse.
13. Delivered the charter* to hold a fair to Sam Mathis.
22. Billy wounded with a snake.
29. Surveyed buring ground.
July 4. Gave a dinner over the river. Annaversary Am. Independence.
14. Celebration French Revolution at McCaa's.
July 19. Mrs Mortimer & Joshua English died.
20. Began to cut indigo.
21. A meeting of ye citizens on Jay's Treaty.
25. Meeting of ye County on Jay's Treaty.
N. B. There has been this year seven Freshes—distroy'd all the indigo, corn, &c, &c.
Aug. 3. Dined with ye troop at Ross's.
6. Sent Mrs Jarvois Piano Fork home in good tune.
Mrs Thos. Whitaker paid visit.
29. M. K. took ague—very peevish.
Oct. 9. Cut the last vat indigo.
Oct. 10. Opened ye road to ye Warehouse field: McRae, Broom & Col. Brisbane Comrs. p. order of Court.
22. Gen. Gunn passed through Camden on Aristocrat.
Dec. 5. Attended Mrs Blake's exhibition

1796.

Jany. 18. Wyly's warehouse swept by fresh & 80 hhds. tobacco. M. K. & others went in flatts to Indian Mounts.
Mch. 4. Took a sale with Miss Patsey Brevard.
30. Married men's dance at Dinkins.
Apr. 22. Mr Broom's dance.
25. Col. Cantey's dance.
May 11. Meeting of Town on address to Representatives in Congress.
17. Mrs. Atkins & Miss Smith pd. a morning visit.
23. Captn. Rob Thomson & 8 other Chickasaws arrived here. Brot. letter from Bro. Jno. at Cataba.
27. Made settlement with McRa & Cantey.
June 20. M. K. began quilt.
July 14. Anniversary of ye French Republic. A dance in ye evg.
20. Joe started to Columbia on Mohawk.
Aug. 4. Fishing party at Belton's Spring.
Sept. 23. Regimental muster p. Gen. Winn.
Oct. 4. Sheriff's sales. John, Syphax & Ned for £300.
Nov. 22. The woods on fire all round. Dined at Dubose's. A large party.

---

*The old charter granted by the King to Jos. Kershaw and others in Oct., 1774.

27. Dined at McRa's. Introduced to Mrs James Chestnut.*
Dec. 5. Tuned Miss M. Chesnut's Piano Forté.
7. Attended Committee Thespian Society to fix play house.
20. Fixed ye scenes at ye Court House.
22. Performance Thespians—Cato & Vilage Lawer.

1797.

Jany 2. Rented ye Ferry for £40 to the Rev. Thos. Adams.
18. Dined at Wm. Keneday's.
19. Coleman's boat launched.
26. James Polk married to Miss Martha Moore.
Feb. 5. Began to haul ye seine. Caught no fish.
16. Dance at Fisher's.
Mch. 3. Godwin's Benefit—Revenge & Love a la Mode.
13. Sewed five acres flax.
21. Dubose launched boat "La Belle Catherine."
Apr. 24. Planted the cotton† round the Warehouse, Westerham.
June 3. Sent June, Charity & Primus to Perkins.
July 4. Annaversary Orphan Society. Brevard dld oration.
5. Old John Flinn married to Dorcas Minton—87 & 30.
6. Isaac Dubose married to Catherine Dubose.
19. Robin Hood made a new pr. Smith's Bellows & a Shower Bath.
Aug. 5. Removed ye boat into ye creek.
16. Rev. Thos. Adams died.
20. Placed maps &c on ye Schrine.
Sept. 14. Kirkpatrick‡ launched boat "Polly Brisbane"
23. Attended ye funeral Doctor Martin.
30. Kirkpatrick launched Carpenter's Canal boat.
Oct. 12. Engaged 40 pr. Negroe Shoes frm Rees.
23. First meeting Proprietors Navigate on Pinetree Creek.
24. Meeting Pinetree Creek Company.§
Nov. 27. Waited on Mrs. Adams. Tuned Miss Eliza's Spinnet.

1798.

Jany 3. Fire Chesnut's house.¶
10. Went on patrol.
14. Dined abroad.
18. Started ye boat Venture for Charleston.
Mch. 10. Rode to Ross' Fishery. Large party there.
19. Mr. Richard Jennings paid a visit.
26. Surveyed ye town of Camden.
Apr. 6. Jno. Kershaw, Junior, died. Buried in McRa's ground, Peedee.
12. Married to Sarah English.‖
30. Election Light Dragoons for a Cornet. Reuben Arthur elected.
May 2. Met part of Artillery Company in High Germany.
4. Rob. Hood finished checks &c for field piece.
25. Waited on Gen. Winn at Winnsborg & dined with him: gave commission for Compy. Artillery: would write by Mr Fourt to ye Governr. to procure arms &c both for cavalry & artillery. Bro. John applied for comy.

---

*A bride—the charming Mary Cox, of Philadelphia.
†Cotton planting recently introduced.
‡Kirkpatrick a well-known boat builder in Camden.
§Col. Senf engineered this enterprise, never very successful.
¶Stood on north side King street, between Fair and Lyttleton.
‖Great flourishes of penmanship around this and similar entries, marking red-letter occasions.

for the Regiment & Staff department & to approve of the appointments he then proposed, which he acceded to and said that "he had directed the Brigade inspector to draw the lots between Captns. Frierson & Sumpter in the cavalry, which was done and the lot fell to Frierson; that he had also directed him to cast the lot in his battalion of artillery between Captns. Johnson and Moore, and that the lot had fallen to Capt. Moore as Major Commandant."

31. Introduced to Doctr. Perkins.
June 6. Paul Smith finished ye piece Artillery.
9. First parade of ye Artillery.
15. Survey'd ye Indian Camp.
24. Conveyed ye Indian Camp* to McRa & Co. for £126.
26. Play in Camden—Williamson & Co.—"Jane Shore & Spoilt Child."
July 4. Orphan Soc. An. Play "Rode to Ruin."
6. Went to ye Play "Bon Ton" & "Romp."
9. Attended ye play "Bunker's Hill"
17. Miss Eliza Smith married to Mr. Ward.
23. Went to see ye Learned Dog.
29. Mr. Scot, merchant, died.
Aug. 6. Doctor Davaur's fishing party.
7. Swore in as Judge of County.
17. Thespian Society to consider Monsieur Benyon's proposition to paint a new set of scenery, the expense to be £16.
Sept 11. Monsr. Gayetan Alguier died.
16. Attended Methodist meeting.†
20. Sent Guinea Cato‡ to work with Kirkpatrick.
Oct. 1. Bush swore off.
8. Buried Alex. Goodall.
12. Mrs. Broom buried at New Ground.§
26. Mr Belzons began to draw my Picture.
30. Dined at Bro. Johns with Gen. Harrington.
Nov. 9. County Court adj. New clerk Stephen Boykin.
10. Artillery, Cavalry & Infantry parade.
15. Meeting of Comrs. to lay of ye town.
30. The heaviest Fog almost ever known here.
Dec. 6. James Clark married to Nancy Thornton.
29. Mrs. Adamson & Mrs. Belton paid visit.

1799.

Jany 3. Lang, Matheson, Ker & Gow gave a dance at Dinkin's.
14. Prissy Evans came to weave. Adamson, Siples, Arrants & Tho. Dinkins give dance.
Feb. 8. Presented my bond to the Judges—Adamson, Carpenter and John Kershaw.
Mch. 6. James English married to Miss Nancy Darrington.
11. Lay'd of corner lots opposite Court House for Adamson. S. & self attended ye Wax Works.
28. Doctor Trent married to Mary Dubose. Married John Martin to Nancy Payne.

*The tract of land where first the McRa Mill and later the Camden Cotton Mill was located.
†One of the earliest Methodist meetings held in Camden. See Churches, Vol. II.
‡Mentioned in chapter on "Cornwallis House."
§New part of Quaker Cemetery.

31. Planted Jamaica shrubs.
Apr. 3. Granted License to Mr Bracey & Mrs Aiguier.
11. At 20 m. past 3 o'clk in the morn, heard an unaccountable noise like thunder which shook the whole house to such a degree as to rattle the windows; the direction & course was fr. S. S. E. to N. W. At 5 m. before 3 P. m. felt a similar shock.
28. Whiped Isaac, Sam & Ben for stealing Lang's hogs.
31. Dan'l McNeill buried.
June 4. Began to mould bricks.
7. Made cartridges for Infantry. Played ye Engine.
12. John Brown began to raise his house. Sent Sam & Cato to help.
14. Mrs Huger paid visit.
25. Sent Tom, ye Cat, to ye Plantation.
Aug. 22. Surveyed ye lots & laid off DeKalb street
29. Mr Arrants began to get ye kiln brick.
Sept. 29. Thomas Broom died in Charleston of ye Yellow Fever.
25. Mrs Bracey (Aiguier that was) died.
Dec. 14. Gen. Washington died. Aet. 68.

1800.

Jany. 28. Sam Whitaker married to Eliz. Brown.
Feb. 2. Eliz. English married to Thos. Hopkins pr Chambers.
5. Batchellors' Dance. Carter & Matheson managers.
May 10. E. Mortimer paid a visit.
24. Attended Senr. Falconi Exhibition.
June 10. Mrs Yarborough and Miss English arrived in Camden from Bay Honduras.
12. John English married to Eliz. Tucker
23. Josiah Cantey called.
27. Dined at Bro. John's with Capt. Nettles.
July 4. Mr Blanding delivr'd an oration.
6. Stephen Boykin waited on me & brought John McCaa & Thomas Ballard to demand *Cato** the property of James Cary, held in possession by my father. Answer, would not deliver him unless compelled by Law.
9. Mrs David Rudolph buried.
18. Miss A. Belton called in ye evening.
28. S. K. went to quilt for Becky.
Aug. 18. Alexander, Jas. Chesnut & Dubose threw down ye Flag Staff.†
31. Dined at Mathis's Pine Grove.
Sept. 18. Staked out ye Arsenal.
21. Wm. Bracey married to Miss M. Rudolph.
23. Wm. Adamson married to Amelia Alexander.
24. Wm. Luyten died.
Nov. 10. Court opened by Judge Ramsey.
18. Batchellors' Ball.
26. Rec'd orders frm. Maj. Moore to march compy. to Columbia.
Dec. 1. Court Equity opened per Judges Hugh Rutledge & Marshal.
6. Started to Columbia with company Artillery, to be reviewed.

1801.

Jany. 4. Austin F. Peay married to Mary English.
Apr. 2. Got stung by a bee. Inflammation very great, closed ye left eye.
3. Great misery from ye sting yesterday.

---

*Doubtless faithful old Guinea Cato.
†Evidently of some political significance.

27. George started to town in boat Harpoon.
May 15. Doctor Alexander's dance.
16. Painted ye Artillery Guns.
21. Review Col. Cantey's Regiment.
27. James Belton died.
June 9. Census Kershaw County—males 2438, Females 2268, Slaves 2530. Total 7346.
July 4. King & Self gave Artillery Compy dinner.
9. Orange whiped 55 lashes on ac. of Peay. Balatrofaquin.
Aug. 1. Lent Electrical Machine to Lockhart.
Sept. 30. Ye Actors performed for first time.
Oct. 5. Sale of Warehouse, field &c $12,420 to Jno. Taylor.
19. Mr Peay called with Jo. Mickle.
21. S. & Self went to ye play, "She Stoops to Conquer."
24. S. and Self went to ye play "Geo. Barnwell" & "American Tar."
Nov. 24. Dance at Mrs Cantey's. Was not invited.
Dec. 3. Indians paid visit.

1802.

Jany. 13. Camden Races.
Feb. 28. Old Squires stole my sow & 6 pigs. Call'd on him & demanded the same in presence of Sam Brown, which he returned in the evening and call'd the next morning by Sunrise to make an appollogy
Apr. 11. Inoculated Linda & Jack with Vaccine Matter
July 24. Judy ran off. "Conjuration."
26. Miss Brisbane married to Wm. Ancrum, jr.

1808.

Left Lucknow 21 Nov. 1807. Settled Malvern 24 June, 1808
Aug. Delivered powder to Ciples.
Oct. 1. Dined with Artillery Co. at Nixon's, Capt. Ancrum.
31. Sent Poll the parrot home.
Nov. 9. Miss Mary Chesnut married to Jas. Deas.
Dec. 1. Henry H. Dickerson married to Miss Martha Brevard.

1809.

Jany 26. Sent the Music pen to Sam Mathis pr. Mr. Clark.
Feb. 23. Harriet English married to Mr Singleton.
Mch. 5. Mr Eccles paid visit.
16. Camden Races.
Apr. 20. Rochel's Trial.*
May 16. Mr Salmons called.
June 5. Painted a flag for Capt. Coleman's Rifle Comp.
9. Rochelle executed.
29. Went to visit Mr. Adamson at his Retreat.
July 4. Ann. of Independence. Dined in ye Court House. Oration Chapman Levy.
7. Fley executed.†
10. Pul'd ye flax & cut ye oats.
Aug. 8. Capt. Morrison & Esq. Blakeney called.
Nov. 8. Doctor Trent died.
15. Francis S. Lee cut my hair.

1810.

Jany 2. Mrs Balentine, ye Tayloress, arrived.
28. Rec'd bar. Flints for Arsenal.

---

*See "Minton's Mill."
†See "Minton's Mill."

May 4. Mr Abbott married to Miss Lucy Breed.
May 11. Mr and Mrs Thornton paid visit.
19. Camp meeting.
Sept. 22. R. Mc and Miss Jane Alguier called; lent ye chair.
26. Sam Gaunt called.
30. Mr Reed's boy, "Wm. O'Cain," called to apologize for his improper expressions.
Dec. 13. Rich'd L. Champion married to Mrs. M. E. Trent.
22. Review McWillie Reg't.

1811.

Jany 9. Races. Capt. Reuben Stark called; lent my umbrella.*
Apr. 19. Henry Middleton examined ye magazine & arsenal.
May 15. Painted flag for Rev. Mr. Moore's daughter to present to ye Volunteer Co. Infantry.
June 5. Dance at Doby's.
6. Idem at Duncan McRa's.
13. Sarah Adamson married to Lewis Ciples.
July 4. Oration by Wyatt Starke. Hottest day of year, 96°.
26. McRa's Mill burnt.
Oct. 8. Comet very brilliant.
16. Doctor Blanding married to Miss Willet.
Nov. 11. Jo. Doby died.
26. Rev. Mr Smith & Reynolds pd. visit. [lent ye Polite Preceptor.]
Nov. 14. Rec'd 2 elegant pictures fr. Miss Hetty Cummings.
18. Mons. Jumelle called.
26. Doctor Cox pd visit.
Dec. 10. Made return of tax 22 slaves.
12. Rec'd a loom from Bro. John.
16. Appearance of Earthquake.
[This year Extreme Heat and drought. Severe earthquake & comet—portentious events!]

1812.

Jany 8. Camden Races.
13. Doctor Alexander died.
Feb. 7. Severe Earthquake 3:41 a. m. Shocks on 10, 11, & 20, insts.
Mch. 3. Mr Willet pd. visit. Earthquake.
23. Geoffrey Kershaw died.
June 1. Capt. Wm. Vaughan died.
25. Declaration of War.†
July 4. Oration John Boykin.
16. Camp meeting—Saunders Creek.
25. Wolf Hunt.
Aug. 5. Gave Jude a whiping for impudence.
20. Mrs Amelia Adamson buried.
Oct. 22. John Kershaw married to Harriet Dubose.
23. Great Fire in Camden.
Nov. 9. Ballard and Cureton call late.
Dec. 19. Painted a banner for ye Lodge.
28. Consecration Kershaw Lodge No. 55.

1813.

Jany 10. Powell McRa married to Mary Singleton.
Feb. 20. Mr Alexander Young paid visit.

---

*A curiosity at that time.
†Against Great Britain.

Mch. 29. Encampment of ye officers 8th Brigade
Apr. 14. Patriotic Ball.
22. Charlotte Mortimer married to Jno. Boykin.
May 8. Married to Lydia Ann Vaughan.*
24. The parrot died.
July 5. Oration deliver'd by Franklin Brevard.
Aug. 12. Draft of the Militia
16. Delivered 75 lbs. powder to Col. Richardson.
Oct. 9. Col. W. B. Mitchel inspected ye magazine
25. Illumination in Camden.
Nov. 13. Richard Lloyd Champion died
14. Mrs. Ab. Blanding died.
Dec. 16. Sam Mathis' two daughters married. Rec'd no invitation.

1814.

Jany 16. Willie Vaughan & Serrée Dubose dined here.
18. Maj. Mickle called.
Feb. 19. Wm. W. Lang married to Kitty Boykin.
May 2. Shock Earthquake 6:10 a. m.
5. Jno. S. Willet married to Miss Eliza Richardson.
9. Earthquake 5:13 a. m.
May 25. Review Militia
Aug. 24. City Washington burnt by ye British.
Sept. 8. John (Kershaw) started to Congress.
16. Attended review Militia at Hawfields.
30. Last night the smoke house broken and all my Bacon stole.
Oct. 1. Mr. Joshua Reynolds dined here.
6. The Volunteer Companies march for Town, Levy's, Blair's, Douglas', from Lancaster, and Montgomery's. Painted flag for Levy.
Dec. 13. Old Mrs. Rudolph died at F. S. Lee's, Camden. Age 97.

1815.

Jany 15. Got ye shaft of ye chair broke at Pinetree Ford.
24. Mr DeLion and Mrs Levy called.
Feb. 5. For one hour, 43 Minute guns heard distinctly from S. by E. I counted.
20. Rec'd information of Peace. Minute Guns fired in Camden & Columbia.
25. 12 waggons with cotton passed here to Baltimore.
Mch. 29. Thos. Lang married to Mary McRa.
June 27. Caleb Berry gave Jude a whiping for her impudence and abuse to her mistress.

---

*This lady, a widow, was probably the relict of the late Capt. Wm. Vaughan, who died in 1812.

INDEX.

Adair, Lieut. John, 208, 282.
Adamson, Lieut. James, 54; 62-65; 285.
Adamson, John, 104, 130; 281-290.
Adamson family, 76, 99, 290.
Agnes of Glasgow, 291-296.
Aiguier, Gayetan, 189.
Alexander, family, 342.
Alexander, Dr. Isaac, 35, 189, 191, 290, 294, 309, 342.
Alexander, I. B., 25.
Alexander, G. G., 36, 294.
Alexander, David, 68.
Alexander, Colonel, 144.
Allison, Andrew, 87.
Ancrum, family, 344.
Ancrum, William, 11, 12, 88, 125, 130, 286, 298, 380.
Ancrum, Major (or Cadet) George, 125.
Ancrum, Lance & Loocock, 88, 97.
Anderson, Major, 165.
Andrews, Samuel, 205.
Andrews, Thomas, 287.
"Ark," The, 28.
Arledge, John, 71.
Armand, Colonel, 149, 155, 156, 164.
Arrants, family, 354.
Arthur, Reuben, 352.
Arthur Lane, 33.
Arthur, W. L., 33.
Atakullakulla, 63.
Bacot, Samuel, 211.
Ballard, family, 341.
Bank, Camden, 19.
Battles: Camden, Gum Swamp or Sanders Creek, 146-198; Fishing Creek, 200; Rugeley's Fort, 213; Ratcliff's Bridge, 219; Hobkirk Hill, 221-242; Kershaw's Mill, 253; Fourteen in vicinity, 273.
Baum, Plantation, 74.
Beatty, Captain, 233.
Bearfoot, Newel, 384.

Beaumont, H., 393.
Belmont, 68, 369.
Belton, family, 76, 86.
Belton, Abram, 74, 76, 86, 129.
Belton, Hannah, 74, 84.
Belton, John (or Jonathan), 74, 76, 84, 86, 99, 104, 285, 286, 288, 289.
Belton's Branch, 76, 226.
Bennet, John, 69.
Bethune, 329.
Bettie, James, 99, 129.
Bettie's Neck, 303.
Bishop, Nicholas, 208.
Bishopville, 219.
Black, John, 69, 78.
Blair, Gen. James, 325.
Blanding, family mentioned 345.
Blanding, Abram, 19, 35, 330, 345, 390.
Blanding, Dr. William, 27.
Bloomsbury, 370.
Blue House, 188, 353.
Bonney, family mentioned, 353.
Boundary Street, 32.
Boundaries of Camden, 15.
Boykin, family, 345.
Boykin, Burwell, 86, 129.
Boykin, A. Hamilton, 264, 349.
Boykin, Capt. Francis, 104, 110, 117, 349.
Boykin, Capt. John, 104, 144, 287, 302, 350.
Boykin, Capt. Samuel, 104, 110; 116-120; 129, 309, 327, 346.
Boykin, Dr. or Col. E. M., 65, 86, 105, 249, 255, 289, 290, 300.
Boykin, John, 35, 290.
Boykin, William, 85, 287.
Boykin, Stephen, 302.
Bradley, James, 144, 286.
Bradley, Samuel, 108.
Branham or Brannon, Michael, 69, 71.
Bratton, family mentioned, 281.
Bready, William and Daniel, 69.
Brevard, family, 321-326.

Brevard, Judge Joseph, 22, 219, 309; 321-326.
Brew House, 376.
Brisbane, family, 351.
Brisbane, residence, 310.
Brisbane, Adam Fowler, 99, 309, 327.
Broad Street, 10, 31.
Broom, family, 352.
Broom, Thomas, 352.
Broun, Archibald, 129.
Broughton, Lieutenant-Governor, 44.
Brown, family, 341.
Brown, Thomas, 42, 67.
Brown, James, 35, 99, 131, 144.
Brown, John, 380.
Brown, Daniel and Jacob, 393.
Brownfield, Doctor, 136.
Brummitt, William and Spencer, 287.
Bryan, Thomas, 69.
Bryant, Ambrose, 331.
Buford or Beaufort, Col. Abram, 127; 134-139.
Bullard, Royal, 35.
Bull Street, 32.
Bull, Gov. William, 32, 49, 56, 63, 64.
Bull, Stephen, 121.
Burndale, 100, 275, 400, 403.
Burr, Aaron, 29.
Burton, E. P., 280.
Buxton, Samuel, 69.
Bynum or Bineham, Benjamin, 360.
Cain, John, 75.
Camden: Earliest plat of, 12, 90; Royal Charter, 14; Currency, 15, 33; Boundaries, 15; Lottery, 19; Town Records, 22; Created City, 18; Street Lights, 24; Sherman's Raid, 24; Council of 1865, 25; Telephone, Light, and Water Franchises, 26; Fire Department, 26; Squares and Parks, 29; Wards, 30; Streets, 31; Intendants and Mayors, 35; Naming of, 90; Early Inhabitants, 99; Cornwallis Occupies, 142; Fortified as British Post, 143, 203; Battle of, 146; Second Battle of (Hobkirk Hill), 221; Evacuation by British, 270.
Camden, Lord, 91.

Camden, William, 93.
Campbell, Col. Richard, 262.
Cantey, family, 354.
Cantey, Capt. John, 58.
Cantey, John (III), 85, 96, 99, 108, 298, 356.
Cantey, Lieut. James, 96, 104, 133, 248, 301, 304.
Cantey, Gen. Zach., 22, 104, 133, 141, 223, 304, 356.
Cantey, Gen. James W., 256, 358.
Cantey, Samuel, 108.
Cantey, Josiah, 358.
Cantey, James Willis, Jr., 358.
Cantey, Maj. E. B., 14, 248, 256.
Cantey, Maj. Zach., 290.
Carrington, Colonel, 225.
Carrison, H. G., 36.
Carrison's Mill, 130.
Carter, family, 359.
Carter, Robert, 96, 108, 109.
Carter, John, 359.
Carter, John C., 359.
Carter, Capt. Benjamin, 136, 188, 195, 361.
Cary, family mentioned, 104.
Cary, Col. James, 99, 105, 129, 153.
Cary, Nathaniel, 129.
Cary's Fort, 105, 153.
Casity, Thomas, 108.
Cassels, Henry, 108.
Castelo, Shoemaker, 99.
Caston, Glass, 96.
Caston, Mrs. S. A., 399.
Caswell, General, 128, 135, 149, 151, 161, 164, 171, 194.
Catawba Indians, 46, 59, 60, 111; 116-120; 124.
Catawba Path, 10.
Catawba Town, 119.
Catterton, Mark, 69.
Cemetery, 81.
Champion, family, 362.
Champion, Richard, 362.
Champion, Richard Lloyd, 17, 365.
Charlton, Thomas, 99, 104, 110; 111-115.
Charter, Royal of Camden, 14; of Fair, 12; Legislative of Camden, 15, 18.
Chatham, 381.
Chattan, A. L., 23.
Cheraw, 149, 216, 382.
Cheraw Indians, 38.
Cherokee Indians, 60.

INDEX. 417

Cherry, Jacob, 384.
Chesnut, family, 89, 99, 366.
Chesnut, Col. John, 13, 96, 109, 110, 129, 133, 140, 144, 289, 309, 310, 366.
Chesnut, Col. James, 15, 35, 104, 304.
Chesnut, Gen. James, 359, 371.
Chesnut, Capt. John, 375.
Chickanee Indians, 40.
Churches: of England, 95; Quaker, 95; Presbyterian, 95.
Church Street, 31.
Christmas, Jonathan, 75.
Ciples, Lewis, 290.
Clermont, 135, 152, 213.
Clay, Joseph, 99, 129.
Clifton, W. C., 349.
Clock, Town, 22.
Clyburn, Capt. William, 33.
Clyburn Street, 33.
Collins, John, 11.
Colonels Creek, 269.
Columbia, 306.
Conyers, James, 108.
Cool Spring, 237, 351.
Cook, family, 341.
Cook, Lewis, 188.
Cook, John, 75, 99.
Cook, Henry R., 35, 359, 360.
Cook, James, 96, 341, 384.
Cornwallis, Lord, 134, 142, 153, 195, 202, 203, 205.
Cornwallis House, 11, 205; 274-280; 292.
Corbett, Dr. J. W., 36.
Courson, David, 75.
Courthouse, 12, 24, 26, 34, 95.
Court of Piepowder, 13.
Court Inn, 394.
Crane, Mary, 337.
Cummings, Miss Hettie, 276.
Cunningham, family mentioned, 371.
Cureton, family mentioned, 86, 340.
Cureton, Everard, 86, 374.
Cureton, James B., 294.
Daash, William, 26.
Daniels, C. F., 27, 277.
Danzy's Tavern, 329, 331.
Darrell, Edward, 380.
Darrington, John, 35.
Davie, Gen. W. R., 125, 172, 199, 222, 263.
Davis, James M., 36.
Deas, family mentioned, 340.

Deas, Gen. Zach. Cantey, 359.
Deas, Dr. L. H., residence, 274.
Deas, James S., 304.
DeBruhl, Edward C., 331.
DeKalb, Baron, 146, 159, 165, 185; 191-193; 275.
DeKalb Street, 18, 32.
Deloach, Thomas, 87.
Deliesseline, F. A., 290.
DeSaussure, Daniel, 215.
DeSaussure, Maj. John M., 35, 365.
DeSaussure, Dr. Daniel, 390.
DeSaussure, William F., 264.
Devereux, Capt. J. H., 279.
Diary, Mathis, 400-403.
Diary, Kershaw, 405-413.
Dicks, Zachary, 83.
Dickinson, Col. James P., 383.
Dickey, Edward, 108.
Dinkins, Samuel, 141, 287.
Dinkins, Joshua, 129.
Dinkins, John, 287.
Dinkins, Tavern, 319.
Dixon, Colonel, 163, 215.
Doby, family mentioned, 86, 340.
Doby, John, 86, 373.
Doby, James C., 87, 278.
Downey, John, 286.
Downing, Moses, 75.
Downs, Major, 252.
Doyle, Major, 205, 220.
Douglas, family mentioned, 340.
Douglas, James K., 345, 390.
Drakeford, family, 215, 395.
Drakeford, Col. William, 395.
Drakeford, John, 85.
Drayton, Judge W. H., 91, 105, 111.
Dubose, family, 371.
Dubose, Capt. Isaac, 35, 104, 110, 133, 309, 315, 365, 371.
Dubose, John, 372.
Dubose, Elias, 373.
DuBose, H. K. and E. C., 394.
DuBuysson, Chevalier, 189.
Duesto, Anthony, 69.
Dulin, Rice, 392.
Dunlap, family, 373.
Dunlap, Capt. George, 126.
Dunlap, Samuel, 286.
Dunlap, Robert, 373.
Dunlap, James, 26, 35, 373.
Dunlap, Joseph D. and C. J., 36.
Dunn, Sylvester, 108.
Dunsworth, Ann, 75.
Duren, —— 215.

Duyett, Ann, 69.
Edwards, William N., 69.
Eldredge, F. W., 394.
Elbert, Samuel, 129.
Ellerbe, W. C. S., 36.
Elmore, Benjamin T., 326, 351.
English, family, 77, 86.
English, Thomas, 74, 77.
English, Robert, 74, 77, 87, 104, 129, 285, 286, 289.
English, Joshua, 74, 86, 96, 97, 104, 105, 108, 129, 285, 288, 380.
English, James, 278.
English, B. M., 87.
Episcopal Burial Ground, 22.
Essetaswa, Chief, 49.
Eswa-Taroa, River, 47.
Evans, Joseph and Robert, 74, 82.
Evans, Charles, 331.
Fain, Philip, 75.
Fair Street, 31.
Fair, Royal Charter, 12; Grounds, 13,31.
Falconer, William, 322, 330.
Factory Pond, 89.
Few, Colonel, 144.
Ferguson, Colonel, 212.
Finin, Thomas, 75.
Fires, in Camden, 26.
Fire Companies, 28.
Fisher, James, 380.
Fishing Creek, battle, 200.
Fletcher, 215, 333.
Fley, Jesse, 332-339.
Ford, Colonel, 166, 263.
Fortifications (see Redoubts), 105, 153, 204, 205, 312 (note).
Fraser or Frazer, Major, 219.
Fredericksburg, Township, 10. 11, 68.
Friends Neck, 74.
Frierson, Aaron, 108.
Frow or Prow, King, 57, 320.
Furguson, Capt. C. W., 25.
Furman, Wood, 286.
Furnass, John, 74, 84.
Galbraith, ———, 287.
Gamble, James, 71.
Gamble, John, 96, 108, 286.
Gates, Gen. Horatio, 147-149; 164-173; 178-185.
Gaunt, Nebo, 67, 74, 77, 80.
Gaunt, Zebulon and Zimri, 74, 80.
Gayles, Kit, 141.

Gayle, Josiah, 205.
Gayle, Caleb, 287.
Genet, Citizen-Minister, 314-320.
Gerald, W. J., 35.
Gervais, John L., 135.
Gibson, Roger, 71.
Gibson, Luke, 71.
Gill, Robert, 209.
Gilman, Miss, 343.
Gist, Gen. Mordecai, 161.
Glasgow, Samuel, 134.
Glasgow, Agnes and Robert, 295.
Glenn, Governor, 48, 49, 50.
Goodwin, Uriah, 384.
Goodwyn, Col. A. D., 25, 35.
Goodie Castle, 394.
Goodale, J. R., 26, 36.
Gordon Street, 31.
Gordon, Captain, 286.
Gordon, Chief Justice, 31.
Gordon, Moses, 31, 96, 108.
Grannys Quarter Creek, 71, 166.
Grant, William J., 371.
Granby, Fort, 218, 306.
Gray, William, 69.
Gray, John, 80, 384.
Greene, Gen. Nathaniel, 173, 215, 243-245; 259, 270.
Greene's Bridge, 225.
Greene's Road, 223.
Greene, Mrs. General, 278.
Gregory, Richard, 71.
Gregory, General, 193.
Groves, Mary, 336.
Gum Swamp, battle, 146-198; 157.
Gunby, Col. John, 166, 238; 245-248; 260.
Gunby, A. A., 247.
Guess, William, 69.
Habbersham, Joseph, 129.
Haiglar, King of Catawbas, 20, 51, 52, 55, 56.
Haile, family, 373.
Haile, Benjamin (I), 373.
Haile, Benjamin (II), 87, 289.
Haile Street, 33.
Haile, Capt. C. C., 374.
Haley, James, 75.
Hampton Square, 30.
Hampton, Anthony, 304.
Hampton, Col. Wade, 276.
Hannahan, Thomas, 67.
Harlestone, Paul, 69.
Harper, Thomas, 69.
Harris, Michael, 68.
Harrison, William, 71.

INDEX. 419

Hart, Rev. Oliver, 111.
Harvin, John, 287.
Havis, John and Thomas, 336.
Hatley, R. P. H., 377.
Hawes, Col. Samuel, 263.
Heard, John, 90.
Henry, Robert, 352, 380.
Hermitage, The, 130, 275, 400.
Heyward, Mrs. Savage, 290, 351.
Hill, Nathaniel, 71.
Hill, Capt. Joseph, 287.
Hilton, ———, 215.
Hobkirk Hill, 224, 225; 221-242; 250-252.
Hobkirk, Thomas, 225.
Hobkirk Inn, 257, 279.
Holmes, James, 330.
Hope, John, 69, 129.
Hopkins, Thomas and T. A., 28, 87.
Hopkins, Mary E., 349.
Hotels, 27, 28, 227, 257, 279, 394.
Horse Branch, 18.
Howard, Edward, 71.
Howard, Gen. John E., 166, 216, 262.
Hough's Bridge, 151.
Hudson, John, 69.
Huger, Daniel, 135.
Huger, Gen. Isaac, 172, 243, 261.
Huck (or Hutt), Capt. Christian, 140, 282.
Hughson, Spy, 154.
Hughson, W. E., 25.
Hunter, family, 341.
Hunter, Colonel, 144.
Hunter, Henry, 108.
Hunter, Humphrey, 186, 210.
Hutchins, John, 130.
Hutchins, Misses S. and Ann, 380.
Hyco, 45, 393.
Indian, Figure on steeple, 20.
Indians, tribes of South Carolina, 37, 50, 57.
Indian Mounds, 61.
Intendants, list of, 35.
Irvin (or Irwin), connection, 352, 391.
Irvin (or Irwin), Mr., 144, 368.
Irvine, Dr. Matthew, 222.
Jackson, Andrew, 28, 208.
Jacksonboro Assembly, 286.
Jail (or Gaol), 12, 19, 26, 144.
James, Col. John, 109, 286, 287, 304, 305.
Jenkins, Isaiah, 382.
Jenkins, Rev. James, 252.

Johnson Springs, 226.
Jones, Gen. Allen, 264.
Jones, James, 36.
Jones, Maj. Samuel, 188.
Jones, Thomas, 97, 99.
Jones, the traitor, 228.
Jumelle, Pierre Laurent, 388.
Jumelle Hill, 394.
Jumping Gully Creek, 303, 327.
Jury, Grand, presentments, 95, 96, 106.
Kadapau Indians, 47.
Kegg, Gen. Jim, 58.
Kelley, Abram, 120.
Kelley, Samuel, 74, 84.
Kelley, Timothy and Walter, 74, 78.
Kelley, William, 69.
Keowee, 55, 63, 64.
Kennedy, A. D., 33.
Kennedy, David, 294.
Kennedy, Gen. J. D., 346.
Kennedy, John, 80.
Kennedy, R. M., Sr. 25, 35.
Kennedy, William, 373.
Kershaw, family, 99, 375.
Kershaw, Col. Eli (or Ely), 104, 109, 110, 123, 128, 130, 203, 381; roll of company, 384.
Kershaw, James, 87, 276, 319; Diary, 405-413.
Kershaw, John, 15, 35, 276, 327, 372, 381.
Kershaw, Rev. John, 279, 294. 381.
Kershaw, Col. Joseph, 11, 35, 87, 104, 109, 110, 111, 116, 118; 121-123; 126; 127-128; 129, 130, 131, 132, 142, 144, 203, 274, 278, 280, 308, 376, 378, 379.
Kershaw, Gen. (or Judge) J. B., 35, 294, 310, 381, 355.
Kershaw, Miss Mary, 205, 275.
Kershaw, William, 144.
Kershaw & Wyly, 125, 132.
King Street, 32.
Kirkland, Richard and Joseph, 85, 96, 215.
Kirkley, D. C., 36.
Kirkwood, Capt. Robert, 166, 216, 228, 231, 265.
Kirkwood, 17.
Kirkwood Branch, 249.
Kirkwood Heights Hotel, 227.
Knights (or Nights) Hill, 357, 367, 401.
Lafayette, Marquis, 19.

Lafayette Avenue, 33.
Lafayette Hall, 360.
Lance, Lambert, 12, 88, 89.
Lanier, Dr. Thomas, 374.
Lang, family, 86, 385.
Lang, Thomas, 386.
Lang, William W., 15, 86, 99, 129, 287, 309, 385.
Lang, James W., 385.
Lang, Mrs. William, 141.
Langley, William, 35.
Laurens Street, 32.
Lausanne, 388.
Lawson, John, 40, 41.
Leadom, Thomas, 69.
Leconte, William, 129.
Lee, Col. Henry, 167, 175, 221.
Lee, family, mentioned, 340.
Lee, Joseph, 286.
Lee, Francis, 85.
Lenoir, Isaac, 87, 289, 374.
Lenoir, Thomas, 287.
Leonard, Coleman, 287.
Leitner, W. Z., 36.
Levy, Hayman, 35.
Levy, Chapman, 387.
Levy, family, mentioned, 387.
Levi, slave, 169.
Liberty Hill, 371, 393, 395.
Lide, Charles Mott, 322.
Lights, town, 24, 26.
Lindsay, James, 295.
Lincoln, General, petition to, 133.
Little, Samuel, 109.
Little, G. T., residence, 255.
Lizenby, 329.
Logtown, 18, 90, 99, 152, 209, 224.
Loocock, Aaron, 12, 88, 97, 109, 286.
Lottery, town, 19, 22.
Loudoun, Fort, 64.
Lyles, family, mentioned, 86.
Lyles, James, 392.
Lynches Creek, 47, 151, 225, 330.
Lyttleton Street, 31.
Lyttleton, Governor, 31,63.
Maddox, John, 69.
Mahaffy, Oliver, 71.
Magazine Hill, 11, 34, 88.
Magazine, 127, 128, 132.
Malloy, Edward, 69.
Malloy's Pond, 70.
Man, Robert, 24, 25.
Manning, family mentioned, 356.
Marion, Gen. Francis, 150, 159, 160, 211, 215, 222.

Market, town, 19, 27.
Market Street, 19, 31.
Marshall, John, 109.
Martin, Dr. James, family, 389.
Martin, John, family, 342.
Martin, James, 99.
Martin, Captain, 172.
Martin, John, 287.
Masonic Lodge, 24.
Matheson, Farquhar, 375.
Matheson, Christopher, 20, 290, 374.
Mathis, family, 75, 86, 99.
Mathis, Daniel and Sophia, 74, 86, 380.
Mathis, Samuel, 17, 23, 99-103; 104, 133, 276; Diary, 400-403.
Mathieu, J. B., 21.
May, John, 129.
Mayors and Intendants, list of, 35.
McCaa, family, mentioned, 340.
McCaa, Dr. John, 349, 375.
McCain, W., 209.
McCalla, Thomas, 207.
McCandless, Leslie, 25.
McClelland, Maj. John, 360, 372.
McConnel, John, 69.
McCormick, Patrick and Thomas, 69.
McCreight, E. O., 36.
McCutchin, Hugh, 68.
McDaniel, Daniel, 69.
McDowall, W. D., 26, 35.
McGirtt (or McGirth), Daniel, 104, 115, 123; 297-305.
McGirtt, James, 77, 96, 297.
McGowan (or McGowen), James, 68.
McGraw, ——, 69.
McIntosh, George, 129.
McKain, family mentioned, 340.
McKain, James R., 23.
McKain, W. J., 35.
McKenzie, John, 71.
McKinney, Benjamin, 69.
McLaney, family mentioned, 64.
McRa, John and Colin, 389.
McRae, family, 387.
McRae, Duncan, 104, 289, 330, 387.
McWillie, family mentioned, 387.
McWillie, William, 387.
Meeting Street, 32.
Meeting House, Quaker, 32, 81.
Melone, Cornelius, 75.
Meroney, John S., 279.
Meroney's Hill, 223.

INDEX. 421

Mickle, family, 86, 215, 390.
Mickle, Joseph (I), 85, 390.
Mickle, Maj. Joseph, 391.
Mickle, Robert (I), 23.
Miles, John, 205.
Milhouse (or Milhous), family, 74, 76, 99.
Milhouse, Robert, 16, 74, 77.
Milhouse, Samuel and John, 78.
Milhouse, Dinah, 74, 86.
Mill Street, 31.
Mills, 71, 77, 89, 223.
Millbank, 249.
Miller, family mentioned, 102.
Miller, Gov. S. D., 349, 371.
Milling, Dr. John, 391, 396.
Minton, David, 327-339.
Minton's Mill, 327-339.
Moffatt, Keith S., 23.
Monument Square, 30.
Moon, Thomas, 75.
Moore, Isham, 108.
Moore, Dr. A. A., 26, 35, 208.
Moore, C. C., residence, 255.
Morgan, Gen. Daniel, 148, 212, 216.
Morong, P., 99.
Morgridge, Timothy, 75.
Mortimer, Edward, 290.
Mortimer Springs, 226.
Mounds, Indian, 61.
Moultrie, General, 121.
Mulberry, 11, 76, 304, 370.
Mulberry Street, 16, 18, 33.
Murchison, tailor, 99.
Murphy, Malachi, 130.
Murray, family, 354.
Murrell, William, 99.
Natchez Indians, 38.
Neilson (or Nelson), David, 108, 129.
Neilson, Samuel, 69.
Nelson, John J., 392.
Nettles, family, 392.
Nettles, Capt. William, 86, 99, 392.
Nettles, Jesse S., 393.
Nicholls, Richard, 384.
Nixon, family mentioned, 393.
Nixon, Col. William, 27.
Nixon, Henry G., 28, 375, 393.
Nobkehea, Chief, 49, 50.
Nullification, 386.
O'Cain, Elder, 209.
Oconostota, 63.
Odam, Abraham, 87.
Ogilvy, William, 125.
Ogilvie, Charles, 130.

O'Neall, John Belton, 84.
Opera House, 20.
Orphan Society, Camden, 278, 377.
Ousley, James, 67.
Pace, Nathan, 287.
Paget, Roger, 69.
Paget, Thomas, 71.
Paine, William, 71.
Parks of Camden, 29.
Patton, Robert, 109.
Patterson, family, 393.
Payn (or Pain), John, 108, 129, 384.
Peay, Austin F., 87.
Peedee Indians, 38.
Perkins, family, 393.
Perkins, Benjamin, 393.
Perkins, Benjamin (II), 394.
Perkins, Mrs. Benjamin, 276.
Perkins, Caroline Jumelle, 394.
Perkins, James, 333.
Perkins, John, Sr., 108.
Petition, of Provincial Militia, 133.
Pickens, Gen. Andrew, 216.
Pinckney, Gen. C. C., 122.
Pinckney, Gen. Thomas, 163, 177, 196.
Pine Tree Hill, 11, 88, 90.
Pine Tree Creek, Big, 10, 40, 44, 68.
Pine Tree Creek, Little, 17, 40.
Pine Flat, 256.
Plane Hill, 349.
Platt, John, 129.
Pleasant Hill, 348.
Plunkett, Timothy, 75.
Porterfield, Colonel, 149, 156, 157, 193.
Postell, family mentioned, 99.
Postell, James C., 323, 325.
Potter's Raid, 25.
Pratt, Charles (Lord Camden), 12, 91.
Presbyterian Burial Ground, 31, 95, 257, 291.
Presentments, of Grand Jury, 95, 96, 106.
Prevost, General, 123, 300.
Prisoners, at Camden, 144; 208-211.
Prow (or Frow), King, 57, 320.
Pulaski, Count, 125.
Purrysburg, 121.
Quakers, 11; 73-87.
Quaker Meeting House and Cemetery, 77-81.

Ragland (or Raglin) Creek, 71.
Ramsey's Mill, 218.
Ratcliff, Charles, 11, 69.
Ratcliff (or Radcliffe's) Bridge, 219.
Rattray, Alexander, 69, 71.
Rawdon, Lord, 132, 143, 161, 204, 207, 214, 218, 219, 230, 258, 271.
Rawdon Town, 272.
Rectory Square, 30.
Redoubts, 132, 204.
Reed, Isabella, 129.
Reese, Huberd, 287.
Reese, William, 290.
Regulators, 347.
Reynolds, Dr. Joshua, 86, 103, 400.
Reynolds, Dr. George, 371.
Richardson, Gen. Richard, 55, 109, 121, 286, 287.
Richardson, Richard, Jr., 109.
Richardson, John S., 325.
Richardson, William, 55, 109, 287.
Ripponden Street, 16, 32.
Rives, Martha, 349.
Roberts, Roger, 71.
Rochelle, Lovick, 329-339.
Rollings, J. C., 36.
Rork, Bryan, 69. -
Ross, Isaac, 109.
Ross, family, 342.
Rosser, John, 35, 209.
Royall, Mrs. Anne, 257, 277.
Rudulph, family, 353.
Rudulph, Zebulon, 23, 189, 353.
Rugeley, Col. Henry, 104, 135, 152; 212-215; 286, 289.
Rugeley's Fort, 152, 212, 213, 238, 268.
Rugeley, Roland, 212.
Russell, family mentioned, 215.
Russell, Charles, 71.
Russell, Samuel, 74, 80.
Rutherford, General, 123, 128, 135, 185.
Rutledge, Gov. John, 32, 118, 127, 128, 135, 285, 378, 379.
Rutledge Street, 20, 32.
Saarsfield, 227.
Salley, A. S., 295.
Salmond, Thomas, 35, 352, 368.
Salmond, E. A., 35.
Salmond, H. C., 26.
Salmond, family mentioned, 340.
Sanders Creek, 10; Battle, 146-198; 157, 237.
Sanders, George, 96.

Sandy Hill, 369.
Saunders, family mentioned, 215.
Sawney Creek, 45, 268.
Schrock, family mentioned, 359.
Schrock, Capt. J. A., 26.
Scott, William, 71.
Seawright, William and Robert, 68.
Seal of Town, 89.
Seesom, James, 129.
Seminary, Episcopal, 25.
Senf, Col. Christian, 156.
Senior, George, 11, 69.
Sessions, Samuel, 384.
Settlers, first near Camden, 67-73.
Shannon, C. J. (I), 20, 87.
Shannon, Col. W. M., 83, 209, 256, 386, 391.
Shannon, Thomas E., 375.
Shannon, C. J., Jr., residence, 274.
Shawnee Indians, 38.
Shelton, Ann, 69.
Sherman's Raid, 24.
Singleton, ——, 87.
Singleton, Matthew, 108, 109, 287.
Singleton, John, Sr., 287.
Sizer, Mrs., 23.
Smallwood, General, 165, 174, 205.
Smith, Capt. John, 264.
Smith, Judge William, 333.
Spears Creek, 77.
Springdale, 227.
Squares and Parks, 24, 26, 29.
St. Julien, James, 9.
St. Marks Parish, 95, 109, 296.
Starke, family, 342.
Starke, Douglas, 309.
Star Redoubt, 132.
Stateburg, 268.
Stedman, Extracts from, 142, 167.
Steele, John, 201, 384.
Stevens, General, 152, 158, 161.
Steward, Charles Augustus, 388.
Stockton, 346.
Stockton, family mentioned, 357.
Strain, Adam, 68.
Streets of Camden, 31.
Strother, Mr., 144.
Sumter, Gen. Thomas, 96, 109, 152, 200, 215, 218, 219.
Sutton, Jasper, 89, 96, 99, 108, 366.
Swift Creek, 77.

INDEX. 423

Tarleton, Col. B., 134, 155, 161, 194.
Taverns, 319, 327, 329, 331, 337.
Taylor, Thomas and John, 207.
Team, Adam, 188.
Telephone, Franchise, 26.
Tennant, Rev. William, 110.
Terraces, The, 349.
Thomas, Samuel, 74.
Thompson, family mentioned, 395.
Thompson, Col. William, 110, 115, 116, 117.
Thornton, family mentioned, 340.
Thornton, Phineas, 19.
Tod, John, 75.
Toland, Bryan, 75.
Tomlinson, Josiah, 73, 74.
Tomlinson, William, 74, 80, 99.
Town Creek, 11.
Trantham, family, 215, 395.
Trantham, Dr. John I., 395.
Trent, Dr. John, 365, 372.
Truesdale, Miss, 374.
Tuck or Huck, Capt. Christian, 139.
Tucker, Richard, 205.
Tuscarora Indians, 58.
Twenty-five-mile Creek, 269.
Uphton or Upton Court, 394.
Upton Mills, 225.
Valentine, William, 286.
Vaughan, family mentioned, 215.
Vaughan, Virginia, 23.
Vaughan, Wilie, 365.
Vaughan, Mrs. Lydia Ann, 380.
Vaughan, Mrs. Wilie, 23.
Villepigue, Capt. James I., 21.
Villepigue, Gen. J. B., 24.
Von Tresckow, E., 33, 274.
Wade, Joseph, 208.
Wadison, Richard, 99.
Wards of Camden, 30.
Ward, Henry Dana, 189, 353.
Ward, Henry Dana Artemas, 189.
Warren, Capt. Peter, 20, 35.
Warren, Thomas J., 35.
Washington, Col. William, 212, 216, 236, 237, 261.
Washington, George, 160, 182; 306-313; 368.
Wateree Street, 33.
Wateree River, 9, 47.
Wateree Indians, 39-46.
Watson, Archibald, 75.
Watson, Colonel, 220, 268.

Waxhaw Indians, 38, 41, 47.
Weatherspoon, David, 134.
Weatherspoon, 69.
Weir, George, 209.
Welsh, William, 286.
Westerham, 67.
West, J. C., 35.
Whitaker, family, 396.
Whitaker, James, 129, 396.
Whitaker, William, Sr., 129, 397.
Whitaker, William, Jr., 130.
Whitaker, Maj. Willis, 104, 133, 396.
Whitaker, John, 104, 133.
Whitaker, Thomas, 397.
White Oak Creek, 71.
Widos, William, 75.
Willett, family, 354.
Williams, John, 11, 69.
Williams, Gen. Otho, 148, 156, 162.
Williams, Gen. D. R., 370.
Williamson, Gen. Andrew, 115, 121, 127.
Wilson, David, 108.
Wilson, William, 109.
Wilson, Robert, 210.
Winn, Colonel, 144.
Winnsboro, 214, 216.
Wisacky Indians, 47.
Withers, Judge T. J., 349.
Witherspoon, John, 96, 108, 134.
Witherspoon, J. K., 24.
Witherspoon, James H., 137.
Woodford, General, 128.
Woolford, Colonel, 152.
Workman, William C., 252.
Workman, John, 278.
Wright, Anthony, 71.
Wright, John, 74, 384.
Wyly or Wylie, family, 86, 99.
Wyly or Wylie, Samuel, 51, 52, 66, 75, 78, 86, 89, 94, 104.
Wyly, Samuel, Jr., 133; 139-141.
Wyly, John, 104, 129, 140.
Wyly, William, 204, 287.
Wyly Street, 31.
Yarnall, Peter, 210.
Yemassee Indians, 38, 41.
Yenabe-Yetangway, Chief, 49.
York Street, 32.
Young, Alexander, 20, 22.
Young, J. A., 25, 35.
Young, Robert, 381.
Young, G. G., 22.
Young, Miss Mary, 275.
Zemp, Dr. F. L. (1), 103.
Zemp, F. L., 36.
Zemp, Miss Sophia, 86.

INDEX TO ILLUSTRATIONS AND DIAGRAMS.

	Facing Page
Diagram No. 1—Fredricksburg Township	10
Diagram No. 2—Lots in Fredricksburg	11
Diagram No. 3—Earliest Plat of Camden, 1774	12
Diagram No. 4—Plan of Camden, 1798	15
Diagram No. 5—Copy of Champion Plat	17
Diagram No. 6—The Mathis Plan of Camden	18
Diagram No. 7	19
Illustration A—Old Market and Courthouse, 1836	20
Illustration B—Tower of Present City Hall	21
Diagram No. 8—Chart of Indian Tribes	37
Illustration C—Effigy of King Haiglar—Vane on Tower of City Hall	55
Diagram No. 9—Grants to Earliest Settlers of Camden and Vicinity	69
Diagram No. 10—Quaker Cemetery	81
Illustration D—Lord Camden	91
Diagram No. 11	130
Diagram No. 12—Line of Gates's March and Chart of Military Operations Around Camden	149
Illustration E—Battle of Camden	157
Diagram No. 13—Battle of Camden, August 16, 1780	161
Illustration F—Gen. Horatio Gates	171
Illustration G—Baron DeKalb	186
Illustration H—Lord Cornwallis	195
Illustration I—Gen. Nathaniel Greene	215
Illustration J—Hobkirk Hill	221
Diagram No. 14—Battle of Hobkirk Hill	233
Diagram No. 15—Captain Vallancey's Map, 1783	235
Illustration K—Revolutionary Sword	256
Illustration L—Lord Rawdon	258
Illustration M—Cornwallis House	274
Illustration N—The Grave of Agnes of Glasgow	291
Illustration O—Joseph Brevard	321

www.ingramcontent.com/pod-product-compliance
Lightning Source LLC
Chambersburg PA
CBHW030901080526
44589CB00010B/88